To [illegible],

With wa[illegible]
fascinating [illegible]
visit.

Larry Altman
Davis
May 20, 1988

# Who Goes First?

# WHO GOES FIRST?

## The Story of Self-Experimentation in Medicine

LAWRENCE K. ALTMAN, M.D.

Random House
New York

Published in the United States by Random House, Inc., New York, and simultaneously in Canada by Random House of Canada Limited, Toronto.

Altman, Lawrence K.
Who goes first?

Bibliography: p.
Includes index.
1. Self-experimentation in medicine. 2. Medical research personnel—Biography. 3. Medical research—History. I. Title. II. Title: Story of self-experimentation in medicine.
R853.S44A57 1985 619'.092'2[B] 83-43178
ISBN 0-394-50382-1

Manufactured in the United States of America

24689753

First Edition

This book is dedicated
TO MY MOTHER, AND TO MY FATHER,
WILLIAM S. ALTMAN, M.D.,
who taught me that a physician should
first and always place himself
in the role of a patient.

# Foreword

## BY LEWIS THOMAS

As an experimental pathologist, I have been engaged, off and on for most of a professional lifetime, in research on the mechanisms of human disease. I have always been aware of the occasional contributions made by physician-investigators who used themselves as experimental subjects, and I have carried along in my memory of old medical school lectures the usual anecdotes about such experiments —John Hunter, for instance, and Walter Reed. I was an intern at the Boston City Hospital when John Crandon was his own guinea pig for research on vitamin C. I thought the stories were interesting but relatively unimportant anomalies in the annals of research, a sort of scientific exotica. I was skeptical about the reliability of most of the anecdotes, and I saw no way to verify any of them by perusing the standard literature of biomedical science.

But now, seen as a whole, autoexperimentation emerges as a highly significant branch of medical history, with its own continuity and coherence. With the unique vision of a skilled physician, a meticulous scholar and a professional journalist, Lawrence K. Altman, M.D., has put the history together and uncovers a solid but previously unrecognized part of the underpinning of modern medical science and technology. Like any scholarly account of history, it presents the two sides of medical research—a flattering view of courageous, devoted, insatiably curious scientists willing to risk anything, including their lives, to get at the truth, but also the seamier side of human nuttiness and grabbiness at its most fallible.

For all that it informs, *Who Goes First?* also entertains. These are dramatic stories, not only because they are about people willing to risk death but also because they recount the efforts of medical investigators to conquer disease. Ultimately, the results gained from self-experiments affect all of us. Perhaps most important, Dr. Altman raises timely questions about the ethics of human experimentation, questions we as a society must evaluate and eventually answer.

*Who Goes First?* ought to be fascinating reading for almost anyone —the general public, physicians and other professionals, people interested in science and its history, and readers fond of solid documentation and original sources. It ought to be required reading for undergraduates hoping for medical school and medical students themselves. It will, I predict, come as a surprise.

# Acknowledgments

Over the years, many people have told me anecdotes about self-experimentation and those who did it, and many others have provided support in additional ways. I am indebted to them all, and with hopes that I have not slighted anyone, I wish in particular to thank:

Donna Anderson; Howard Angione; Robert S. and Mary Ascheim; Judy Baggot; William B. Bean; Gunnar Biorck; Michael Bliss; Mark and Kay Bloom; John Z. Bowers; Robert A. Bruce; Roger J. Bulger; Veronique Buttin; Eli Chernin; Matt Clark; Ronald Clark; William J. Darby; Lena Daun; Hilary Davies; Gail de Avillez; Friedrich Deinhardt; Joe Elia; Leif Erhardt; Myron and Sabine Farber; Saul A. Farber; Agustin M. Florian; Ben and Arna Goffe; Richard A. Frank; Silvio Garattini; Alex Greenfield; Laurence A. Harker; Theodore Hauschka; David Hendin; John and Marty Herbert; Robert and Sheilah Hillman; James G. and Beate Hirsch; Dorothy M. Horstmann; Edward J. Huth; Glenn and Ginger Irvine; Thomas H. Jukes; Lucy Kroll; Vladislav O. Kruta; David and Joanne Kudzma; Dominique and Olivier L'Ecrivain; Richard I. Levin; Anne Liebling; Richard J. Litell; F. C. MacIntosh; George and Arlette Miller; Louis Nelson; Barbara Oliver; Robert G. Petersdorf; Chase N. Peterson; Carl and Betty Pforzheimer III; Ronald R. Roberto; David E. Rogers; Stanley Rothenberg; Guillermo C. Sanchez; Richard Schatzki; Jonas A. Shulman; Margaret Stanback; Andreas Sjogren; Carl and Susan Steeg; James H. Steele; John and Susan Talbott; Lewis Thomas; Jurgen Thorwald; Fred and Carol Valentine; Kenneth S. Warren; Stephen and Dorothy Weber; Paul E. Wiseman; and Richard J. Wolfe.

. . .

My thanks also to the library staffs of the following institutions for their help at various times in this project: Centers for Disease Control in Atlanta; Francis A. Countway Library of Medicine in Boston; Karolinska Institute in Stockholm; Mount Zion Medical Center in San Francisco; Mario Negri Institute of Pharmacologic Research in Milan; National Library of Medicine in Bethesda, Md.; New York Academy of Medicine; *New York Times;* New York University School of Medicine; St. Luke's-Roosevelt Hospital Center in New York; Royal Society of Medicine in London; Tufts University School of Medicine in Boston; University of California Medical School at San Francisco; University of Virginia Medical School at Charlottesville; University of Washington Medical School in Seattle; The Wellcome Trust in London; and the World Health Organization in Geneva.

A special thanks go to research librarian Judy Consales, for her diligence in checking obscure points and the references that were misplaced in all my travels over the years, and to my editors, Rob Cowley and Carol Tarlow.

A grant from The Josiah Macy, Jr., Foundation helped support this project.

# Contents

# Contents

# Prologue

In Lima, Peru, there stands what may be the only statue in the world of a medical student. It memorializes a young man named Daniel Carrión and the dramatic experiment he performed on himself in 1885, an experiment that solved a great mystery about a disease that was killing people in South America. Carrión's research conclusively linked, for the first time, a disease of the skin called verruga peruana and another of the blood called Oroya fever (because it had struck workers of the Oroya railway line in the Peruvian Andes).

For years doctors had been trying to find out the cause of puzzling bumps that would erupt on the skin and in the mouths of people living in the steep valleys of the Andean cordillera in Peru, Ecuador, and Colombia. These small bumps, which to victims looked like red warts and to doctors like tumors of blood vessels, were inevitably accompanied by fever and severe joint pain. The rash of bumps was called verruga from the Spanish word for warts, and the sometimes fatal condition was known to have existed in the region for centuries. Epidemics suggested that the disease might be infectious, perhaps caused by the microscopic organisms scientists were just starting to discover. But no one had yet found the organism.

A worldwide search for clues to the puzzling disease began. Researchers from as far away as Europe sent to South America for specimens of skin with the verruga bumps to study in their laboratories, and a Peruvian medical society set up a prize competition with the hope it would spur interest in the disease. Daniel Carrión, a twenty-six-year-old Peruvian medical student, decided to enter this competition. As a youth, Carrión had often accompanied his uncle on trips through the Andes Mountains, where he had seen verruga sufferers firsthand and had been deeply impressed by their affliction. Now in his sixth year of medical training, he had spent the previous three years studying the geographic distribution and the pattern of symptoms of verruga peruana in preparation for the thesis that was required for his medical degree.

Carrión was vaguely aware that some verruga patients developed anemia, a deficiency of oxygen-carrying hemoglobin in the red blood cells, before they developed the bumps on the skin. He also knew that some doctors believed Oroya fever, a disease of the blood, was actually verruga peruana, while other doctors did not believe they were even related. Carrión's chief interest was not in solving this controversy. He wanted to study the evolution of the eruption of the skin bumps to see how the onset of verruga peruana differed from that of other diseases such as malaria. By clarifying the earliest phases of the disease, Carrión thought he could help doctors treat patients more effectively.[1]

The more he studied the disease, the more he became convinced that he needed to inject material from a verruga into a healthy person. In this way he believed he might learn whether the disease could deliberately be given to a human and, if so, document the length of an incubation period and the progression of symptoms. He decided to do the experiment on himself. His friends and professors tried to dissuade him, but Carrión insisted on going ahead. He believed verruga peruana was primarily a Peruvian disease, and he was obsessed by the belief that it should be solved by a Peruvian. The prize competition had been his final impetus.

On the morning of August 27, 1885, in a hospital in Lima, Carrión examined a young boy whose skin was affected by the disease. Carrión's professor and three of his assistants were with him. All expressed disapproval of what he was about to do and refused to help. Determined, nonetheless, to go ahead, Carrión took a lancet and drew blood from a verruga over the boy's right eyebrow. Then, unsuccessfully, he tried to inoculate the material into his own arm. At this point, one of Carrión's colleagues overcame his misgivings and helped the medical student finish the inoculation.

What Carrión thought about his experiment during the next three weeks remains unknown. It was not until September 21 that he recorded his first entry in his diary. He told of feeling a vague discomfort and pains in his left ankle. Two days later, that discomfort had worsened to a high fever and teeth-chattering chills, vomiting, abdominal cramps, and pain in all his bones and joints. He was unable to eat or to quench a strong thirst. By September 26, he could not even maintain his diary, and his classmates assumed the task. Carrión's doctors had no therapy to offer other than herb poultices, comfort, and prayers. Carrión was not dismayed; he believed he would recover. But tests showed that his body had suddenly become alarmingly anemic, with many millions fewer red blood cells than normal. We now know they were being destroyed by bacteria whose existence was unknown at the time. The anemia was so severe that it produced a heart murmur—an abnormal sound usually produced by a disorder of a valve in the heart. Carrión could recognize it himself by listening to the sounds transmitted from his heart to the arteries in his neck.

Although Carrión's condition weakened each day, his mind remained alert. As he lay sweating and feverish in a rooming house, he began to understand the implications of what he had done. He remembered the varying theories about the links between Oroya fever and verruga peruana and recalled the recent death of a friend. On October 1, Carrión told his friends: "Up to today, I thought I was only in the invasive stage of the verruga as a consequence of my inoculation, that is, in that period of anemia that precedes the eruption. But now I am deeply convinced that I am suffering from the fever that killed our friend, Orihuela. Therefore, this is the evident proof that Oroya fever and the verruga have the same origin."[2]

Carrión was right. He had shown that verruga peruana and Oroya fever were in fact one disease. Whatever caused the mild skin condition of verruga peruana could also cause the high temperatures, bone pain, and fatal anemia of Oroya fever. It was yet to be discovered that both are manifestations caused by a bacterium *(Bartonella bacilliformis)* which is spread by sandflies.[3]

Carrión's condition rapidly worsened, and he was finally admitted to the same hospital where he had first inoculated himself. There, his physician prepared a blood transfusion to help correct the anemia, but for unknown reasons a committee of doctors decided to delay giving it to him. It may seem today that Carrión's medical care was bungled when he was denied a transfusion that might have saved his life, but the necessary blood typing tests were unknown then and transfusions were risky. As it was, he went into a coma and died on October 5—thirty-nine days after performing his self-experiment.

Although Carrión was eulogized profusely after his death, at least one prominent doctor publicly criticized the experiment as a "horrible act" by a "naive young man" that "disgraced the profession." And there were some who said Carrión had committed suicide. To complicate the situation, when the police learned the identity of the physician who had helped inject the verruga material into Carrión's arm, they charged him with murder. Carrión's professor, who had originally opposed the self-experiment, came to the defense of his student and the assistant. The professor cited the many physicians in other countries who had risked their lives in self-experiments. As a result of his arguments, the murder charge was dropped. Today, Carrión is an unqualified hero in Peru, where medical students sing a ballad to his memory.

The verruga story did not end with Carrión's death. In 1937, Dr. Max Kuczynski-Godard, a physician and bacteriologist in Lima, repeated Carrión's self-experiment.[4] Kuczynski-Godard used pure cultures of the *Bartonella bacilliformis* bacterium in what seems to have been a crude attempt to study immunity to the infection. (The identity of the bacterium had been discovered in 1909 by Alberto Barton, a Peruvian physician.[5]) Kuczynski-Godard took skin biopsies from the area where he had injected the organisms into himself and then examined them under the microscope. Seventeen days later he became seriously ill with what had come to be known as Carrión's disease. Max Kuczynski-Godard was apparently luckier than Daniel Carrión—there is no record that he died from his self-experiment.

Now we know that the *Bartonella* bacteria invade the red cells in the first and most dangerous stage of the disease (bartonellosis); it can often be fatal, but in mild cases the individual may not be aware of the infection. Then, from two to eight weeks later, it goes on to cause the bumpy skin rash (verruga peruana), which may last for up to a year. This second stage is a milder form of the disease, which now occurs only rarely in South America and can be cured with antibiotics. The self-experiments of Carrión and Kuczynski-Godard led public health officials to knowledge that has enabled them to control the disease.

Moreover, by showing that one organism could cause two vastly different diseases, Carrión gave scientists insights into the enormous diversity of human biology. His discovery set the stage for others to learn, for example, that chicken pox and shingles are different manifestations of the same herpes virus. And the ramifications of Carrión's finding can be appreciated by its application to a newly recognized disease, Acquired Immune Deficiency Syndrome, or AIDS. Scientists have learned that the feline leukemia virus can cause not only leukemia in cats but also a wasting disease and suppression of the immune system resembling AIDS. The visna virus can cause neurological damage and also a wasting disease in sheep. Both the feline leukemia virus and the visna virus are members of the retrovirus family and thus have become models to study another retrovirus—the one that causes human AIDS.

Was Carrión foolish? What if his experiment had proved nothing at all? Like all acts of courage, self-experimentation straddles the fine line between heroism and foolishness. When the experiment goes well, scientists heap praise on the researcher who did it; when disaster occurs, some critics are quick to denounce the self-experimenter and his methodology. Carrión's experiment was no different. Once he had made the decision that experimentation on a human was necessary, he must have asked himself: On whom? Carrión answered that question in the only way his conscience would allow: Myself.

My interest in self-experimentation and physician-investigators who deliberately choose to do their experiments on themselves stems from a discussion during my first days at Tufts Medical School in 1958. After an embryology class a few of us gathered for an informal explanation of how doctors had learned so precisely some of the steps in the anatomical development of fetuses. We were told that several years earlier a small team of Harvard doctors had asked a group of women to cooperate in a research study. The doctors asked the women not to practice birth control during the month before their scheduled hysterectomies. Following the operations, researchers examined the uteri for indications of pregnancy and then made microscope slides from the thirty human embryos that were found. Technically, the Harvard doctors had performed abortions on the women. The research project became a subject of public and religious controversy, and because statutes then prohibited abortion in Massachusetts, some critics charged that the researchers had broken the law.

For me, the discussion raised nagging questions about the nature of research on humans, then in its halcyon period. Did doctors customarily choose to skirt the law or commit crimes in the name of clinical research (experimentation on humans)? What was the process by which researchers sought and chose human volunteers for experiments? In the case of the Harvard project, how had the doctors explained it to their patients?[6]

These questions were in the back of my mind a few weeks later when a lecturer, apparently trying to point out that doctors make mistakes in research, sometimes fatal ones, told us about a physician who had used himself as a volunteer for his own experiment. He was John Hunter, a surgeon to King George III and one of the most celebrated anatomists and medical teachers of his day. He pioneered in transplant surgery by placing a human tooth in a cock's comb, made some of the finest, most detailed anatomic descriptions of the body's lymph system, and helped us understand how bone grows.

In 1767, Hunter contracted gonorrhea and syphilis, but not in the usual way. Then as now, these two diseases were among the most common ailments doctors treated, and in Hunter's era there were almost as many theories about their cause as there were physicians. In an attempt to understand gonorrhea, Hunter took pus from an infected patient and injected it into two places on his own penis in expectation of producing the same infection in himself.[7] Two days after inoculation, the injected areas began to itch, redden, and become moist. A week later, pus formed. There was irritation on urinating. The thirty-nine-year-old surgeon had been successful; he had contracted gonorrhea.

Unexpectedly, however, a few weeks later, the characteristic sores of syphilis also developed. Hunter treated himself with calomel ointment and other standard but useless remedies of his day. The syphilitic sores "healed" or, as we now know, naturally disappeared for a time. Four months later the sore on the tip of the penis recurred. Once again it healed on its own. It was to reappear and heal several more times. Meanwhile, a lymph gland in Hunter's right groin swelled. He treated the swelling by rubbing mercury on the leg and thigh as an experimental "cure." The swelling subsided considerably. When it returned two additional times, he applied increasingly larger doses of mercury for symptomatic relief.

Unfortunately for Hunter, the patient from whom the venereal pus was taken probably had a dual infection—both gonorrhea and syphilis. We now know that syphilis, over the span of decades, passes through three stages and ultimately damages many tissues, such as the heart and the aorta, the main artery leading from the heart. Also, long-term syphilis can be one of the several causes of angina, a painful condition that results when the heart is deprived of an adequate supply of oxygenated blood. Hunter suffered from attacks of angina for the last fifteen years of his life. The least exertion, physical or emotional, was apt to induce spasms ending in unconsciousness. Often, the mere act of undressing at night precipitated an attack, as did heated discussions, drinking wine, performing a difficult operation, concern over an experiment in progress, or climbing stairs. As he said, "My life is in the hands of any rascal who chooses to annoy and tease me."[8]

Indeed, his death at age sixty-five followed an argument during a meeting at St. George's Hospital in London, where he practiced. An autopsy showed that he had a ballooning of the aorta known as an aneurysm. Many modern-day doctors would attribute his death to the third stage of syphilis, and some would conclude that the syphilis resulted from his self-experiment.

Today there are conflicting theories about whether or not the experiment Hunter performed was actually done on himself or someone else, since he wrote about it in the third person and did not identify the individual who became infected. Yet all major medical historians have stated flatly, without further supporting evidence, that he did it on himself.[9]

Puzzled by the discrepancy and by the lack of facts, when I was later in London I went to the Hunter Museum in search of supporting evidence. There was none. How, then, did the experts come to take Hunter's self-experiment as truth? One explanation, which is still debated in the pages of current medical journals and texts, is that in lectures Hunter told his students that he was the subject of the experiment. But there are many more questions to which I could find no answers:

> If Hunter contracted gonorrhea from a self-experiment, was the patient who supplied the injected material in fact also the source for Hunter's syphilis? Or might Hunter have acquired gonorrhea experimentally and syphilis naturally? How could he be certain?
>
> Why did Hunter choose to do the experiment on himself? He had performed other experiments on servants. Why not this one? Was it for reasons of risk? If reliability was a crucial factor, did Hunter practice abstinence to insure it? Did he keep just one sexual partner?
>
> Did Hunter discuss the experiment with his wife before they were married in 1771? Was he aware of the risks to her? If so, was

she made aware of them? Did she become infected? What happened to her? Were their children affected?

Whatever the answers, the experiment is regarded as a classic in the history of medical research and in the tradition of self-experimentation. But over the years Hunter has been criticized not only for setting back progress in venereal disease research by a century because he drew false conclusions from his experiment (that he was dealing with one, not two, diseases) but also for his methodology—self-experimentation. I believe the critics have lost sight of the state of knowledge that existed at Hunter's time.

Hunter and his colleagues had nothing more than crude suspicions about the infectious nature of disease and no clear idea of its long-term consequences. No one knew about incubation periods—the interval between exposure to an infectious organism and the onset of symptoms. The concepts of contagion and communicability could not have been understood because the link between microbes (germs) and disease was unknown. The microscope had existed for a hundred years, but it would be another century before the connection between microorganisms and disease was discovered. Hunter's experiment was doomed to failure no matter who was chosen as the subject because of the scientific ignorance of the era. Were Hunter alive to conduct his experiment today, the pus from the patient would be cultured in a laboratory to determine whether only gonococcal bacteria were present or also syphilis-causing *Treponema pallidum* spirochetes and other infectious organisms. The experimental inoculation would contain only pure cultures of gonococci.[10]

Hunter's story made me wonder how widespread self-experimentation was. To find the answer, I consulted a professor who was interested in medical history. He declared emphatically that while self-experimentation may have been practiced with some frequency in the past, it was no longer common. I then sought help from medical librarians, usually an almost endless source of information. To my surprise, not one could provide a single reference to the subject of self-experimentation. Apparently there had never been a thorough study of what seemed such a fundamental issue in medical research.[11] Further, no index, reference book, historical text, catalogue, or computer system existed then—or exists now—to classify how experiments are done. I was fascinated with why doctors self-experimented, but I was frustrated right from the start by this lack of information. I would have to do my own detective work. This book is the result of nearly three decades of investigative study covering self-experimentation and those physician-researchers who, like Daniel Carrión, chose to go first.

Whenever doctors discover a new drug, develop a new test, introduce a new therapy, or try to unravel a mystery about physiology or disease, human experimentation is necessary. Even after thousands of animal tests, our biologic uniqueness requires human experiments. Someone, then, must be the first human subject to try an experimental drug, vaccine, or device or to test a scientific theory. Everything that is now standard in medical practice was once experimental. Moreover, our good health is largely due to the cumulative knowledge gained from the millions of experiments in which our forebears participated. When we take a pill, get an immunization, eat something, or drink water free from the hazards of typhoid, cholera, and other diseases, most of us overlook the fact that those who lived before us took risks in order to prove the safety and value of the foods, therapies, and preventions from which we now benefit.

Medical progress leads to the fundamental question of human experimentation: Who should be that first human guinea pig? Who goes first?

According to the medical tradition Carrión exemplified, the first human volunteer for an experiment should be the researcher. And, in fact, despite emphatic declarations to the contrary by many contemporary physicians and medical researchers, self-experimentation has been, and *continues* to be, a medical tradition.

Throughout history, medical researchers have deliberately served as human guinea pigs in their own experiments. This does not include accidental exposure to disease, nor does the list encompass those physicians who caught some infection while caring for patients. Self-experimentation means that the experimenter deliberately volunteers to take the risk of going first.

No one knows how many self-experimenters there have been over the years, nor how many there are today. When I began my own search for them, I quickly became aware of the decided lack of precise data not only about self-experimentation specifically but also about human experimentation in general. This deficiency has helped foster many misconceptions and myths about the way research is carried out and has led many people to the mistaken impression that all experiments can be—and are—done on animals. Ultimately, however, humans must become test subjects, and the leap from experimenting on animals to experimenting on humans (clinical research) is always a huge one.

Self-experiments in clinical research can be divided into two types. In one, the volunteer is suffering or dying from an untreatable disease and is motivated to participate in an experiment by the hope that he might personally benefit and also help others. The second type involves normal, healthy volunteers like the women who participated in the fetal research at Harvard and who are largely altruistically motivated. If the experiment is a success, it is conceivable that knowledge gained from the experiment might contribute to their own recovery should they become ill at a later stage in life, but these are not the major motivating factors.

No one knows how much research falls into either category because statistics are not kept on the number of experiments that are done each year. Beyond this, doctors often mask the fact they are carrying out human experimentation by using substitute terms such as "tests," "studies," and "research projects." One reason they avoid the phrase "human experimentation" is because, in the minds of many people, it conjures up memories of Nazi atrocities. Further, scientists differ in their definition of an experiment. As if this were not complicating things enough, the definition changes with time. What was an experiment one day may be standard therapy the next.

Publicity about experiments done in correctional institutions has created another widespread erroneous impression that most clinical research in the United States is done on prisoners. To be sure, many experiments were done in prisons in years past, in return for shortened terms. But because of severe criticism of the ethics of this practice, little research in America is now done behind bars. An even more common error is the belief that many experiments are done on charity patients in hospitals. That, too, was the situation at one time, but no longer, largely because charity medical care for Americans has been vastly reduced, if not eliminated, by the introduction in 1966 of Medicare and Medicaid.

Doctors regard the medical literature as their scientific Bible, and reading it can give a distorted impression of both the merits of self-experimentation and its frequency. The few articles I found lack incisive analysis and focus on a select number of self-experimenters, such as John Hunter, who are regarded as foolish.[12] Most of these discussions overlook the fact that experiments without scientific merit need not be self-experiments. Bad experiments can be—and have been—done on many people. No guarantee exists that because an experiment is done on someone other than the researcher it will be scientifically valid. Nor is there reason to believe that if a researcher experiments on himself the results will be scientifically invalid just because it was done that way.

As I continued my investigation I discovered that although a researcher might mention in the text of a scientific article that he or she was one of the volunteers, most references to self-experiments were not clear. The most useful clues were found in the tables in the medical journal articles where the scientific data were listed case by case. It was a long-standing practice to use the initials of volunteers as a means of identifying them in a particular case. When the initials of an author of a paper matched those in any of the cases listed in the tables of the thousands of journal papers I read regularly as a physician, I could presume that self-experimentation was involved. I would then write to the investigator to verify the fact.[13] Several of these researchers told me about other self-experimenters. It was a rewarding beginning. And it had an abrupt ending. As my research reached material from the mid-1960s, I found that for ethical and legal reasons medical journal editors had changed the system of identifying volunteers. To protect the identity of those involved in research projects, the editors began substituting numbers for initials in the case listings. This conscientious policy deprived me of my chief research tool! But it did nothing to daunt my interest.

Additional self-experiments came to light in conversations with my teachers and with other professional colleagues who learned of my interest. In fact, when I did an internal medicine residency at the University of Washington in Seattle, I found that some of my professors there had experimented on themselves.[14]

After I had finished my medical training and become a specialist in internal medicine, I began to analyze the examples of self-experimentation I had collected. Strongly encouraged by Dr. Franz J. Ingelfinger, a former professor and self-experimenter in his own right, who had become editor of *The New England Journal of Medicine,* I published an article on the subject in his journal.[15]

This book is the result of more than a decade of further effort. As a physician and medical journalist, I have traveled from the Arctic to the tropics, and everywhere I have heard whispers about self-experiments. I have made it my business to seek out all the details, interviewing young doctors embarking on careers as medical investigators as well as older colleagues. Some stories began as anecdotes at dinners or in hallway conversations. Many proved accurate; others I could not substantiate. Scientists are human. They have their jealousies. They gossip. They spread rumors. They exaggerate. Sometimes they treat hearsay as fact. I interviewed many of the self-experimenters long after the actual experiments were done. I recognized that some of their recollections might be distorted by the vagaries of memory. When possible, I sought confirming accounts from other researchers who, even if they had not witnessed the self-experiment, had worked in the same hospital at the same time.

In almost all the interviews, one theme became clear. Self-experimentation is an expression of the Golden Rule: "And as ye would that men should do to you, do ye also to them likewise."

Finally, my research into self-experimentation led me to practice it myself. At the University of Washington I did clinical research on a rare genetic disease that blinds, causes bleeding, damages the skin, and leads to heart attacks and strokes at a premature age. It is called PXE, for pseudoxanthoma elasticum.[16] The study required that a skin biopsy be performed. I did on myself first what I would do for experimental purposes on my patients. Another doctor removed a piece of my own skin, which served as a normal control for comparison with those of patients in the experiment. The biopsy was technically simple, left only a tiny scar in my left elbow crease, and involved no unusual risk. But it had an unexpected dividend. The fact that I had done it made it easier for me to explain the process to patients, and a bond developed between me and the people who volunteered for my research project.

I would later find that it was a bond familiar to other self-experimenters. Before Sir Douglas Black became Chief Scientist in the British Ministry of Health in 1973, he had been a frequent self-experimenter. As Black told me, "It's much easier to get the volunteer's cooperation for a study if you sit by the bedside and say that you have done the same experiment on yourself and are none the worse for it. And if you do it on yourself first, it gives you a wonderful chance to iron out any bugs."[17]

This book is about some of the doctors and scientists who went first. There are hundreds more who, for reasons of space, I was unable to include. I was impressed by their numbers as well as by their diversity. Self-experimenters are the leaders of medicine: Nobel Prize winners, deans of medical schools, editors of medical journals, surgeon generals, and heads of health organizations, as well as ordinary doctors. They come from virtually all the specialties of medicine. The ones I met and talked with were serious-minded and dedicated. Most were altruistic and regarded the risks they took as just part of the business of research. They went ahead and experimented on themselves despite the fact that there was no organized mechanism in research to compensate them for any injuries their experiments might cause. Their courage has brought a spirit of adventure to the laboratory and to clinical research.

Clearly, without self-experimentation we might never have discovered the true nature of some diseases, determined the length of the incubation periods of others, learned how still others are spread, and recognized that a few are due to nutritional deficiencies. Drugs might not have been developed to relieve the pains of angina pectoris and heart disease and to help alcoholics refrain from drinking. Surgery would be prohibitively painful without the variety of anesthetic gases developed by experiments doctors did on themselves. Immunizations to prevent crippling and potentially fatal viral and bacteriologic infections would not exist. If a doctor had not put a tube into his own heart, we might not have open-heart surgery to repair birth defects in children and damaged cardiac valves in adults as well as bypass operations to relieve the pain from angina caused by arteriosclerotic damage to the coronary arteries. Our obligation to self-experimentation, to those who went first, is immense.

# Chapter One

## AN OVERVIEW

Human experimentation began when the first doctors treated the first patients. Until recently, however, it was largely a trial-and-error process and, by today's standards, hardly scientific. For hundreds of years physicians made little effort to formally coordinate knowledge, relying instead on intuition from personal experience. It was not until the first medical journals appeared in the late seventeenth century that doctors began to systematically report cases. At first, these reports tended to be anecdotal accounts and isolated testimonials, not full-blown scientific studies.[1] Then, as the rudiments of the scientific process took hold, doctors began collaborative efforts. Many were simply marginal variations on standard therapies.

For most of history, medical research was passive, reflecting straightforward observation and description of the course of events in disease. Rarely did doctors intervene to influence nature's course in any other way than by giving herbs or applying poultices and other concoctions that were the forerunners of today's pharmaceuticals. Only in recent history have doctors tried to learn how to manipulate physiological processes in expectation of curing disease or improving the course of a patient's illness. This move to deliberate experimentation was an escape from the limitations of the methodology of observation. Purposeful tampering with the natural course of disease came late because it must be based on human experimentation, which exposes the patient to possible harm and which runs counter to the traditions of the medical profession. When it was first done, it was on criminals, not patients.[2]

The cardinal rule of medicine—to do no harm—has been taught from the time of Hippocrates in 460 B.C. "I will . . . abstain from whatever is deleterious and mischievous," the Hippocratic Oath says.[3] Yet literal interpretation of this oath would wipe out a large part of research.

The ancient Greeks and Romans did not attempt serious experiments as we know them. For instance, while treating a boy whose brain had been exposed as the result of an injury, Hippocrates picked out the fragments of bone that had lodged in the brain and also "gently scratched the surface of the cortex with his fingernail."[4] Hippocrates observed the convulsions that occurred on the opposite side of the boy's body. Today, that act would be a teaching exercise. In Hippocrates' time, it amounted to an experiment because so little was known about the brain and the function of the central nervous system.

The ancient medical philosopher also warned in his famous First Aphorism that "life is short, the art long, opportunity fleeting, experience treacherous, judgment difficult."[5] Our interpretation of that aphorism depends on the translation. The words "experience treacherous" can also be translated from the Greek as "experiment perilous." This latter translation has been cited as a warning to doctors against experimenting with new and unknown therapeutic measures. It describes an attitude that undoubtedly contributed to the lack of progress in medicine for many centuries.

Those doctors who experimented did so at their own peril. The risks were emphasized in a British court decision in 1767: "Many men very skillful in their profession have frequently acted out of the common way for the sake of trying experiments . . . they have [acted] ignorantly and unskillfully, contrary to the known rule and usage of surgeons."[6] The warning was repeated as late as 1918 in a legal encyclopedia: "While it is the duty of a physician or surgeon to keep up with the advancement made by his profession, it is also his duty not to attempt to forge ahead of it by trying experiments on his regular patients."[7]

Nevertheless, movement developed toward a more liberated attitude about human experimentation. One of its proponents was the celebrated French physiologist, Claude Bernard (1813–1878), whose classic experiments demonstrated several functions of the liver, the digestive properties of the pancreas, and the nervous system's control of blood circulation. He stated his opinion on the subject in 1865: "Physicians make therapeutic experiments daily on their patients, and surgeons perform vivisections daily on their subjects. Experiments, then, may be performed on man, but within what limits? It is our duty and our right to perform an experiment on man whenever it can save his life, cure him, or gain him some personal benefit. The principle of medical and surgical morality, therefore, consists in never performing on man an experiment which might be harmful to him to any extent, even though the result might be highly advantageous to science."[8]

But in recognizing the need to experiment on humans, Bernard emphasized the importance of self-experimentation: "Morals do not forbid making experiments on one's neighbor or on one's self. In everyday life men do nothing but experiments on one another. Christian morals forbid only one thing, doing ill to one's neighbor. So among the experiments that may be tried on man, those that can only harm are forbidden, and those that may do good are obligatory."[9]

By the end of World War II, such principles had been defiled by doctors in Nazi Germany, who invoked the name of science to justify atrocities labeled "experiments" that involved hundreds of thousands of victims, most of them Jewish. The Nazi doctors were not the first to betray their training as healers, but their experiments were the most horrible, at least in recent times. They were sadistic human torture under the guise of medical research. Among the twenty Nazi doctors who were tried at Nuremberg was an eminent malaria expert, Dr. Klaus Karl Schilling. A former member of the League of Nations Malaria Commission, Schilling infected more than one thousand prisoners at Dachau with the parasitic disease. More than four hundred died, many from complications of treatment with experimental antimalarial drugs, often given in excessively large doses. He was hanged.

Brigadier General Telford Taylor, the United States chief war crimes prosecutor at Nuremberg, testified that among the "experiments" Nazi doctors performed were:

> Locking prisoners into airtight chambers and then rapidly changing the pressures to duplicate the atmospheric conditions which an aviator might encounter in falling long distances without a parachute or oxygen.
>
> Infecting individuals with cholera, diphtheria, paratyphoid A and B, smallpox, typhus, and yellow fever and then testing experimental and mostly useless vaccines on them. Some inmates at Buchenwald and Natzweiler "were deliberately infected with

typhus with the sole purpose of keeping the typhus virus alive and generally available in the bloodstream of the inmates."

Injecting phenol or gasoline into the veins of prisoners, who died within sixty seconds.

Testing to determine how long humans could survive without water and after eating huge amounts of salt.

"These experiments revealed nothing which civilized medicine can use," and among the physicians who did them were leaders of German medicine, Taylor said.[10]

At the time of the Nuremberg Nazi war crimes trials, there was no formal code of ethics in medical research to which the judges could hold the accused Nazi doctors accountable. The Nuremberg trials forced doctors and scientists to consider openly for the first time the value, ethics, and limits of human experimentation, and made the medical profession realize that serious breaches of medical ethics had occurred in the past.

Out of the Nuremberg trials in 1947 came the Nuremberg Code, the first code to deal specifically with human experimentation. It created ethical guidelines for the conduct of medical research throughout the world. The Nuremberg Code recognized that human experimentation could yield results for the good of society unobtainable by other means. Although many researchers had customarily obtained consent from volunteers in the past, it was the Nuremberg Code that first established the practice formally. The code deals with self-experimentation in Article 5, which states: "No experiment should be conducted where there is an *a priori* reason to believe that death or disabling injury will occur; except, perhaps, in those experiments where the experimental physicians also serve as subjects."[11]

Dr. Leo Alexander, an American psychiatrist serving as a consultant to General Taylor, prepared the memorandum on which the Nuremberg tribunal based the code. Alexander told me that in drafting the memorandum he had recalled several famous self-experiments from medical history, and, with them in mind, he wrote: "It is ethically permissible for an experimenter to perform experiments involving significant risks only if the solution, after thorough exploration along all the other lines of . . . scientific investigation, is not accessible by any other means, and if he considers the solution of the problem important enough to risk his own life along with those of his non-scientific colleagues . . ."[12]

Most people believed that unethical research could not happen in a democratic society. Yet, in the 1960s, only two decades after the adoption of the Nuremberg Code, there were shocking disclosures of glaring breaches of ethics that had been committed by a small number of American doctors just after World War II. These breaches came to attention largely through an article by Dr. Henry K. Beecher, an anesthesia and pain researcher at the Massachusetts General Hospital in Boston.[13] Beecher cited fifty unethical studies, among them:

> Deliberately withholding penicillin from 109 servicemen who suffered streptococcal infections, thereby exposing them to the risks of rheumatic fever.
>
> Administering several chemicals of no benefit to patients with advanced cirrhosis to determine their effect on the liver disease.
>
> Exposing twenty-six normal newborn infants to extensive X rays so their urinary bladder function could be studied.[14]

Most of this post–World War II criticism about breaches of scientific ethics involved civilian researchers working in private institutions. However, government researchers came under attack in 1972 when the public learned that United States Public Health Service officials had withheld antibiotic therapy from a group of syphilis patients whose medical histories they had carefully followed for more than forty years. The patients, who had acquired syphilis naturally, had been asked to volunteer for what came to be known as the Tuskegee Study.[15] Its aim was to observe the natural course of the infection and to further medical knowledge about the disease. In return for their cooperation, the volunteers—mostly poor and black—were to be given free medical care and free burials. The ethics of the study would not have been questioned except for a major development that occurred during its course. It was discovered that when penicillin was administered in the early—but not late—stages of the infection, syphilis could be cured. To be sure, most patients in the study were already in the late stages of the disease by this time, probably too late for them to have benefited from the discovery. Nevertheless, the researchers did not offer treatment to any volunteer.

Further erosion of the public's faith in the ethics of research came from revelations that Pentagon officials, in order to simulate a germ warfare attack, had purposely spread microorganisms and other biological substances in eight areas of the United States, including a simulated poison through two New York City subway lines.[16] Only after the organisms were released did doctors learn that some of these bacteria could cause disease in humans. More recently it was disclosed that officials of another American government agency, the Central Intelligence Agency, secretly conducted experiments on Americans across the country, "slipping" LSD and other mind-affecting drugs to numbers of people without their knowledge or permission. At least one person committed suicide as a result.

News accounts of these experiments stimulated intense debate about the ethics of human experimentation. Scientists insisted that such examples of unethical behavior were rare exceptions, but the breaches made it clear that medical researchers did not always live up to their ethical pledges.

In the wake of the syphilis scandals, the federal government began to issue regulations in an attempt to legally enforce the principles set out in voluntary codes. Formal rules were adopted that drastically changed the role of human experimentation. Laws in the United States and some other countries now *require* human as well as animal experimentation. The Food and Drug Administration, a federal agency acting under a legal mandate, requires extensive experiments on humans to prove safety and efficacy before any drug or medical device can be marketed for general use. Additionally, the public endorses human experimentation via taxpayer funding for such research at medical centers throughout the country. Society clearly accepts, even encourages, ethical experimentation on humans toward gaining new knowledge against disease, but only within strict parameters and under clearly defined rules.

Since 1966, each medical center that receives federal funds for research has had to comply with federal regulations and to organize committees that go by various names such as Institutional Review Board or Ethics Committee. Before experimenting on humans, American research physicians must obtain prior approval from these groups, followed by written informed consent from each volunteer. These regulations were created to protect volunteers from participation in unethical research projects. There are about 550 review boards in the United States, and they have become the standard formal review mechanism at all American research institutions. Similar committees now exist in England and other countries.

These committees were conceived to address all ethical issues of human research, but, surprisingly, the question "Who goes first?" is not usually discussed. The review committee at the Johns Hopkins Hospital is an exception. In 1983 this committee sent a memorandum to the faculty of the medical school reminding members that proposed self-experiments must be submitted for review in the same way any investigation using human volunteers needed to be submitted. One stated purpose of this requirement was to protect an overenthusiastic self-experimenter from taking unwarranted risks. "Under these circumstances most of us are so excited about the prospect of new knowledge [that] the fact that there is any risk associated may be minimized or escape our attention," said Dr. Thomas R. Hendrix, the chairman of the Hopkins committee.[17]

Another regulation, issued in 1967 by the National Institutes of Health, specifically approves the practice of self-experimentation with the aim of providing "the same safeguards for the investigator-subject as for the normal volunteer." The regulation includes, among other things, a requirement that the self-experimenter undergo a complete medical examination beforehand.[18]

Nevertheless, in 1974, when Congress established a commission to review specific areas of human research, such as on prisoners and fetuses, no attention was directed to the subject of self-experimentation or to the question of who goes first. Still, the federal regulations that resulted from the congressionally mandated review were a recognition of the revolutionary changes in medical science that had occurred over recent decades, and they were to allow research and human experimentation to flourish on an unprecedented scale.

Earlier in this century, there were few researchers in the United States and they did their medical investigations in their spare time. Research was often a hobby for doctors with independent incomes or those who could support experiments through fees from private practice. These well-heeled individuals were members of an informal "gentlemen's club" that viewed research more as a luxury than a necessity. They would tend to visit their laboratories at leisure to solve puzzles that happened to intrigue them. Undoubtedly, there were many more doctors who had an interest in doing research but simply could not afford it.

The revolutionary change came in the latter part of the twentieth century, particularly after World War II, when Congress began to grant large sums of money to researchers in medical centers and universities.[19] For the first time, doctors were paid salaries to do research full time in what became a respected, even coveted, career. Today, government grants support the salaries of most researchers as well as the costs of their experiments. The increased budgets led to the creation of new medical schools and to the vast expansion of research programs in most existing ones.

Today research is highly competitive, and the fierce competition for the shrinking research dollar has changed the gentlemen's club atmosphere. Research is often done by teams because, given the increased complexity of the nature of science, few medical investigators can truly work alone. A scientist cannot dream up an experiment in a few days and proceed with it. It can take years to acquire the basic information necessary to begin to comprehend the facts behind a research project, to plan the experiments, and to apply for funding to perform them.

Researchers, supported by public funds, are under constant pressure to produce results that justify taxpayer funding. Their careers are linked to getting new grants, and the applications for many of these grants are based on the ability to convince a sufficient number of volunteers to participate in a particular project.

This situation imposes new dangers. Researchers have become increasingly dependent on their ability to publish in the medical literature in order to win promotion and continued financial support. As Dr. Oscar D. Ratnoff, a leading blood researcher, and Marian F. Ratnoff have written: "Despite miles of verbiage about the need to recognize fine clinical teachers, the route to promotion is all too often dependent upon the production and publication of experimental results. Even disregarding promotion, the economic well-being of the member of a clinical department may be inextricably hitched to his ability to carry out experimental work. . . . Research, it would seem, must be conducted not only for its own sake but to gain both salary and advancement. No wonder the desire for short cuts to attractive answers blunts the investigator's judgment about what is and what is not appropriate."[20]

There are various motivations—sometimes hidden, sometimes overt—to entice other people to volunteer for research projects. Medical researchers may have much to gain personally in terms of career advancement and even monetary profit by doing something to someone else that they would not do to themselves or to family members. But in the midst of this situation, self-experimentation continues, a testimony to man's nobler instincts.

. . .

The earliest recorded self-experimenter I know of, Santorio Santorio, shared few of the concerns of his contemporary counterparts. He worked alone, without fanfare and with little reward, in Padua, Italy. Regarded as the father of the science of metabolism, Santorio Santorio (also called Sanctorius) lived from 1561 to 1636, the age of Shakespeare and of William Harvey's discovery of the circulation of the blood.[21] The great difficulty of scientists in Santorio's era was finding suitable instruments to measure changes in basic physiologic functions. Santorio was perhaps the first physician to use a thermometer to measure the temperature of the body. He also used a steelyard, a type of large portable balance, to discover what is called "insensible perspiration," the continual process by which the body loses large quantities of fluid that cannot be seen by the naked eye.

Santorio placed his worktable, his bed, and all his other daily necessities upon his steelyard balance. Over a thirty-year period, he experimented on himself to determine how his body responded to various physiological and pathological conditions. Each day he weighed himself and the amounts of food he ate and drank, as well as his bodily discharges. From these measurements he determined that there was always an appreciable difference between the weight of the food and drink he consumed and what his body lost as waste and sweat. This difference is insensible perspiration. Today, the knowledge gained from Santorio's self-experiments is applied in hospitals whenever doctors operate on patients or treat victims of burns, heart attacks, or other serious problems. Because the amounts of fluid lost through insensible perspiration can be critical in the care of such patients, doctors routinely prescribe extra amounts of intravenous fluids to compensate for what is lost.

It is said that Santorio's experiments were the first in which a physician thought of verifying theoretical statements by testing and retesting. Medical history books show a picture of the bearded physician seated in a chair facing a table, which is resting on balances hanging from the ceiling. On the table are several plates of food and some wine. Santorio's chair "was at a finger's height from the floor," according to a leading twentieth-century medical historian, Dr. Arturo Castiglioni.[22] When Santorio ate, Castiglioni said, "the chair lowered itself somewhat, and he was easily able to establish when he had taken the right quantity of food and drink. The elevation of the chair indicated the quantity of perspiration, since the sum of the excretions was deducted from the total amount of the loss of weight.

Assuming that the healthy adult body generally retains the same weight for twenty-four hours, the experimenter indicated with his balance the absorbed substances, the secretions and excretions, noting the rest of the loss until he obtained the actual weight effective on the next day."

More than two hundred years later another self-experimenter, Max Josef von Pettenkofer, was probably very much aware of Santorio's experiments and contribution to medical research.

Max von Pettenkofer is one of those scientists whose fame is based more on one mistake than on his several solid scientific triumphs. Pettenkofer was a public health pioneer who developed the first large city pure-water system, in Munich, Germany. He was one of the most influential scientists of his era and a man who at various times was a chemist, pharmacist, actor, and poet. As a scientist, he established basic facts and concepts about nutrition. He discovered a new amino acid, creatinine, that he detected in human urine; today doctors routinely test for it as a measure of kidney function. Pettenkofer also developed a color test for bile. In nonmedical areas, he created methods to retrieve precious metals used in minting coins and an industrial technique to make cement. Pettenkofer improved the illuminating power of wood gas, and his new method was used to light several German cities as well as the Munich railway station.

His famous mistake resulted in part from a self-experiment. In 1892, at the age of seventy-four, eight years after another German scientist, Dr. Robert Koch, had identified the bacterium that causes cholera, Pettenkofer swallowed a pure culture of the microorganism. For many years before Koch's discovery, Pettenkofer had believed that cholera was caused by a microorganism, but he was convinced that it took more than the cholera bacterium alone to cause the disease.[23]

Cholera kills by producing such severe diarrhea, quarts of it, that it dehydrates the body. It can strike suddenly, while the victim is in bed or walking the street. In the late nineteenth century, recurrent cholera epidemics were one of the grimmest challenges to public health. During one outbreak in Munich, Pettenkofer and his young daughter came down with the infection, and their cook died of it. This led Pettenkofer to begin an intensive study of ten cholera outbreaks, including the one that had affected his family. While investigating an epidemic in France in 1892, he noted that certain regions escaped, despite the presence of cholera bacteria in the water. He developed a theory that a combination of four conditions was essential for an epidemic to occur: (1) a specific germ referred to as *X;* (2) certain local conditions, chiefly affecting the soil; (3) certain seasonal conditions; (4) certain individual conditions.

Pettenkofer became embroiled in a controversy that had been going on for decades. No one could agree whether cholera was spread directly from person to person or whether it struck many people at the same time due to a combination of atmospheric, climatic, hygienic, and other environmental factors. Only the waterborne nature of cholera had been clearly documented. In 1854, in one of the most dramatic applications of the principles of epidemiology, Dr. John Snow had traced an epidemic of cholera in London to drinking water obtained from a feces-contaminated well and particularly to a pump on Broad Street. Snow gained fame for halting the epidemic by having the Soho parish councillors remove the pump handle. Thirty years before Koch's identification of the cholera-causing bacterium, Snow argued that cholera was caused by a specific waterborne microorganism, yet to be discovered.[24] However, Snow had many critics, and Pettenkofer was among them;[25] he pointed out that the epidemic had been on the wane by the time the pump handle was removed.

The controversy was fueled by Koch's discovery in 1884 of the bacterium that he described as "a little bent, comma-shaped" and that is called *Vibrio cholerae.* Koch saw it through the microscope and also grew it from samples of drinking water obtained from a pond in India during an epidemic. Koch believed the disease spread when cholera patients excreted the bacterium into the soil or when it came into contact with drinking water. Koch postulated the bacterium was the sole cause of cholera.

Pettenkofer accepted Koch's organism as the *X* factor. But Pettenkofer believed that subsoil water, not drinking water, played the principal role, and he held to his four conditions. According to Pettenkofer, the bacterium alone would not cause cholera. Pettenkofer was convinced the germ could be spread not just by patients but also by apparently healthy individuals traveling among cholera localities. We know today that Pettenkofer was describing the carrier state, which, because of the peculiarities of the body's immunologic defense system, allows some people to harbor the bacterium in their intestines without developing full-blown symptoms of the disease.

Instead of reasoning that the carrier state was due to an immunologic phenomenon, Pettenkofer attributed the carrier state to environmental factors. According to Edgar E. Hume, Pettenkofer's biographer: "So certain was Pettenkofer of his ground that the vibrio [the causative bacterium] cannot of itself cause cholera, that he resolved to perform what he termed the *experimentum crucis* on his own person, i.e., to swallow the comma bacillus. If this bacillus were the only cause of cholera, he could not escape the disease. Even the bacteriologists were willing to admit this and warned Pettenkofer that his experiment would prove fatal."[26]

On October 7, 1892, Pettenkofer swallowed one cubic centimeter of bouillon laced with cholera bacilli derived from a patient who had died of it. Koch had claimed that stomach acid might kill cholera bacteria. So, after neutralizing with sodium bicarbonate whatever acid might be present on an empty stomach, Pettenkofer took a swig of the contaminated water. He would allow no one to cast doubt on his challenge to Koch by saying the dose was weak; Pettenkofer emphasized the fact that the number of bacilli swallowed was of course far greater than the number ordinarily taken into the body under normal conditions of exposure. The next day he began to experience abdominal colic from extensive gas pains and diarrhea. The diarrhea lasted almost a week. He also had an enormous proliferation of the cholera bacteria in the stools, but he never became seriously ill.

The general conclusion of Pettenkofer's critics was that he had escaped cholera through luck, possibly coupled with some immunity from his earlier attack. Today, with a better appreciation of the spectrum of symptoms produced by cholera, most would agree he had contracted an extremely mild case of the disease.

Although Pettenkofer was confident of his theory, he said he was prepared to get a severe case: "Even if I had deceived myself and the experiment endangered my life, I would have looked Death quietly in the eye for mine would have been no foolish or cowardly suicide; I would have died in the service of science like a soldier on the field of honor. Health and life are, as I have so often said, very great earthly goods but not the highest for man. Man, if he will rise above the animals, must sacrifice both life and health for the higher ideals."[27]

Pettenkofer's cholera self-experiment was repeated by several other scientists with similar results. One was a Pettenkofer student,

Rudolph Emmerich. Another, Elie Metchnikoff, would later win a Nobel Prize for his studies on immunology. All three erred in the conclusions they drew from their experiments—not because they were done on themselves, but because parts of their theory that the bacterium was not the sole cause of cholera were wrong and because they did not accumulate enough data on a sufficient number of volunteers.[28] Even today the factors that allow one person to develop a full-blown case of cholera and others like Pettenkofer, Emmerich, and Metchnikoff to escape with trivial symptoms are poorly understood. Pettenkofer was correct in believing that cholera was due to the bacterium Koch discovered. He was wrong in his stubborn persistence that it was also caused by a factor in the subsoil, an error that, like John Hunter's, can be attributed in part to the scientific ignorance of his time.

The nineteenth-century tradition of self-experimentation embodied by Pettenkofer is as strong as ever. Self-experiments were not rare earlier in the twentieth century, and they have been anything but rare in recent years. Consider these several examples:

Acquired immune deficiency syndrome was first recognized in New York and California in 1981; no one knows whether it is a truly new disease or whether it has infected people in remote areas of the world for centuries. Clearly, infections with the AIDS virus have spread to almost every country, and it is now a scourge that threatens to kill millions of people.

In 1986, Dr. Daniel Zagury, a French physician, became the first to test a candidate AIDS vaccine on humans by injecting it into his own arm. That act quickened the pace of AIDS vaccine research. And in the scientific investigations to learn more about this fatal disorder that cripples the immune system and leaves the infected individual prey to a wide variety of opportunistic infections, researchers surely will continue to experiment on themselves.

Proof that AIDS is caused by a virus has led to an unparalleled worldwide effort to develop a vaccine to protect against it. The endeavor will take many years, even decades, with no guarantee that the research efforts will be successful. As scientists explore a wide variety of approaches, they are using molecular biology techniques to carve out selected proteins from different areas of the AIDS virus. The hope is that at least one of these small pieces of the virus will be harmless yet sufficient enough to stimulate protection against invasion of the body by the entire lethal virus.

In 1986, Dr. Zagury of the Pierre-et-Marie Curie University in Paris and his French and Zairian colleagues began the first reported human experiments with an AIDS vaccine in Kinshasa, Zaire. Zagury, whose blood tests showed no evidence that he was infected with the AIDS virus, injected himself with what he hopes will be an effective AIDS vaccine. The vaccine he used had been made by harnessing sophisticated modern genetic techniques to the oldest vaccine, the one that uses the harmless vaccinia (cowpox) virus to protect against smallpox. To create the experimental AIDS vaccine, the scientists inserted a protein called gp 160 that is located in the outer coat of the AIDS virus into live vaccinia virus.

After the injection of the experimental vaccine, Zagury tested his blood every week for nine weeks. Results showed that the experimental vaccine stimulated the production of the desired gp 160 antibody. Furthermore, since Zagury did not develop any toxic reaction or any symptoms of AIDS during the first several months after he took the injection, he felt his self-experiment indicated the safety of the vaccine for humans, at least in the short term. Zagury reported confirmatory results from injections of the experimental AIDS vaccine in "a few other" uninfected human volunteers. Nevertheless, because the incubation period of AIDS is so long—at least several years—dangerous reactions might show up in the future.

In fact, Zagury did not inject himself with the AIDS virus. His self-experiment was not designed to test the efficacy of the vaccine. Rather, its purpose was to test the vaccine's ability to produce an immune reaction in humans and to determine its safety. The experimental injection came after his team had tested a form of immunization known as immunotherapy on a small number of Zairians with AIDS and after the experimental vaccine had been tested on animals. Zagury said the results of these experiments led to his self-experiment.[29]

No one fully understands how the AIDS virus infects the body or how the body might protect itself against progression from infection to disease. No one even knows how many strains of the AIDS virus there are. Therefore, research into a number of different candidate vaccines is being conducted. Scientists often have looked to the envelope, or protective coat, of a virus as the most likely part of the infecting agent to stimulate production of protective antibodies. The gp 160 protein used in Zagury's experimental vaccine comes from this outer envelope. In the United States, Dr. Allan L. Goldstein of George Washington University in Washington, D.C., heads a team of scientists who have developed another candidate AIDS vaccine that uses a synthetic protein which he hopes will protect by mimicking one in the inner shell of the AIDS virus. Because the core proteins of the AIDS virus are believed to be more stable than those on the surface, Goldstein theorizes that his experimental vaccine might protect against a wide variety of strains of the AIDS virus.

Goldstein's team has applied for permission from the Food and Drug Administration to test the vaccine on humans. If it is given, Goldstein says he will be the first to take the vaccine.

Dr. William Randolph Lovelace II, whose family founded the medical clinic that bears his name in Albuquerque, New Mexico, combined his interests in medicine and aviation by investigating the problems of high-altitude physiology and pilot fatigue. Early in his career he was a surgeon at the Mayo Clinic, and then, during World War II, he became head of the Aero-Medical Laboratory at Wright-Patterson Air Force Base in Dayton, Ohio.[30]

Flights above 35,000 feet in pressurized cabins are routine now. But when airplanes first reached those heights in World War II and an aviator was forced to jump, he would lose consciousness within a minute due to lack of oxygen. He could not pull the rip cord of his parachute. Even if he could pull it, another five to ten minutes would pass while he dropped to an altitude where he would have enough oxygen to survive, and then there would be little chance of regaining consciousness. There was an urgent need for special oxygen inhalation equipment. Lovelace became his own test subject to learn the problems of high-altitude escape and parachuting and to develop such a device. It contained about a fifteen-minute supply of oxygen, enough to keep an aviator who parachuted from 35,000 feet conscious until he reached the 15,000-foot level, at which height he would be safe.

On June 24, 1943, above Washington State, the thirty-five-year-old surgeon and army lieutenant colonel bailed out of a B-17 bomber at 40,200 feet. It was his first jump, and he wanted to convince himself and everybody else that the emergency oxygen unit he and his colleagues had devised worked in a real jump as well as it did under laboratory conditions. "We had believed that the shock of the opening parachute would put a force of less than eight *g*'s on the jumper at that high altitude, but we were wrong." Lovelace said. (The earth's forces of gravity act on humans to give them the weight to which they are accustomed; under normal circumstances this is one *g*. But the effects of acceleration on the body are measured in weight. At two *g*, body weight doubles; at three *g*, it triples; and so on. Humans can easily withstand acceleration of up to ten *g* for several seconds because the physiologic effects are reversible. But acceleration of more than twenty *g*, even for only fractions of a second, may damage bone and tissues.) Computations later showed the force on Lovelace was thirty-two *g*. The shock of the opening parachute knocked him unconscious in forty-degree-below-zero temperatures, and his glove was torn away. His left hand was instantly frostbitten. Somewhere in his descent he regained consciousness, and at 8,000 feet he waved to a smaller plane that was following his path. Twenty-three minutes and fifty-one seconds after he dropped out of the bomber, Lovelace landed in a wheat field with a thump and a wrenched back. The test prompted development of delayed automatic opening devices for parachutes. Lovelace was awarded the Distinguished Flying Cross.

Automobiles, airplanes, and spacecraft are safer now because of the scores of deceleration experiments that Dr. John Paul Stapp, an Air Force physician, did on himself on fast track and rocket sled rides to determine the human tolerance limits to crash forces.[31]

Stapp became known as "the fastest man on earth" for having sped faster than a forty-five caliber bullet on a rocket sled that was mounted on heavy rails set in concrete at Holloman Air Force Base in New Mexico. There, on December 12, 1954, the forty-four-year-old Air Force colonel reached a peak velocity of 632 miles per hour in five seconds as the wind and sand stormed at his body. Then he slammed to a stop in one and a half seconds, withstanding pressure almost forty times his own weight. Bucket scoops underneath the sled allowed him to come to such an abrupt halt at such fantastic speeds. They dug into a trough of water, stopping the sled with about the same force as a car hitting a stone wall at fifty miles per hour. A web of straps locked Stapp in place, his head protected by a helmet and his teeth by a rubber bite. The five-foot-eight-inch Stapp suffered only a black eye and several bruises from the historic run. Stapp's contorted face became familiar to Americans in pictures in magazines, and his self-experiments became the basis of a 1956 movie, *On the Threshold of Space.*

John P. Stapp was born on July 11, 1910, the son of American Baptist missionaries, in Bahia, Brazil, where he spent the first twelve years of his life. After moving with his family to the United States, he earned a Ph.D. in biophysics in 1939 and then, in 1943, a medical degree at the relatively late age of thirty-four. During World War II, Stapp was drafted by the Air Force as a general duty medical officer before he completed his internship. Later, as an industrial medical officer and flight surgeon, he became interested in safety, particularly in helping to develop planes that could fly faster and at higher altitudes.

In April 1947, he was sent to Muroc (now Edwards) Air Force Base in California, where one of his first tasks was to collect data for improving the design of aircraft safety harnesses. He did it in part by participating in ejection seat experiments and by conducting twenty-two rocket sled experiments on humans. "They did not order me to get on the sled and expose myself," Stapp told me. "They ordered me to see to it that the project got carried out. I felt fortunate that my goal was to save lives, not to shoot. I went on orders and did it in the same way that a soldier charging a hill gets shot at. I saw no difference between doing a human experiment and leading a military charge to take a military objective because all of this was in a military context. I was expendable."

He used dummies for thirty-two trial runs before he made his own first rocket sled run on December 10, 1947. At the time, most experts believed that the human body could not stand accelerations or decelerations that were more than eight *g*. Stapp disagreed, drawing clues from reports of individuals who had surprisingly survived falls from high roofs and bridges. For about another decade, Stapp allowed his body to be slammed and stressed hundreds of times at increasingly greater *g* forces, measured by sensors strapped to his body and the sleds. The aim of all these severe jolts was to determine how the tissues of the human body react to various *g* forces and sudden stops and to document how sudden a deceleration humans can withstand. His efforts provided engineers with the specific data needed to build safer airplanes and automobiles; until then, much of this type of engineering had been based on observations and guesswork, often scientifically unreliable.

Experimenting on humans, Stapp believed, was far superior to experimenting on dummies because the latter cannot describe feelings; thus, valuable insights that come from actually going through a test are not available with dummies. Furthermore, dummies cannot describe the specific anatomic location of pain. "You can design harnesses and restraints that are far better after you ride with one of your mistakes," Stapp explained.

As the experiments progressed, Stapp let others join in on the project, but only after he vividly described the experience. "They all knew they were gonna get hurt, but they accepted it," Stapp said.

Stapp took every precaution to minimize the risks. He experimented on humans only when necessary; primates were used for many sled runs, and every experiment was conducted according to a research protocol.

For several days before a deceleration run, Stapp abstained from alcohol and any medication, even aspirin. On the day of the experiment, he fasted to avoid the possibility that, if injured, he might, as a complication, inhale food into his lungs, causing a potentially fatal aspiration pneumonia. Moreover, an empty stomach and bladder reduced the chances of their rupture in the experiment. When he was offered water or food before the runs, he refused them, saying, "My experience is that a full stomach makes a messy autopsy."

Stapp believes he avoided potentially catastrophic accidents by confining experiments to the midweek—Tuesdays, Wednesdays, and Thursdays. He insisted on doing the experiments only after at least one day of preparation, and Mondays were saved for that purpose. He also insisted on no distractions. No experiment was performed on a Friday because, he said, "Everybody's mind was on what was gonna happen when they left for the weekend." As a further precaution, an ambulance was always at the site.

Yet for all this, Stapp was nervous each time he waited for the rockets to blast the sled down the track. As he looked at the New Mexico desert, he would think of death. His heart would beat faster. He would feel depressed. To Stapp, the experiments were reminders of the childhood experience of misbehaving and knowing in advance that he was going to get a whipping. Stapp developed a fatalistic approach to all the rides, and immediately afterward he would experience what he called "survival euphoria." But he also had the discipline of a trained scientific observer. "I consciously made every effort to be alert," he told me, "and to precondition myself to recall everything so that I could write it down afterward." He carried the discipline over to his personal life; he refused to marry until after he stopped the sled runs because he "didn't want anything to interfere with getting those experiments done."

Stapp's twenty-nine rocket sled experiments left him with retinal hemorrhages in one eye that limited some of his vision; a concussion; an abdominal hernia; many bruises and several broken ribs; a fractured coccyx; and a shattered right wrist. The deceleration experiments also permanently damaged his sense of balance. When he stands on his left foot with his eyes closed, he must lean on something to keep from falling. The problem, though not major, is still enough to make him rely on a walking stick to climb hills.

One of his greatest concerns was that the public would perceive his experiments as stunts, and for that reason he said: "I devoutly wished I would outlive any experiment by at least six months so that no one could link whatever caused my death to the experiment. I didn't want to cast any aspersions on the research."

Stapp's wish has been fulfilled. When I last talked with him he was in his mid-seventies, enjoying retirement in Los Alamos, New Mexico.

Cyclosporine is a drug that has given a successful new boost to transplanting organs through its powers to fight off the rejection phenomenon.[32] Since its introduction on an experimental basis in 1978, it has helped more people to live longer with transplanted kidneys, hearts, and other organs than was possible with older immunosuppressive drugs. Cyclosporine's discovery came about in 1969, when employees of the Sandoz Corporation in Basel, Switzerland, went to Wisconsin and Norway and brought back soil samples from these two diverse areas that yielded two new strains of fungi. It was these strains that produced cyclosporine. Initial hopes were that the drug would be useful as an antibiotic. While extensive tests did not bear out that possibility, animal experiments by Dr. Jean Borel, a Sandoz researcher, showed that cyclosporine was a powerful immunosuppressive drug, one that could decrease the production of the natural hormones and biochemical substances that defend the body against invasion by foreign agents. Cyclosporine showed distinct promise as a drug to help the body counteract the rejection phenomenon which is the transplant surgeon's major obstacle. Borel's observations were verified in further animal studies, but in moving on to humans, Sandoz researchers found that cyclosporine, when swallowed in the form of a gelatin capsule, was not absorbed into the blood of several healthy volunteers, including Borel himself. This posed a major problem. Could it be that the drug worked in animals but not in humans? If so, its promise was indeed a hollow one. But Borel, remembering that there were significant variations in the way animals absorbed different preparations of cyclosporine, was confident that it would be absorbed most easily by humans if it were mixed as a cocktail with alcohol, water, and a solvent. One day in 1977, Borel drank such a mixture. He became a bit high, but he was happy for another reason—the drug got into his blood. Transplant surgery would not be what it is today without Borel's willingness to experiment on himself with a new drug.

Henle-Koch postulates are named for Dr. Robert Koch, the German scientist, Nobel Prize winner, and self-experimenter, and for his teacher, Jakob Henle. The postulates that form the basis of proof of bacterial diseases in humans and animals state that: (1) a specific organism must be identified in all cases of an infectious disease; (2) pure cultures of the organism must be obtained; (3) organisms derived from pure cultures must reproduce the disease in experimental animals; (4) the organism must be recovered from the experimental animal.[33]

In 1980, in order to fulfill Koch's postulates in the case of a bacterium called *Campylobacter jejuni*, Dr. David A. Robinson of the Public Health Laboratory at Withington Hospital in Manchester, England, experimented on himself. He recovered *C. jejuni* from individuals whose gastrointestinal illness was attributed to drinking cow's milk that contained these bacteria. Then Robinson prepared a purified culture of the bacteria in the laboratory, thereby fulfilling the first two steps of the Henle-Koch postulates. Next, he added five hundred of these microorganisms to a glass of pasteurized milk, which he then swallowed. Robinson, too, became sick. For the next few days, he experienced abdominal cramps and a mild attack of diarrhea, fulfilling step three. Finally, the organisms were isolated from Robinson's stools, thereby fulfilling all the Henle-Koch postulates for that organism in humans for the first time.[34] There was no point in feeding the bacteria to a cow because these organisms often live in cattle without causing illness.

Robinson's self-experiments helped doctors understand the public health importance of *C. jejuni*. Subsequent research has shown that it is one of the common causes of diarrhea.

A newly described bacterium, *Campylobacter pyloridis*, may be the cause of a common inflammation of the stomach called gastritis and possibly of duodenal ulcers, according to an Australian researcher and self-experimenter, Dr. Barry J. Marshall. Researchers in several countries have confirmed Marshall's studies linking *C. pylori-*

*dis* and gastritis, but more research is needed to be certain the bacterium is the primary cause, not a secondary invader.

In one step, in an attempt to fulfill Koch's postulates, in 1984 Marshall swallowed a gastroscope tube through which tiny pieces of the lining of his stomach were removed in several places, all to prove that he had no known disorders of his intestines and did not harbor the bacterium.

The thirty-two-year-old Marshall waited a month to allow healing and then swallowed *C. pyloridis.* A week later, he had an unusual sensation of fullness in his stomach after eating supper, felt hungry on awakening, became irritable, and felt ill. Friends told him he had developed halitosis.

Ten days after his symptoms began, Marshall had another gastroscopy, biopsies were taken, and bacteriological tests were conducted. The studies were done on three occasions, and the results indicated he had developed gastritis. Marshall cured it by taking the drug tinidazole, which made his symptoms disappear within twenty-four hours. Marshall's experiment presented strong evidence that *C. pyloridis* could be the cause of gastritis. According to his theory, many people who come in contact with the bacterium get rid of it on their own but others, for unknown reasons, are unable to do so. He further theorizes that some people go on to develop chronic gastritis and that this can predispose a person to ulcers.[35]

The practice of blood transfusions was made possible by a Nobel Prize–winning self-experiment conducted in Vienna in 1900. Today, eight decades later, dramatic advances in this lifesaving technique may come from experiments being carried out in New York City by researchers on themselves.

In 1900, Dr. Karl Landsteiner, an Austrian physician, discovered the ABO human blood group system, a breakthrough that made it possible to separate blood into the four groups and, later, to safely transfuse blood from one person to another. Researchers then learned how to store blood, leading to the creation of blood banks to store supplies for daily needs and catastrophes.

Landsteiner made his discovery from tests of blood samples collected from himself and five associates.[36] After allowing the blood samples to clot, Landsteiner separated the sticky fluid part (known as the serum) at the top of the test tube from the red cells which had settled at the bottom. In further experiments, Landsteiner mixed his own serum with the red cells from each of his colleagues and, in turn, tested the blood of each individual with each other. Then he looked for a reaction. He observed that the mixtures caused the red cells of some individuals—but not others—to clump.

Landsteiner concluded that these reactions were due to the presence or absence of two antigens, A and B, that were present on the surface of the red cells. (Antigens are foreign substances that lead the body to produce natural protective substances called antibodies.) Landsteiner found that two of his colleagues had what he called the A antigen (group A) and two others had the B antigen (group B). Since Landsteiner and another colleague had neither of the two antigens, he classified their blood as group O (for null). Later research showed that there was a fourth blood group called AB.

Landsteiner was lucky in these experiments. Because they involved such a small number of people, there was a chance that all could have had the same blood group. If they had, Landsteiner might have come to a quite different conclusion. As it happened, however, two had group A, two group B, and two group O blood.

The existence of blood groups is the reason doctors must match the blood types of the donor and recipient before transfusions are given, if potentially fatal reactions are to be avoided. All four major blood groups—A, B, AB, and O—have the same basic structure; the distinction is made on the basis of minor chemical changes on the chains of carbohydrates that are attached to fats and proteins on the surface of red cells. What characterizes each blood group is the specific sugar that is attached to the end of the chain. Blood group B has a sugar called galactose at the end of the chain; it is the B antigen. Blood group A has *N*-acetylgalactosamine at the end of its chain; it is the A antigen. Blood group AB has both compounds, thus having A and B antigens. Blood group O has only the basic unit without either the sugar or the amine attached. At the same time, group A blood has antibodies against antigen B, and group B has antibodies against antigen A. It was the reaction of group B antibodies with group A antigen, and of group A antibodies with group B antigen, that caused the clumping of cells that Landsteiner had observed. Group AB has no antibodies, and group O has antibodies to both antigens A and B. Thus, group O blood is the so-called universal donor because it has no antigens to cause reactions. Individuals with group AB are the universal recipients because they have no antibodies to react with recipient cells of any other type.

In 1981, members of a small team of researchers at the New York Blood Center deliberately transfused themselves with blood of a different type from their own. It was the first of a series of experiments planned for the next several years that, if successful, could revolutionize blood transfusion practices by making it possible for any individual to give blood to anyone else without danger of a potentially lethal transfusion reaction.[37]

The leader of the New York Blood Center team, Dr. Jack Goldstein, a biochemist, has devised a way to chemically transform group B into group O blood without damaging the red cells. He has found that an enzyme called alpha-galactosidase, which is naturally present in coffee beans, breaks the chemical bond between galactose and the end of the long chain on the group B red cell, thus chemically snipping the B antigen and turning the B cell into a group O cell. Experiments in test tubes have shown that the transformed group O red blood cells cannot be distinguished from the original group B cells. In further experiments on gibbons, Goldstein's team found that the transformed animal red cells could safely be given back to the gibbons. But gibbons and humans differ in their blood groups (gibbons have no group O blood), and other primates that do have type O blood cells were not available to Goldstein. There was no choice but to do the definitive experiment on humans.

To learn whether the transformed cells could be given safely and would survive in human recipients, Goldstein chose three people from the New York Blood Center with different blood groups. Goldstein himself was group O, Mrs. Rosa Hurst was group A, and Richard Bonomo was group B. Each researcher received transfusions of about 11.5 billion group B red cells that had been transformed into group O cells. Since Goldstein was group O, he had antibodies to both A and B. Hurst, having group A, had antibodies to B. Bonomo was at no risk because he was group B and the donor of the B red cells. If the group B cells that were to be injected had been successfully transformed into group O cells, there should be no adverse reactions in the experiment, Goldstein reasoned, since group O contains neither A nor B antigens.

When no volunteer developed a transfusion reaction, Goldstein knew no one had developed antibodies to the transformed O cells, indicating that the antigen had been successfully removed. The tests demonstrated that the technique can provide group O red cells of a quality that can be transfused safely. It offered the possibility of a larger pool of donor blood that could be used for anyone. Nevertheless, it will take further research and more tests on human volunteers to determine whether the method can be used in blood banks throughout the world. The next step will be to develop a method to transform group A into group O red cells through an enzyme that removes the A antigen.

In choosing themselves for their experiments, the New York Blood Center researchers were following the leadership of Karl Landsteiner, who was honored for his early work with a Nobel Prize in 1930.

Since Landsteiner, hundreds of doctors have stuck needles in their own veins to collect samples of blood to carry out their experiments. Hematologists, the doctors who specialize in caring for blood disorders, have been forced to do most of their experiments on humans because animals are susceptible to only a very few of the blood disorders that affect humans. In fact, the practice of taking one's own blood samples and injecting oneself for experimental purposes has become so common that many of the doctors who have done it consider it routine; they overlook the fact that they are self-experimenting. Are they foolish or are they heroic? The controversy continues.

In the chapters that follow we will look closely at a number of doctors who experimented on themselves in a wide variety of medical fields. Their willingness to go first not only serves as an example to future physician-investigators but also acts as a catalyst for discussion of the broader issues raised by the methodology of self-experimentation.

# Chapter Two

# DON'T TOUCH THE HEART

Civilization has discarded many of the taboos of primitive societies, but some have survived into modern times. As late as the 1920s, for example, it was taboo for a doctor to touch the living human heart. By that time surgeons, aided by advances in anesthesiology, had invaded most areas of the body. They had begun to operate routinely on the abdominal organs, limbs, the face, even the brain—but not the heart. In the few instances in the preceding centuries when, in emergencies, surgeons had entered the chest to cut and sew the heart, the patient generally had died.

Well into the twentieth century, to touch the heart was to molest a sacred area of the body, its spiritual center, and most doctors feared to tamper with it. Even if they had not been afraid of incurring God's wrath, there were seemingly unsolvable physical problems. The heart constantly pumped blood; when cut, it bled profusely. How could anyone survive such a hemorrhage?

Furthermore, the heart seemed inaccessible. It lies at most three inches beneath the skin, but it is enclosed by a bony cage of ribs that protects both it and the lungs. Were a surgeon to open the chest cage to operate on the lungs or heart, air could suddenly rush in, collapsing one lung and possibly both.[1]

By World War II, knowledge of the heart's functions and the physiology of the lungs was still rudimentary, much of the intimate physiological relationship between the two yet to be revealed. In 1628, when William Harvey discovered the circulatory system, he taught us that the heart pumps blood over and over again through a closed system of arteries and veins. But for hundreds of years that was all doctors knew. Even three centuries after Harvey's discovery, few doctors could consistently diagnose a heart condition. Physicians could rely on little more than their hands and ears as diagnostic aids.[2] Too often, the correct diagnosis emerged only after an autopsy.

With the discovery of anesthesia in the mid-nineteenth century, surgeons experimented and devised new operations, but touching the heart remained taboo. In 1880 Dr. Theodor Billroth, the most influential European surgeon of his time, said: "A surgeon who tries to suture a heart wound deserves to lose the esteem of his colleagues."[3] The medical profession adopted an attitude about heart surgery so fatalistic that in 1896 Dr. Stephen Paget, a noted English physician, wrote: "Surgery of the heart has probably reached the limits set by Nature to all surgery: no new method, and no new discovery, can overcome the natural difficulties that attend a wound of the heart."[4]

By the turn of the twentieth century, surgeons had opened the chest, but not the heart. Then, in 1903, Dr. Ferdinand Sauerbruch, a famous German surgeon, performed an operation that was to make history—and it came about accidentally. One of Sauerbruch's patients was a woman with heart failure, and Sauerbruch believed it was due to constriction of the pericardium, the membrane that covers the heart. He decided to relieve this constriction. Sauerbruch, a great teacher, operated in an amphitheater before a group of observant doctors. When he cut open the woman's chest, he saw what he thought was a cyst in her pericardium and he began to cut it out. Suddenly blood spurted. Sauerbruch realized immediately that it was not a cyst in the membrane but a ballooning of the heart wall itself, known as an aneurysm, and the pericardium had become attached to it. This brutally bold, fearless surgeon quickly repaired the aneurysm and sewed the heart. The patient recovered.[5]

Others must have tried, but failed, to duplicate Sauerbruch's success. Although these presumed failures were not reported in medical journals (surgeons prefer to report successful operations), the failures must have been known through the medical grapevine and they must have perpetuated Billroth's and Paget's earlier warnings. It would take twenty-six more years and the courage of a twenty-five-year-old surgical intern to change things.

Werner Forssmann received his medical degree from the University of Berlin in 1929, and that summer he began his internship in surgery at the Auguste Viktoria Home, a small Red Cross hospital in Eberswalde, Germany, fifty miles outside Berlin.

During his studies, Forssmann had been deeply impressed by a sketch in his physiology textbook that showed French physiologists standing in front of a horse, holding a thin tube that had been put into the jugular vein in the animal's neck and then guided into the heart. An inflated rubber balloon recorded the changes in pressure inside one of the heart chambers. The horse's heart was not disturbed by the procedure.[6] Forssmann became obsessed with the potential value of putting a tube into the human heart. He thought that the technique could be used as an emergency measure to speed delivery of drugs to the heart of a dying patient and as a means to further understanding of the diseases of the heart and circulatory system.[7] He could not understand why this simple technique, which would avoid the complications of opening the chest, had not already been tried on humans.

The more Forssmann thought about the horse experiment, the more he became convinced that it would work on humans as well. But he believed that neck veins would be unsuitable; patients might object because the incision would leave a scar. For cosmetic reasons, then, he focused on the veins in the elbow crease as the point of entry for the tube that would reach the heart.

Forssmann decided to wait a few weeks before asking his superior for permission to try his experiment. He would need a little time to get to know the other doctors at Auguste Viktoria, and to learn the routine.

In the 1920s, the German medical system favored those with independent financial means, and Forssmann, from a middle-class background, was at a disadvantage. His father had been killed in World War I, and he had been raised by his mother and grandmother. When Forssmann decided to emulate a physician-uncle and become a doctor, his mother worked to pay for his medical studies.

In Forssmann's time, paid medical training jobs for postgraduate medical students were rare. But Forssmann was lucky; he found a job for $50 a month—a pittance even then—as an apprentice to Dr. Richard Schneider, a general surgeon at the Auguste Viktoria Home and a friend of the Forssmann family. Then as now, the internship is an intensive training period designed to teach the accepted techniques of medicine or surgery with little or no time for devising or executing experiments. Nevertheless, not long after joining Schneider's staff as an apprentice, Forssmann approached the elder doctor and asked permission to insert a tube through the arm of a human in an effort to reach the human heart. He carefully explained to his superior that since it was too dangerous to touch the beating heart directly, perhaps a less dangerous approach would be to put a tube inside the heart.

How would he reach this vital organ that was so well protected by the ribs?

The same way the French physiologists had reached the horse's heart—through the veins. Forssmann showed Dr. Schneider the sketch from his physiology textbook. Schneider was sympathetic to Forssmann's proposal but advised the young doctor to experiment on animals first. Forssmann countered that the animal experiments by the French physiologists had already proved the technique safe. But he admitted to Schneider he did not know what would happen when the tip of the rubber tube touched the sensitive inside lining of the human heart. So he offered to do it on himself first. "I was convinced that when the problems in an experiment are not very clear, you should do it on yourself and not on another person," Forssmann recalled years later.[8]

But Schneider refused. Forssmann then suggested doing the experiment on a dying patient. Schneider rejected this as well. He forbade Forssmann to do the experiment at all on any person, including himself. As a friend of the family, Schneider feared that Forssmann's widowed mother would have no means of supporting herself if something happened to her only child. The risk was too great, not only to Forssmann but also to Schneider's reputation. An accident would create a scandal.

Forssmann decided to do the experiment anyway—in secret. He would need equipment: sterile scalpels, sutures, and a painkiller to anesthetize the area in the elbow crease he would pierce. He would also need a long piece of sterile rubber tubing, and he knew that only the ureteral catheter, the thin tubing urologists use to drain urine from the kidneys, was long enough for his purpose. This crucial equipment was kept locked in the operating room under the care of Gerda Ditzen, a nurse of about forty-five who had a keen interest in medicine.[9] Forssmann would need her assistance.

"I started to prowl around Gerda like a sweet-toothed cat around the cream jug," he said. He lent her medical books about anatomy and physiology and dropped by the cafeteria after she had finished lunch, ready to talk about what she had read. And each time they met, Forssmann would tell her a little more about his idea. He showed her the picture of the tube in the horse's heart and explained how the same technique could be performed on humans. She was captivated. Forssmann took her to dinner, and during the evening she asked more and more questions about his experiment. She liked the vision and passionate conviction of this young doctor, and, yes, she could clearly understand the importance of his idea. When Forssmann told her he was forbidden to do the experiment, she immediately suggested that they do it together; she would be his human guinea pig.

Forssmann had something else in mind.

A few days later, sweating from the summer heat as well as from his own excitement, he visited Nurse Ditzen in the small operating room. It was the noon break, and she was alone. He asked her to unlock the cabinet and get him a set of sterile surgical instruments —a scalpel, a hollow needle, sutures, and a ureteral catheter. Knowing no operations were scheduled for that afternoon, she asked Forssmann why he needed them. Then she realized what he was going to do. Convinced that she would be the first human to have a tube in her heart and excited by the knowledge that she would be making medical history, Gerda prepared everything Forssmann needed and willingly followed his command to climb onto the surgical table.

Forssmann strapped her arms and legs to the table, then stepped out of her view, toward the surgical workbench. He peeled the white towel from the instrument tray and examined the scalpel, the thin rubber ureteral tube, and the sutures Nurse Ditzen had sterilized. He glanced briefly across the room at the back of Gerda's head. She rested comfortably, expecting him to return at any moment with the novocaine.

Forssmann turned back to the surgical tray and briefly studied the ureteral tube. It was sixty-five centimeters long, just shy of thirty inches. Long enough, he estimated, to push through the hole in the vein in the elbow crease, slide up the arm, and twist across the shoulder, down a large vein in the chest, and into the venous connection to his heart.

His heart, not Gerda Ditzen's.

As the nurse adjusted her body to the tight-fitting straps, Forssmann worked confidently. He dabbed iodine over his left elbow crease and injected the novocaine to numb his skin. While he waited for the local anesthetic to take effect, he returned to the surgical table. Slowly and ceremoniously, he rubbed Nurse Ditzen's arm with iodine. He smiled reassuringly at Gerda, patted her arm gently and returned to the workbench, out of her sight.

Forssmann picked up the scalpel and cut through his skin. When he reached a large vein, he put down the scalpel, picked up the hollow needle, gently pushed it into the vein and left it in place. A small amount of blood spilled over his arm. Forssmann reached for the rubber tubing and pushed its tip through the hollow needle to guide it into the vein. The tube slithered along. There are valves in the veins that close when blood flows away from the heart, but because the tube was moving in the direction of the blood flow, the valves opened naturally and offered no resistance to Forssmann's tube. As he pushed the tube along the course of the vein in his upper arm, he felt a slight warmth, but no pain. Forssmann was learning that nature keeps the veins devoid of pain fibers.

When the tube reached the level of his shoulder, he stopped. Once it got to his heart, he would need documentation, an X ray of his chest to show the tube's precise location. The X-ray machine was in the basement of the hospital. He would need Nurse Ditzen's assistance.

Just then she called to him from across the room. Was anything wrong? When would he begin?

Forssmann went over to the table. As he loosened the straps, he replied, "It's done."

Gerda pushed herself off the table and stared at the tube in Forssmann's arm. She realized immediately that she had been duped.

"She was furious," Forssmann recalled. "I told her to relax and asked her to put a handkerchief around my arm and call the X-ray technician. Then we walked together down a flight of stairs to the X-ray department in the cellar."[10]

There, Forssmann went behind the fluoroscopic X-ray screen and ordered Nurse Ditzen to hold up a mirror so he could look over the screen and see the position of the catheter on the fluoroscope. The two were silent, completely engrossed, as they watched the tube move through Forssmann's vein. Neither noticed the X-ray technician slip out of the room.

Forssmann jiggled the catheter and inched it toward his heart; still there was no pain, only the continued feeling of warmth. On one occasion the tube hit something sensitive, for he had an urge to cough. He restrained himself.

The stillness was abruptly broken when Dr. Peter Romeis and the X-ray technician burst into the room. The frightened X-ray technician had woken Dr. Romeis from a nap. Romeis was Forssmann's friend and colleague and had expressed support for Forssmann's idea when Forssmann had first confided it to him. Now, to Forssmann's dismay, a bleary-eyed Romeis was yelling at him, telling him he was crazy.

"Romeis tried to pull the catheter from my arm," Forssmann recalled. "I fought him off, yelling, 'Nein, Nein. I must push it forward.' I kicked his shins and pushed the catheter until the mirror showed that the tip had reached my heart. Take a picture, I ordered. I knew the main point was to get radiographic proof that the catheter was indeed in the heart, not in a vein."

The X-ray technician snapped the picture. When it was developed a few minutes later, Forssmann had his proof. The catheter was in his right auricle, the first heart chamber that he could reach through the arm vein. The tube was too short to be pushed further into the heart.

Satisfied that he had the X-ray documentation he needed, Forssmann pulled the tube out of his heart, slid it back through the veins in his chest and arm and out of his elbow crease. A few drops of blood oozed out of the hole where the tube had pierced the vein, and Forssmann put a suture or two into the wound to stop the bleeding. Then he bandaged his elbow. The incision would turn red a few days later from a mild infection. But no further complications developed.

Forssmann was luckier than he could have known. Because so little was understood about the functions of the heart, he was oblivious to the dangers that can occur when anything touches the sensitive endocardium, or inside lining of the heart wall. Abnormal, potentially fatal heart rhythms can develop. Forssmann could have died suddenly, on the spot.

Oblivious to all this, Forssmann faced a more immediate problem: Dr. Schneider. The chief surgeon summoned the young intern to his office and started to give him a lecture about disobedience.

Forssmann was deeply concerned. He knew his career was at stake. Then Schneider asked to see the X ray.

As he told me the story years later, Forssmann burst into a roaring laugh. "When Schneider saw the X-ray pictures," Forssmann said, "he agreed the experiment was a good one and decided to celebrate. That evening we went to Kretchmer's, an old-fashioned, low-ceiling wine tavern where the waiters wore formal evening dress. We had a good dinner and several bottles of fine wine."

Forssmann repeated his experiment on himself five more times over the next four weeks. Each time, he went through the same procedure, and each time he successfully pushed the catheter through his arm to his heart.

Schneider urged Forssmann to write a scientific paper describing his experiments. The older doctor knew that Forssmann's technique was revolutionary, and as the word spread he feared others would steal the idea and claim credit. Schneider also anticipated the furor that would come when the medical profession learned of the daring experiments. He told Forssmann to stress the potential therapeutic applications of catheterization and its perceived usefulness for the emergency administration of drugs to the heart, and to minimize its usefulness for research purposes. "As a method of investigation, it is too revolutionary for doctors to understand," Schneider pointed out to his young apprentice. "Say that you tried it on cadavers before you did it on yourself. The reader of your paper must have the impression that it is not too revolutionary and that it was not made without a lot of forethought. Otherwise, the critics will tear you to pieces."

Decades later, Forssmann was criticized by those who said he had pursued the catheter technique for unmerited impractical ideas and not as the valuable physiological tool it came to be. Nevertheless, Forssmann did report some of the research potential he foresaw from his experiment. In his paper, he wrote, "The method opens up numerous prospects for new possibilities in the investigation of metabolism and of cardiac function." To counterbalance this and in an effort to comply with Schneider's suggestions, Forssmann invented a story. He claimed in his report that a colleague had been with him for the experiment and had, in fact, inserted the catheter into Forssmann's arm. At that point, according to Forssmann's report, the colleague became so frightened by the whole procedure that he ran away, leaving Forssmann alone, the catheter dangling from his arm. Forssmann went on to say that he did not continue with the experiment at that time, but a few days later he decided to do it again, alone. Forssmann also claimed in his report that he had tried the technique first on a cadaver. But, as he told me much later, he catheterized a cadaver only *after* he had put the tube into his own heart. Even today, textbooks describe the fictitious, aborted first effort and the nonexistent preliminary test on the corpse.

On September 13, 1929, Forssmann sent his paper to the *Klinische Wochenschrift,* the leading German medical journal. When it appeared in November, it caused the furor that Schneider had feared. Newspaper accounts sensationalized and distorted the technique. A

Berlin paper offered Forssmann a thousand marks to publish pictures of the X rays showing the catheter in his heart. Forssmann declined.

Then, Forssmann's priority in performing the experiment was challenged by Dr. Ernst Unger, the senior surgeon at another, more prestigious German hospital. In 1912, seventeen years before Forssmann's paper appeared, Unger and Fritz Bleichroeder and another colleague had published a series of papers in *Klinische Wochenschrift* in which they had reported inserting tubes into the arm and leg veins of four human volunteers.[11] Unger now claimed that in one experiment he had pushed the catheter through an artery into Bleichroeder's heart. Bleichroeder backed him up, arguing that the stabbing pain in his chest indicated that the tube had reached his heart. But if indeed it had, they had not mentioned it in their report. Furthermore, they had taken no X rays. Without them, there was no proof.

Unger wrote to the *Klinische Wochenschrift,* charging that its editor had shirked his journalistic duties in failing to note the previous claim. Forssmann explained that because the titles of the previous papers had given no hint that they were related in any way to his project, he had not read them before publishing his own paper. The editor printed a brief note from Forssmann that explained the situation but did not yield priority.[12]

On October 1, 1929, a month before his report would be published, Forssmann moved from Eberswalde to Dr. Ferdinand Sauerbruch's clinic at the Charité Hospital in Berlin, where he took an unpaid position in the expectation of working closely with the renowned surgeon.[13] Sauerbruch's clinic had become the mecca of German surgery, but from the start Forssmann was unhappy. He seldom had a chance to operate on patients, and he rarely saw Sauerbruch. When he did manage to corner him for a few minutes to outline his plans for further experiments, Sauerbruch rejected them. Sauerbruch, the great teacher and the surgeon who had performed pioneering heart operations, failed to appreciate the potential benefits of cardiac catheterization. When Forssmann's paper was published, his superiors at Charité accused him of seeking publicity. A little more than a month after he had started work, Sauerbruch summoned Forssmann to his office and fired him.

Happily for Forssmann, his old position with Schneider was vacant, and he returned to Eberswalde. There he outlined a second experiment with implications as revolutionary as his first. It was an experiment in angiocardiography, a technique in which a radiopaque substance that blocks X rays is injected into an artery or a vein so that the circulatory system can be outlined on the pictures. The areas in which the substance is present appear white on the X-ray films.

Forssmann's proposed technique not only was different but also involved considerable risk. Instead of squirting contrast material into the arm vein so that it would disperse into the blood, Forssmann wanted to put a tube directly into the heart and squirt a different type of contrast material through it. He hoped that the contrast material would outline the anatomy of the chambers of the right side of the heart. Unlike his first experiment, this one required prior work with animals. Because the facilities at the hospital in Eberswalde were too small for this type of research, Forssmann arranged to do the studies with Dr. Willy Felix at Neukölln Hospital in Berlin. He began with rabbits, but they proved unsuitable. When Forssmann's thin catheters touched the animal's hearts, abnormal heart rhythms developed and the rabbits died.

Forssmann then tried dogs. At that time hospitals were not equipped, as they are now, with special quarters for experimental animals. Forssmann's mother cared for the dogs at her apartment. There he would inject a dog with morphine, put the sleepy animal into a potato sack and take it by motorcycle to the hospital. In experiments that recalled those of the French physiologists, Forssmann would push a catheter through a vein in the dog's neck and into its heart.

Radiopaque chemicals were just beginning to be used to help X-ray the urinary system and the stomach. Forssmann knew it would be much more difficult to use the technique with the heart, because the heart moves so rapidly. The X-ray exposure would have to be made quickly and at the precise moment. Forssmann chose an arbitrary dose of one of the radiopaque chemicals and injected it into the dogs. He took X rays, hoping that by luck he would catch a flash of the chemical rushing through one of the chambers of the heart. The first chemical he used killed several dogs, and he switched to another, sodium iodide. This proved to be safe and he managed to get the X rays he wanted. By putting about thirty of them in sequence, he showed that the heart actions could be demonstrated radiographically. Now, at least, he knew that the technique was feasible. But would it be safe on humans?

Forssmann wasn't sure. "I didn't know what the reaction of the intima [the inner lining of blood vessels] would be when the chemical was injected," he said. "I was a little anxious, more nervous than I was before the first self-experiment. You can pull a catheter out of the body, but what is injected into the heart stays in. So I experimented for a few days. I pressed the solutions of sodium iodide against my buccal mucosa [the inside of the mouth] for several hours. I also tested it with samples of blood in the laboratory. There were no reactions. Then I thought: Now I can do it on man." There was never any question in his mind who that man would be.

On the first attempt, a bent catheter tip caused the tube to deviate into a neck vein instead of going into the heart. When the tip reached the middle of the neck, it produced a dull pain in his ear. He tried again. This time the tube went smoothly to the heart. He injected the sodium iodide and felt only a mild irritation of the nasal membranes, an unpleasant transient taste in his mouth, and a slight feeling of dizziness, which passed quickly. Disappointingly, the X rays were unsatisfactory.

Forssmann repeated the experiment. At this point, he was no longer threading the catheter through the veins in his elbow crease because the most readily accessible of these blood vessels had been sewn closed after his previous catheterization experiments. Instead, he was injecting a local anesthetic into the skin around his groin and inserting the catheter into a vein in his upper leg. He would then push it up along the veins in his thigh to the abdomen and further into the main vein that drains blood from the lower half of the body and on into its connection with the heart.

Fifty years later the experience was still vivid in Forssmann's mind. As he watched one of his grandchildren crawl across the living room floor, he explained to me why he had had to be the subject of such a messy and technically difficult experiment: "Nobody else," he said, "would dirty his fingers with such experiments."

On that second try, he experienced the same fleeting light-headed feeling and a warm sensation in his mouth. Once again, the X rays were of poor quality. All that could be seen was a little cloud at the end of the catheter. The pictures were useless for diagnostic purposes. By this time Forssmann had put a tube into his heart *nine* times.

Shortly before Forssmann's report of his angiographic experiments appeared in a medical journal, he presented his findings at a scientific meeting in Berlin.[14] Ferdinand Sauerbruch heard his paper and invited him to return to his clinic. Forssmann, believing that Sauerbruch would now encourage his research, accepted and returned to the Charité Hospital, still as an unpaid assistant. The year was 1931.

Unfortunately, it was more of the same. In the next sixteen months, Forssmann performed just three operations, about as many as he might do with Schneider in a week in Eberswalde. Sauerbruch delegated the running of his clinic to a group of subordinates who neither accepted Forssmann nor believed that he was cut out for scientific research. Forssmann was fired again. As a medical friend told him many years later, "Be happy Sauerbruch and his staff did not understand. Had they, they would have won the Nobel Prize, not you."[15]

By 1935 Forssmann was back in Berlin, this time working with another physician, Dr. Karl Heusch, at the Rudolf Virchow Hospital. And he was ready for another self-experiment. Others had reported the technique of aortography (X rays of the aorta, the main vessel leading from the heart), but only under general anesthesia. Forssmann and Heusch wanted to learn if they could perform this technique using a local anesthetic. The two doctors decided to try it on each other. Aiming with a needle for Forssmann's aorta, Heusch pierced an area between his shoulder blade and a vertebra in his spine. Each jab at the aorta caused Forssmann excruciating pain. After the third unsuccessful attempt, Forssmann took to his bed with headaches and a stiff back.

By now Forssmann was married and had small children. When he suggested repeating the experiment, his wife, who was also a doctor, asked him not to go on. This time Forssmann listened. He had performed his last self-experiment.

To support his family, Forssmann decided to specialize in urology and general surgery. But in spite of his research successes, or more accurately because of them, he had great difficulty getting established. In one town, officials who had read his medical papers turned down his application for the job of chief surgeon. They reasoned that if he had done all these experiments on his own heart, what might he do to the hearts of his patients?

Not only did Forssmann's self-experiments create unexpected difficulties, but so would another experience. At Sauerbruch's clinic, Forssmann had been impressed by a senior staff member, a surgeon who now urged him to join the Nazi party. Forssmann's new Nazi affiliations led to an offer of the very thing his medical colleagues would not grant—the best available scientific equipment and plenty of human guinea pigs with which to carry on his research. Forssmann rejected the opportunity. "To use defenseless patients as guinea pigs," he said, "was a price I would never be prepared to pay for the realization of my dreams."[16]

World War II broke out and Forssmann served with the German army on the Russian front. In 1945 he avoided capture by the Russians by swimming across the Elbe River. On the other side he was taken prisoner by the American Army.

Later, because of his Nazi associations, West German officials forbade him to practice medicine. In the 1950s, when they rescinded the order, Forssmann found work as a urologist in a small German farming community, where his name was not known. It remained for others to apply his revolutionary techniques to the everyday practice of medicine.

Two of the crucial figures in that effort—Dr. André Cournand and Dr. Dickinson Richards—were based in New York City. During the early 1930s they had read Forssmann's papers on cardiac catheterization and angiography. Although they attached little value to his suggestion of using the technique for emergency administration of drugs, they saw enormous potential in catheterization as a technique to obtain blood samples from the heart in order to study the blood concentrations of oxygen and carbon dioxide, the chief respiratory gases in the blood. In 1936 they began a series of experiments in which they catheterized the hearts of dogs and a chimpanzee; they discovered that the concentrations of the gases changed drastically as blood passed from the body into the lungs and back into the heart.[17] In order to understand the physiology of the heart and lungs, doctors needed to know how much these concentrations differed in humans.

But it was four more years—1940—before Richards and Cournand felt confident enough to experiment on a human. Their first human catheterization was performed on a patient dying of cancer at Columbia-Presbyterian Medical Center; the attempt failed because cancerous growths obstructed passage of the tube through the veins. Later Richards and Cournand, working at Bellevue Hospital, used the technique experimentally in patients who were suffering from heart failure due to advanced stages of high blood pressure. By 1942 the New York team had perfected the technique for use in measuring blood components in the right side of the heart and later in the pulmonary artery that delivers deoxygenated blood from the heart to the lungs.

Neither Cournand nor Richards did what they knew Forssmann had done—neither put a tube into his own heart.

As a young man, it is true, Cournand had experimented on himself, allowing dozens of blood samples to be taken from an artery in his wrist; he had also breathed nitrogen and other gases. In an interview with me he said his superiors had rejected his offer to have his heart catheterized as a normal volunteer because of his age; he was then approaching fifty. However, a scientific paper published about those experiments, and coauthored by Cournand, lists the age range of the subjects as thirty-eight to seventy-three.[18] That omission was to haunt Cournand for the rest of his life. "My regret," he admitted, "is from a psychological point of view—that people said, well, he did it on other people but not on himself."[19]

In 1956 Forssmann was plucked from obscurity when he, Cournand, and Richards shared the Nobel Prize in Physiology or Medicine. At the Nobel Prize ceremonies in Stockholm, Professor Göran Liljestrand, an official of the Nobel Committee, paid tribute to Forssmann's courage in doing the "by no means harmless" experiments on himself: "It must have required firm conviction of the value of the method to induce self-experimentation of the kind carried out by Forssmann. His later disappointment must have been all the more bitter . . . Forssmann was not given the necessary support; he was, on the contrary, subjected to criticism of such exaggerated severity that it robbed him of any inclination to continue. This criticism was based on an unsubstantiated belief in the danger of the intervention, thus affording proof that—even in our enlightened times—a valuable suggestion may remain unexploited on the grounds of a preconceived opinion."[20]

After winning the Nobel Prize, Forssmann was asked to head a German cardiovascular research institute and to perform open-heart surgery. But he recognized that he was not qualified for either position. He returned to his small farming town and continued to practice urology. "I was conscious that the others had made so much progress I could not catch up on the basics," Forssmann told me. Leaning back in a chair in his living room, glancing a little wistfully at the snowdrifts outside his picture window, he continued, "The basic sciences had become so developed that I would have needed ten years to learn the math, chemistry, and physics necessary to run an institute." Forssmann's deep voice gave way to a chuckle as he told me that even experts sometimes forget what they learn. In 1971, he said, he learned that 140 years earlier another German physician, Johann Dieffenbach, had deliberately put a catheter into the heart of a patient near death from cholera. The aim was to drain thick blood from the heart.[21]

A few months before his death in 1979 at age seventy-four, Forssmann said what must have been on his mind for nearly half a century: "It was very painful. I felt that I had planted an apple orchard and other men who had gathered the harvest stood at the wall, laughing at me."

Today the importance of Werner Forssmann's seedling apples is universally recognized. His techniques have become standard in medical practice. Without them, birth defects affecting the heart would be irreparable and there would be no lifesaving operations on patients whose heart valves have been scarred by bouts with rheumatic fever or other diseases. Nor would heart surgeons be able to do coronary bypass operations to relieve the crushing chest pains of angina pectoris or to minimize the chances of a heart attack. Forssmann's techniques are the basis of many tests, now routine, done in coronary care units to monitor the recovery of patients from heart attacks or in cardiac catheterization laboratories to diagnose heart ailments. Without his work, it would be impossible to implant pacemakers to electronically control the beats of a heart whose rhythm is too slow or erratic. His experiments were as courageous—the results as far-reaching—as any in the annals of medicine.

# Chapter Three

# THE PERILOUS ROUTE TO PAINLESS SURGERY

On October 16, 1846, Dr. John C. Warren, a professor of surgery at Harvard, entered the surgical amphitheater of the Massachusetts General Hospital. Attired in the nonsterile formal garb worn by surgeons of his day, Warren waited by his patient, twenty-one-year-old Edward Gilbert Abbott, who since birth had had a large tumor under the left side of his jaw. Dr. Warren was going to remove it.

Warren glanced about uneasily. He wondered if perhaps he had not been too hasty in granting permission for this first public demonstration of the use of ether in an operation. He looked at his watch. Where was Morton?

Dr. William T. G. Morton was an unusual second-year student at Harvard Medical School, one who already had an established dental practice and who also ran a factory that mass-produced false teeth. The income he received from these endeavors was paying for his medical education. Morton had performed several experiments with ether and had used it successfully to eliminate pain in dental extractions. The amount of ether necessary, however, to anesthetize someone for a short dental extraction was one thing. The longer, deeper anesthesia needed to do extensive surgery was another. Even so, Morton was confident ether would work in surgery as well as in dentistry and he had convinced Dr. Warren to let him prove it. Now, however, it looked as though Morton had changed his mind.

Warren glanced again at his watch. Becoming impatient, he told the audience, "I presume he is otherwise engaged," bringing "derisive laughs" from the assembly of senior physicians and Harvard medical students. After waiting fifteen more minutes, Warren put his watch into his pocket, picked up his scalpel, and turned to make an incision.

Just at that moment, a breathless Morton arrived. He had been delayed, he said, making last-minute adjustments to the apparatus he held in his hand. It consisted of a tube connected to a glass globe, with which he would administer the ether. Warren pulled back his scalpel, retreated, and said in a strong voice, "Well, sir, your patient is ready."

Morton assembled his apparatus and administered the ether to Abbott, who said he was not afraid of the experiment. Within five minutes, the patient felt no pain from a sharp pinch; soon after, he became unconscious. "Dr. Warren," Morton said, *"your* patient is ready."

Thus began a tradition that continues today. When the anesthesiologist believes that enough anesthetic has been delivered to the patient for the operation to begin, he informs the surgeon: "Doctor, your patient is ready."

The spectators were silent—"the stillness oppressive," one of them remembered.[1] As Warren picked up his scalpel again, strong men stood by, ready to grab young Abbott's arms and legs in case the anesthetic did not work. But the surgeon's slashes drew no cries. The doctors and the students in the amphitheater bent forward, straining to follow each step. Warren skillfully removed the tumor in a few minutes. When the operation was finished, Morton aroused Abbott. The account of the operation in the records of the Massachusetts General Hospital reads: "To the surprise of Dr. Warren and the other gentlemen present, the patient did not shrink, nor cry out, but during the procedure he began to move his limbs and utter extraordinary expressions, and these movements seemed to indicate the existence of pain; but after he had recovered his faculties, he said he had experienced none; but only a sensation like that of scraping the part with a blunt instrument, and he ever after continued to say he had not felt any pain."[2]

When Abbott was fully awake, Dr. Warren turned to the audience and announced: "Gentlemen, this is no humbug."[3]

And it wasn't. But it had been a long time coming.

In the days before anesthesia, a surgeon's reputation was determined by the swiftness of his scalpel. It usually took less than a minute for Alexander Pope's friend William Cheselden to cut and then use his fingers and a forceps to extract a stone from the urinary bladder of a patient at St. Thomas Hospital in London.[4] That was in the early eighteenth century. By the nineteenth century, Dr. Robert

Liston was amputating legs at University College in London in less than thirty seconds.[5] Liston, who died just one year after Morton's dramatic demonstration of the efficacy of ether, was considered the finest and swiftest surgeon of his day. A showman with extraordinary manual dexterity and great physical strength, he would begin each operation by exclaiming, "Time me, gentlemen, time me." There are descriptions of Liston amputating a leg at the thigh by compressing the artery with his left hand and sawing with his right.

From the earliest days of medicine, surgeons had tried all manner of primitive techniques to ease their patients' pain. The Egyptians, for example, used diluted narcotics. Other surgeons made their patients drunk with brandy and then tied them to wooden benches that served as operating tables. In Europe, some surgeons choked their patients unconscious before operating. Still others applied pressure to a nerve or artery to make an area "fall asleep." In the sixteenth century, the French surgeon (and barber) Ambroise Paré devised a novel expedient: He put a wooden bowl over the head of a patient and pounded a hammer against it to knock him unconscious.[6]

Because there was little that could be done to make operations bearable, surgeons were limited to performing very simple ones; only the rare human could tolerate any procedure that required more than a few minutes. Even when a patient was able to withstand the pain of prolonged surgery, he was very apt to die of infection in the following days.

It is striking how long it took for people to see that common anesthetic agents might have a use in surgery. For decades self-experimenters had suspected the powers of these agents, and ultimately their observations played a crucial role in the development of surgical anesthesia. In fact, there is perhaps no other area of medicine where the tradition and pattern of self-experimentation has been so prominent. It was there from the earliest days of modern chemistry when Joseph Priestley, an English cleric, experimented on himself with oxygen and nitrous oxide. For Priestley, chemistry was an avocation. Nevertheless, he discovered a number of gases, two of which are among the most important agents now used in anesthesia.

In 1774, when Priestley prepared pure oxygen, he called it dephlogisticated air, after the Greek word for inflammation and because it lacked phlogiston, a hypothetical substance thought to be released during combustion. Priestley conjectured that his new discoveries might be useful in diseases of the lungs, and after breathing oxygen he related: "I fancied that my breast felt peculiarly light and easy for some time afterwards. Who can tell but that, in time, this pure air may become a fashionable article in luxury. Hitherto, only two mice and myself have had the privilege of breathing it."[7]

Oxygen and nitrous oxide—or "laughing gas" as it was later called—attracted the interest of another Englishman, Dr. Thomas Beddoes, a leader in the then fashionable use of gases to treat many medical conditions. The practice was known as pneumatic medicine, and Beddoes urged a more scientific approach. Following Priestley's suggestion, in 1799 Beddoes founded the Medical Pneumatic Institution to make inhalation gases and to investigate their use in medical treatment. He appointed as the director of the institute twenty-one-year-old Humphry Davy, an exuberant artist, fisherman, and lover of nature, who had turned from poetry to chemistry.

Davy immediately found himself in the midst of controversy. Some years earlier, Samuel Latham Mitchill, an American physician who had never himself experimented with nitrous oxide, had branded the gas as dangerous. Mitchill believed that nitrous oxide, which he called oside of septon, was a "principle of contagion." He theorized that even the smallest amounts could produce the most terrible effects when breathed by animals or when applied to the skin or muscles. Partly to test Mitchill's hypothesis, Davy decided to breathe nitrous oxide himself. He wanted to measure how long he could safely inhale the gas and to study its effect on his pulse and on his body.[8] "I was aware of the danger of this experiment," Davy wrote. "It certainly would never have been made if the hypothesis of Dr. Mitchill had in the least influenced my mind."[9] In fact, there were other potential dangers of which he could not have been aware. For example, impurities in nitrous oxide can lead to the production of nitrogen peroxide, an insidious lung irritant.

Davy started cautiously, with a single inhalation of the gas. Once assured it was safe to breathe, he inhaled progressively larger amounts. "Between May and July, I habitually breathed the gas, occasionally three or four times a day for a week together; at other periods, four or five times a week only."[10]

The gas, he discovered unexpectedly, had certain pleasurable side effects. He tried it on some of his friends, among them the poets Samuel Taylor Coleridge and Robert Southey and Dr. Peter Mark Roget, the compiler of the *Thesaurus.* Davy, careful to observe the effects, discovered the painkilling, or analgesic, properties of nitrous oxide on himself:

"In one instance when I had head-ache from indigestion, it was immediately removed by the effects of a large dose of gas; though it afterwards returned, but with much less violence. In a second instance, a slighter degree of head-ache was wholly removed by two doses of gas.

"The power of the immediate operation of the gas in removing intense physical pain, I had a very good opportunity of ascertaining.

"In cutting one of the unlucky teeth called dentes sapientiae [wisdom teeth], I experienced an extensive inflammation of the gum, accompanied with great pain, which equally destroyed the power of repose, and of consistent action.

"On the day when the inflammation was most troublesome, I breathed three large doses of nitrous oxide. The pain always diminished after the first four or five inspirations; the thrilling came on as usual, and uneasiness was for a few minutes swallowed up in pleasure. As the former state of mind however returned, the state of organ returned with it; and I once imagined that the pain was more severe after the experiment than before."[11]

The conclusion from his self-experiments seemed inescapable: "As nitrous oxide in its extensive operation appears capable of destroying physical pain, it may probably be used with advantage during surgical operations in which no great effusion of blood takes place."[12] No one knows why Davy qualified his recommendation.

Davy inhaled nitrous oxide almost daily and also breathed other gases. He nearly lost his life breathing water gas, which is a mixture of hydrogen and carbon monoxide. He is credited with the discovery of two elements, sodium and potassium, and was knighted for inventing the miner's safety lamp. As a popular lecturer and a prominent society figure in London, Davy had the ear of England's scientific and cultural leaders. Yet for more than four decades doctors paid no attention to his suggestion that nitrous oxide be tried as an anesthetic —and he never pursued it himself.

Nor was there serious interest in the observations that Dr. Henry Hill Hickman made a few years later. Hickman, a physician in an English farming town, noted that no experiments had been done to determine whether operations could be successfully performed on animals under carbon dioxide. In 1824, he administered carbon dioxide to mice, dogs, and chickens, and apparently subsequently performed painless amputations on them. "I feel perfectly satisfied," Hickman wrote, "that any surgical operation might be performed with quite as much safety upon a subject in an insensible state, as in a sensible state . . ."[13]

Hickman went to Paris, then the leading medical center, to plead for further experiments on suspending sensation. His appeal was referred to the French Royal Academy's Section of Medicine. A committee was appointed to investigate, but nothing further was heard from it or from Hickman.

Untold suffering could have been prevented if the medical men of the time had taken the implications of Davy's or Hickman's work more seriously. But the relief of suffering was not the highest priority in a society that routinely put children to work and that callously disregarded pain and affliction. Nitrous oxide would eventually become one of the most widely used anesthetics, but the stimulus for making it so would come from the pleasurable use of another gas—ether.

Ether frolics—or "jags" as they were also called then—were as popular in mid-nineteenth century America as marijuana smoking or cocaine sniffing is today, the difference being that ether was entirely legal and ether frolics were held wherever people socialized. Nevertheless, ether was dangerous. Participants who inhaled too much risked complications ranging from vomiting to death. Still, showmen moved from village to town to city, encouraging people to sniff the gas and allowing them to inhale only enough to produce exhilaration, not enough to make them unconscious.

Physicians were among the eager participants. Dr. Crawford W. Long, who had learned about ether frolics as a medical student at the University of Pennsylvania in Philadelphia, was one. In 1841, at twenty-six, Long returned to his home state of Georgia and set up practice in Jefferson, a rural cotton farming village, about sixty-five miles north of Atlanta. When an itinerant showman came through the town demonstrating nitrous oxide, the neighbors challenged the young physician to match the laughing gas performance with ether.

Long took a bottle of ether off his shelf and gave a few whiffs to a man who, the day before, had inhaled nitrous oxide at the show. Then Long inhaled it himself before handing it to others in his office. The ether must have compared favorably to the nitrous oxide for ether frolics soon became a fad in Jefferson and before long it had spread to other parts of Georgia.

A tall, dashing man, something of a womanizer, Long thought up another social use for ether. When the young practitioner wrote to a druggist-friend in nearby Athens for a fresh supply of the drug, he confided his purpose: "We have some girls in Jefferson who are anxious to see it taken, and you know nothing would afford me more pleasure than to take it in their presence and to get a few sweet kisses."[14] One of these girls, Caroline Swain, the niece of the governor of North Carolina, later became his wife.

Long wrote that his frequent use of ether led to ". . . bruised or painful spots on my person which I had no recollection of causing and which I felt satisfied were received while under the influence of ether. I noticed my friends while etherized received falls and blows which I believed were sufficient to produce pain on a person not in a state of anesthesia, and on questioning them they uniformly assured me that they did not feel the least pain from these accidents."[15]

Clearly there was a pleasure-seeking element to Long's self-experiments. But there was a serious side, too, and this was where serendipity played its role. Long did not dismiss the painless bruises as a trivial observation. The more he thought about his experiences, the more he wondered whether ether could be used to relieve the pain of surgery.

Then, in 1842, a patient, James M. Venable, asked Long to remove two small cysts from the nape of his neck. They arranged a day for the operation, but, dreading the pain, Venable postponed it. This happened several times before Long, knowing that Venable was fond of inhaling ether, mentioned to his patient the painless bruises that he and others had acquired in the frolics. Long proposed giving Venable ether before removing the tumors. Venable agreed.

That evening, March 30, 1842, Long poured ether on a towel and held it with one hand under Venable's nose. The doctor used his other hand alternately to feel his patient's pulse and to prick his skin with a pin to test his sensitivity to pain. When Venable could no longer feel the pinprick, Long picked up his scalpel and successfully removed the first cyst in about five minutes. Later, in the presence of witnesses, he removed the second. Since correct dosages of ether were unknown, Long and Venable had taken an enormous risk, a risk much greater than they could have imagined.

By 1846, the year Morton publicly demonstrated the use of ether for the first time, Long had already used the gas for six operations. But he had not communicated his successes to the medical profession.

Meanwhile, others had discovered the benefit of nitrous oxide in relieving dental pain. On December 10, 1844, a newspaper advertisement heralded the arrival in Hartford, Connecticut, of "Professor" Gardner Q. Colton. "Professor" Colton was an entrepreneur who had begun his career as a five-dollar-per-year apprentice to a chairmaker. Colton had studied medicine for a period, but he had not earned a degree. However, during his studies Colton had learned of the exhilarating effects of inhaling nitrous oxide. He left the chairmaking business and went on the road. Public demonstrations of nitrous oxide were a great deal more profitable than chairs; one show in New York yielded $535. Colton traveled throughout New England giving exhibitions, inhaling the substance first himself to show his audience that it was safe.

The advertisement in the Hartford paper attracted a twenty-six-year-old dentist, Dr. Horace Wells. To Wells, Colton's laughing gas exhibition was a welcome distraction from financial worries following the recent dissolution of his partnership with the same Boston dentist who, two years later, would keep Dr. Warren waiting in the surgical amphitheater of the Massachusetts General Hospital, Dr. William T. G. Morton.

When the "Professor" called for volunteers, Wells went up on stage. He watched a drugstore clerk inhale nitrous oxide, then run across the stage to battle one of the strong men hired to protect people under the influence of the gas. The volunteer tripped, gashing his leg. Blood spurted. Wells noted that it was not until the effects of the gas wore off that the clerk began to suffer pain from his injury.

After the performance, the scientifically minded Wells asked Colton why teeth could not be extracted while a person was under the influence of the gas. Colton had never thought of the possibility. Wells was fascinated by the potential of the gas and decided to experiment on himself. Not only would he inhale nitrous oxide, but while anesthetized he would allow a colleague to pull one of his own teeth. Wells asked Colton to bring a silk bag of the gas to his office (in those days nitrous oxide was sometimes stored in silk bags). Colton hesitated at first, but was easily persuaded when Wells explained that there was a fortune to be made from painless dentistry.

The self-experiment was done the next day, December 11, 1844. Colton was not trained to pull teeth, so Wells asked a dentist-friend, Dr. John M. Riggs, to anesthetize him and take out his tooth. When the effects of the nitrous oxide wore off, Wells looked up at Riggs, who held the extracted upper molar, and exclaimed: "It is the greatest discovery ever made. I didn't feel as much as the prick of a pin."[16]

Over the next several days Wells removed teeth painlessly from about fifteen patients. A month later, accompanied by his former partner, Morton, he went to the Massachusetts General Hospital in Boston to demonstrate his nitrous oxide technique. During his lecture Wells was struck by the skepticism of doctors and students alike, many of whom had inhaled the gas for fun. None seemed willing to assist him. He was finally invited to administer the gas to a patient who was about to have a leg amputated, but the patient decided not to go through with the operation. Instead, Wells prepared to extract a tooth from another volunteer. He described what happened next: "Unfortunately for the experiment, the gas bag was by mistake withdrawn much too soon, and he [the patient] was but partially under its influence when the tooth was extracted. He testified that he experienced some pain, but not as much as usually attends the operation . . . several expressed their opinion that it was a humbug affair."[17] Humiliated, Wells returned home.

Wells did not know what has been learned since—that some patients need larger doses of anesthetics than others.

The next year, 1846, William Morton took up where Wells had left off. Presumably Morton's problems with Wells and Wells's own failed demonstration with nitrous oxide led Morton to use another gas. After consulting his chemistry teacher and preceptor, Dr. Charles T. Jackson,[18] and after convincing himself of its safety by reading about the frolics, Morton chose pure sulfuric ether, which he called "the toy of professors and students."

Morton was a peculiar man. His wife wrote, "never shall I forget my sensation as a young bride at sleeping in a room where a tall, gaunt skeleton stood in a big box near the head of the bed."[19] Morton's wife may have grown accustomed to the skeleton by the bed, but she never grew to like the smell of ether that came to saturate her husband's clothes. She merely tolerated it. And Morton persisted in his investigations of the effect of the gas on green worms, bugs, the family dog, cats, and other animals.

Initially, ether was considered dangerous because it was theorized that the vapor would mix with room air and explode when exposed to the flame of a candle. "To satisfy myself upon this point," Morton wrote, "I placed an ounce of ether upon a shovel, fastened to a pole eight feet long; I then placed the shovel under a lighted gas lamp, so that the ethereal vapor was exposed to its blaze; and, finding that it did not ignite, I inhaled it for a minute or two, and found that I could breathe directly against the flame of a lamp without any danger. I afterward held a lighted paper over a saucer of ether, and found that, at the distance of two inches, no effect was produced, but, that when the flame was brought within half an inch of the ether, it immediately ignited."[20] So Morton simply avoided bringing the flame very close to a patient or a bottle of ether. Still, Morton was extraordinarily lucky.

"Finding that when closed up in a hollow tooth, and sealed with wax, ether would gradually destroy the sensibility of the part, I reasoned that perhaps when inhaled it might destroy or greatly alleviate sensibility to pain generally," Morton said. So he inhaled from a handkerchief that had been saturated with ether and the effect, he said, suggested that "a tooth could have been drawn with but little pain or consciousness."[21] Small doses of ether could kill pain. Morton offered a five-dollar reward to any person who would allow him to extract an aching tooth while under ether. When no one answered his advertisement, his two assistants volunteered. But because the ether was impure, it was ineffective, and both operations proved painful.

Undaunted, Morton went on to perform an experiment on himself. His wife described it. "My husband, with characteristic persistence, at once procured a supply of pure ether, and, unwilling to wait longer for a subject, shut himself up in his office, and tested it upon himself, with such success that for several minutes he lay there unconscious. That night he came home late, in a great state of excitement, but so happy that he could scarcely calm himself to tell me what had occurred; and I, too, became so excited that I could scarcely wait to hear. At last he told me of the experiment upon himself, and I grew sick at heart as the thought came to me that he might have died there alone."[22] His watch, Morton said, showed he had been unconscious for seven to eight minutes.

Shortly thereafter, still unable to find anyone willing to accept his five-dollar offer, Morton planned another self-experiment. According to his wife, "He was on the point of etherizing himself once more, and having one of his assistants extract a tooth from his own head, when there came a faint ring at the bell . . ." and a patient with a toothache. The operation was successful.

Morton's next success was with Dr. Warren's patient Edward Gilbert Abbott at the Massachusetts General Hospital. That success led to a second painless operation the following day, the removal of a fatty tumor from the arm of a woman.

A new era of medicine had begun. Oliver Wendell Holmes, wanting to have some stake in the discovery, wrote to Morton suggesting the new technique be called *anesthesia* from the Greek, meaning a feeling of insensibility.[23]

But now a bitter fight—as acrimonious as any in the annals of medicine—began, as four men scrambled to win credit for the discovery of anesthesia.

Morton, seeking profit, refused to disclose the composition of his anesthetic agent, and he gave it a mysterious name, "letheon." Just after the successful operations at the Massachusetts General Hospital, he and his former professor, Jackson, attempted to patent it. Their secret compact was soon broken, and "letheon" was identified as ether. Jackson, Long, Morton, and Wells and their respective supporters petitioned Congress separately for rewards. Eight years later, Congress dropped the matter, with no resolution.

In fact, Crawford Long's operation on James Venable had been the first, but he lost full credit because he failed to publish his results. Wells did much dental work on patients under nitrous oxide anesthesia, but he was unlucky in his public attempt to perform surgical anesthesia at Massachusetts General, and he did not push his experiments to a successful conclusion. It is doubtful that Jackson did more than suggest pure sulfur ether to Morton. Morton first demonstrated surgical anesthesia publicly and was responsible for gaining its acceptance elsewhere. His name is usually placed at the top of the list.

Wells became increasingly frustrated as he watched ether, not nitrous oxide, become the popular anesthetic for general anesthesia in the United States. He stopped practicing dentistry and became a salesman for chloroform, which European doctors would come to prefer over ether. He inhaled it to determine the dose and the duration of its effects, but in a short time he became addicted to it. "Insanity seems to have been produced," commented the *Boston Medical and Surgical Journal* in Wells's obituary in 1848.[24] That year, at the age of thirty-three, Wells had been arrested for hurling sulfuric acid at two prostitutes on Broadway in New York City. He was sent to the Tombs on a Friday: The following Sunday, after listening to a sermon in the prison chapel, he somehow obtained a razor blade and chloroform. After writing a long letter to the newspapers and to his family, he committed suicide. He apparently inhaled the chloroform and then cut the main artery in his left thigh; he bled to death. A few days later his widow received a letter addressed to Wells. From it she learned that the Paris Medical Society had credited her husband with being the first to discover and successfully use anesthesia for painless surgery.

Thereafter Morton was accused widely, though unfairly, of being responsible for driving Wells to suicide. He tried to profit from the manufacture of the apparatus to deliver ether, but could not; anyone now could make it. Morton, who never did complete his medical degree, resumed his dental practice, only to find that he no longer had an advantage over his competitors, who also used anesthesia. In 1868, after the claims and counterclaims had dropped out of the news, Morton read a magazine article that supported Jackson as the discoverer of surgical anesthesia. It "agitated him to an extent I had never seen before," his wife said.[25] Morton went to New York to confront the editors. A few days later the forty-eight-year-old dentist suffered a stroke while riding in a carriage through Central Park.

Meanwhile Jackson declared himself the discoverer of surgical anesthesia and won support from the Academy of Sciences of the Institute of France at a time when the French strongly influenced American medicine. But by this time Jackson was an alcoholic, and after Morton's death he was found screaming at his former student's graveside in Mount Auburn Cemetery in Cambridge. Jackson was committed to the McLean Asylum, a part of the Massachusetts General Hospital, where he spent the last twelve years of his life. He died at the age of seventy-five.[26]

Of the four principals, Long fared the best. He continued to practice medicine and to own a pharmacy in Georgia. He died in 1878 at age sixty-two as he was about to administer ether to a woman in childbirth.

Word of the marvels of ether spread quickly, and, as it did, doctors began to learn that the gas was by no means perfect. When sulfur dioxide or other impurities got into ether, the subdivisions of the windpipe, known as the bronchi, through which oxygen and carbon dioxide pass into and out of the lungs, could become irritated. Worse, too much ether could kill a patient.

So doctors looked for other anesthetics, a hunt that was itself full of risks because most of the newer chemicals tested were even more dangerous. One who joined the search was Sir James Y. Simpson, an Edinburgh obstetrician, who wrote in 1847: "I have tried upon myself and others the inhalation of different other volatile fluids, with the hope that some one of them might be found to possess the advantages of ether, without its disadvantages. For this purpose, I selected for experiment and have inhaled several chemical liquids of a more fragrant or agreeable odor, such as the chloride of hydrocarbon (or Dutch liquid), acetone, nitrate of oxide of ethyle (nitrate ether), benzin, the vapor of iodoform, etc. I have found, however, one infinitely more efficacious than any of the others, viz., Chloroform . . ."[27]

Chloroform, the anesthetic that drove Wells to kill himself, had been discovered by Eugène Soubeiran in France in 1831 and a year later by Justus von Liebig in Germany. In those days it had limited application to medicine, although some doctors prescribed its inhalation on the presumption it might help lung disorders. Others used it to relieve nerve pain. In March 1847 Pierre J.-M. Flourens reported to the French Academy of Sciences on his experiments on animals using chloroform and other anesthetics. Although several doctors had observed the anesthetic properties of chloroform, it fell to Sir James Simpson to use it in surgery.

In the week following Simpson's self-experiments with chloroform, the Edinburgh obstetrician administered it to about thirty women just before childbirth. All of the women delivered their babies painlessly.[28] This miraculous advance was regarded as a scandal by the Edinburgh medical establishment; most doctors considered pain in labor a biological necessity. The Scottish doctors were influenced by the Presbyterian clergy, who derided the abolition of pain in childbirth as heresy. But Simpson was resourceful and tenacious. He convinced the public that God had intended women to benefit from anesthesia. In the twenty-first verse of the second chapter of Genesis, Simpson pointed out, the Lord did the first recorded surgical operation by taking a rib from Adam to fashion Eve—and He used an anesthetic in the process. "And the Lord God caused a deep sleep to fall upon Adam, and he slept: and he took one of his ribs, and closed up the flesh instead thereof."

Despite Simpson's efforts, however, chloroform did not really become accepted in Great Britain until it was used to relieve Queen Victoria's pain when she delivered her last two children, Leopold, in 1853, and Beatrice, in 1857. That ended the debate.

But chloroform itself was soon the subject of doubt; exposure for forty-five minutes or longer could rapidly destroy the liver and also damage the kidneys and heart. Even small doses for a shorter time could lead to jaundice from liver damage. It took an extremely skilled anesthesiologist and a careful selection of patients to reduce these risks. Because of this, American doctors preferred ether and nitrous oxide. British doctors and those in some other countries stuck by chloroform for a longer period, perhaps because they found it difficult to change their habits, perhaps because they were more skilled in the administration of chloroform. It was not until 1980 that anesthesiologists in Simpson's hometown of Edinburgh stopped using chloroform. In June of that year, Dr. H.W.C. Griffiths, an Edinburgh anesthesiologist who was about to retire from practice, gave chloroform anesthesia for the last time. He had used the gas several thousand times on obstetrics patients, and he must have been a very skillful anesthesiologist, because few of them suffered complications from it.[29]

General anesthesia, however, is not always appropriate. There are countless operations for which it is impractical to put a patient to sleep and many minor problems for which the dangers of general anesthesia are not justified. Soon after the discovery of general anesthesia, doctors started to ask whether a chemical might be dropped into the eye or injected beneath the skin to anesthetize a specific local area for a minor operation while the patient remained conscious. Despite these early speculations, it was almost forty years after the introduction of general anesthetics before the first local anesthetic was successfully tried. That anesthetic was cocaine, and its use for such a purpose was suggested by Sigmund Freud. The year was 1883, and Freud was a twenty-seven-year-old physician in Vienna, his psychoanalytic research still in the future.[30]

Cocaine, a derivative of the coca leaf, has been used for pleasure as well as for medicinal purposes for centuries in South America. Europeans began using coca just after the discovery of America, though it was almost another three hundred years—1855—before pure cocaine was isolated.[31] By the mid-1870s several doctors had testified in scientific journals as to its benefits for a wide variety of conditions. Sir Robert Christison of Edinburgh, a seventy-eight-year-old physician who was president of the British Medical Association and had been a famous athlete, reported that coca had helped him walk fifteen miles in one day. On another occasion, Christison climbed the 3,224-foot peak of Ben Vorlich in Scotland—also under the influence of the coca leaf.[32]

Across the Atlantic, cocaine had become an officially accepted drug in the United States pharmacopoeia by 1880. In the next four years the *Detroit Therapeutic Gazette* published sixteen reports in which coca purportedly cured an opium habit.[33] In 1883, Parke-Davis, the American manufacturer of cocaine, advertised it in medical journals as a treatment for morphine addiction and alcoholism. It even became, for a time, an ingredient in Coca-Cola.

Two reports about coca leaves and cocaine particularly impressed the young Sigmund Freud. One was an essay written in 1859 by a prominent Italian neurologist, Paolo Mantegazza, who extolled the virtues of coca on the basis of self-experimentation. He noted that with small doses, digestion was promoted and both pulse and breathing were quickened. Larger doses caused flashes of light, headache, and increased physical and mental vigor.[34]

The second report was published by Dr. Theodor Aschenbrandt in 1883.[35] Aschenbrandt described experiments in which he had surreptitiously administered small doses of cocaine to Bavarian soldiers while they were on maneuvers. It was, Aschenbrandt said, "the only way in which objective observations can be made, and the only way in which objective descriptions of the behavior of subjects can be achieved." Aschenbrandt credited the cocaine with helping soldiers overcome fatigue.

At the time, Freud was financially dependent on loans from wealthier colleagues, among them Dr. Ernst von Fleischl-Marxow. The discovery of a specialized medical use for cocaine, Freud thought, might bring him not only fame but also the financial security he felt he needed to get married. On April 21, 1883, Freud, describing himself as someone with "an explorer's temperament," wrote his fiancée, Martha Bernays, that he was "toying now with a project and a hope. . . . It is a therapeutic experiment."[36] Nine days later, on April 30, 1883, he took cocaine for the first time.[37] Unlike Christison and most other experimenters who had chewed coca leaf, Freud used pure cocaine. This allowed him to relate effects to specific doses, even to test the pharmacological equivalence of two different brands. "These experiments established appropriate dosage and a time course of the drug's action—a critical relationship in human experimentation," Dr. Robert Byck, the editor of Freud's "Cocaine Papers," later wrote, pointing out that in 1883 those were remarkable steps, ones that made Freud a pioneer in psychopharmacology.[38]

In experimenting with cocaine, Freud was also motivated by a desire to help his friend, von Fleischl-Marxow, a twenty-five-year-old researcher in pathology in Vienna. Von Fleischl-Marxow's right thumb had become infected and had had to be amputated. To kill the intolerable nerve pain he suffered from the phantom thumb and from the neuromas—the nerve growths—for which he had repeated operations, von Fleischl-Marxow began taking increasingly larger doses of morphine. Despite the amputation, von Fleischl-Marxow kept on working in the pathology laboratory. In May 1883, with less than a month's personal experience with the drug but relying on the published recommendations of American doctors, Freud began treating von Fleischl-Marxow with cocaine as a substitute for morphine. It was no solution: Von Fleischl-Marxow simply became addicted to cocaine instead of morphine.

Freud was not discouraged. He hoped that cocaine might be used to combat not just nervous disorders but physical illnesses such as heart disease as well. He had associated his own depressions with severe stomach cramps. When he took cocaine, however, both the cramps and the depressions vanished.

As a scientist, Freud was not satisfied with merely reviewing reports of the experiments that his predecessors had done or with experimenting on others. He was a physician who trained himself to be an experimental subject, and he carefully recorded self-experiments that were designed to show the effects of cocaine on his mind and body. To obtain the most accurate physical and psychological measures, Freud tested the effects of cocaine with two devices. Both were crude by our standards but they were the most sophisticated measuring instruments available to him. One was a dynamometer, which he described as "a spring-metal clasp which upon being pressed together moves a pointer connected to it along a graduated scale. The pointer remains locked at peak pressure."[39] He used it to measure pressure exerted by muscles.

The other instrument was a neuroamoebimeter, which measured psychic reaction time. Freud described it as consisting "of a metal strip that vibrates one hundred times per second. The subject stops the vibrations as soon as he hears the tone caused by the release of the set strip. The time elapsing between the perception of the tone and the completed action of stopping the spring is the reaction time. The number of vibrations is recorded directly in hundredths of a second by a pen."[40]

After measuring the effects of cocaine on his muscular reactions over a period of several weeks, Freud was struck by two facts. Firstly, he said, "the figures for the motor energy of a muscle group reveal a regular fluctuation in the course of a day; secondly, the same figures reach quite different absolute values on different days."[41] Further, he noted that "under cocaine my reaction times were shorter and more uniform than before taking the drug; but sometimes, in a more cheerful and efficient mood, my psychic reactions were just as good. Change in reaction time is then a characteristic of cocaine euphoria to which I have also ascribed the increase in muscular strength."[42]

In 1884 Freud wrote a scientific paper in which he recommended coca or cocaine for a variety of illnesses.[43] He based his claims on "some dozen" experiments on himself as well as additional ones on others. Most important, Freud and his colleagues observed that cocaine numbed their tongues and cheeks. Others had described the same lack of sensation in the past, yet none had had the ingenuity to apply it to surgery.

At the time, eye surgery was all but impossible because there was no way to prevent eye movement during an operation. The few eye operations that were done were limited to draining abscesses with the aid of an ether spray that froze the surface of the eye briefly—but not long enough to perform major surgery. Although general anesthesia eliminated pain, a patient under the influence of ether or nitrous oxide could not cooperate with the surgeon's command to gaze in a specific direction, limiting what the ophthalmologist could do. Nitrous oxide and ether (particularly) often caused retching, vomiting, and restlessness, which could raise the pressure in the eye and destroy all the work the fastest and most skilled ophthalmologist had done, since healing of the eye requires rest and immobilization.

Freud mentioned cocaine's tongue-numbing effects to a friend, Dr. Carl Koller, who was an ophthalmologist. Koller himself had been looking for an anesthetic for eye surgery and had already tried morphine, bromide, and other drugs without success.[44] Any substance that paralyzed the sensory nerve endings on the tongue, he assumed, would have a similar effect on the surface of the eye. He immediately went to his laboratory, prepared a solution of cocaine, and dropped it into the eyes of a frog. Because of the initial irritation, the animal blinked for up to thirty seconds; then the blinking stopped and its eyes assumed a staring appearance. The frog remained still when Koller pricked and scratched its eyes with a pin or applied electricity or heat.

He repeated the experiments on guinea pigs, rabbits, dogs, and, finally, on himself. As his assistant, Dr. Joseph Gaertner, later wrote: "We trickled the solution under the upraised lids of each other's eyes. Then we put a mirror before us, took a pin in hand, and tried to touch the cornea with its head. Almost simultaneously we could joyously assure ourselves, 'I can't feel a thing.' We could make a dent in the cornea without the slightest awareness of the touch, let alone any unpleasant sensation or reaction."[45]

Koller tried the experiment on colleagues and patients. It worked. He had found a local anesthetic that would serve two purposes: It was a painkiller for people with eye conditions, and it was an anesthetic agent for eye surgery. Now an eye surgeon could work unconstrained, without fear of sudden movements from a terrified patient. In a play on the trade name of the soft drink, Koller became known as "Coca Koller."

Freud regretted that he had abdicated the discovery of the use of cocaine in surgical anesthesia to Koller. He later blamed it, ungallantly, on a visit to Martha that had interrupted his work. But Freud also recognized that he had been too "lazy" to pursue the key studies.

He continued experimenting with cocaine until 1895. But he came under attack for promoting what turned out to be a worthless therapy for anything other than local anesthesia and for overlooking the potential for abuse of cocaine. That criticism later made it more difficult for him to gain acceptance for his theories of psychoanalysis.

Nevertheless, Freud's experiments with cocaine and his immediate understanding of its application to surgery were a great contribution to medicine. Robert Byck concluded: "It can be said that Freud's work on cocaine was pioneering in many respects; that the errors he made in judgment and advocacy of the drug were mistakes that have since been made by many persons who have worked with centrally active drugs [those that affect the central nervous system]; and that the difficulties he created for himself by his advocacy were relatively minor when compared to the importance of his introduction of a systematic scientific methodology into the study of centrally active drugs."[46]

Others now began to wonder whether they could do minor surgery after cocaine had been injected under the skin. They experimented with the hypodermic syringe that Alexander Wood, a leading physician of his time, had introduced in Scotland in 1853.[47] In 1884 two surgeons at Roosevelt Hospital in New York reasoned that injections of cocaine through the skin into or near nerves would block pain sensations so that the removal of abscesses or moles or other minor operations could be done with local anesthesia on conscious patients. The doctors were Richard J. Hall and William S. Halsted, and though they did not cite Freud or Koller in their scientific papers, they must have known about the work of these Viennese physicians to whom they were indebted.[48] Halsted went on to become the first chief of surgery of the Johns Hopkins Medical School in Baltimore. He also invented rubber surgical gloves and developed the radical mastectomy operation that until recently was the standard one for breast cancer. Hall and Halsted used cocaine as a local anesthetic for thousands of operations in New York. Before doing so, they experimented on themselves.

An injection of cocaine into Hall's forearm caused complete loss of sensation in the area around the point of injection. It had no effect elsewhere.

Hall had a dentist inject cocaine into a nerve in his mouth when he had his left first upper incisor tooth filled. He wrote that the dentist "was then able to scrape out the cavity in the tooth, which had previously been so exquisitely sensitive, and to fill it, without my experiencing any sensation whatever. The anesthesia was complete until about twenty-six minutes after the injection, and sensibility was much diminished for ten or fifteen minutes longer."[49]

Hall and Halsted repeatedly tested the effects of different doses of cocaine after injecting it at varying depths into their arms and legs; they used strong and weak solutions of cocaine as well as sterile water and salt solutions. Their experiments made a major contribution to surgical anesthesia.[50] But they paid a heavy price; both became addicted to cocaine. Halsted apparently believed that morphine would stop his habituation to cocaine; it was Freud's mistake, with his friend von Fleischl-Marxow, in reverse.

Sir William Osler, one of the pioneering doctors at the Johns Hopkins Medical School in Baltimore, said, "When we recommended him [Halsted] as full surgeon to the Hospital in 1890, I believed . . . that he was no longer addicted to morphia. He had worked so well and so energetically that it did not seem possible that he could take the drug and do so much."[51] About six months after Halsted's appointment, some of his colleagues learned he was still addicted to morphine, but they kept it a secret. He continued to work at Hopkins for thirty-two years, and until his death in 1922 he remained addicted.

Halsted also disclosed: "Poor Hall and two other assistants of mine acquired the cocaine habit in the course of our experiments on ourselves—injecting nerves. They all died without recovering from the habit."[52]

Hall's and Halsted's discovery of nerve block, or conduction anesthesia, also spurred further investigation into a new area—spinal anesthesia. Once again, self-experimentation played an important role.

In 1886 doctors discovered that a needle could safely be inserted through the space between two vertebrae in the back and into the spinal canal to collect spinal fluid. It was a procedure that came to be known as a spinal tap or lumbar puncture.[53] Dr. August Bier, a surgeon in Kiel, Germany, was among those who reasoned that the spinal tap could be used to produce regional anesthesia for surgery. In this procedure, some spinal fluid that bathes the spinal cord is withdrawn and is replaced with an equal amount of drug. The local anesthetic paralyzes the nerves serving the muscles in the lower half of the body and blocks the pain resulting from nerve impulses conducted between the brain and the nerves.

Bier and his assistant, Dr. August Hildebrandt, did major operations on five patients using spinal anesthesia.[54] However, Bier noted that the patients suffered from postoperative effects comparable to those following general anesthesia. "To reach a valid conclusion on this," Bier said, "I decided to carry out some experiments on myself."

Bier and Hildebrandt gave each other spinal anesthesia through injections of cocaine solution into the lower (lumbar) areas of their backs; the aim was to block the nerves in the lower part of the body. They took careful notes of the experience. The initial thrust of the needle caused no pain beyond the usual jab and a short, mild stabbing sensation in one leg. Bier felt a mild tugging sensation when Hildebrandt began the injection. But Hildebrandt was nervous, and much of the solution trickled down Bier's back. They waited ten minutes before Hildebrandt pricked Bier's thigh with a pin. It hurt: not enough cocaine had penetrated the spine.

When the more experienced Bier injected the solution into Hildebrandt's back just a few drops escaped. Within seven minutes Hildebrandt could feel pinpricks only as pressure; tickling of the sole of the foot hardly bothered him. A minute later Bier drew a large curved needle through the skin of Hildebrandt's thigh. Again his assistant sensed no pain. Two minutes later Bier thrust a needle into Hildebrandt's thigh bone; he felt nothing. Bier squeezed Hildrebrandt's skin between the teeth of a hooked forceps. Hildebrandt perceived the pinching only as pressure.

Thirteen minutes after the spinal injection, Bier put the lighted end of his cigar on Hildebrandt's legs. The burn caused no pain. Hard hammer blows against his shins were painless. On and on, Bier battered Hildebrandt. Pulling out pubic hair felt like lifting a skin fold, whereas plucking hairs from the chest was painful. Strong pressure and tugging on Hildebrandt's testicles produced no sensation.

It took forty-five minutes for the effect of the drug to wear off and normal sensitivity to return.

The two doctors dined together that evening, drinking wine and smoking several cigars. They went to bed about eleven o'clock. Bier, whose body had absorbed almost no cocaine, slept soundly and awoke refreshed. When he finished his customary morning stroll, he found he had a slight headache.

At the clinic he found Hildebrandt looking wan; he had not slept and was able to stand only with great effort. Later that morning Hildebrandt had a severe headache, which may have been due to a hangover or to the spinal injection, followed by an attack of vomiting. By midafternoon he was forced to go to bed. Although still suffering from a headache, he returned to work the next day.

There could no longer be any question about the effectiveness of spinal anesthesia. Its application opened up a new era in surgery. It saved many people from the potential dangers of general anesthesia, and eventually it allowed surgeons to develop new techniques for gynecological, urinary, pelvic, and other surgery of the lower part of the body. Today drugs with less severe side effects than cocaine are used in spinal anesthesia, and the technique has become common practice with surgery in American hospitals, largely because anesthesiologists consider it almost free of complications.

It soon became clear that general anesthesia could be divided into four stages, from the first or "lightest" stage, when the individual is still conscious and can later recall what happened, to the fourth or "deepest" and potentially most dangerous stage, when the vital centers in the brain are most depressed. Once these stages had been recognized, anesthesiologists could begin to regulate more accurately the amount of gas a patient could inhale. They learned that it is not until the third stage that the anesthetic agent abolishes sensation and spinal reflexes, producing muscular relaxation and making the third stage the stage of surgical anesthesia. In retrospect, this explained why Wells's demonstration at the Massachusetts General Hospital failed; he had given only enough nitrous oxide to put his patient into the first stage.

In addition, doctors learned the importance of maintaining adequate blood pressure, pulse, respiration, and normal heart rhythm during surgery. By 1940 anesthesiology was becoming established as a separate specialty of medicine. At that time ether and nitrous oxide were still the most commonly used anesthetic gases. They were effective, but they had to be given in large amounts to put a patient into the third stage and to sufficiently relax the muscles. As long as the patient's muscles remained taut, it was more difficult for the surgeon to make the delicate maneuvers precisely. "He's too tight. Give me more anesthesia," the surgeon would yell at the anesthesiologist at the head of the operating table. The anesthesiologist would then give the patient more gas until the surgeon was satisfied with the degree of muscle relaxation.

Anesthesiologists worried about such high doses. The patient paid a great physiologic price for increased muscle relaxation: the longer the patient was under deep anesthesia, the greater the risk of vomiting, and each time a person recovering from an operation vomited, the chances of aspirating stomach contents into the windpipe and lungs with resultant pneumonia increased. Also, the longer the period of deep anesthesia, the longer the patient had to lie flat in bed with a depressed ability to cough. The immobility increased the chances of bacteria remaining in the air sacs, growing in the mucus that the patient could not cough up and producing pneumonia.

So, while it was no longer necessary for a surgeon to be as swift an operator as London's Robert Liston, the new anesthetic agents did not eliminate the need for speed. Surgeons and anesthesiologists eagerly sought new ways to minimize the amount of gas the patient had to breathe during an operation. One approach was to administer a substance that would relax the muscles. It did not have to be a true anesthetic agent, but, if it worked, it would be just as valuable as the anesthetic itself.

This relaxing substance turned out to be curare, the South American arrow poison that had acquired the nickname "Flying Death." For centuries Indian tribes in the Amazon and Orinoco basins had depended on crude curare for hunting and for war. Curare is a gummy substance that can be extracted from many plants. As a poison, it acts rapidly, so rapidly that it had gained a reputation as the most terrifying poison known. Curare's powers had become legendary when Sir Walter Raleigh, among other explorers, returned from South America relating stories of how Indian hunters, by smearing the dark brown extract on the tips of their arrows, paralyzed the strongest and swiftest animals so they fell dead the moment they were hit.[55] A man wounded with a curare-tipped arrow would suffocate from the paralysis of his breathing muscles.

The Indians knew that curare was poisonous only when it penetrated the skin. The substance was harmless if it was rubbed on unbroken skin or if eaten in small amounts. The Indians ate with impunity the flesh of animals killed by curare. They also knew that many curare arrow injuries could be treated successfully if the poison was sucked out of the wound. But they knew, too, that paralysis could strike anyone who did the sucking if he had a cut or sore in his mouth.

Curare fascinated European scientists, who studied samples brought back by explorers. Doctors observed that an animal's heart would continue to beat after curare poisoning caused breathing to stop. From experiments on cats, donkeys, and other animals, Sir Benjamin Brodie, a British scientist, discovered in 1811 that artificial respiration with a bellows attached through a hole in the windpipe would keep alive an animal paralyzed by curare, proving that the effects of the poison were temporary and that recovery was possible if the animal's respiration could be maintained.[56]

In the 1840s and 1850s, the pioneer French physiologist Claude Bernard studied the effect of curare on frogs. He showed that the principal pharmacologic action of curare occurred at the anatomical area where a nerve stimulated a muscle to contract. Later studies by other researchers showed that curare concentrates at this point, blocking the transmission of nerve impulses that signal a muscle to contract, thus causing muscle paralysis. We now know that the paralysis is temporary because the body quickly breaks down and removes curare. If adequate breathing can be maintained for as long as the curare has effect, the muscle strength returns to normal as soon as the body eliminates the drug.

Curare is a nonspecific term used to describe a group of South American arrow poisons, all derived from plants. These poisons, as made by South American tribesmen, were of markedly different composition and potency because each tribe's witch doctor had his secret recipe and the preparations were contaminated with extraneous plant and animal materials. Chemist after chemist failed to isolate the basic ingredient until 1935 when Dr. Harold King, a Welsh chemist, isolated *d*-tubocurarine from a museum specimen of crude curare that had been stored in a tube and that was still active.

Curare was first used in medical practice in 1912 to relax muscles during surgery by a German physician, Läwen, whose suggestion was overlooked for many years.[57] In 1938 two doctors in Nebraska, Archibald R. McIntyre and A. E. Bennett, began experimenting with it as a means of reducing the hazard from a new treatment for mental depression, electroshock therapy.[58] McIntyre and Bennett believed that curare's muscle-relaxing properties might prevent the broken arms and legs or fractured spines many patients suffered as a result of convulsions during electroshock treatment.

McIntyre prepared a crude extract of curare from the bark of specimens of *Chondodendron tomentosum* imported from Ecuador. In 1939, E. R. Squibb and Sons manufactured it for experimental therapeutic use as Intocostrin, the first so-called biologically standardized curare preparation. Although Intocostrin was supposed to consist primarily of the pure *d*-tubocurarine isolated by Harold King, it was a mixture of similar compounds. Each batch was standardized by the rabbit head-drop test—the point at which a rabbit's head dropped from paralysis of its neck muscles was the unit reference point—but McIntyre said tests later showed the potency actually ranged widely, from 0.15 to 3.3 milligrams per unit.

Four years later, in 1943, the botanical source was identified with certainty. Two other scientists, Oskar Wintersteiner and James D. Dutcher, who worked at the Squibb Institute for Medical Research in New Brunswick, New Jersey, detected *d*-tubocurarine in the stem of the same plant McIntyre had used to prepare his crude extract—*Chondodendron tomentosum.*

Before that important step was made, there were those who believed that a crude preparation was better than none at all. Two Canadian physicians, Dr. Harold R. Griffith and Dr. Enid Johnson, first tried curare in an attempt to paralyze the abdominal muscles so they would remain limp as the surgeon cut. Griffith, an anesthesiologist, had already put himself to sleep several times with a new anesthetic called cyclopropane, but there is no record of his having self-experimented with curare. These doctors from the Homeopathic

Hospital in Montreal administered curare to a patient who was having an operation on January 23, 1942. They found that by providing artificial respiration as required, they could administer substantially less anesthetic gas during the operation if curare was used at the same time.

However, there was much research still to be done before curare could be widely used in surgical anesthesia. Two dramatic self-experiments performed independently in England and the United States provided this necessary research.

Although British anesthesiologists were impressed with the potential importance of curare in medicine, they considered Intocostrin dangerous because of its lack of purity. Scientists at the headquarters of Burroughs Wellcome, the giant British drug company, independently prepared *d*-tubocurarine in pure form. It was called Tubarine. Workers at Burroughs Wellcome had experimented with Tubarine on animals and had convinced themselves that it was safe; now in 1944 they were ready to push on with clinical tests on humans.

The director of clinical research at Burroughs Wellcome, who was responsible for work on Tubarine, was Dr. Frederick Prescott, a forty-year-old physician who also had a Ph.D. in chemistry.[59] He felt that his team could not test Tubarine on patients during surgery because the other drugs they would be receiving with their anesthesia would interfere with studies aimed at determining the effects of specific doses of purified curare. Prescott doubted that anyone not connected with the experiment would volunteer to be a subject because of curare's notorious reputation. He was hesitant to test it on a medical student or a laboratory assistant, even if such a volunteer were paid. "Perhaps foolishly, I consented to be the human guinea pig," Prescott said.

Burroughs Wellcome, unlike some drug companies, did not discourage employees from experimenting on themselves, and, in fact, a few years earlier Prescott had been injected with morphine and methamphetamine (later known as speed), in a self-experiment performed at his home. He had been interested in testing a theory some scientists had that a combination of these two drugs would help maintain blood pressure during surgery. When Prescott's blood pressure suddenly rose to 250, about double the usual level, and he developed what he said was "a terrific manic reaction," his medical colleagues hospitalized him as a precautionary measure. The reaction, fortunately, was only temporary. Prescott was back at work in a few days.

Now, for the experiment with curare, he and his colleagues at Burroughs Wellcome drew up a protocol, or scientific blueprint. They would be testing the drug's safety, and the experiment would be done in an operating room, because the scientists wanted to mimic actual conditions of surgery. The researchers chose Westminster Hospital in London where Dr. (later Sir) Geoffrey S. W. Organe, among the most respected anesthesiologists in London at the time, agreed to administer the drug.[60]

According to the protocol, Prescott was to lie on a table while his breathing rate, blood pressure, and pulse were continually recorded on a sheet of paper on a revolving drum. There would be a full tank of oxygen on hand. Organe and other doctors would be there, ready to insert a tube and breathe for Prescott if he turned blue and stopped breathing—or if something else went wrong. The experiment would be done in four stages with gradually increasing doses of curare. The medical team was certain it had planned for everything.

The experiment began with an injection of ten milligrams of *d*-tubocurarine into a vein in Prescott's arm. It was a small dose, not enough to paralyze him totally. But, Prescott recalled: "It made me feel very weak. I could move my arms and legs, but my facial and neck muscles were paralyzed . . . I could not speak properly. I could just mouth my words. I saw double because my eye muscles were weak. I could still breathe, but shallowly. I could swallow and cough. Within fifteen minutes, power started to return to the muscles. Strength developed in the reverse order to which the paralysis had developed."

About a week later, they stepped up the dose to twenty milligrams; it produced strikingly different results. "Within less than a minute," Prescott said, "I saw everything as double. I was weak. Then, within two minutes, the muscles controlling my face and neck were paralyzed. I could not speak. Then my arms and legs were paralyzed. Yet I could still breathe, but it was difficult. I could still cough and swallow."

Again, within fifteen minutes, Prescott's paralysis was over. The muscles regained their usual strength in the reverse order that they had become paralyzed. So far, it was an extraordinary experience, but not a frightening one.

They were now ready for the third stage, a thirty milligram injection that was given about two weeks after the first. "That was a real knockout dose. Within two minutes, the muscles of the face, neck, arms and legs were completely paralyzed. I could not speak or open my eyes. Within three minutes my breathing muscles were paralyzed."

At this point, Prescott was unable to communicate with his colleagues who were busy watching the graphs being recorded on the revolving drum. They glanced at him every few seconds, but because he did not turn blue, they assumed everything was fine. Objectively, they were correct. But not subjectively. They had forgotten the most critical factor in the protocol—a means of communication. The tracings they watched showed that Prescott was receiving enough oxygen, although his breathing was shallow and rapid at twenty-five breaths per minute, more than double his usual eleven per minute.

"I was not going blue, but I had the feeling I was suffocating," Prescott recalled.

The paralysis of his respiratory muscles made his breathing still more shallow. Now he was gasping for air at the rate of fifty breaths per minute. He was accumulating too much carbon dioxide, and he thought he was beginning to lose consciousness. The back of his mouth and voice box were clogged with saliva and mucus. "I felt that I was drowning in my own saliva because now I could not swallow or cough."

The doctors attending him were breathing for him by compressing with their hands a breathing bag that was attached by a tube to his mouth. That measure provided sufficient oxygen. Still, Prescott continued to feel that he was suffocating. There was nothing he could do about it. He could not move a limb, finger, or toe. He stared at the ceiling but could see little because he could not raise his drooping, paralyzed eyelids. He was terrified. His blood pressure and pulse rate, which had risen dramatically, showed his fear, but his colleagues failed to realize how frightened he was. Organe, the anesthesiologist, said he believed he was in full control at all times.

Once the medical team had collected the data it sought, Organe injected a dose of an antidote called neostigmine to counter the curare. But the dose was not large enough. For seven additional minutes, the doctors continued to give Prescott artificial respiration. That was enough time for his own breathing muscles to take over. It was about a half hour before he could speak properly. In another forty minutes, his muscle power began to return to normal, and after forty-five minutes, he was able to walk—a bit unsteadily, like an alcoholic. About two hours after the experiment ended, he went home. Yet he continued to see double for four hours after the curare had been injected. For several days he had a persistent tight feeling across his chest.

In addition to testing the safety of curare in humans, another aim of the research was to test the ability of curare to deaden pain. It had none. Prescott recalled how "Strips of adhesive plaster were applied to my chest and legs. When they were torn off my body, they produced considerable pain."

As frightening as the experience had been, Prescott was to repeat it. According to the scientific protocol Prescott and his fellow researchers had designed, the fourth and final stage would study what would happen when one-half the total dose was injected into the muscles and the other half into the veins. The purpose was to determine whether the effects from the intramuscular and intravenous injections of curare would last for the same amount of time. Prescott agreed to do the experiment because, as a good scientist, he would live up to the agreement he had made, but another six weeks passed before he was able to face it. This time it was with the benefit of signals. They were not needed. The effects of the final experiment were similar to those produced by two-thirds of the dose that had been given intravenously, but the final experiment lasted much longer—forty-five minutes compared with twenty-five minutes. So the researchers recommended that doctors inject the first dose intravenously and reinforce it with additional doses intramuscularly, if the operation was likely to last longer than forty-five minutes.

Prescott had achieved his purpose; the dose of pure curare had been roughly correlated to the degree of paralysis in a human and he had proven that with controlled doses the drug was safe. Tubarine was soon marketed in England.

Meanwhile, in Salt Lake City, Utah, another researcher was carrying on parallel experiments with curare that were designed to answer different scientific questions. His name was Dr. Scott M. Smith.[61] Smith had grown up on a farm in Missouri and had become a registered pharmacist to help pay his tuition at the University of Louisville Medical School. He had started out to become an orthopedic surgeon, but he had been forced to abandon that goal because of a then frequent occupational hazard—radiation damage. At that time, it was standard practice to fluoroscope broken bones. But the constant radiation exposure from fluoroscopy—a technique in which X rays are shown continuously on a screen that is coated with a fluorescent substance—had burned his hands. He had failed to protect himself adequately, and his sensitive skin could no longer tolerate the scrubbing that was a prerequisite to entering the operating room. So instead of becoming an orthopedic surgeon, he became an anesthesiologist.

When Smith finished his training in 1943, he accepted an offer to work in Salt Lake City, where he took charge of anesthesiology at the University of Utah Medical School. There he read the report of Griffith and Johnson, the two Canadian physicians who had successfully used curare in surgical anesthesia. When the medical director of E. R. Squibb and Sons sent a supply of Secostrin (the commercial form of curare in North America) to the head of the anesthesiology department, Smith and a few other anesthesiologists used it. In some cases, Smith even used the drug surreptitiously because the more conservative surgeons on the staff did not want curare injected into their patients; they still considered it too experimental. Smith would tell these surgeons that their patients were getting "a relaxant." He did not say which one, and he certainly did not tell them it was curare. The results of the anesthesia were excellent, and most surgeons were happy.

One surgeon, however, mentioned a curious circumstance to Smith. A patient of another anesthesiologist had been able to recall some of the events toward the end of an operation, a period when the dosage of anesthetics and curare was reduced. Smith was puzzled. Could lowering the dose of the anesthetic—or of the curare itself—permit the patient to remember his ordeal? He did not want his patients, particularly children, to experience any more painful memories than necessary from their anesthesia and surgery.

At the time, there was a debate in the medical literature about the effects of curare on the central nervous system. A few investigators thought it caused complete unconsciousness and amnesia and abolished the electrical activity of brain cells. Others could detect no evidence that brain function was affected by curare. Smith was uneasy: Might curare have some unknown effect on the brain? And, like Prescott's team at Burroughs Wellcome, he had an additional question: Could curare alone abolish pain? The answer to Smith's questions would require an experiment on a human under the influence of a large dose of curare—someone who could communicate his sensations. Smith did not know that Prescott had already done a similar experiment, because Prescott's report would not be published for another six months.

"I did not think about using somebody else," Smith recalled when we talked one summer day, thirty years after the experiment. "It did not occur to me, but even if it had, I doubt I could have convinced anyone else to participate."

Dr. Louis S. Goodman, an internationally recognized expert in the actions of drugs, was the pharmacology professor at the University of Utah Medical School. He and Dr. Alfred Gilman wrote a textbook that became the pharmacological Bible for generations of doctors. Goodman encouraged Smith to do the curare experiment and volunteered his cooperation.[62] Goodman would check the protocol that Smith had drawn up and would assist during the investigations. In addition, two anesthesiologists, two pharmacologists, and other assistants, including medical students, would be at Smith's side during the experiment. His secretary would be there to record the events.

In the hope of getting a clear-cut answer to his questions, Smith decided to take a dose three times larger than he had ever administered to a patient. "It may sound funny," he said, "but I did not think that I was experimenting on myself. I believed the drug was safe because I had used so much of it already and had observed its action. And there was an antidote—neostigmine—available."

The experiment was scheduled for January 10, 1946, a Thursday afternoon. The procedure was clear. Smith, who was then thirty-four years old, would receive a total of five hundred units of curare, to be given in his veins in increments on that one afternoon. The researchers devised a set of signals so that they could get clues to what Smith was experiencing and would know when to continue or to stop. When speech was lost, Smith would wiggle his fingers. When power over those muscles was lost, he would blink his eyelids, and so on, until he could contract no muscle in his body.

Smith's blood pressure, pulse, respiration, and other physiologic functions were carefully recorded as he rested flat on his back on a bed. Electrodes were placed on his scalp and on the skin over his chest and arms so machines could constantly record the rhythm of his heart and his brain waves. Smith's attendants slowly began injecting the first two hundred units of curare over a fifteen-minute period.

Seven minutes later, Smith asked for oxygen. "Can hardly bring teeth together," he said. Smith could no longer speak, but he could hear distinctly and he could nod his head and move his hands slightly. The assistants began to force air into his lungs because his breathing was shallow.

After eleven minutes the paralysis was spreading rapidly. Three minutes later he could no longer move his head but he could still wrinkle his forehead slightly. An assistant raised the eyelids that Smith could not open; he saw clearly.

Fifteen minutes into the experiment, when he had received all of the first two hundred units, Smith could still comprehend and answer questions accurately by signals; he could move his feet and hands slightly.

Two minutes later the doctors stuck pins into his skin. The pins felt sharp. Smith had discovered what Prescott already knew: Curare afforded no pain relief. He received another two hundred units.

After twenty minutes his muscles for breathing were totally paralyzed. The doctors inserted a stiff tube through his mouth and into his windpipe to give him artificial respiration. They squeezed air into his lungs through a rubber bag. His color was good. More curare was injected. Smith saw double. Again the doctors tested curare's anesthetic effects by pricking his skin with a pin or twisting his skin with a set of clamps. The provocations were painful. But, as Smith was paralyzed, he could not wince or jump in response. When it was time to inject the final one hundred units, Smith still had enough control to signal that he approved by "slight movement" of the inner aspect of his left eyebrow. The attendants injected the final dose. Thirty-four minutes after the experiment began, Smith lay motionless, unable to signal a response to any inquiry.

Six minutes later, forty from the initial dose, the researchers began giving Smith the same neostigmine antidote that had reversed Prescott's paralysis. The signaling system the team had worked out had spared Smith the terror and helplessness that Prescott had experienced. Within two minutes the paralysis eased. Smith still could not open his eyes, but he could now wrinkle his forehead.

Gradually Smith's muscle function returned. His speech, slurred at first, became more intelligible. Although he now had the normal power of his breathing muscles, he still felt he needed artificial respiration, and though he could open his eyes, he preferred to keep them shut. The doctors injected more antidote to speed up Smith's recovery. Two hours and nine minutes after he had first received curare, and eighty-nine minutes after the first of six doses of antidote had been administered, Smith could lift his head from his pillow. A half hour later, although dizzy, he sat with assistance on the edge of his bed. For twenty minutes he dictated a report of his experiences. "A little bit dizzy and quite a 'glow,' " he said. "A little hard to focus on anything. Weakness in jaw muscles noted. Hard to talk. Difficulty in swallowing and keeping eyes open. No unpleasant sensations, legs feel weak . . ." Fifteen minutes later he felt nauseated, drowsy, and uneasy and had to lie down. In ten more minutes the nausea passed and he began walking unassisted. His legs felt heavy and weak, as they would for several more hours.

That evening, when he told his wife about his self-experiment, she was unhappy. "She thought I was really a bit touched in the head," Smith recalled. "She needled me, saying, 'I suppose you are after publicity.' That thought had never entered my mind. She felt I was unfair for not having talked it over with her first. The message was clear: I had damned well better not do anything like that again."[63]

There was no need to. Smith had learned that curare neither killed pain nor altered consciousness. Clearly, it could not be given alone. The surgeon's patient had remembered part of what had happened during surgery because he had received curare and an anesthetic without additional medications to dull his memory. Smith himself, like some other doctors, had always prescribed scopolamine, morphine, or other drugs in addition to curare, to ensure that the patient's memory would be dulled. Without it some patients might remember the events of surgery. From now on he could tell the medical profession that anesthetic agents and drugs would *have* to be administered in addition to curare.

The medical profession's understanding of a drug or a class of drugs can come only from a combination of experiments, each of which is designed to answer rather limited questions about the nature of a pharmacologic substance. Although Prescott and Smith had different objectives in experimenting with curare, the results were the same and they were important.

In time, when newer curarelike drugs and newer anesthetic agents were ready for testing in humans, other researchers would carry on the tradition of self-experimentation that is so striking in the history of anesthesia. Eventually, these newer drugs replaced curare because anesthesiologists found it easier to control them during surgery. But curare revolutionized the practice of medicine. The profound muscle relaxation it provided removed for all time the need for deep anesthesia and led to a drastic decrease in the number of pneumonias and other complications following surgery.

The search for anesthetics is not over. The uses of ether, nitrous oxide, cocaine, and curare have all undergone change; new drugs are now available, and newer ones are under investigation. Self-experimentation remains at the center of these investigations.

# Chapter Four

# THE CASE OF THE QUEASY CHEMISTS

"A desire to take medicine is, perhaps, the great feature which distinguishes man from other animals."[1]

—Sir William Osler, 1891

Despite advances in anesthesia and surgery, the scalpel remains a risky solution to many medical problems, and it can do little to benefit the myriad conditions that are caused by biochemical, not anatomical, defects. So the quest for drugs, almost as old as disease itself, continues. It began self-experimentally with a trial-and-error search for safe and nutritious foods. Before long our ancestors discovered that some plants also had medicinal value. Ancient civilizations learned about hundreds of substances; most were botanical derivatives of common items from the garden. Juice of the skammonia plant, which belongs to the morning glory family, was prescribed as a drastic purge, and senna as a milder laxative. Dill was used to relieve gas and colic. Flax was prescribed for disorders of the womb.[2] Cannabis, or marijuana, which was known in central Asia and China as long ago as 3000 B.C., was regarded as having medicinal value for such widely disparate ailments as gout, "female weakness," rheumatism, constipation, and asthma.[3] The Ebers Papyrus, which dates from 1550 B.C. and which was discovered at Thebes, describes prescriptions of castor oil, opium, and other drugs that are still in use or that were used well into the twentieth century.[4]

In the second century A.D. the Greek physician Galen expounded the theory that four natural humors—blood, phlegm, yellow bile, and black bile—were responsible for health. Galen believed that disease should be treated with remedies that had qualities opposed to those of the disease. For example, a head cold was characterized by an overabundance of phlegm, which is cold and moist. Therefore, reasoned Galen, it should be treated by a remedy that was hot and dry. Drugs were classified according to their qualities, and Galen customarily combined different drugs, sometimes as many as twenty-five in one prescription.

Galen's humoral theories dominated therapeutics in Western medicine for fourteen centuries. It was not until the Renaissance that more modern notions began to surface, and it was a Swiss physician who was most responsible for the change. Born in 1493, Theophrastus Bombastus von Hohenheim, better known as Paracelsus, argued that qualities such as hot and cold were only the products or effects of a disease, not the cause. He introduced the concept of the body as a chemical laboratory, and he stressed the localized nature of a particular disease rather than considering it a disequilibrium of the whole body. He emphasized that remedies were specific for specific diseases.[5] Paracelsus' theories gained support in the seventeenth century, when drugs from the New World were first introduced into European medicine. The two most important were cinchona bark (quinine) and ipecac (emetine). Cinchona bark checked malaria; ipecac was prescribed to induce vomiting, as well as for treatment of parasitic infections such as amebic dysentery.[6]

At this point in medical history, the cause-and-effect relationships of the administration of a drug were not measured scientifically. Doctors and pharmacists did not have the knowledge or the technology to isolate the active ingredients from the plant and botanical substances they prescribed. Because the strength of a potion depended entirely on how it was prepared, its effectiveness varied widely. It is easy to understand how one doctor could believe in the benefits of a drug that was denounced by a colleague. Each time a doctor prescribed a drug it was tantamount to an experiment. And yet only through such a hit-and-miss approach could doctors learn how to treat disease.

Scientists have always been among the first to test new drugs, and many pharmacologists have tested newly invented drugs on themselves. Physician-researchers have learned that if they really want to know what their patients are going to experience, there is no substitute for taking a drug themselves. Those who are observant, perceptive, and good reporters can detect valuable clues to potentially dangerous effects. They can also become aware of trivial but bothersome effects that can be corrected easily, but only if they are recognized and not overlooked.

Through self-experimentation doctors have learned that the action of drugs can vary depending on how a particular drug is administered. Some drugs are ineffective when swallowed because stomach acid inactivates them. Yet injections of the same drugs into a vein or muscle can be lifesaving. Self-experimentation has provided crucial insights into the ways new drugs can be used in the practice of medicine.

The first deliberate self-experiment with a drug that I know of was reported by Dr. Anton Storck in 1760.[7] Storck, a nineteen-year-old Viennese physician, was fascinated by the blackish-green drug circuta vulgaris, or hemlock. He noted that it grew abundantly in the shade, flowered in July, and had a "disagreeable and stinky" smell. "We all know, nevertheless, that nothing has been created by God, which was not designed for some good, and use."[8]

To prove the useful purpose of hemlock, Storck reviewed what the ancient and contemporary writers knew about the herb. He made no mention of Socrates, who had committed suicide by drinking hemlock, but he cited how, for centuries, doctors had used it "with great effect" as an external application to the skin in the treatment of cancers and other diseases.[9] Indeed, then and for many more decades doctors considered hemlock useful in the relief of the pain of cancer as well as a powerful and direct sedative to the nervous system when taken internally, and they prescribed it to allay spasms, particularly of the respiratory system.[10] Storck decided to experiment on himself to discover the effects of hemlock when swallowed. He wrote: "As it would, however, have been criminal to have made the first trial of the extract on men, I gave a scruple of it, with a piece of flesh, three times a day to a little dog that was hungry. I then watched carefully, what changes might be produced in him. He remained, nevertheless, well, lively, and waiting with eagerness for the piece of flesh."

Storck repeated the experiment on the dog for two more days with the same results. Encouraged, he began the experiment on himself.

Each morning and evening for eight days he took one grain of a hemlock extract with a cup of tea and proceeded with his normal schedule. He noted no unusual effect. "I was active and strong; had my memory perfect; enjoyed good stomach; and slept soundly."

The next week Storck doubled the dose and rubbed some on his tongue, which became swollen, stiff, and painful. He could not speak, but it was fright, not the hemlock, that caused his muteness. After the symptoms wore off, leaving no ill effect, Storck said: "I was, therefore, now justified, in reason and conscience, to try this on others."[11]

Storck and other prominent Viennese physicians went on to prescribe hemlock for cancers, tumors, ulcers, and cataracts. Their hemlock prescriptions probably harmed many people and cured no one. But because pharmacology and science were in those days so primitive, the doctors had no way of knowing, as we do now, that hemlock has no medicinal value.

Less than half a century later, another self-experiment with a drug was reported by a German researcher named Friedrich Wilhelm Adam Serturner. Few scientists have taken more risks than Serturner, who had numerous close brushes with death as he experimented on himself to produce the drug that continues even today to be *the* sovereign painkiller—morphine. Serturner's research was, in fact, a turning point in the history of pharmacology. Serturner began his research on opium in 1803 as a twenty-year-old apprentice at a pharmacy in a town in Westphalia.[12] He had observed that some samples of the drug could rapidly and almost completely blunt pain, while others did not. He theorized that opium contained a specific active component that was responsible for this effect—but only if its concentration was powerful enough. In his quest to find this active substance, Serturner was one of the first to apply the basic techniques of chemical analysis to pharmacology. He used ammonia to separate the components of opium, and discovered the specific narcotic substance of the drug. Serturner named the pain-killing substance he isolated "morphine" after Morpheus, the god of sleep.

At the time, the concept of isolating the active constituents of a medicinal plant was only a theoretical possibility. Serturner's discovery required no sophisticated equipment, just the patience to go through a series of experimental steps, fifty-seven in this case. Yet even the first step was one that took thousands of years for someone to make.

Once he had isolated morphine, Serturner began testing it with cautious experiments on animals. He put crystals of pure morphine in food for the mice in the cellar and in food for some unwanted dogs in the neighborhood. In both cases, the crystals put the animals to sleep and ultimately killed them. Undaunted by the powers of the drug, Serturner decided to test it at a greatly reduced dosage on himself and three young friends, each just seventeen years old, "because experiments on animals do not give exact results."[13]

Forewarned by the deaths of the animals, Serturner began with a half grain of morphine, dissolved in a mixture of alcohol and water. He called his three friends together, and all four of them drank the mixture. Immediately their faces became flushed and they felt feverish. A half hour later, each took another half grain of morphine, and their feverish state increased. In addition, they began to feel nauseous and dizzy.

Fifteen minutes passed and then they swallowed another half grain of the drug. This time all four experienced a sharp pain in the stomach and a feeling that they were about to faint. Serturner himself lay down and fell into a dreaming state. "I felt a sort of palpitation in the extremities," he reported, "principally in the arms."

Concerned by these symptoms, which he recognized as evidence of poisoning, Serturner swallowed six to eight ounces of a strong vinegar and gave the same amount to the three young people. Violent vomiting occurred, and one of the young men became seriously ill. Serturner gave him some carbonate of magnesia, which temporarily stopped the vomiting. "He spent the night in a deep sleep," Serturner wrote. The following morning the vomiting returned but ceased soon after another dose of carbonate of magnesia. However, all four men experienced lack of appetite, enervation, headache, and stomachache for several days. They had swallowed about ten times the amount of morphine now recommended.

Serturner then concluded "that the principal effects of opium are dependent on pure morphine . . . My own experience has taught me that a very violent toothache, which did not yield to opium, went away with a dissolution of morphine in alcohol, although this liquid did not contain much of it. . . . It is to be wished that qualified physicians soon might concern themselves with this matter because opium is one of our most effective drugs."[14]

His discovery excited much interest. Its importance was recognized in 1831 when the Institute of France awarded Serturner, then fifty, a two-thousand-franc prize "for having opened the way to important medical discoveries." His isolation of morphine led to the discovery of other important alkaloids. (The alkaloids—organic bases containing nitrogen and usually also oxygen that occur in seed plants—were the first important class of drugs to be isolated, and morphine is one of the most important members of the alkaloid family.) As it turns out, opium contains more than twenty distinct alkaloids. One, codeine, was quickly isolated by other researchers. In the course of the next century, other alkaloid compounds such as emetine, strychnine, caffeine, atropine, cocaine, eserine, muscarine, pilocarpine, nicotine, and ephedrine were discovered.

As important as drugs themselves are the means by which they are administered. For example, morphine given in pill form is only about one tenth as effective as an injection of the same dose. Other opium derivatives such as paregoric are more effective when taken orally. An important step in expanding the routes of administering a drug came in 1821 from self-experiments by Dr. Enoch Hale, Jr. Hale, the son of a minister in West Hampton, Massachusetts, was a sickly child, a factor that led him later to study chemistry and medicine at Harvard; he would become one of the first doctors to practice at the Massachusetts General Hospital in Boston. As a twenty-nine-year-old physician, Hale set out to find an alternate route of administering a cathartic, emetic, or other drug when "some powerful obstacle" prevented a patient from swallowing the medication. No one knew whether it was safe to inject a drug by vein; whether the veins, as a reaction, would become inflamed; whether the veins would tolerate a substance that had not been digested through the bowel; whether the drug delivered through the vein would have the same action as it did when it was swallowed. Hale recognized that the practice of such injections was "highly dangerous, or at best, of very doubtful safety."[15]

He decided to try castor oil, then known to be an effective cathartic, and he experimented on himself only after he had injected it into the veins of rabbits over an eleven-day period and observed no adverse effects. Even so, his experiment sounds crazy today. But considering how little was known about drugs in his time, it was not.

In fact, Hale won the prestigious Boylston Prize for his self-experiment.[16] It was an example of practical research. His experiment was a forerunner of what was to be a major focus of modern pharmacologic research—finding new, safer, and more effective ways to deliver existing drugs to specific regions of the body. Hale's final product was a well-reasoned report that formed a basis for the injection of drugs by vein, a standard modern medical practice today which was then unknown.[17]

On the day of the experiment, Hale was nervous. Despite the

assurance gained from his tests with the rabbits, he was still anxious when an assistant injected the castor oil slowly into the vein in his arm. Some of the oil went into the vein but some leaked under the skin of his arm because it was difficult to inject the heavy liquid through the primitive needle. Apart from some swelling at the injection site, Hale felt all right at first. Then he began to notice an oily taste in his mouth and to experience abdominal cramps and a feeling of nausea. He developed a headache. "I felt a slight stiffness of muscles of the face and jaw," he wrote, "which cut short my speaking in the middle of a word, accompanied by a bewildered feeling in my head, and a slight faintness. I sat down and in a few moments recovered myself a little."[18]

Hale's injection was given slowly over a twenty-five-minute period and completed by noon. The initial symptoms continued to get worse, reaching a peak around one-thirty. Then they began to abate.

By three o'clock he was able to eat some pudding. At four o'clock he answered an urgent call to examine a patient, accompanied "by my assistant, to guard against accidents."[19] But the effects of the experiment lingered, and even after four weeks Hale had not yet recovered his usual strength. "I am more easily fatigued, and am obliged to pay more careful attention to my diet than before," he said.[20]

Doctors had transfused blood before, but they had never injected medicines. A reviewer of Hale's prize dissertation noted in *The New England Journal of Medicine and Surgery:* "Although the injection of foreign substances into the veins of animals in various physiological investigations has been a frequent experiment among philosophers. . . . This is, we believe, the only well-authenticated one upon record, in which any medicinal substance has been introduced into the veins of any individual of our own species."[21]

Hale had made a beginning, and an extraordinarily important one. Without his work on intravenous injection, many more people would die today of heart attacks, diabetes, infections, and complications of surgery, among other conditions.[22]

Meanwhile, another self-experimenter, a Czechoslovakian, Jan Evangelista Purkinje (also spelled Purkyne), was doing experiments that were to establish him as a pioneer in pharmacology as well as in physiology and psychology.[23] Born in 1787 in a castle in Bohemia, where his father managed an estate, Purkinje became a monk but left the order to turn to medicine. At that time medicine was the only way to acquire a knowledge of the natural sciences, and in 1819, at the relatively advanced age of thirty-two, Purkinje became a doctor. His aim was a career in scientific research rather than the practice of medicine—an effort encouraged by his friend, the poet Goethe.[24] Purkinje's self-experiments began when he was a third-year medical student and would visit the "Golden Crown" pharmacy in Prague, where the owner, the father of a friend, allowed him to taste, smell, and collect drugs.

Purkinje was dissatisfied with the medical research of his day. Guidelines for prescribing drugs for different diseases were based on simple descriptions and crude tests on animals. He was skeptical of the effect of the small doses that were then prescribed, considering them "to be nothing but mysticism."[25] Driven by his belief in the indivisible unity of the body and mind, Purkinje wanted to know how drugs acted on humans. Although he recognized the value of making drug experiments on animals, he worked in a period when there was strong opposition to vivisection. He repeatedly tested drugs on himself and paid particular attention to their sensory and mental effects. He took risks, but he was a cautious investigator. "Since experimentation is done on the living body," he said, "one will have to exercise care lest he offer himself as a sacrifice by exposing himself to danger."[26] As a good Catholic he was not about to risk suicide.

His most famous and daring drug self-experiment was with digitalis, a substance that is derived from the foxglove plant and that for more than a century has been one of the physician's chief tools in the treatment of heart disorders.[27] From the beginning, doctors knew that too large a dose of digitalis could blur a person's eyesight. Purkinje used digitalis to study the physiology of vision. "I could not resist the temptation to look for a more exact explanation of the phenomenon," he said.[28] Over a four-day period, he deliberately swallowed an overdose of digitalis—the equivalent of nine times the lethal dose for a cat. For fifteen days he suffered from flickering vision and black spots before his eyes. The sketches he made of what he saw while poisoned with digitalis are among his fundamental contributions; they gave clues to the toxic effects of the commonly prescribed drug and insights into the physiology of vision. Although his heart slowed and skipped many beats during the experiment, he suffered no permanent adverse effects. Fortunately, Purkinje's heart was normal; we now know that for unknown reasons the action of digitalis is weaker on a healthy heart than on a damaged one.

Purkinje's chemistry teacher, Pleischl, learned about his student's self-experiments with drugs and asked him to compare the effects of several extracts of ipecac (emetine). Purkinje did six experiments within a three-week period, describing his feelings of nausea, vomiting, salivation, cramps, and diarrhea. By the end of the experiment he had developed a feeling of nausea as a conditioned reflex whenever he saw a brown powder resembling ipecac.

In another experiment he tested belladonna, which is derived from a plant known as deadly nightshade. Purkinje put drops of belladonna in his eyes and described the blurred vision that resulted. Then he swallowed it. Among the effects were the drying up of his mouth, because he stopped secreting saliva, and a speeding up of his heart rate. These experiments led other researchers to discover related drugs such as atropine, which is used in ophthalmology to dilate the pupil and to relax stomach and bowel muscles in treating ulcers and spasms.

In an additional experiment, Purkinje studied the effects of ingesting turpentine. At that time, turpentine was used to treat worm infections, and because some patients had described peculiar effects after taking large doses, Purkinje decided to try it on himself. He took varying doses of the drug on three successive mornings, describing its hypnotic effects and the unusual euphoria that lasted several days after he took it with wine. Next he tested the toxic effects of nutmeg. When he became stuporous, he attributed the effects to the herb.[29]

In all these tests, Purkinje had to keep increasing the dosage in order to observe the gradation of symptoms. Some experiments proved especially dangerous. While testing camphor, which is used as a component of paregoric and was occasionally prescribed as a stimulant, Purkinje took different doses on at least five occasions. After one, he became totally unconscious for about half an hour. It was another full day before he regained his sense of time and awareness of the environment.

Purkinje's self-experiments in pharmacology had value far beyond the various descriptions of the actions of individual drugs. He helped introduce a more systematic basis to the practice of prescribing drugs, and he was probably the first to describe the principle of drug interactions. Now, when doctors write a prescription, they consider the possible harmful influence of one drug on another. Furthermore, his exceptional powers of self-observation, all the more remarkable because one eye had been defective since childhood, enabled him to discover many physiological phenomena. For example, Purkinje used the carousels and swings in Prague amusement parks to study vertigo (the phenomenon that occurs after an individual rotates around his own axis) as well as to learn how the body maintains posture and equilibrium. From such studies he developed a law of vertigo now known by his name that pertains to the way the head perceives position when the body rotates. He found that the involuntary muscular reactions of the eyes, or nystagmus, depend on the position of the head during rotation, a finding that doctors rely on in examining a patient's eyes and neurological function. These experiments were difficult to do and dangerous. Some researchers had to practice for a year before they could master the techniques Purkinje used and others were blinded in trying to repeat Purkinje's experiments.[30]

Purkinje eventually stopped experimenting on himself because of increasing age and family obligations. When his wife died in 1835 and he became solely responsible for the care of their two sons, he announced that self-experimentation was something he was "leaving to the young, more agile" scientists.[31] He could be pardoned. He had, after all, done thirty-five experiments on himself, probably more than any other researcher in history.

By modern standards little progress was made in pharmacology over the next several decades. Then, in 1879, one of the "younger scientists" to whom Purkinje had left self-experimentation made an important discovery. The young doctor was twenty-six-year-old William Murrell, who discovered that nitroglycerin could relieve the pains of angina pectoris. It is a therapy that remains standard today.[32]

Murrell, a London physician, became interested in a medical controversy over the effects of nitroglycerine, which some doctors, over the objections of their colleagues, suspected would be valuable in the treatment of spasms and in a large class of nervous diseases. The controversy had begun in 1858 when another London doctor, A. G. Field, had allowed a colleague to put two drops of nitroglycerine on his tongue.[33] Field described a sensation of fullness in both sides of his neck, followed by nausea and a loud rushing noise in his ears like steam passing out of a kettle. His head drooped back, his jaw dropped, and he turned white. When Field's physician-friend could detect no pulse, he thought he had killed him. He poured a stimulant into Field's mouth. Field recovered and went on to do further experiments on himself and others to demonstrate the great variation in the strength of different specimens of the drug.

Twenty years later, Murrell, who had read Field's reports and had followed the controversy, tested nitroglycerine on himself to make up his own mind about its effects. "One afternoon, whilst seeing out-patients, I remembered that I had the bottle in my pocket," Murrell wrote. "Wishing to taste it, I applied the moistened cork to my tongue, and a moment after, a patient coming in, I had forgotten all about it. Not for long, however, for I had not asked my patient half a dozen questions before I experienced a violent pulsation in my head, and Mr. Field's observations rose considerably in my estimation. The pulsation rapidly increased, and soon became so severe that each beat of the heart seemed to shake my whole body. I regretted that I had not taken a more opportune moment of trying my experiments, and was afraid the patient would notice my distress, and think that I was either ill or intoxicated." Murrell could feel his pulse beating to the tips of his fingers. "The pen I was holding was violently jerked with every beat of the heart."[34] He barely got through the consultation.

To confirm his findings, Murrell took nitroglycerine another thirty or forty times; it always produced the same symptoms. He also tested it on thirty-five other people. He noticed that nitroglycerine's physiological actions were similar to those of another drug, amyl nitrite, which had been used in the treatment of angina pectoris. Murrell concluded that nitroglycerine could also be valuable in the treatment of the condition. His theory proved correct. Since then, tens of millions of people have relied on nitroglycerine to relieve the crushing chest pains of angina, a common manifestation of arteriosclerosis. Nitroglycerine and amyl nitrite relax the muscles in blood vessels, allowing blood to pass more freely through arteries that have been narrowed by arteriosclerotic heart disease.

While Murrell, Field, Purkinje, and other researchers focused their attention on trying to ascertain more precise reasons for prescribing drugs and increasing their safety, others were trying to find effective antidotes to poisons. One such antidote was activated charcoal, which can rapidly absorb as much as half its weight in various substances. Although charcoal was already being used as early as the time of Hippocrates, the first systematic studies of its use as an antidote were done by French scientists in the nineteenth century.[35] In 1813 the chemist M. Bertrand, after showing that he could use charcoal to prevent arsenic poisoning in animals, gave a public demonstration of its benefits to humans.[36] Bertrand swallowed five grams of arsenic trioxide mixed with charcoal without ill effect. Other researchers had difficulty confirming his findings, probably because the absorbing quality of the charcoal varied according to preparations. But in 1852 a chemist named Pierre-Fleurus Touéry confirmed once and for all the benefits of charcoal in a bold demonstration before the French Academy of Medicine.

Touéry had begun his studies of charcoal in 1830 with experiments on dogs, and he continued them until 1852. He learned that charcoal was an effective antidote against the toxins of mushrooms and other poisons. But skeptical members of the French Academy of Medicine demanded that Touéry repeat the experiments after having tied the dog's esophagus. The eminent scientists reasoned that the dog would vomit any poison fed it. By tying the gullet, this could be prevented. Touéry, insulted by the Academy's attitude, decided to perform the experiment on himself. In front of a large audience he swallowed one gram of strychnine (ten times the fatal dose) mixed with fifteen grams of charcoal. Members of the Academy sat on the edge of their chairs watching in stunned silence. Many of them must have thought the chemist mad. Touéry stood there calmly. Ten minutes passed, fifteen minutes. Touéry smiled. Nothing was going to happen to him.

In the nineteenth century most scientists, like Murrell and Touéry, worked alone, although some, like Pasteur, formed small teams. There were no rules regarding self-experimentation, and, while it was often viewed as too risky or even foolish, the self-experimenter was free, for the most part, to conduct his experiments as he wished. The development of drug companies was to profoundly change all this. By the end of the nineteenth century the economics of an industrialized society had transformed pharmacology into a full-time business. The increasing scarcity of quinine, for example, essential in the treatment of malaria, inspired the first search for a potentially therapeutic substance not found in nature. The search was led by dye manufacturers, mainly German, who were leaders in the chemical industry, and who began to synthesize new compounds. None were successful in treating malaria, but several shared with quinine the ability to reduce fever and relieve pain. The most famous of these synthetic drugs was acetylsalicylic acid, first used in 1899, and known to most people as aspirin.

Largely as a result of the success of aspirin, it was not long before pharmacology itself became a huge industry. More and more chemists became industrial pharmacologists, and other scientists who at one time might have pursued research alone or in universities now began working for drug companies. No longer spirited amateurs making discoveries in private pharmacies and laboratories, they became professionals, paid to work as members of large teams. It was a switch symptomatic of the twentieth century, as inevitable for those studying drugs as it was for people in other professions.

Still, within this industrial setting, many scientists continued to carry on the tradition of self-experimentation in their search for new drugs. There is no better example of this than the development of Antabuse (disulfiram), a drug that is now used throughout the world to help treat alcoholism.

During World War II, at a Danish company called Medicinalco, now known as Dumex, it was customary practice for pharmacologists and technicians to experiment on themselves when a new drug was being tested. The employees who did so were admitted to a group that jokingly called itself the "Death Battalion." Medicinalco employed about three hundred people, which, although small by today's standards, made it a rather large firm then. The employees were a congenial group, and for many workers the practice of self-experimentation helped form a bond of camaraderie.

Dr. Erik Jacobsen, the company's medical research director, was a gregarious physician who had a Ph.D. in pharmacology. As a youth in Copenhagen, where his father was a lawyer, Jacobsen had given up thoughts of becoming a professional saxophone player or an astronomer for the more secure life of medicine. He lived by a strong moral code. In his work, he believed that pharmacologists should test a drug on themselves before doing so on another human. He practiced what he preached. Medicinalco paid none of the members of the "Death Battalion" for their participation, but it offered those who gave a blood sample a glass of port. As a further reward and goodwill gesture, Medicinalco treated the group to a lavish dinner dance at least once a year. Jacobsen was one of the group's most active members; it was he, in fact, who had coined the name "Death Battalion." At each banquet, a small plastic skeleton nicknamed "Jacob" was awarded to the member who had been the Battalion's most ardent participant since the previous festivities. Jacobsen had already won a "Jacob" several times for his self-experiments with vitamin B-12 and barbiturate sedatives.

One member of Jacobsen's research team was Dr. Jens Hald. He had read a report that stimulated him to think about research possibilities with the drug disulfiram against intestinal parasites. The report described the successful treatment with disulfiram of the parasitic skin disease scabies, which caused itching and often severe scratching that triggered infections which left scars. Scabies was epidemic throughout wartime Europe, and Swedish researchers had reported success in treating it by putting an old chemical to a new use. They had applied disulfiram (or tetraethylthiuram disulfide), long used as a chemical in the rubber industry, as an ointment to the skin of patients with scabies.

Hald knew that disulfiram had a strong affinity for copper. And he had a hunch. Somewhere he had read that some intestinal parasites needed copper to live, and he wondered if the drug, when swallowed, would interfere with copper metabolism in intestinal worms. Could disulfiram be made into a pill that would also be effective against intestinal worms?

Jacobsen and Hald decided to find out. They made disulfiram into pills and, as was standard for the day, fed them first to rabbits. The animals remained content, munching as usual on carrots in their cages. Nothing adverse happened, at least as far as the investigators could tell. Next, the two Danes found some rabbits infected with an intestinal parasite, and fed these animals the disulfiram pills. The drug seemed to work. Now the medical investigators had to determine disulfiram's safety for humans. They knew it was safe when used topically; but what would happen when it was swallowed? And on whom would they test the drug first?

"Just to be safe, we took some of the tablets ourselves," Jacobsen told me when I first met him in Copenhagen in 1972.[37] "We regarded the drug as innocuous, or we wouldn't have done so. Yet even if we had suspected a side effect, that wouldn't have stopped us. We would have started more cautiously, of course. It never occurred to us to ask others to volunteer first. We would have regarded that as unethical. And it was convenient—we were near at hand."

The scientists began taking disulfiram pills as a daily regimen while they continued their regular tasks in different sections of the drug company.

At lunchtime one day, shortly after the pill experiment had begun, Jacobsen picked up the brown paper bag that contained the sandwiches his wife had made for him that morning and stopped to remove a bottle of Tuborg beer from the refrigerator. Then he walked down the corridor to the library to have lunch and talk with fellow workers.

By the time lunch was over, Jacobsen felt slightly groggy. His head throbbed, he felt nauseated. Gradually the symptoms disappeared and he returned to his laboratory to work. Could a "bug" or virus be spreading through the Jacobsen household? he wondered. That was unlikely. His wife and two daughters had felt fine when he had left home that morning. When he returned home that night, he found them still healthy. The next day at work, he ate an open-faced shrimp sandwich and coffee. Nothing happened.

As Medicinalco's research director, Jacobsen lunched with the managing director once or twice each week at a restaurant in Copenhagen. This particular week, upon returning from one such lunch, Jacobsen appeared unusually red-faced. A worried colleague asked: "Have you been fired?"

"No," a startled Jacobsen replied. "Why?"

The lunch, in fact, had been so friendly that Jacobsen and the director had raised their glasses of aquavit to propose an extra "skoal." Although Jacobsen could not see how red his face had become, he did feel unusually flushed. He thought it was peculiar that his head throbbed. But again the symptoms, which included nausea, disappeared and he shrugged it off.

That Friday, while a fellow pharmacologist gave an informal luncheon talk, Jacobsen sipped a beer and ate the meatball sandwich his wife had made. Shortly afterward, he had another attack and went home early. It was a trip of several miles, and as he weaved on his bicycle through Copenhagen's narrow streets, he wondered: Could it be those meatballs? He asked his daughters what they had eaten for lunch. Meatballs, just like their father. They were fine; the meatballs could not be responsible.

On Monday morning, he grabbed the brown lunch bag and bottle of beer and pedaled off to the laboratory. Again he felt mildly ill after lunch. This time he noticed that his heart seemed to speed up and to pound a little more than usual.

The attacks continued, but they were only mildly annoying, and Jacobsen did not think too much about them until one day he met Hald in the corridor. They compared notes about the disulfiram that both were taking. "We were just chatting and I mentioned this curious affair that I had been through. Hald smiled and said, 'That's funny. I have had the same bug.' "

Hald related an incident that had occurred when an old friend, a sailor, had come to visit, and he opened a bottle of cognac to celebrate. Hald had become sick, his friend had not. Now in talking with each other, the two researchers realized that they had shared a common reaction. Had the alcohol caused it?

It was well known that drinking too much alcohol over a period of years could permanently damage a portion of the brain, even to the point of psychosis. Alcohol could destroy the liver, producing jaundice; the resulting damage could lead to fatal bleeding. But neither man was a heavy drinker, and how to account for the sudden nausea, sweating, and rapid heartbeats? These symptoms suggested sensitivity to a compound, a reaction unheard of in relationship to alcohol alone. Could the mysterious culprit be the disulfiram pills? The animals had displayed no symptoms. But how could they? The rabbits had not been fed a cocktail or a beer with their carrots.

At the time, doctors knew about drug side effects and routinely checked for the well-known ones—itching, rashes, nausea, hair loss, impotence, visual disturbances, and so on, when they tested compounds. There was not a hint of any of these with disulfiram, except the nausea which they had experienced after drinking alcohol.

Here was a startling finding—a pill that seemed to do nothing, unless alcohol was consumed with it. It was an unusual form of drug interaction. The new findings forced the two Danes to draft another protocol.

First each researcher avoided both the drug and alcohol. Nothing happened. Then each drank alcohol but still avoided the drug. When they had a beer or drank a cocktail, the sickening symptoms did not return.

In the third phase they abstained from alcohol but resumed taking the drug. They waited for several days, and nothing happened except that Jacobsen had an embarrassing experience. One night, he gave a public lecture at the Tuborg Breweries and he was offered the customary complimentary beer. The scientist did not want to tell his hosts about the experiment, nor did he want to offend them by refusing a beer. "So I had to pass my beers along to my wife, who drank them," Jacobsen said. As he recalled the incident, both he and his wife laughed about it.

In the final phase, Jacobsen and Hald resumed taking the drug and a few days later began drinking small amounts of alcohol. Both investigators became sick.

Just to be certain that the combination of drug and alcohol was responsible for the reaction, they repeated the experiment on a laboratory colleague. The results were the same. And in all cases the alcohol triggered a reaction only after the person had been taking the drug for a few days. Somehow the body needed enough time to break down disulfiram to trigger the drug-alcohol reaction.

The results of the experiment dealt a devastating blow to the potential marketing of Jacobsen's and Hald's proposed antiparasitic drug, but by this time the two Danes had made a more important discovery—one that could only have been made as a result of testing the drug on humans. Further, it could only have happened by accident. Even the most clever, knowledgeable researcher could not have predicted it. Nor could anyone have devised a scientific protocol sufficiently ingenious to discover that disulfiram, a drug that was nontoxic when taken by itself, could make even the smallest amount of alcohol toxic.[38]

At first the two Danes were less than enthusiastic about capitalizing on their serendipitous discovery and changing the focus of their research. Although Jacobsen himself was extremely interested in alcoholism and had already written a book on the subject, alcoholism was not then considered an important medical problem in Denmark.[39] "There was a high tax imposed on alcoholic beverages," Jacobsen explained. As a result, the authorities felt that few Danes could afford to drink enough alcohol to cause alcoholism. There was no practical or commercial reason to develop an antialcohol drug."

So disulfiram remained a drug with fascinating properties that a few pharmacologists were testing on themselves in the laboratory, but not on any patients. That final step, like the original discovery, came almost by accident.

On October 11, 1947, Jacobsen, who was interested in civic affairs, found himself the unscheduled speaker at a public meeting when a well-known Danish educator had to cancel an appearance at the last minute. During the course of his impromptu speech, Jacobsen told his audience about the disulfiram experiments he and Hald had conducted and how as a result of these experiments neither of them could stand alcohol—a sudden change for both.

To Jacobsen's surprise, his comments were reported the following morning in the *Berlingske Tidende,* a Copenhagen newspaper, by a journalist who had been in the audience. Jacobsen was even more surprised by the extent of the reaction to the article among Danish alcoholics. Some of them wrote, pleading for pills as "a last chance." This reaction made it clear that alcoholism was more common in Denmark than anyone had thought.

As a further experiment Jacobsen gave Dr. Martensen Larsen, a psychiatrist, a supply of the pills to treat his alcoholic patients. Larsen was a specialist in aversion therapy, a crude and unpleasant treatment that was then the chief one for alcoholics. Jacobsen heard nothing for two months. Then Larsen called to report that five of ten chronic alcoholics had remained sober over Christmas and New Year's, something they had not done for years. He asked for more pills.

The results sparked a new series of experiments, some of them self-experiments, to learn more about how the drug worked in the body. "We took the tablets," Jacobsen said. "We took some alcohol. We measured skin temperature, counted the pulse rate, and determined the dosage. We thought the sensitivity reaction might be due to the effects of [a natural chemical in the body called] histamine that could also cause the heart to pound. But we couldn't find any increase in the histamine content of the blood."

Hald and Jacobsen were puzzled. They knew something in the body, perhaps an enzyme in the bowel, must be interacting with the drug to cause such a reaction. They decided to swallow disulfiram pills, then inject alcohol intravenously and record the effects. "I was the victim at that point," Jacobsen said. "I took the alcohol—not much more than the equivalent of one beer. It was given intravenously, slowly."

The effect was much more dramatic and potentially dangerous than Jacobsen had supposed it would be. He became seriously ill. When his blood pressure was taken it showed no diastolic pressure. (Blood pressure measurements are recorded as a fraction. The top number is called systole, the bottom number diastole. The zero reading was a sign of a potentially serious, if not fatal, reaction.)

Two hours later, Jacobsen recovered. He was lucky. The injection could have killed him, since the interaction of disulfiram with alcohol can be fatal.

The interaction of alcohol and the drug produced an odor on Jacobsen's breath, and when a chemist, Tind Christensen, paid him a surprise visit, he startled Jacobsen's team by identifying the source as a chemical called acetaldehyde.

Scientists knew that the body ordinarily metabolizes, or biochemically converts, alcohol to acetaldehyde and then to acetic acid. Normally, the metabolic reaction occurs so rapidly that acetaldehyde does not have time to concentrate in the body or leave a trace on the breath. Christensen's observation led to the identification of acetaldehyde as the metabolic product primarily responsible for the effect of disulfiram on humans.

Jacobsen chose the simplest trade name he could think of—Antabuse—to describe the new use for disulfiram, a drug to combat alcohol abuse. Now, nearly a half century later, alcoholism is becoming recognized for what it is—a major public health problem. It is probably the most common form of drug abuse in virtually every developed non-Islamic country. As doctors have taken a greater interest in treating alcoholism, Antabuse has become a major part of their efforts to discourage impulse drinking among alcoholics who have committed themselves to sobering up permanently.

And how effective is disulfiram against the parasitic diseases for which it was originally developed? "Unfortunately," Jacobsen told me, "it turned out to be useless."

Antabuse might never have been discovered if the research were done today. Medicinalco eventually merged into a company called Dumex, and about 1970 Dumex officials disbanded the "Death Battalion." As Dr. Tage Hansen, the research director, explained: "At a medical meeting we were criticized by a pharmacologist who said the practice of using company employees should be stopped because as employees they were forced to participate in experiments. This was not the case. But because it was perceived that way, we stopped the practice. I believe other drug companies in other countries have done the same for similar reasons. Now the policy at Dumex is to pay medical students up to several hundred dollars, depending on the complexity and demands of the experiment."[40]

Although some drug companies continue to approve of the tradition of self-experimentation, others have drastically curtailed or stopped the practice. The reasons are both legal and financial; a company might be held financially responsible if the researcher-employee were to suffer adverse reactions while experimenting on himself.

There are good reasons for drug company executives to insist that research employees who experiment on themselves abide by certain rules. It is wise, for example, that self-experiments be conducted under adequate medical supervision. But to the extent that drug companies discourage or prohibit self-experimentation simply as a reflection of the trend for concern over the threats of litigation, it is a bad industry policy. Not only has self-experimentation led to the discovery of drugs; the methodology has helped keep potentially dangerous drugs from reaching the market because self-experimenters have identified adverse effects that were not detected in animal studies.[41] Furthermore, who knows how many beneficial drugs are being withheld from the public or remain undiscovered because curious scientists are inhibited from following their scientific instincts?

## Chapter Five

# THE PASTEURIAN CLUB

Medicine's ultimate goal is prevention, and the best prevention against a disease is, of course, to eradicate it so it can never harm anyone again. But only once in history have doctors been able to play a symbolic taps for the death of a disease. In 1980 the World Health Organization declared smallpox eradicated after an army of its workers had used a derivative of a vaccine developed nearly two centuries earlier to wipe the viral disease off the face of the earth. Before that time, smallpox killed about one in four of its victims, scarred most survivors for life, and blinded others. Moreover, smallpox, like many other viral infections, could not be cured, nor could it be effectively treated once it came on. But it could be prevented.

The weapon against smallpox was a vaccine developed by Dr. Edward Jenner in 1796.[1] Jenner's discovery became a model for all the immunizations that are used in medicine today: immunizations that mean children no longer risk choking to death from diphtheria or being brain damaged as a complication of measles or paralyzed from poliomyelitis; no longer are people in danger of getting "lockjaw" (tetanus) from stepping on a rusty nail; and many fewer babies are gasping for breath from the severe paroxysms of whooping cough.

Edward Jenner, an English country physician, took his cue from milkmaids who noted that people who came down with cowpox often escaped subsequent infection from smallpox. Jenner spent years developing a vaccine from matter derived from the sores of cowpox patients; along the way he was encouraged by John Hunter, the same John Hunter who in a dramatic self-experiment had purposely injected himself with pus from a patient infected with gonorrhea.[2] (See Prologue.) Jenner inoculated eight-year-old James Phipps with the cowpox matter; young Phipps got cowpox and recovered. Then, in the next and most crucial step, Jenner, on July 1, 1796, inoculated the boy with the smallpox virus. He repeated the inoculation about twenty times over the next two decades; Phipps did not get the disease.

Jenner never reported testing the vaccine on himself, and he left no historical records to explain why he had not done so. Because he had had smallpox at age eight, he might have thought that he had acquired lasting immunity to the disease and therefore believed that self-experimentation would not test the efficacy of the vaccine.

When Jenner published a report on his smallpox vaccine, doctors in other countries began using his technique. This grandfather of all vaccines worked because the cowpox and smallpox viruses were so closely related that when cowpox virus was injected into a human, it tricked the body's immune system into producing antibodies that defended against future invasion not only by the cowpox virus but also by the smallpox virus. It was an unusual way to make a vaccine; most of the ones developed since have been based on the disease-causing organism itself, which is either weakened during growth in eggs or cells in test tubes or killed by chemicals, before being used to immunize.

In light of the success of Jenner's vaccine, it is surprising that it was not until eighty-nine years later that the second vaccine against a human disease was developed. The disease was rabies, and the vaccine was developed by Louis Pasteur.

The relative risks and benefits of rabies immunization were controversial from the earliest days, and no vaccine has undergone more modifications. From the start, self-experimentation played an important role. It all began with Louis Pasteur, who expressed a willingness to do daring experiments on himself but was discouraged by his colleagues, who then bravely did experiments on their own bodies. Their names are not well known, but their efforts did much to assure a wider use of the vaccine.

Rabies affects animals primarily and humans only accidentally, usually from infected animal bites. It kills people slowly and horribly by destroying the brain and central nervous system. As the victims try to breathe, their bodies can twist with jerky spasms, their arms shake, and the head is thrust backward involuntarily. Rabies is often called hydrophobia (dread of water) because many human victims (but not animals) become terrified as they start to swallow. They cough, inhale liquid into the windpipe, and regurgitate water through the nose. But hydrophobia is a misnomer for rabies because not all victims get this aversion to water, while others experience the same violent reactions from the mere flow of air across the face.

Rabies has been dreaded far out of proportion to its true incidence, in part because of the horrible way it attacks its victims and in part because of the terrible forms early attempts at treatment took. The disease has been known in western Europe since at least 1271, and treatment over the centuries has been extreme. Victims were often thrown in the water to cure both their hydrophobia and their thirst; affected limbs were sometimes amputated, and a few rabies victims were even murdered. Everywhere, rabid animals created hysteria, and because the incubation period can last several months, many bite victims waited in terror, not knowing when, or if, they would get the disease.[3]

In 1880, when Pasteur began directing his attention to rabies, the only treatment was cauterization of the bite with a red-hot iron, a fearsomely painful procedure.[4] It is said that when Pasteur was a child, he witnessed cauterization in a blacksmith's shop, where several neighbors were being treated after having been bitten by a rabid wolf. By the time he began his rabies research, Pasteur was fifty-eight years old and famous. A chemist and physicist with no medical training, he was entertained by royalty and honored by his professional peers. From his early research on the structure of crystals, he had moved to fermentation studies on vinegar and wine; his "pasteurization" research had helped the beer industry and led to healthy milk. Then Pasteur turned his efforts to medicine. By the time he began working with rabies, he had already developed vaccines for animals against anthrax and fowl cholera.

Yet it was the antirabies treatment that "made of him a hero in the golden legend of science" and for which the French public would honor him by underwriting the costs of a network of Pasteur Institutes throughout the world.[5]

Pasteur and his colleagues were well aware that the dangers in developing the rabies vaccine were great. They took precautions to avoid being bitten, but rabid animals were treacherous. A bite, even a lick, could transmit the fatal disease. Even after the animals were dead the researchers risked infection from work with the tissues, which contained rabies virus.

It had been known from at least the first century A.D. that the saliva of rabid animals contained the invisible agent that caused rabies, and for more than a year Pasteur tried to implicate a "saliva microbe" as the causative agent.[6] Rabbits inoculated with the "saliva microbe" died, but they did not have the cardinal symptoms of the disease, and Pasteur soon realized that the "saliva microbe" had no connection with rabies. The "microbe" turned out to be the pneumococcus bacterium, which also happened to be in the saliva that Pasteur tested; it caused the overwhelming infections that killed the rabbits. Pasteur was unable to implicate any other organism. The reason is apparent today: The bullet-shaped rabies virus can be seen only under an electron microscope, and it would be decades before such a high-powered instrument was invented.[7]

Other French scientists, who were doing research on rabies at the same time as Pasteur, tried unsuccessfully to induce the disease in animals by injecting them with blood from rabid dogs.[8] Then in 1881 a veterinarian in Lyons named Victor Galtier succeeded in transmitting rabies to rabbits.[9] That same year, Pasteur found a consistent method of transmitting the disease to animals: Brain matter was extracted from a rabid dog and then inoculated directly into the brain of a healthy animal.[10] The next year, 1882, Pasteur succeeded where others had failed—he transmitted rabies to animals by intravenous injections of infected material.[11] These direct injections reduced the time it took for the exposed animals to become ill to about six days, considerably less than the several-week incubation period they experienced when bitten under real-life conditions. The overwhelming majority of the inoculated animals died. But Pasteur found that those animals that did not get the infection were immune to subsequent injections of the rabies virus. This boosted his confidence that a vaccine could be produced.[12]

In May 1884, Pasteur prepared rabies viruses with varying degrees of virulence. He inoculated the material into an animal and allowed it to grow, then recovered it and inoculated it into another animal through a technique known as "passage." Each transfer is called a pass, and passaging in some animals can weaken, or attenuate, the virus. Pasteur passed rabies viruses from dog to monkey and then on to other monkeys. The virus was still too strong; instead of simply being immunized, all the monkeys actually came down with the disease.

As he continued his experiments, Pasteur found that the length of incubation time varied among species. In some animals it sped up, in others it slowed down. In the process, the incubation period in each successive animal changed until it could be "fixed" within a certain number of days. Pasteur discovered that the incubation period of the natural so-called "street" rabies virus was long and variable, but that in experiments on rabbits it shortened and became "fixed" at about six to eight days. The "fixed" virus often failed to infect animals unless injected directly into the brain. After about one hundred passes in rabbits, for instance, the "fixed" rabies virus could sometimes be injected into dogs without producing rabies.[13]

Crucial to Pasteur's success was his finding that if he suspended rabies-infected spinal cords of rabbits in a vapor of a chemical, potassium hydroxide, he could reduce the number of virus particles in the tissue. Pasteur believed that if he used this treatment over a long period of time, he could inactivate the rabies virus. Pasteur now thought he had a means of immunization. He would give an animal a series of injections with varying strengths of rabies vaccine. He would start with the weakest and then proceed in a step-wise manner to the most virulent, thereby stimulating the body to gradually form antibodies to increasing strengths of rabies virus. The same technique, he reasoned, could be used to protect humans *after* they were bitten by rabid animals, because rabies was a disease with an unusually long incubation period; the vaccine, he theorized, would invoke antibodies *before* the virus itself did its damage. But, Pasteur stressed, "proofs must be collected from different animal species, and almost ad infinitum, before human therapeutics can make bold to try this mode of prophylaxis on man himself."[14]

Pasteur carried out a scientifically controlled experiment involving forty-two dogs. Twenty-three were vaccinated with a series of injections, and nineteen were not. All forty-two were then exposed to the rabies virus by one of three procedures—injections into the brain, injections into the blood, or actual bites from rabid animals. Of the nineteen not immunized, thirteen developed rabies. None of the twenty-three immunized dogs came down with the disease. Pasteur announced this finding at the International Congress of Medicine in Copenhagen in August 1884.

He was still terrified at the prospect of experimenting on people. Pasteur was the leading world expert on vaccines, but the two he had successfully developed were aimed at protecting animals, not humans. He explained to the Copenhagen audience that there were tremendous difficulties in extending the rabies vaccine to humans.

"Experimentation permitted on animals," Pasteur said, "is criminal when it concerns man."[15] Pasteur reiterated these anxieties a month later in a reply to the emperor of Brazil, who wrote asking when rabies vaccine would be tried on human patients.[16]

In December 1884, four years after the beginning of his project, the conservative scientist in Pasteur maintained that his experiments had not yet been carried on long enough to establish the efficacy of the vaccine in animals. "It is only when I can tell that I can vaccinate for sure dogs who have been bitten," he wrote, "that I would dare to experiment on man, and yet my hand would shake because what is possible on the dog may not be so on man."[17]

At this point Pasteur contemplated an experiment which, had he carried it out, would have been one of the most daring in the history of medicine. In a letter to a friend on March 28, 1885, the scientist wrote: "I have not yet dared to treat human beings after bites from rabid dogs; but the time is not far off, and I am much inclined to begin with myself—inoculating myself with rabies, and then arresting the consequences; for I am beginning to feel very sure of my results."[18] His proposal went far beyond testing the safety of a single dose or two of the vaccine. He also wanted to prove its efficacy. If Pasteur inoculated himself with the rabies virus, the risk was almost certain death unless his vaccine worked. It would be the ultimate test.

But events took another turn.

On July 6, 1885, nine-year-old Joseph Meister and his mother made a surprise visit to Pasteur's laboratory in Paris.[19] Two days earlier, the boy had been severely bitten by a ferocious dog that was believed rabid. A local doctor had cauterized the wounds with carbolic acid. Then, knowing of Pasteur's work, he sent the boy to him for consultation. Joseph's mother pleaded with Pasteur to do something for her son. The scientist was tormented. He was almost certain that the boy would die from rabies. But he knew that the moment he inoculated Joseph, his reputation and that of the vaccine would be at stake. Moreover, if he treated the boy on his own, he might be attacked for practicing medicine without a license. Pasteur immediately consulted his assistant, Edmé-Felix-Alfred Vulpian, a physician and physiologist. Vulpian urged Pasteur to use the vaccine because there was no other effective treatment. Pasteur still hesitated. He consulted another assistant, Dr. Jacques J. Grancher, a physician, who also urged that the vaccine be given immediately. Pasteur decided to proceed, estimating the dosage from the animal experiments. Each succeeding day, a more virulent rabies virus was injected into young Meister's body.

Pasteur waited. The boy's family waited. Joseph suffered painful red swellings around the sites of the thirteen injections he received over a twelve-day period. Midway through, the boy developed a headache, and Pasteur worried that it heralded the onset of rabies or of an adverse reaction to his vaccine. But neither developed. The vaccine was credited with saving Joseph Meister's life. Soon after, Pasteur treated another lad, and he, too, did not become rabid.

Pasteur is noted for the thoroughness of his laboratory notes and for the voluminous correspondence that he left for historical examination. Yet nothing tells us why he did not carry out his proposed self-experiment at the same time he treated Meister. Almost certainly, there was enough vaccine for both Meister and himself. Was this proposal merely a self-serving dramatic gesture? Had his colleagues swayed him against his plan? According to Adrien Loir, a nephew of Madame Pasteur who worked with Pasteur, the scientist later did, in fact, attempt to take the vaccine. Loir recorded the circumstances that occurred as a result of a laboratory accident.

Jacques Grancher, the physician who gave the first injections of the vaccine to Meister, accidentally stuck his thigh with a syringe containing live rabies virus.[20] Pasteur, who was standing near Grancher, immediately commanded that his colleague receive the vaccine, not as an experiment but to save his life. Grancher, who was fully confident of the immunization method, agreed. Loir asked another assistant, Eugene Viala, for a supply of the vaccine, and when Loir told Viala about the accident, the two men, perhaps as a show of confidence, decided that they, too, should take the full series of rabies immunization shots.

In this moment of crisis, Pasteur announced that he was ready to experiment on himself. He met with his colleagues in his office and insisted that he go first. He pulled off his shirt to bare his skin for the injection. But Grancher refused to give it to him. He contended that no reason existed for Pasteur to take the immunization since he had not been infected. Pasteur then turned to his wife's nephew and demanded that Loir give him the vaccine.

By this time Pasteur was a national hero in France. Who was brave enough to risk the life of such a famous man? What if something went wrong?

The syringe was loaded with the rabies vaccine. Loir said he would give the injection only on Grancher's command because he himself was not a physician. Grancher refused to give the order. It was Grancher, not Pasteur, who received the first injection. Then, without sterilizing the needle, Pasteur and Grancher injected the next doses into Loir and Viala. "My uncle [Pasteur] was mortified, putting his shirt back on," Loir said. Weeks passed; the three men remained healthy. Pasteur and his colleagues concluded that the vaccine was effective and would have no serious adverse effects.

Word about the success of Pasteur's vaccine began to spread throughout the world.[21] But it turned out that his original fears about its safety were well founded. The immunization therapy involved a series of injections lasting for as long as twenty-one days. During this time the patient received up to two and a half grams—a very large amount—of animal brain tissue, as well as weakened rabies virus, in the vaccine. Just a few molecules of brain tissue were enough to incite a fatal allergic reaction in some people.

Over the next two years, 350 people were treated with Pasteur's vaccine. In 1886 Pasteur reported that of the 350 treated cases, only one person had developed rabies—a child whose therapy had been delayed.[22] But a few of the patients treated with the Pasteur rabies vaccine developed permanent damage to the brain and central nervous system. Some died because of the vaccine. Pasteur was now severely criticized for having experimented prematurely on humans.[23] He was still working to improve his vaccine when he died in 1895.

Following the rabies vaccine, Pasteur's disciples developed other immunizations, and sometimes the scientists who made these new vaccines tested them first on themselves. Although Pasteur never actually experimented on himself, those researchers who do self-experiment in their search for new vaccines qualify for membership in what has become known as the "Pasteurian Club." This is not a formal institution, and there are no meetings. It exists because when scientists do experiments with new vaccines they feel a bond to Pasteur's original work. Members of the Pasteurian Club share a fraternal spirit; they read each other's scientific papers, and they try to improve existing vaccines or make new ones.

In Pasteur's time, there was no large pharmaceutical industry to mass-produce his new rabies vaccine. Instead, as news of the treatment spread, scientists throughout the world made their own vaccines. Some followed Pasteur's method as they would a recipe from a cookbook, and, like chefs preparing their versions of standard dishes, they added their own ingredients to Pasteur's original "seed" or mother virus. Some scientists used phenol and other chemicals that killed most of the rabies virus yet maintained its ability to produce antibodies.[24] Researchers adapted Pasteur's techniques to develop the first rabies vaccine used for mass immunization of dogs. It was a significant step, because by controlling the infection in animals, it greatly reduced the threat to humans.

For decades the Pasteur rabies vaccine, or variations of it, continued to be used, but concern remained about the paralysis and other serious damage to nerves that sometimes followed a course of treatment with the vaccine.[25] It was not until 1945 that a significantly different rabies vaccine was developed. It became known as the Flury rabies vaccine because it had its origins in a strain of rabies virus that Dr. Harald N. Johnson of the Rockefeller Foundation isolated from the spinal cord of a fourteen-year-old Georgia girl whose last name was Flury.[26] In 1939, shortly before she died, the girl confided to her mother that she had allowed a dog to lick her vagina on several occasions. The dog died from rabies five days before the girl became ill. A little more than a week later, Miss Flury was dead herself.

Johnson wanted to try a new approach in the preparation of the vaccine. He injected the virus taken from the dead girl into one-day-old chicks; it took thirty days to produce signs of rabies in the birds. Then he transferred the Flury rabies virus from the brain of one chick to that of another, shortening the incubation period to six days. Johnson passed the Flury virus among chicks 136 times, thereby fixing the virus in avian, not mammalian, brain tissue. For the first time there was the possibility of developing a vaccine that was less likely to cause dangerous allergic reactions, because it used nonmammalian nerve tissue.

In 1945 Johnson took some samples of the Flury virus to Dr. Hilary Koprowski, a virologist at Lederle Laboratories in Pearl River, New York. Koprowski was trying to achieve the dream of all rabies vaccine researchers: a single-injection vaccine that would confer a lifetime immunity to dog bites.

Koprowski's interest in vaccines had begun in medical school in Poland, where he had studied under a member of the Pasteurian Club, Professor Romuald Nitsch. In 1903 Nitsch developed his version of the Pasteur rabies vaccine. Although this vaccine had killed rabbits in preliminary tests, Nitsch was convinced it was safe for humans and was willing to prove it by testing the first batch on himself. He injected a large dose of his rabies vaccine beneath the skin of his abdomen and suffered no ill effects.[27] Soon after Koprowski learned about this experiment, he began his own self-experiments. Some of his first research projects concerned the amount of ammonia in the blood. In keeping with the principles he had learned from Nitsch, Koprowski used his own blood for these tests.

After the Nazi invasions Koprowski fled Poland and spent several years in South America, where he worked with a team of scientists from the Rockefeller Foundation on a number of viral diseases.[28] In 1949, shortly after his arrival in the United States, he joined the Pasteurian Club. He prepared what he thought would be a weakened vaccine against a different viral disease—Colorado tick fever—and then he and his colleagues took the vaccine.[29] Unfortunately, it caused side effects—transient fever, malaise, and headache—but several months later, when five of the group exposed themselves to a challenge dose of Colorado tick fever virus, they had no reaction. The vaccine was effective.

A virologist must be extraordinarily patient, because it takes time to weaken the virulence of a microorganism; years and years may be needed to pass a virus from animal to animal time and time again. Koprowski spent seven years working with the Flury rabies virus that Johnson had given him. He used chick eggs because they were easily available. Still, each time he injected them he had to wait weeks for the eggs to incubate, then pass the virus on to incubate in the next set of chick eggs. Meanwhile, he tested the virulence of the passed virus by injecting it into guinea pigs, mice, and other laboratory animals and determining their fate. Koprowski was taking a scientific gamble; he was investing years of work in the belief that he could produce a safer rabies vaccine. But in truth, because of the nature of biology, he could not know what would happen; he might very well have been wasting years of his professional life.

Finally, after the one hundred eightieth pass among chick eggs, Koprowski noticed a remarkable change. The passed virus not only failed to produce rabies when injected into the laboratory animals, it actually began causing the production of large amounts of antibodies.

In 1954 Koprowski and his colleagues prepared two forms of the

Flury vaccine: The form passed from between forty and sixty times was called LEP, for low egg passage, and the form passed 180 or more times was called HEP, for high egg passage. Although the LEP vaccine protected dogs and produced no rabies in animals, the researchers were concerned that the live virus vaccine might still be virulent enough to pose serious risks if injected into humans. However, it did not produce any harmful reaction when tested on cancer patients at Memorial Hospital in New York.[30]

In 1955 the World Health Organization sponsored a course on rabies for African scientists in Kenya. The course was designed to teach the latest advances in rabies prevention in an area where the disease was rampant among wildlife and therefore a major public health problem. Two of the experts who taught the course were Koprowski and Dr. Martin M. Kaplan, a Philadelphia-born and -educated veterinarian and a rabies expert for the World Health Organization in Geneva. Out on the Kenyan savanna, the two men would relax by playing chamber music—Kaplan the cello, Koprowski the piano.[31]

Pasteur's rabies vaccine was still being used throughout Africa, but because both Kaplan and Koprowski were concerned about the potentially lethal adverse reactions that often complicated its administration to humans, they limited the demonstration of the vaccine to animals. At the same time Kaplan and Koprowski believed it was important to show the African scientists how to prepare a vaccine for human use under field conditions. Koprowski, believing that his HEP Flury vaccine, the one that had been passed 180 times, was safer than the Pasteur vaccine and eager to prove its potential for human use, decided to use it to carry out an experiment in front of his African students. There was no Flury vaccine on hand, but Koprowski had brought with him the seed virus from which it could be made. There were excellent laboratory facilities available in Kenya, and Kaplan and Koprowski used them to prepare the vaccine from the seed virus in chick eggs.

The doctors injected the rabies virus into eight-day-old chick embryos and let the virus incubate for about ten days. Then, on the eighteenth day, three days short of hatching, they cracked the eggs, ground up the chick embryos in blenders, and filtered the material that included the rabies virus. From the filtered substance they made a crude experimental vaccine, which contained decimated beaks, feathers, and other anatomical parts.

Kaplan and Koprowski were not allergic to eggs, but, as part of the course, they injected a small amount of egg into their skin as a test for allergy. Then, with their scientist-students looking on, the two doctors injected the first doses of the impure vaccine into their own skin. Neither Koprowski nor Kaplan had ever been immunized against rabies; therefore both were susceptible to the virus. They had refused to take the Pasteur rabies vaccine in the past because of the risk of adverse neurological reactions. Since their modified Flury virus did not kill animals even when injected directly into their brains, Koprowski and Kaplan felt it would be safe for humans. The beaks and other impurities created a risk, but the doctors believed it was less of a danger than if they had used the Pasteur rabies vaccine. Furthermore, both Kaplan and Koprowski believed strongly that self-experimentation was essential. "If those of us who developed the vaccine were going to recommend that other humans take it," Koprowski said, "it was incumbent on us to show our own confidence in it by injecting it into ourselves first. It was only fair that we do it on ourselves—to say that we had put ourselves on the line first and that we were not afraid."

To document whether their own experimental vaccine offered any protection against rabies, the two doctors had taken samples of their own blood before giving themselves the injections. Thereafter, they took additional blood samples at specified intervals to test the amount of antibody they produced. Indeed, their crude vaccine did provide immunity.

Except for a large area of swelling and redness around the injection site on their forearms, the doctors experienced no adverse reactions. The injection, however, left a scar. In Kaplan's case it was about an inch long and had a black spot in the middle of it. For many years thereafter, Kaplan jokingly said he "saw the feathers of the chick embryo coming out of this scar."

Then Koprowski and Kaplan asked their students to follow them in volunteering to take the vaccine, called the living attenuated Flury virus vaccine. Most did so; in a continent where they risked repeated exposure to rabies, it seemed a sensible precaution.

Koprowski's vaccine was an improvement on Pasteur's because it produced fewer adverse reactions. However, although both the LEP and HEP vaccines were licensed in a few countries for animal use and the LEP had been tested on some humans, they were considered too risky for standard use. Moreover, Koprowski still dreamed of a vaccine that would provide immunization against rabies with just a single inoculation.

In 1957 he moved from Lederle to become director of the Wistar Institute in Philadelphia, one of the oldest and most important private research centers in the world. A few years later he formed a team of scientists to develop a new rabies vaccine that he hoped would replace one prepared in duck embryos that was being marketed in the United States. Besides himself, the team included Dr. Tadeusz Wiktor and Dr. Stanley Plotkin from the Wistar Institute, and Koprowski's colleague in Africa, Martin Kaplan, who often visited the Wistar Institute from Geneva.

The Wistar researchers had developed a new technique of growing human embryo cells in the laboratory; fetal cells were used because they thrive in a test tube environment, unlike adult cells, which do not. Koprowski's team adapted the technique, and in 1964 they found they could get a strain of rabies virus to grow in the cells; they called it the WI-38 strain. (The WI stood for Wistar; the number thirty-eight was used because it took that many attempts to grow the virus in the laboratory.) The Wistar scientists added chemicals to kill the rabies virus and prepared an experimental vaccine. Because it contained much less potentially dangerous foreign protein, much more rabies virus could be given with each dose. The researchers discovered that a single injection of the Wistar rabies vaccine protected some monkeys after they had been exposed to natural rabies virus.

By December 1971 the new rabies vaccine was ready for the first tests in humans. Koprowski was joined in the experiment by Kaplan, Wiktor, and Plotkin, all of whom had protection from previous inoculations with another rabies vaccine. Still, there was a risk. The amount of antibody might not be enough to protect them from rabies in case something was wrong with the new experimental vaccine and the rabies virus was still capable of transmitting rabies instead of protecting against it. Also, even if they had enough protective antibodies, they could develop adverse or allergic reactions to the new vaccine.

But none of the four men experienced any negative reactions to the new vaccine, and the scientists went on to test four more Wistar staff members who worked with rabies and who had received immunization against the disease with other vaccines.[32] They waited several weeks to make certain there were no unexpected complications. There were none. Now the researchers felt justified in injecting the experimental rabies vaccine into a second group of eight volunteers —staff members of the Institute selected because they were so-called "immunological virgins," that is, none had antibodies to rabies.

The scientists were elated by the results of their experiments. The tests showed that in most volunteers a single dose of the new vaccine provided greater protection than did the long series of shots required with other rabies vaccines. Now eighty-nine veterinary students at the nearby University of Pennsylvania volunteered to take the Wistar rabies vaccine.[33] Virtually all recipients of the vaccine developed antibodies to rabies that persisted for at least two years. And, except for headaches, there were none of the neurological symptoms, or paralysis, that complicated immunization with the Pasteur vaccine.

One question remained. Was the new Wistar vaccine truly effective for use in someone who had been bitten by a rabid animal? The surest way to answer this would be to inject actual rabies virus into those who had received the rabies vaccine, challenging the immunized individual with the real disease. Koprowski had taken a similar step when he was developing the Colorado tick fever vaccine.

But rabies and Colorado tick fever are strikingly different diseases, and self-experimenting with each involves drastically different risks. Colorado tick fever is rarely fatal; rabies usually is. Koprowski and the Wistar researchers had been willing to receive the experimental vaccine, but there they drew the line. Rabies was just too deadly. What if the vaccine failed? Experiments to measure the Wistar vaccine's ability to protect against rabies would have to be done under natural conditions.

The vaccine was first tested in West Germany, where forty-two people who had been bitten by rabid dogs received six injections of the Wistar vaccine. All survived. The vaccine was also tested on forty-five people in Iran who had received vicious bites, mostly from wolves. None developed the disease.[34]

In 1977 France became the first country to license the Wistar rabies vaccine, and soon thereafter it was also licensed in England, West Germany, and Switzerland. Paradoxically, it was not until 1982 that it was licensed in the United States, where it had been developed.[35]

The advantages of the new rabies vaccine have made it more practical to give it in countries where rabies is a major public health problem but where immunization was given sparingly before because the risks and costs were so great. Eventually the Wistar rabies vaccine may become one of the standard immunizations that pediatricians give in the developing countries of Africa, Asia, and South America, where children are constantly in danger of contracting the dread disease.

The Wistar team faced the risk of getting rabies at each step of their research. Yet these scientists did not hesitate to go first. In so doing they continued the tradition of self-experimentation in the development of vaccines and became members of the Pasteurian Club. The development of another vaccine to fight another deadly disease produced still another Pasteurian Club member. The disease was cholera and the scientist was Dr. Waldemar Mordecai Haffkine, a colleague of Pasteur.

The modern cholera vaccine traces its history to the crude, live version that Dr. Jaime Ferrán y Clua prepared and tested in 1884 during an epidemic in Tortosa, Spain.[36] Cholera, which is caused by the cholera vibrio bacterium, produces a severe diarrhea and is spread by poor sanitation. For reasons doctors do not understand, it appears and disappears in epidemic cycles. Ferrán had observed that guinea pigs surviving injections of living cholera organisms became resistant to developing disease from further injections of cholera material. Borrowing Pasteur's techniques, Ferrán developed a vaccine that immunized the animals. Next he tested the vaccine on himself and on a co-worker. But, faced with the urgency of the epidemic, Ferrán apparently did not feel that he had the time to make further experiments. That year fifty thousand people received three injections of his cholera vaccine—a total of one hundred fifty thousand doses. The result was disastrous. Ferrán's methods were primitive, the dosage wrong, and his cultures impure. He had not inactivated the vaccine completely, and virulent organisms had survived, leading to a number of deaths among the recipients of the "vaccine."[37]

Ferrán's failure was an object lesson in human experimentation: There are risks in drawing conclusions from a limited number of experiments on animals and only a few tests on humans. When those tests are further limited to those done by researchers on themselves, there is even greater need to be scientifically critical of the results: Investigators who are too eager to expand the scope of their research can be lulled by the false security that comes from favorable results on too small a sample. Nevertheless, it is understandable that scientists, when confronted by epidemics and public health threats, sometimes feel the need to take shortcuts.

The 1884 cholera outbreak faced by Ferrán was just that kind of major public health problem, and in the early 1890s cholera flared up again. Ferrán's failure notwithstanding, the urgency of the epidemic encouraged other scientists to develop a successful cholera vaccine. One such scientist was Waldemar Mordecai Haffkine, a Russian émigré who joined Pasteur's team in Paris.

Haffkine found that he could decrease the virulence of the cholera vibrio bacterium by inoculating the organism into the abdominal cavity of a guinea pig, letting it grow, and then taking it from the dead animal and culturing it in the laboratory. After about twenty such passes, the cholera bacteria reached the "fixed" stage, as had happened to Pasteur's rabies virus. Haffkine's experimental vaccine protected guinea pigs. But Haffkine, like Pasteur, recognized that successful experiments on animals did not necessarily mean that his vaccine would be safe for humans. Without hesitation Haffkine first tested the vaccine on himself, becoming a member of the Pasteurian Club.

On July 18, 1892, one of Haffkine's Russian friends injected him in the flank with a weak dose of the vaccine.[38] He experienced a very mild fever of 99.5 degrees Fahrenheit, headache, dryness of the mouth, and tenderness at the site of injection. Six days later, Haffkine tested a stronger vaccine with an injection into his opposite flank. For a day or two his fever hovered at 100.5 degrees Fahrenheit, and he again experienced local tenderness, but that was all. Pasteur offered his congratulations.

After Haffkine repeated the experiments on three Russian friends, none of whom suffered any adverse reactions, he believed his vaccine was safe. We know now that his group represented a regrettably small sample, but vaccine development was in too early a stage for Haffkine to understand that. Now it was time to test the efficacy of the initial tests under epidemic conditions.

Haffkine did not have long to wait. In 1893 he decided to go to Siam to test his vaccine under epidemic conditions, but when Lord Dufferin, ambassador to France and formerly viceroy of India, learned of Haffkine's project, he persuaded him to try it in India, where cholera was raging. Compared with the cholera vaccine used today, Haffkine's was weak and not totally effective. Nevertheless, it was a significant advance for the time and possibly saved millions of lives.

Moreover, his constant effort to improve the method of field studies of vaccines set a standard: Haffkine was the first to develop the method of randomly allocating the test vaccine or a placebo in strictly controlled trials to determine its efficacy. However, the significance of his contribution was not recognized at that time. Haffkine also set a pattern for cholera immunization: The first injection was a weak dose, followed by a stronger one five or more days later.[39]

The vaccine Haffkine developed continues, with modifications, to be used today, but even with improvements it is one of the least effective common vaccines now available.

Haffkine remained in India, turning his attention to plague. Known as the Black Death, plague had already killed millions of people in Europe and had become epidemic in Bombay. In 1896 the Indian government asked Haffkine to find a way to control the infection.[40] Haffkine improvised a laboratory in Bombay where, within a few months, he had developed an experimental antiplague vaccine which was effective in animals. On January 10, 1897, another doctor secretly inoculated Haffkine with the first dose of the vaccine; it was four times stronger than what was later used on the Indian population. Within a few hours Haffkine experienced high fever and pain at the spot where he had been injected. But he kept on working. The next morning, his fever was reduced and he suffered no further reactions. That day, in a lecture at Grant Medical College, Haffkine disclosed the details of the experiment and his reaction to the injection. He concluded that his vaccine was as harmless to humans as it was to animals.[41] When he appealed for volunteers for further tests, hundreds responded.

Soon after, the Aga Khan, who was to become the leader among Muslims in India and elsewhere, was inoculated, not only to protect himself but also to set an example for his followers.[42] Proponents of the vaccine claimed it prevented up to ninety percent of deaths from plague; certainly it saved lives, but how many is not clear.[43]

Haffkine's technique seems crude by today's standards. Modern experts look back with astonishment at the imprecise criteria he used to set the first doses of the vaccine.[44] Still, Haffkine's successes against cholera and plague opened the door to the universal acceptance of the use of vaccines against bacterial diseases. By 1915 the number of people who had been inoculated with Haffkine's vaccines was second only to those who had received smallpox vaccinations, and by the time of Haffkine's death in 1930 at age seventy, he had stimulated the public to support attempts to develop vaccines against other diseases, among them typhoid fever.

The leader in developing the modern typhoid vaccine was Dr. Almroth E. Wright, who was working at the Army Medical School in Netley, England, in 1893. Pasteur was still alive then, and although he had not visited Wright, through his scientific papers the French master's imprint was in Wright's laboratory when the British researcher began his work on vaccines. It was Pasteur who had challenged Haffkine to develop cholera and plague vaccines. Now it was Haffkine who challenged Wright to make a vaccine against typhoid fever. While on his way to India in 1893, Haffkine visited Netley, where he talked with Wright about making a typhoid vaccine from dead bacteria.

Here were two scientists from diverse cultures and backgrounds. Haffkine was a persecuted Russian who had emigrated to France, where he had become a scientific troubleshooter, applying his talents wherever they were needed. Wright was the privileged son of an Irish Presbyterian minister. Educated at Trinity College in Dublin, Wright had studied literature, languages, and law before turning to bacteriology and medical research. He was a man well known to his generation. In fact, George Bernard Shaw, who admired Wright's scientific abilities, caricatured him as Sir Colenso Ridgeon in *The Doctor's Dilemma.* In the play, Sir Colenso must choose between saving the life of an honest but ineffective doctor and a scoundrel artist. It is hard to imagine members of the Pasteurian Club more different than Wright and Haffkine. Yet for all their differences the two scientists both chose to do their research by experimenting on themselves.

Until Haffkine's visit, Wright's research had focused on bleeding, diabetes, and other problems related to chemistry and physiology. But when Haffkine began suggesting a radically different technique for the development of a typhoid vaccine, one that would use killed bacteria, Wright was fascinated.[45] He believed that a vaccine made from dead bacteria would be cheaper to manufacture and safer to use: Unlike a living typhoid vaccine, it could not lead to a severe, and possibly fatal, attack of the disease. But although vaccines made from dead bacteria protected animals, no one had shown that such nonliving vaccines would effectively immunize humans.

Wright's idea was to trick the body into producing the same protective antibodies that it would have made if the typhoid bacteria were living enemies. Documentation of that effect required measuring antibody production in humans. Wright turned to himself to help provide the evidence. As the development of his killed typhoid vaccine went through different stages, he pricked his finger thousands of times and added drops of his own blood to test tubes which contained samples of his vaccine to try to determine if under laboratory conditions there was enough protective antibody.

The effort was long and tedious, but by 1897 he had his vaccine. He tested it first on horses and other animals and then injected it into himself and ten fellow laboratory workers.[46] Three of his volunteers "looked somewhat shaken in health for some three weeks after," Wright reported, but none was made seriously ill.[47]

The typhoid vaccine was tested on larger groups in several areas of the world over the next five years, with mostly favorable results. Wright prepared large amounts of vaccine for use by the British army in the South African Boer War, but many refused to take it. Some who opposed the principle of immunization dumped boxes of vaccine overboard from ships in Southampton. Others did not want to experience the transient headaches, fevers, and sore arms that went with the injections. By war's end, only 14,628, or four percent, of the 328,244 army personnel had volunteered to take it. An effective vaccine would have been valuable because typhoid infected about one in six members of the military. As it was, there were fifty-eight thousand typhoid cases in the British military during that war, including nine thousand deaths.

The data from immunization of the fourteen thousand-plus soldiers suggested that Wright's vaccine was protective, but the information was collected under conditions of war in less than scientifically satisfactory ways. The value of Wright's vaccine and how many cases of typhoid fever it actually prevented became the target of statistical debates and medical and military politics. Despite the controversy, Wright had established the feasibility of killed vaccines. The more potent modern typhoid vaccines are patterned after Wright's.

Subsequent to his self-experiments with the typhoid vaccine, Wright experimented on himself to test a vaccine he had developed against brucellosis, a bacterial disease that is characterized by spiking fevers—those that shoot up for a few hours and then return to normal or near normal. Although seldom fatal, brucellosis can make a victim extremely ill for weeks. At the turn of the century, brucellosis was known as Malta fever, because doctors mistakenly believed it was mainly confined to that island. In 1897 Dr. David Bruce, one of Wright's army medical colleagues at Netley, discovered the bacterium that causes Malta fever. Soon thereafter, doctors learned that cases diagnosed under different names in many other places were in fact brucellosis and that "Malta fever" was a public health problem throughout the world. Wright had taken an early interest in brucellosis and had already developed a diagnostic test for the disease—one of the earliest diagnostic blood tests in medicine—that helped to distinguish it from typhoid fever.[48]

Then Wright developed a killed brucellosis vaccine. After tests on monkeys showed that it worked, he inoculated himself with a moderate dose. A week later, he gave himself a larger dose, and two weeks later a third, even stronger, one.

His self-experiments showed that the killed brucellosis vaccine was safe for humans. But he had yet to solve a second problem: Would it protect them against the disease? To find out, Wright did the riskiest of experiments on himself—the same one that Pasteur had proposed with his rabies vaccine but had not been allowed to carry out and the same one that Jenner had done on the Phipps boy. Wright challenged the vaccine with living brucellosis organisms. Two weeks after receiving the third dose of the brucellosis vaccine, a colleague injected Wright with live brucella bacteria.[49] He came down with a severe and painful case of brucellosis, one that caused him acute muscular pains and incapacitated him for months. As strong as Wright had made the vaccine, it was too weak. Nevertheless, his self-experiment removed any doubt that Bruce's bacterium was the cause of Malta fever.

Wright continued to self-experiment with both successes and near successes, the latter earning him the nickname Sir Almost Wright. He perfected techniques for taking blood samples using a broken-off piece of glass pipette or similar sharp tool to prick the finger and draw just enough drops of blood for diagnostic testing. Wright took blood from his own fingers about twenty thousand times, making them "so scarred as to be nearly insensitive."[50]

The Pasteur tradition has persisted throughout the twentieth century, and disease prevention by inoculation has become the underpinning of modern medicine. It is the main reason our life expectancies have expanded not just by years but by decades. Newer members of the Pasteurian Club continue to search for new vaccines against other major killers, and older members, as long as they are able, remain tireless in their search for ways to stop disease. We have already seen how Dr. Hilary Koprowski used self-experimentation in his efforts to develop a safer, easier-to-use rabies vaccine. He self-experimented again as he tried to fight a newer, and in some ways an even more frightening, disease—poliomyelitis.

In 1934 in Montreal, Dr. Maurice Brodie of McGill University Medical School ground up the spinal cords of polio-infected monkeys and added formalin (formaldehyde) with the hope that the chemical would weaken the polio virus enough to produce an effective killed vaccine. This vaccine became known as the Park-Brodie vaccine when Brodie moved to join Dr. William H. Park, director of the Bureau of Laboratories of the New York City Department of Health. Brodie injected his experimental vaccine into monkeys, the only animal besides man known at the time to be susceptible to poliomyelitis, and found that the vaccine produced immunity in the monkeys but also caused severe skin irritation, even sloughing of areas of skin.[51] Then he reduced the amount of formalin in the vaccine; the skin reactions ceased, and no other adverse reactions occurred.

Brodie told the annual meeting of the American Public Health Association on September 3, 1934, that when it came time to test it on humans: "It was deemed advisable to try it upon ourselves, not that we had misgivings about the possibilities of infection, but rather to determine whether the vaccine produced any disagreeable local or general reactions." Brodie, Park, and four other colleagues from the New York City Health Department were injected with up to three doses of the vaccine. Soreness and swelling developed at the injection site and lasted several days, but there was no evidence of a systemic reaction. Blood tests showed that antibodies had been produced. "It was now evident," Brodie wrote, "that the vaccine could be administered with perfect safety and so it was given to twelve children, aged one to six years." Apparently all the children responded well.

Many were enthusiastic and championed Brodie as a new Pasteur. The vaccine was given to several thousand children before other scientists suspected that it was not as safe and effective as Brodie had reported it to be; just how many cases of poliomyelitis actually occurred among the children is not clear, but there were several.[52]

Brodie was in fierce competition with Dr. John A. Kolmer of Temple University in Philadelphia, who was pursuing another way of developing a vaccine against poliomyelitis. Where Brodie's was a killed vaccine, Kolmer's was a live one. Kolmer used a chemical, sodium ricinoleate, to weaken, rather than kill, the poliomyelitis virus, believing that "the vaccine to be effective must contain some living but devitalized virus."[53] Kolmer tested his vaccine on monkeys without noting any adverse reactions. Then, according to Kolmer, he and his laboratory assistant, Miss Anna M. Rule, "took three doses by subcutaneous [under the skin] injection every five to seven days with no ill effects and with excellent antibody production. I then vaccinated my own two sons and twenty-three additional children with absolutely no ill effects."[54]

Kolmer had moved with what, in retrospect, was clearly undue haste. That haste may have been caused by the great fear polio inspired at that time. Children were forbidden to swim in lakes or pools or go to movies. Everyone knew someone who had died or been severely paralyzed from polio. Scientists wanted to convert new knowledge into something useful as quickly as possible.

Challenged by Brodie's reported success, Kolmer's live, "attenuated" vaccine was injected into more than ten thousand children throughout the country.[55] It is an open question whether the injections did them any good; clearly they did some harm. Dr. James P. Leake, a U.S. Public Health Service epidemiologist, determined that at least twelve children who had taken Kolmer's vaccine became paralyzed and five died.[56] Beyond the dangers of the vaccine, its efficacy had not been tested because it was given in areas where no other cases of poliomyelitis had occurred during the same year. When the facts were disclosed at a scientific meeting later in 1935, Kolmer reportedly replied to his critics that he wished the floor would open up and swallow him.[57]

Brodie and Kolmer pioneered in an era when the odds were overwhelmingly against the successful production of a polio vaccine. Their techniques proved too crude to grow the virus or to measure the amounts of chemicals needed to tame it to the point where the resulting vaccine would be both safe and effective. Scientists later learned why Brodie had failed: He had not used the right amount of formalin. Too much formalin destroys the virus to the point where there is not enough virulence left to stimulate immunity; too little formalin makes the vaccine unsafe because too many virulent polio viruses remain in the product.

Brodie and Kolmer, like Dr. Ferrán before them, had also shown that self-experimentation was not a foolproof research step, particularly in dealing with a vaccine or a drug. Brodie, Park, and Kolmer took their own vaccines, suffered no adverse effects, and assumed the same would be true for other subjects. But they were wrong. They had simply been lucky in escaping the paralysis that struck down others who took the same vaccine.

The pilot studies that the Park and Kolmer groups performed were simply too small to test the relative benefits and risks of the polio vaccine. When the time came to evaluate the efficacy and safety of the currently used Sabin and Salk vaccines, the trials were much more rigorous. Nevertheless, after the Salk polio vaccine was licensed and marketed, some recipients of the early batches also developed polio.[58] This time extensive epidemiologic investigations were conducted, which showed that a technical failure to inactivate some of the polio virus used in the vaccine was at fault.

Following in the footsteps of Brodie and Kolmer, other scientists experimented on themselves in the search for a safe polio vaccine. One of these scientists was, again, Dr. Hilary Koprowski. In 1951, while Dr. Koprowski was still working at Lederle Laboratories in Pearl River, New York, he tried to develop a polio vaccine made from live but weakened virus, using a different technique from Kolmer's. Koprowski competed with two other scientists who became famous for their work in developing polio vaccines, Dr. Albert Sabin and Dr. Jonas Salk. Koprowski was the first to swallow such a live polio vaccine; he said it tasted like cod liver oil.[59]

Sabin also took his own vaccine—though only to test its safety. He had antibodies to polio from a childhood infection and therefore could not determine anything about its efficacy on himself.[60] Salk, who injected his own children with his vaccine, has told conflicting stories about trying it on himself. At first he said that he had not taken his own vaccine, but later he reversed himself and claimed that he had.[61]

Today the polio vaccine is usually administered orally in the United States. It is a safe, effective vaccine that has thwarted the paralyzing disease and ended the polio scare in most developed countries. Though the number of cases each year approaches zero in the United States, thousands of cases still occur elsewhere in the world due to inadequate immunization programs. The new push to immunize all children in the world promises to make polio a rare disease, and perhaps someday the vaccine will eradicate polio just as the derivative of Jenner's vaccine eradicated smallpox.

# Chapter Six

# THE MYTH OF WALTER REED

The name of Dr. Walter Reed is synonymous with self-experimentation. He was at the head of an American military medical team that went to Cuba in 1900 and proved through daring human experiments that mosquitoes transmitted yellow fever and that something submicroscopic in the blood caused the disease. The agent is now known to be a virus, and for centuries this particular microbe had caused a great scourge in the western hemisphere. Yellow fever savaged armies, decimated populations, wrecked national economies, and changed the course of history.

North America, for example, might have become a largely French continent had it not been for the decimation of Napoleon's troops in Santo Domingo by yellow fever. Napoleon's losses became a crucial factor in his decision to sell the Louisiana Territory in 1803. Later, in the 1880s, yellow fever again killed tens of thousands of Frenchmen and prevented the first attempt to build a Panama Canal, by Ferdinand DeLesseps. The Reed team's experiments led to health control measures that in effect supplied the silent dynamite that allowed the Panama Canal to be built. Those measures also brought down the yellow flag—known as the yellow jack—which for more than a century had been hoisted wherever quarantines were imposed during yellow fever epidemics.[1] Areas such as Panama and Cuba where the disease occurred continually became safely habitable for the first time.

Because yellow fever was endemic in Cuba, it was a source of danger to all countries having commercial relations with that island country. In 1898, with the outbreak of the Spanish-American War, the disease became a primary concern of the U.S. Army. Yellow fever even struck officers who lived in the best quarters under the most advanced hygienic conditions of the time. It often claimed more lives than the enemy did. Whenever it broke out, it caused panic since it was untreatable and had a high death rate. There still is no effective treatment once the illness sets in, although there is now a vaccine to prevent it.

When the Reed team began its work in Cuba following the war, it noted that outbreaks of yellow fever had occurred in the United States at least ninety-five times over the preceding 208 years. The infection was frequently called the American plague, usually killing one in five victims.[2] Yellow fever broke out almost every year in at least one southern seaport and often occurred in the interior of the country as well; epidemics extended up the Mississippi River and along the East Coast as far north as Portsmouth, New Hampshire. New Orleans was the hardest hit, with 41,348 deaths from 1793 to 1900, followed by Philadelphia, with 10,038.[3] Yellow fever's "ravages," Reed wrote, "were such as to completely paralyze both the social and commercial interests in a given city, and even of an entire section of our country."[4]

The human volunteers in the Reed yellow fever experiments included three members of his medical team and more than a score of soldiers. In scientific articles, as well as plays, movies, novels, and paintings, they were lauded for their heroism, courage, and selflessness. The popular stories and dramatizations made Reed, as captain of the team, the symbol of the most famous set of experiments, not to mention self-experiments, in medical history. The widespread publicity of the yellow fever experiments helped create the heroic popular image of the medical researcher as a valiant investigator who, in hopes of improving human welfare, willingly risks contracting a fatal disease.[5] Ironically, it was a group of modern medical researchers who became a prime source of perpetuating Walter Reed's reputation as a heroic self-experimenter by forming the Walter Reed Society. Sponsored by the National Society for Medical Research, the group was formed to recognize the contributions of self-experimentation to medical science.[6]

So legend was built. The Walter Reed Army Medical Center in Washington, D.C., perpetuates Reed's memory. His name appears in history books, his story is taught to schoolchildren. Yet few ever hear the names of the three other team members, Drs. Aristides Agramonte, James Carroll, and Jesse W. Lazear. Lazear died from a yellow fever self-experiment, and Carroll may have developed long-term fatal complications from one. Agramonte, too, experimented on himself. But because he was possibly immune to yellow fever, it is not known whether he was exposed to the same degree of risk as were his colleagues. Legend notwithstanding, the person most people remember—Walter Reed—never experimented on himself, the only member of the team not to do so. His death in 1902 was due to a ruptured appendix, not to yellow fever as many people believe.[7]

For reasons that even today are not clear, the medical establishment did all it could to perpetuate the myth that Reed was directly involved in the on-the-scene experiments in Cuba. For example, Reed was the focus of a popular painting, "Conquerors of Yellow Fever," by Dean Cornwall that Wyeth Laboratories commissioned and made famous through frequent advertisements. Reed, in the center, watches as Lazear applies a mosquito to Carroll's forearm. The fact that Reed was a thousand miles away at the time of this self-experiment was omitted from most of the notes Wyeth distributed about the painting.

The image was also inaccurate in other respects. Much of what Reed's team—known variously as the Yellow Fever Commission, the Yellow Fever Board, or the Reed Board—did was to confirm findings made almost a century before by another brave self-experimenter, Stubbins Ffirth, of Salem, New Jersey. Had more people known about and believed the results of Ffirth's earlier experiments, control of yellow fever might have come much sooner.

Until the Reed team's experiments in 1900, no one knew what caused yellow fever. In the preceding century, observers had noted that nurses and others who attended yellow fever patients rarely came down with it. Nevertheless, it was considered communicable by clothing, bedding, and other inanimate objects, which are known as fomites, and by person-to-person contact (contagion). Furthermore, several doctors had actually shown by self-experiments that yellow fever was *not* contagious. Despite this evidence, many continued to shun the clothing and bed linen of infected patients, and Reed himself in his Army entrance examination, expressed belief that fomites were a main means of spreading the disease.[8]

Yellow fever damages the liver and derives its name from the resulting jaundice—a buildup of bile pigments in the blood which gives the skin a yellow hue. Because damage to the liver can interfere with the production of the substances that make blood clot, victims of yellow fever often bleed into their stomach and then vomit a dark material. Thus, the disease was also known as black vomit, particularly among Spanish-speaking people. Many investigators tried to determine what role, if any, the vomitus played in transmitting the disease, and one, an American physician, Dr. Isaac Cathrall, self-experimented with black vomit. In 1800, in what he considered "an hazardous undertaking," he repeatedly put black vomit from several patients to his lips and tasted it. The immediate sensation must have been unpleasant, to say the least, but he did not develop yellow fever.[9]

In 1804 Stubbins Ffirth provided even more convincing evidence against fomites and contagion in the thesis he wrote for his M.D. degree at the University of Pennsylvania.[10] When Ffirth began his work as a student at the college, he was convinced that yellow fever, which he called "malignant fever," was contagious. But careful observations and daring experiments, possibly aided by a degree of luck, changed his mind.

Ffirth noted that seldom was there even word-of-mouth evidence of contagion among nurses, doctors, hospital attendants, household members, and gravediggers who had been exposed to yellow fever. He felt that if he could prove the disease was not contagious, lives would be saved, since relatives and friends of yellow fever victims would understand the disease better and would not abandon the afflicted, depriving them of the good nursing care that, then as now, is the only hope for recovery. Many who might have survived died because they inhaled vomitus into their lungs, setting off a fatal aspiration pneumonia that nursing might have prevented. "Another important advantage," Ffirth pointed out, "will be a revision and alteration of the quarantine laws, which now unnecessarily impede commerce, destroy exertion, injure agriculture, and put the manufacturer to many inconveniences."[11]

Ffirth began his series of experiments in 1802. They were as vile-sounding as any in the history of medicine; they made Cathrall's tasting of black vomit—which Ffirth had cited—seem almost enjoyable. The experiments were done, Ffirth said, "to discover the nature, properties, and qualities of the black vomit; to determine whether it could communicate the disease or not . . ."[12]

But this Philadelphia medical student left no clues as to why he chose to go first. "It is unnecessary to trouble the public with my motives," he wrote, "and as my reasons would not affect the usefulness or duration of this work, I shall decline giving any."[13]

Ffirth purposely exposed himself to yellow fever patients. He said he had "several times slept all night on a bed where a patient lay extremely ill with the disease, attended with black vomit, yet never experienced any ill effects, and I made it a constant practice to receive the breath of my patients in my face . . ."[14]

He then fed black vomit to a cat and a dog for one week. Both animals survived. He cut open the skin of a dog, inserted black vomit, and closed the wound as a pocket to prevent escape of the material. Again, the animals did not become ill. In another experiment Ffirth injected an ounce of black vomit into the jugular vein in the neck of a dog. Ten minutes later, the dog convulsed and died. But when Ffirth saw that death also occurred after he injected water into another dog's neck vein, he attached no specific significance to the dog's death.

Then, on October 4, 1802, Ffirth cut his left forearm and inserted into it some fresh black vomit. He suffered only mild inflammation, which subsided in three days. He repeated the experiment on his right arm, keeping an adhesive plaster around the wound to make certain nothing escaped. He did the experiment again. And again and again. Despite twenty more such attempts during the epidemics of 1802 and 1803, Ffirth remained healthy.

Illness failed to result after he dropped black vomit into his right eye, nor did it occur after he held his head over an iron skillet and inhaled the gas and steam that escaped from heated black vomit. He repeated this experiment, this time staying in the room for two hours. He said he "had great pain in my head, some nausea, and perspired very freely. Towards the close of the experiment, I felt languid and fainty, attended with great oppression at my breast. All these symptoms went off after being some time in the fresh air . . ."[15]

Several times he swallowed black vomit taken directly from a patient, as well as pills he made from black vomit. Still he did not contract yellow fever. "Having proved I hope to the satisfaction of the most skeptical, that the disease cannot be communicated by the black vomit," Ffirth said, he went on to an even more dangerous self-experiment. He injected blood from yellow fever patients repeatedly into himself, and he swallowed both the saliva and blood of victims.[16] Here Ffirth was lucky. He escaped yellow fever, possibly because he had become immune from an undetected case, but more probably because the blood sample he used contained no virus.

"I hope these experiments will have a tendency to allay, if not totally to destroy, that great fear which some have of the disease," Ffirth wrote, "for by these they may be induced to reason for themselves, when they will naturally conclude, that as the disease cannot be communicated by the secretions or excretions, it is at least very doubtful whether it is ever communicated from one person to another, and certainly never by means of contagion; I even doubt its often being communicated by infection, nay believe it very rarely is, which I think has been proved by the arguments already advanced."[17] Ffirth suggested another telling reason why malignant fever could not be contagious or communicable by fomites: Cold weather stopped its progress but had no effect on either smallpox or measles.

Although Ffirth's thesis was known to Benjamin Rush of Philadelphia and other leading physicians of the day, it did not have a major impact. It was one thing to show how yellow fever did *not* spread, but another to show how it *did*—or how people could protect themselves from the disease. Ffirth had associated yellow fever with the weather and environment, but he had not taken it the crucial next step: What exactly caused the disease to be transmitted during the summer and in temperate latitudes?

Others soon took that step. In 1807 Dr. John Crawford of Baltimore, citing the uselessness of quarantine measures, maintained that mosquitoes were responsible for malaria, yellow fever, and other diseases.[18] The theory was renewed in 1848 by Dr. Josiah C. Nott, a gynecologist from Mobile, Alabama.[19] Five years later, Dr. Louis D. Beauperthuy, a French physician working in Venezuela, blamed the domestic mosquito for spreading yellow fever and malaria.[20] Beauperthuy believed the mosquitoes infected themselves by contact with some unknown object or by feeding on the organic material found in the stagnant waters where the insects are hatched and thereafter infected humans through bites, like poison injected by snakes. Beauperthuy's observations were not believed, partly because a commission appointed to evaluate his studies "all but declared him insane" and partly because his ideas were so far ahead of their time.[21] The yellow fever–mosquito link remained entirely theoretical, one of many theories bandied about.

The most conclusive evidence that an insect could transmit a disease to an entirely different species came in 1892 when Dr. Theobald Smith, a microbiologist who worked for the United States Department of Agriculture, and his veterinary associate Frederick L. Kilborne discovered that ticks spread an often fatal parasitic disease of cattle called Texas fever.[22]

Earlier, in 1878, Dr. Patrick Manson, the pioneering Scottish parasitologist, had produced less solid but still convincing evidence of insect transmission when he found that mosquito bites played a key intermediate role in a disease called filariasis by carrying the microscopic worm *Wuchereria bancrofti.*[23] The disease, passed along when the worm-carrying mosquito bites an individual, is also known as elephantiasis because the parasites block the lymph channels, leading to an accumulation of fluid and a grotesque swelling in the arms and legs. In 1894 Manson discovered a second insect-borne parasitic disease, this one spread by the tsetse fly. It was called n'gana, a parasitic disease of animals that is the counterpart of human sleeping sickness, or trypanosomiasis. Then in 1896 Manson guided Dr. Ronald Ross, who worked in India, to the discovery that mosquitoes transmitted the parasites that cause malaria.

A few years after Patrick Manson discovered the role of mosquitoes in causing filariasis, Dr. Carlos Finlay, an American-educated physician who practiced in Havana, began trying to convince his colleagues that the common house mosquito transmitted yellow fever.[24] Finlay was influenced by his own observations over many years and possibly by Manson's discovery. He waged his campaign by doing what Crawford, Nott, and Beauperthuy had not done—putting his hypothesis about mosquitoes to experimental tests. In so doing Finlay tried to infect humans with bites from the household mosquito (then called *Stegomyia fasciata* and now *Aedes aegypti*). In Finlay's experiments, a few volunteers developed fevers and then seemed immune to subsequent challenges from mosquito bites. But there was not one incidence of what other experts would accept as a case of yellow fever. Only later would doctors learn that Finlay's mosquitoes were not capable of producing infection; he had not kept them long enough before allowing them to bite the volunteers.

Yellow fever was rife all around him, and mosquitoes were abundant. Over the next nineteen years Finlay tried again and again. But in 104 experiments he failed to transmit yellow fever to humans. Apparently Finlay did not include himself in these experiments. He persisted in his belief, though, and continued to cultivate mosquitoes. In time he would give the Reed team mosquito larvae from his collection.

Many asked the key question: If mosquitoes caused yellow fever, why had Finlay's human volunteers escaped? The most logical conclusion was that mosquitoes did not transmit yellow fever and that Finlay had disproved his own theory.[25] So scientists sought other explanations for the cause of yellow fever.

One came from an Italian bacteriologist who had gained a favorable reputation from his work at the Pasteur Institute in Paris. He was Dr. Giuseppe Sanarelli, and in 1897, while working in Brazil and Uruguay, he reported that bacillus icteroides, an organism he called "the strangest of all microbes that are known," caused yellow fever.[26] Sanarelli injected what he believed was the yellow fever microbe in five humans and reported that he had "reproduced in man typical yellow fever."

Sanarelli convinced many people, largely because bacteriology was an exploding field and supporters were prepared to believe the discovery of almost any new bacterium. Walter Reed and James Carroll said in 1899, "We hailed with delight Sanarelli's announcement . . . and earnestly hoped that his work would be confirmed by other observers."[27] And "confirmation" did come, from among others, a two-physician commission sent by the U.S. Government to Cuba in 1898.[28]

Sanarelli's claims were greeted with an array of awards on the one hand and a storm of protest on the other. Many considered the experiments unethical because he had injected cultures of his organism into five patients without their permission. Three died. There was no evidence that he had done the same experiment on himself. In a discussion following Army Surgeon General George M. Sternberg's presentation of his scientific report criticizing Sanarelli's work, Dr. Victor C. Vaughan, a prominent bacteriologist at the University of Michigan School of Public Health (see Chapter Eight: Toxic Shocks) and one of the scientists with whom Reed worked on a famous typhoid fever commission, said Sanarelli's experiments were "simply ridiculous."[29] Dr. (later Sir) William Osler, the most renowned physician of his time, charged that they were worse than that: "To deliberately inject a poison of known high degree of virulency into a human being, unless you obtain that man's sanction, is not ridiculous, it is criminal."[30]

One reason Sanarelli's claims attracted wide attention was that they came in the midst of the Spanish-American War. Yellow fever had killed or incapacitated so many American troops in Cuba that when the war was over, Surgeon General Sternberg organized a team of four doctors, including Reed, and sent them to the island in 1900 with a broad charge: to pursue scientific investigations into "the infectious diseases prevailing on the island of Cuba" that affected humans and animals. Despite yellow fever's importance, however, Sternberg did not specify it as the primary focus of the investigations.

At the time, Sternberg was one of the two leading bacteriologists in the United States. Moreover, Sternberg, who had developed immunity to yellow fever after an attack many years before, was an authority on the infection and had worked directly with Finlay on the first yellow fever commission in Cuba in 1878.[31]

The 1900 Yellow Fever Commission organized by Sternberg consisted of four doctors: Aristides Agramonte, James Carroll, Jesse Lazear, and Walter Reed. Agramonte and Lazear had been classmates at Sternberg's alma mater, the Columbia University College of Physicians and Surgeons in New York. And three of the men (Reed, Lazear, and Carroll) had worked with Sternberg either in Baltimore or in Washington.

The four men could not have come from more diverse backgrounds. Reed was born in 1851 in Belroi, Virginia, where his father was a circuit-riding Methodist minister.[32] At the age of seventeen Reed completed a one-year medical school course at the University of Virginia. Because the University was not affiliated with a hospital and had few facilities for clinical teaching in Charlottesville, medical graduates usually moved on to Philadelphia or New York for further training. Reed went to New York, where he thought he would spend the rest of his life. A year later, in 1870, the tall, slender physician obtained a second M.D. degree, this one from Bellevue Medical College (now New York University). Reed spent five years working in hospitals and as an official of the Boards of Health of New York and Brooklyn. Then, in 1874, Reed joined the army, telling his fiancée, Emilie Lawrence, that he would spend only three or four years in the service.[33] Eighteen years later he had gone through fifteen changes of station in various posts, mostly in the West, where his duties were clinical and military rather than scientific. During this period Pasteur, Koch, and other European scientists were making important discoveries in bacteriology, immunology, and preventive medicine.

In 1890 Reed went to Johns Hopkins for what was essentially a sabbatical, and there he made rounds with the renowned Osler and received fundamental training in pathology and bacteriology under Dr. William H. Welch.[34] It was this training that would give Reed a reputation as the best sanitary inspector in the army and the court of last resort on all sanitary questions.

In 1893 he was appointed curator of the Army Medical Museum and professor of bacteriology at the Army Medical School, which Sternberg had recently created. This was an assignment that allowed Reed to renew his ties with the Johns Hopkins faculty as well as with Sternberg. Over the next several years Reed traveled to Cuba and did some outstanding work in investigating typhoid fever there and in the United States with two other epidemiologists, Victor C. Vaughan and Edward O. Shakespeare. These three researchers concluded that spread of the causative bacterium from person to person was much more important than through contaminated water. They also recognized that human typhoid carriers, who shed billions of typhoid bacteria, were important sources of the infection.[35]

The only other regular army member of the Yellow Fever Board was James Carroll, who had been born in England. Carroll described himself as "a wandering good-for-nothing who fell in love at fourteen and left home at fifteen, roughed it in the Canadian backwoods for several years and finally drifted into the Army."[36] While serving as a hospital steward at Fort Custer, Montana, he decided to become a doctor, and Reed helped him in his fight to overcome the army bureaucracy to do so. Carroll studied in St. Paul, Minnesota, at Bellevue Medical College in New York, and at the University of Maryland before he took up bacteriology and pathology at Johns Hopkins, where he, like Reed, came under the influence of William Welch. In 1897 Carroll became Reed's laboratory assistant. Carroll, who was appointed second in command of the Yellow Fever Board, was the team's bacteriologist. He was tall, thin, and bald, had a light red mustache and projecting ears, wore glasses, and had a rather dull expression. To Jesse Lazear, he was "a bacteriologist pure and simple" and "not a very entertaining person."[37] Carroll was never promoted for his part in the yellow fever experiments, and as the years rolled on he became increasingly bitter about the credit that went to Reed and that he believed was denied Lazear and himself.

Jesse Lazear was born in 1866 to a wealthy family in Baltimore, where he grew up on the estate of his retired grandfather. After graduating from Johns Hopkins University, he entered the Columbia University College of Physicians and Surgeons but interrupted his courses to go to Europe to study anatomy and to travel. He returned to New York in 1892 to earn his M.D. degree and to intern at Bellevue

Hospital. Following his internship, he spent another year in Europe, this time learning the new techniques of growing pure samples of bacteria in cultures in the laboratory, chemical staining, and animal experimentation. These were "state-of-the-art" disciplines that were giving doctors a better scientific understanding of disease. On his return, Lazear became the first chief of clinical laboratories at the newly opened Johns Hopkins Medical School, where he, too, met and worked with William Welch.[38] He was described by a senior colleague: "Quiet, retiring and modest, almost to a fault, he was yet essentially a manly man with a good, vigorous temper, well controlled, and rare physical courage . . ."[39]

Early in 1900 Welch gave Lazear a strong recommendation when he applied to the army for work in Cuba in a civilian position known as a "contract physician." Before he left the United States, Lazear discussed mosquitoes and possibly their relationship to yellow fever with Leland O. Howard, an entomologist in Washington to whom he would later send specimens of insects from Cuba.

Aristides Agramonte had been born in Cuba and had been brought to New York as an infant after his father was killed fighting in a revolt for his country's independence from Spain in the 1870s. A tall, energetic man, Agramonte earned his M.D. from Columbia and worked as a bacteriologist in the New York City Health Department. In 1898 he wrote the surgeon general seeking a job as a contract surgeon with the army in Cuba. In reply Sternberg asked him whether he had had experience with yellow fever or had recovered from the disease.[40] No record exists of Agramonte's response, but he was assigned to work for two months with Reed in Washington before going on to a yellow fever hospital in Cuba. While there, in 1899, Agramonte solicited a recommendation from Sternberg for the position of professor of bacteriology at the University of Havana. Sternberg wrote favorably, but by the time his letter arrived in Cuba someone else had been chosen. When Agramonte was appointed to the Yellow Fever Commission, he was a pathologist in charge of the laboratories at Military Hospital No. 1 in Havana and chief physician on a ward where yellow fever patients were treated.

Because he had been born in Cuba and had spent the first few months of his life there, he was presumed to be immune to yellow fever and was assigned to do the autopsies on patients who had died of the disease. However, because there is no record that Agramonte had come down with yellow fever as an infant, and because no diagnostic test was available then to determine whether he had had a mild case, as children sometimes get, no one knows what his true immune status was. Possibly he was susceptible to the disease.

Most accounts portray the Reed team as a harmonious group, and that may have been true while they worked in Cuba. But, as often happens when scientists work for long periods in teams that meet with sudden success and fame, some members come to believe their contributions outweigh the credit they receive, and they begin to criticize their colleagues. Feuds develop. Key figures may die soon after the event, leaving others to tell the tale. Crucial evidence disappears, and the deceased individuals cannot defend themselves against new attacks. The longest-living survivors of the Yellow Fever Commission, Carroll and Agramonte, complained bitterly in later years that Reed had been given too much credit, that they had not gotten their fair share, and that if any member deserved to be singled out it was Lazear.

Carroll and Reed arrived in Cuba on June 25, 1900, to join Agramonte and Lazear. The four met for the first time on the veranda of the officers' quarters at the hospital at Columbia Barracks, a military reservation outside Havana, and immediately decided on their first order of business—to give undivided attention to studying Sanarelli's bacterium. Agramonte did not believe the organism caused yellow fever, because he had found it in autopsies of persons who had died of other diseases.[41]

During their first weeks on the island, Reed and Carroll gained considerable experience with a disease that neither of them had ever seen, although Reed had been in Cuba in 1899 to investigate typhoid fever. Reed's first yellow fever patient was Major Jefferson R. Kean, a ranking surgeon with whom Reed would work closely in Cuba. An epidemic of yellow fever was in progress in the nearby town of Quemados. The researchers tested blood cultures from people who survived attacks of the disease, as well as from those who died of it, and made additional bacteriological studies of autopsy specimens. Sanarelli's bacillus icteroides was not to be found consistently in the blood of yellow fever patients. By August the commission had demolished Sanarelli's claim.[42]

Absence of the bacillus in specimens taken from victims of the Quemados epidemic surprised some members of the team. But there was another surprise. The commission members soon recognized that yellow fever was not contagious or communicable by fomites. As Reed told a medical meeting in Baltimore, he was embarrassed "to confess his ignorance" but said that "candor compels me to record my very great surprise, when brought face to face with yellow fever, to learn that attendance on patients by non-immune nurses in every stage of the malady, involved no danger."[43]

Despite the rudimentary medical library system then available, it is astonishing that this finding should have surprised the leader of a major scientific investigation. True, many other yellow fever experts had ignored Ffirth's work showing that yellow fever was not contagious. But Reed was a leading bacteriologist and medical school professor. And as curator of the Army Medical Museum, Reed, more than others, might have been expected to know the history of the disease he was studying. Moreover, Reed and his team worked closely in Havana with Finlay, who, while developing his theory of mosquito transmission, had relied heavily on Ffirth's experiments.[44]

If Sanorelli's bacterium did not cause yellow fever and neither did fomites, the commission was left with two choices: to study the bacteriology of the intestines of yellow fever patients in an attempt to detect the specific agent of yellow fever, or to consider Finlay's mosquito theory. They chose mosquitoes, and a major factor in the decision was a recent publication by Dr. Henry R. Carter, a physician and pioneering epidemiologist who spent two decades as a career officer in the U.S. Public Health Service investigating yellow fever.

In a study of two northern Mississippi towns, Carter observed that a minimum interval of two weeks occurred between the first case of yellow fever and subsequent ones. He concluded that an incubation period was required outside the body for the spread of yellow fever from person to person. Carter repeatedly mentioned contaminated objects and said that though he considered Finlay's theory plausible, he found his observations "not convincing."[45]

The commission members were divided in their feelings. Agramonte said that "neither Drs. Reed, Carroll nor myself [sic] believed in said theory, the only one of us inclined to consider it favorably being my friend and classmate, Dr. Jesse W. Lazear."[46] That may have been because Lazear was the only one among the four who had worked with mosquitoes, though, aside from his brief meetings with Leland O. Howard, the entomologist in Washington, his experience was limited.

No animal was known to be susceptible to yellow fever. Thus, to test the mosquito theory, the members of the commission would have to resolve the tremendous ethical and moral questions that are involved in human experimentation.

Reed might have ordered soldiers to volunteer for the experiments. But he must have been aware of the letter that Surgeon General Sternberg had sent to Agramonte on May 14, 1900, nine days before he created the Yellow Fever Board. If Agramonte carried out such tests on humans, the surgeon general had warned, he must first obtain the volunteer's "full knowledge and consent."[47]

The Reed commission clearly knew about the dangers of such experiments.

None of the researchers was enthusiastic about taking the risk of catching yellow fever. At one point for example, Agramonte, who because of his presumed immunity was considered useless as a human guinea pig for the yellow fever experiments, admitted that he "would not like to have tested" the supposition that he was immune.[48] Because all four members had families, they certainly had pressing reasons to avoid risking their own lives. Carroll had five children; Lazear had one, and his wife was expecting another; Agramonte had one; and Reed had two, one of whom was serving as a soldier in Cuba.

But the personal risks to the four were offset by moral and practical reasons for using themselves as volunteer subjects. As Reed and Carroll pointed out: "In experimentation on human beings, aside from the grave sense of responsibility, at times well-nigh insupportable, which the conscientious observer must always feel, even with the full consent of the subjects to be experimented upon, there must be added another factor, viz., the difficulty of finding willing and suitable non-immune individuals for experimentation just at the proper and urgent moment."[49]

In early August, the commission members visited Finlay in Havana. He was elated to learn that the Americans would test his theory. He instructed them about the peculiarities of the implicated species of mosquito and gave them several mosquito eggs that he kept in a bowl of water on his bookshelf. When the eggs hatched, the Reed team placed the mosquitoes on people ill with yellow fever. Because almost no one—certainly no one on the Reed team—was an expert on mosquitoes at that time, they sent these mosquitoes to Lazear's former colleague, Leland O. Howard, for identification. Howard identified them as *Stegomyia fasciatus,* the type that was later proved to spread yellow fever.

Around this time added pressure was put on the commission from a rival British Yellow Fever Commission composed of two well-trained scientists, Herbert E. Durham and Walter Myers, who were sent out by the University of Liverpool to visit research centers in Canada and the United States and Reed's team in Cuba.[50] Wherever they went, the British researchers were alert for any clues they might pick up about the disease, and in Cuba they met Finlay and discussed the theory that mosquitoes might spread yellow fever.

The ten-day visit in July 1900 of Durham and Myers to Cuba must have spurred Reed to speed up the pace of his team's research, for just a few days after the British researchers left, the Reed team members made their now-famous pledge to experiment on themselves. It is not certain when the idea of self-experimentation was first proposed or who made it. In his later years, Carroll maintained that he had twice proposed the idea before Reed himself raised it for the first time at a meeting, apparently on the night of August 3, "as the best atonement they could offer for subjecting others to the risks entailed thereby."[51] According to Carroll, Reed, Lazear, and Carroll (Agramonte being absent and considered immune) "agreed that the members of the Board would themselves be bitten, and subject themselves to the same risk that necessity compelled them to impose on others."[52] Unknown to the Reed team, they would risk more than the possibility of contracting yellow fever or malaria, as mosquitoes can also transmit many other diseases.

Reed agreed to the pledge, but as soon as he did he went back to Washington, leaving his three teammates in Cuba. Why Reed left the scene is one of the most perplexing aspects of the yellow fever story. Reed has left us no clues, although many of his letters remain. Biographers say that Reed was summoned back to Washington on direct order of Surgeon General Sternberg to join Victor C. Vaughan, one of Reed's colleagues on the Typhoid Fever Commission, to finish a report on their investigations. (Edward O. Shakespeare, the other member of the Typhoid Commission, had recently died.) If so, such a summons must have been given orally or in papers that have been lost. Certainly, there is no hint of it in Reed's official summary of his activities for the month of August.[53] Reed said that from August 10 to 31 he was on duty as curator of the Army Medical Museum according to orders of 1893, which had been issued five years before creation of the Typhoid Fever Commission and which he had used for routine travel to Washington in April; he did not cite specific orders of the surgeon general, as he did in subsequent reports when he traveled between the United States and Cuba. The lack of evidence of such specific orders raises questions about the accuracy of the claims that Reed was summoned to Washington under official military orders instead of going voluntarily.

Moreover, Carroll later presented a differing view. On August 4, the morning after the team pledged to self-experiment, Reed sailed for Washington "without a word of explanation so far as I knew," Carroll wrote in a letter in 1906. "He was given carte blanche by General Sternberg to go and come as he pleased," and in no way was he forced to return to the United States.[54]

Just after Reed arrived in Washington to resume his work on typhoid fever, his teammates began carrying out their pledge in Cuba.

Perhaps because Jesse Lazear gave more credence to the mosquito theory than did the other commission members, he was the most anxious to probe its validity. Lazear apparently self-experimented on several occasions. In the first set of mosquito experiments, he used himself and eight other volunteers in a very simple procedure that Agramonte described. "Each insect was contained in a glass tube covered by a wad of cotton, the same as is done with bacterial cultures. As the mouth of the tube is turned downwards, the insect usually flies towards the bottom of the tube (upwards), then the latter is uncovered rapidly and the open mouth placed upon the forearm or the abdomen of the patient; after a few moments the mosquito drops upon the skin and if hungry will immediately start operations; when full, by gently shaking the tube, the insect is made to fly upwards again and the cotton plug replaced without difficulty."[55]

None of the nine came down with yellow fever.

Now it was Carroll's turn. Later he wrote that on August 27, 1900, "I reminded Dr. Lazear that I was ready, and he at last applied to my arm an insect that had bitten a patient with a severe attack twelve days previously."[56] Carroll assumed that the bites he received that afternoon would be innocuous, because Finlay's evidence had left him unconvinced of the mosquito theory. Nevertheless, Carroll later wrote, "I was perfectly willing, however, to take a soldier's chance."[57]

The insect that bit Carroll had been hatched and reared in the laboratory and had fed on four individuals with yellow fever. Once again, Agramonte described the experiment: "The tube was carefully held first by Lazear and then by Carroll himself, for a considerable length of time, upon his forearm, before the mosquito decided to introduce its proboscis."[58]

That night Carroll wrote Reed about the incident: "I remarked jokingly," he recalled, "that if there were anything in the mosquito theory I should have a good dose. And so it happened."[59]

Two days later, on August 29, Carroll began experiencing the earliest, vague symptoms of yellow fever, symptoms so mild that they did not prevent him from taking his customary daily dip in the ocean, a mile and a half from the camp. On August 31, four days after the bite, the symptoms became much more severe. Carroll became weak and had a chill, and his temperature rose to 102 degrees Fahrenheit. His colleagues suspected he had malaria, not yellow fever.

Agramonte recalled that when Carroll arrived at Camp Columbia that morning, he had already examined his own blood. "Not finding any malarial parasites," Agramonte said, "he told me he thought he had 'caught cold' at the beach: his suffused face, bloodshot eyes and general appearance, in spite of his efforts at gaiety and unconcern, shocked me beyond words. The possibility of his having yellow fever did not occur to him just then; when it did, two days later, he declared he must have caught it at my autopsy room in the Military Hospital, or at Las Animas Hospital, where he had been two days before taking sick. Although we insisted that he should go to bed in his quarters, we could only get him to rest upon a lounge, until the afternoon, when he felt too sick and had to take to his bed. Lazear and I were almost panic-stricken when we realized that Carroll had yellow fever."[60]

Carroll was a thousand miles away from his wife and children, who were in Washington. They learned about his attack and his fight for life through tersely worded cablegrams. These provoked great anxiety because yellow fever usually killed within a week. Beyond good nursing care, all Carroll's medical attendants could do for him was to offer him a hot mustard footbath, which was as much a treatment for themselves as for the patient.[61]

For three days, Carroll said, his "life was in the balance."[62] He was delirious. Beads of sweat covered his skin from his fever, which fluctuated, rising to 103.4 degrees on September 1 and peaking at 104 degrees on September 2. Just a few rays of light were enough to bring on a severe headache. His back ached. His gums were swollen. His skin slowly took on a faint yellowish hue and then turned deep yellow. The nurse who cared for him said that even to the whites of his eyes he was as yellow as saffron.

But Carroll was lucky. He did not bleed severely. By September 7, his temperature was normal. As soon as his colleagues realized he would recover, they sent another terse cable: "Carroll out of danger."[63]

Reed responded immediately, writing Carroll from Washington: "Hip! Hip! Hurrah! God be praised for the news from Cuba today. . . . I shall simply go out and get boiling *drunk!* Really I can never recall such a sense of relief in all my life, as the news of your recovery gives me! And then, too, would you believe it? *The Typhoid Report is on its way to the upper office!* Well, I'm damned if I don't get drunk *twice!!!*"[64]

Reed then urged Carroll to come home quickly to see his family and he penned a note to the back side of the letter: "Did the Mosquito do it?"

Carroll's attack left him so weak that two weeks later he could not stand or change position without assistance. According to one version of the story, Carroll's heart became acutely enlarged at the height of the attack.[65] Yet by September 28 he was attempting to resume his work. He wrote his wife that he had performed an autopsy, although he had felt "too weak to undertake it."[66] Convinced now that mosquitoes did transmit yellow fever, Carroll boldly told his wife that his research was "one of the discoveries of the century."[67]

Carroll was forty-five, just three years younger than Reed, and he had lived up to the pledge to self-experiment. "I was the first to propose that we submit," he said, "and the first to be infected, though not the first to be bitten."[68]

But his illness only supported—it did not prove—Finlay's mosquito theory, because he had carried out his self-experiment more on a whim than under rigid scientific conditions. Carroll had had contact with yellow fever cases in the few days immediately preceding his illness, so skeptics and scientific purists could effectively argue that the mosquito bite had not caused the yellow fever attack but was an incidental factor. For that reason, it was necessary to do a second experiment—to have the same mosquito bite another individual who had no known immunity.

The yellow fever team wasted no time when Private William H. Dean offered to volunteer. On the day that Carroll became sick, Lazear applied to Dean's arm the same mosquito that had bitten

Carroll as well as three others. Lazear added the three others, apparently to provide the greatest chance of transmitting the disease. If Dean got yellow fever, they reasoned, it would be due to mosquito bites. Dean suffered a mild attack and was well before Carroll left his sickbed.

"He thus immediately proved the source of infection in my case and confirmed it at once by producing another case with the same insect. For this he is not given due credit," Carroll said.[69]

Excitement gripped the yellow fever camp in Cuba. Lazear expressed it when he wrote to his wife on September 8. She had returned to the United States to give birth to their second child, a daughter, born on August 23. "I rather think I am on the track of the real germ," Lazear wrote, "but nothing must be said as yet, not even a hint. I have not mentioned it to a soul."[70]

On September 13 Lazear let himself be bitten again, and for the next five days he did not know if his daring experiment would give him yellow fever or not. Then, on September 18, he began to feel ill, and although he stayed in his quarters more frequently and missed meals for two days, he continued to work. Though suffering chills and a fever of 103 degrees Fahrenheit, he did not ask for medical advice or help. Finally, three physicians visited him in his quarters and told him he needed to be admitted to the hospital. Though Carroll was still down with yellow fever, at first Lazear's doctors suspected he had developed malaria, and they examined samples of his blood for evidence of the malaria parasite. There was none. As Lazear became jaundiced, his colleagues were terrified. They realized he, too, had yellow fever.

Cables flashed news of Lazear's illness to army headquarters in Washington and, in turn, to Reed and William Osler. The renowned Johns Hopkins professor described himself as "very anxious" about Lazear's condition in a telegram he sent to Surgeon General Sternberg demanding more news.[71]

Osler had reason to worry, because Lazear's illness was severe. By September 22, black vomit spurted from his mouth, up through the bar over his hospital cot. He was delirious, fighting efforts of the nurses to keep him in bed.

Lazear died on September 25, twelve days from the beginning of his experiment. Later Carroll recalled: "I shall never forget the expression of alarm in his eyes when I last saw him alive in the third or fourth day of his illness."[72]

Lazear's widow learned of her husband's death in a starkly simple one-sentence cable: "Doctor Lazear died at eight P.M. this evening." It was a double shock; although Sternberg had sent orders to tell her Lazear was ill, no one had done so.[73]

Reed had been anxious about Carroll's illness, but not anxious enough to drop the typhoid fever report to rush back to Cuba. He was, however, most definitely concerned about his colleagues. In a letter he wrote just after he had returned to Washington from an outing in the hills of Pennsylvania, he conveyed his guilt about leaving Cuba. Having no way to know he was writing on the very day Lazear took his last breaths, Reed wailed that he was "so ashamed of myself for being here, in a safe country, while my associates have been coming down with Yellow Jack."[74] In the same letter he seemed to reject his pledge to self-experiment: "I certainly shall not, with the facts that we now have, allow a 'loaded' mosquito to bite me! That would be fool-hardy in the extreme. . . . Perhaps I owe my life to my departure from Cuba, for I had agreed to be bitten along with the others—Being an old man, I might have been quickly carried off."[75]

Now, with news of Lazear's death, he made plans to return to the island.

Reed had mixed reactions. He grieved for Lazear. Yet he was jubilant that cases of yellow fever had developed from mosquito bites. Nevertheless, from the limited facts he had received he believed that Private Dean's experiment notwithstanding, the research was flawed because the investigations had not been conducted under strict, scientifically controlled conditions. With good reason, he worried lest some unknown factor other than the mosquito had been involved and that Lazear had died in vain. On September 24, immediately after Reed received Carroll's letter informing him of Lazear's attack, Reed insisted that any experiments on humans be confined to those that would give irrefutable scientific evidence of the mosquito's role in spreading yellow fever.

Reed could not be sure that any of the three cases, except perhaps Dean's, proved anything, and he scolded Carroll for his lack of scientific reasoning, saying that if he had remained in camp for ten days prior to his bite, "then we would have had a *clear* case, but *you* didn't! You went where you *might* have contracted the disease from another source—and unfortunately Lazear was bitten at Los Animas Hospital! *That* knocks his case out! I mean as a thoroughly scientific experiment, that would bear strictest scrutiny. If Dean *did not leave the Post after leaving the Hospital* [where he was bitten] his case is *satisfactory* and proves a *great deal.* If his case will withstand criticism, then your and Lazear's cases would be *confirmatory.*"[76]

Despite his doubts, Reed urged immediate publication. Perhaps he had his British competitors in mind. Shortly after their visit, they had commented favorably on the theory of the mosquito's role in transmitting yellow fever, saying that the scientific report written by Carter, the Mississippi researcher, was "second to none."

When Reed arrived in Cuba on October 4, he immediately set out to get a detailed picture of what had happened during his absence, particularly the circumstances that had led to Lazear's death, but the versions he heard were confusing. Carroll said that Lazear "was bitten by a stray mosquito while applying other insects to a patient in one of the city's hospitals. He did not recognize it as Aedes and thought it was a Culex [another type of mosquito]. It was permitted to take its fill, and he attached no importance to the bite until after he was taken sick, when he related the incident to me."[77]

Another version was that Lazear had purposely enticed the mosquito to bite him in a deliberate self-experiment. Yet Agramonte would write in 1915, "Lazear assured us that he had not experimented upon himself, that is, that he had not been bitten by any of the purposely infected mosquitoes."[78]

But Lazear had kept a pocket notebook, and when Reed examined it, he confided in General Albert E. Truby, the commander of the military hospital in Cuba, who would go on to write the standard account of the yellow fever experiments. Reed told General Truby that some of Lazear's notations indicated that he had applied mosquitoes to himself.[79]

It is not clear why so much confusion existed about the way Lazear contracted yellow fever. There was ample evidence to straighten the matter out. Major General Leonard Wood, a physician who was the U.S. Army commander in Cuba, wrote on November 4, 1900, that Lazear had voluntarily let the mosquito bite him in a self-experiment. "He assumed this risk for the purpose of demonstrating on himself whether or not yellow fever could be directly transmitted in this manner," Wood said.[80] Sternberg in 1901 and Reed in 1902 made similar statements.[81]

Nevertheless, the version that Lazear had been accidentally bitten persisted until 1947, when it was finally dispelled by Dr. Philip S.

Hench, a Mayo Clinic physician who won a Nobel Prize for his research on cortisone and arthritis. Hench was fascinated by the history of the Reed commission and studied it as a hobby. According to Hench, when Reed found Lazear's notebook, it "was vitally useful in solving one mystery but it posed another mystery, for in it Reed found some incomplete entries which appeared to indicate that Lazear had secretly submitted himself to other experimental inoculations. Reed pondered long over these entries and then concluded, according to Dr. (now General) Truby, that when Lazear was taken sick he worried lest his life insurance become forfeited if it became known that he had deliberately infected himself with a fatal disease. The gods of business might not condone human sacrifice no matter how worthy the cause."[82]

Reed believed that at the last fateful hour Lazear withheld facts to protect his loved ones. Ostensibly to preserve Lazear's insurance benefits, Reed decided to let it appear that Lazear was accidentally infected while on duty as a member of the board. That possibility exists, of course. But no life insurance policy was ever found.

One commission member was now dead of yellow fever, another had barely survived a serious attack. Three of the four men had fulfilled their pledge to self-experiment. The commission's leader, Reed, had not. Reed's refusal to self-experiment, for whatever reason, did not, however, cause problems among his colleagues at the time. Agramonte said that after Private Dean's case, "we had agreed not to tempt fate by trying any more upon ourselves, and even I determined that no mosquito should bite me if I could prevent it, since the subject of my immunity was one that could not be sustained on scientific grounds; at the same time, we felt that we had been called upon to accomplish such work as did not justify our taking risks which then seemed really unnecessary. This we impressed upon Major Reed when he joined us in October and for this reason he was never bitten by infected mosquitoes."[83]

Carroll left Havana on October 11 for a month's leave. When he returned he said he was without the "terrors" he had once felt in working on yellow fever. But it is not clear that Carroll ever recuperated fully; his colleagues said he was mentally and physically weakened by the attack.[84]

Having reconstructed the events in Cuba, Reed returned once again to the United States, where he made one of the fastest communications of a scientific discovery in medical history. Despite the fact that he was working from a sample of just three experimental infections, and despite the criticisms he had leveled at Carroll regarding the lack of a thoroughly scientific experiment, Reed stated flatly at a meeting of the American Public Health Association in Indianapolis in mid-October, just two months after the team had produced its first case of yellow fever experimentally by a mosquito bite, that: "The mosquito serves as the intermediate host for the parasite of yellow fever, and it is highly probable that the disease is only propagated through the bite of this insect."[85]

Reed's conclusion, however, was not readily accepted. Editorials appeared in a number of influential newspapers ridiculing the mosquito hypothesis.[86] Furthermore, several scientists immediately challenged the study. Reed acknowledged that he still lacked conclusive proof and after the Indianapolis meeting he returned to Cuba in hopes of locking up the case scientifically through three types of human experiments. One would involve bites from infected mosquitoes, a second would include injection of blood taken from patients during the early stages of their illness, and the third would entail exposure to the most intimate contact with fomites in a repeat of some of Ffirth's self-experiments.

On November 20, 1900, the commission members established another experimental camp in Cuba, building it a mile from the nearest town to avoid any other possible source of infection and to allow for strict quarantine. Named Camp Lazear, it consisted of seven well-guarded army tents that were camouflaged by the surrounding luxuriant vegetation.

When Camp Lazear was created there were only twelve local residents who were judged to be susceptible to yellow fever, all recent immigrants from Spain who knew they might succumb to the disease under natural conditions at any time. Five volunteered for the new round of experiments, apparently in the belief that if they were going to get yellow fever anyway, which was highly probable, it was better to help others than merely to be counted among the hundreds of thousands of victims. They were also enticed by a $100 gold piece, which was perhaps why some of those not chosen "almost wept."[87]

Four of the five volunteers suffered attacks of the disease, from which they recovered. One man did not get sick at all, but it was discovered that he had been bitten by a mosquito that could not have transmitted the infection. "The precision with which the infection of the individual followed the bite of the mosquito left nothing to be desired in order to fulfill the requirements of a scientific experiment," the commission reported.[88]

Additional experiments were carried out in two small frame houses that were specifically built to rule out the possibility that the disease could also be spread by fomites. The first frame building consisted of one room, fourteen by twenty feet, which was called simply Building Number 1, or "Infected Clothing and Bedding Building." Building Number 1 was designed to prevent both the circulation of air and disinfection by sunlight. It had just two tiny, well-screened windows and two well-screened doors to exclude the entry of mosquitoes and thus preclude the possibility of the volunteers getting yellow fever through nonexperimental conditions. Sheets, blankets, and other items that were purposely soiled with black vomit, urine, and feces and taken from the beds of patients with yellow fever were stored in the building for two weeks. Then three volunteers who had never been known to have had yellow fever entered the house. The volunteers had orders to unpack the contaminated bed linens and sleep in the building. Each day the volunteers packed and unpacked the contaminated linens as the yellow fever team watched from outside. They added a fourth box of bedding that had been soiled by the bloody stools of a fatal case. When it was first unpacked, the smell forced the volunteers to retreat from the building. After twenty consecutive days of this filthy routine, none of the volunteers had come down with yellow fever.

The experiment was repeated with two additional volunteers. They handled the soiled linens and slept in the pajamas and other garments worn by yellow fever patients. This experiment lasted twenty-one days, and it was followed by a third, which lasted twenty days. This latter experiment involved an additional two volunteers, who slept on pillows covered with towels that had been thoroughly soiled with blood from yellow fever patients. The attempt to infect a total of seven volunteers who spent sixty-three days in Building 1 "proved an absolute failure," the commission members reported.[89]

Then Building Number 2, or "Infected Mosquito Building," was erected. It was similar in all respects to Building Number 1, except that a wire screen divided the building to keep one part free of mosquitoes. All articles were carefully disinfected by steam before they were admitted. Then fifteen mosquitoes, previously contaminated by being allowed to bite yellow fever patients, were set free in one side of the building. The scientists suspected that of the fifteen mosquitoes, only one—a mosquito that had bitten a patient twenty-four days earlier—was likely to be capable of transmitting the infection. They were learning that the virus had to be present for some time in the mosquito before it could infect a human. Three other mosquitoes had possibly reached the dangerous stage.

One of the new group of volunteers, John J. Moran, was a soldier who was considered susceptible to yellow fever. For the preceding thirty-two days, Moran had been confined to a yellow fever-free area. Now he entered the mosquito section of Building Number 2 on three separate occasions for stays of thirty minutes or less. During this time several insects bit him about the face and hands. Two other volunteers spent the same time with him in the building. However, they were on the mosquito-free side. Within four days of his exposure Moran came down with yellow fever. He recovered. The two other volunteers remained well, even after staying in the mosquito-free area of Building Number 2 for eighteen nights.

The evidence incriminating the mosquito became stronger. But Reed was worried about lack of cooperation and criticism, if not sabotage. "The Marine Hospital Service [now the U.S. Public Health Service] would gladly choke off our experimentation, for it may prove that all their disinfection has been for naught," Reed wrote his wife on December 4.[90]

He was no longer worried, however, about competition from the British researchers, Durham and Myers. They were clearly beaten. Following their visit to Cuba they had gone on to spend five months investigating yellow fever in Brazil. Then, on January 16, 1901, while Reed's team was still carrying out important parts of its research in Cuba, both British scientists came down with yellow fever. Myers died after four days. Durham was more fortunate; he recovered.[91]

In the experiments that showed that yellow fever could not be spread by fomites, Reed's team broke no new ground but rather confirmed what Ffirth had proved a century earlier through experiments on himself. However, the other two categories of the Reed team's experiments went far beyond Ffirth's work. The Yellow Fever Board had unraveled the mystery of how, exactly, the mosquito spread the disease. By an exclusion process, the researchers had learned that the mosquito had to suck the blood of the yellow fever patient within the first two or three days of illness; the infecting agent did not circulate in the blood thereafter. Then they found that the yellow fever victim's blood had to remain in the mosquito for an additional twelve to twenty days before the infection could be transmitted by a bite. That represented the time during which the yellow fever agent went from the insect's stomach to its salivary glands. After the virus was introduced into a human by a mosquito bite, another two to five days passed before he or she became ill. One attack conferred lifetime immunity. However, the ability of the mosquito to infect lasted at least seventy-one days after the insect had initially ingested the organism, a fact that clarified one of the scientific mysteries of the day—how the disease could be conveyed to a second victim long after the first had vacated a dwelling.

The Reed commission also verified Henry Carter's thesis that a period of time was needed for the virus to develop somewhere outside the body in order to continue the spread of the disease. But of course Carter had not fingered the mosquito as the vector.

Moreover, the Reed board's investigations explained why Finlay's theory was correct but why his experiments had failed to produce yellow fever. Reed's team understood that Finlay's theory had not been fully tested: Finlay had not waited long enough for his mosquitoes to incubate the yellow fever agent.

Reed's cable to Sternberg on December 15 summed it up succinctly: "Theory conclusively proven." In return, he received congratulations from Sternberg, who had earlier dismissed the mosquito theory but now began to try to share in the credit for its validation.[92]

When it was clear the mosquito transmitted yellow fever, a new mystery developed: What was it in the mosquito that caused yellow fever? It seemed a bacterium could be ruled out, because the organism was invisible under a microscope. William Welch, the bacteriologist who had trained three commission members at Johns Hopkins, called Reed's and Carroll's attention to some German research which showed that the agent that caused foot-and-mouth disease in animals was so tiny it could pass through a diatomaceous, or earthenware, filter.[93] Perhaps the yellow fever agent was such an organism, Welch suggested, and he urged his former students to search for it.

Sternberg, too, pushed Reed to identify the invisible agent that produced yellow fever. In addition he pointed out that no one knew whether the agent "*must* pass through the body of a mosquito in order to infect susceptible individuals." Sternberg, who only a few years earlier had rejected Finlay's theory of mosquito transmission and who had also believed in the fomite theory, now accepted mosquitoes as the usual way yellow fever was spread. But he urged caution in accepting them as the only way.[94]

According to Sternberg, only one previous attempt had been made to transmit yellow fever by injection of blood from a patient afflicted with the disease, and he himself had witnessed that attempt, made by a Mexican doctor.[95] Carroll decided to try the experiment in Cuba, but Reed objected. As much as Reed wanted to know if the blood from a yellow fever patient would yield the infectious agent that caused the disease, he wrote Carroll that "our work has been too good to be marred now by a death."[96] Had he forgotten about Lazear?

A week later, Reed, realizing that Carroll would proceed despite his advice, reversed his decision and also told him to use his own judgment in the future.

Carroll took a sample of blood from a patient during the first three days of illness and injected it into a volunteer, who then came down with yellow fever. Carroll found that the same result occurred after the blood had been filtered through an earthenware filter. He proved that an infectious agent existed in the filtered portion of the blood and showed that mosquitoes were not necessary for transmission. Carroll's studies also showed why so many others before him had failed to detect a bacterium from blood samples of patients with yellow fever: There was none. The agent was an ultramicroscopic organism which today is known as a virus.

Carroll continued to work with other researchers to expand the scope of the Reed team's experiments. They now tested another of Finlay's theories—that immunity against yellow fever could be produced by the bites of mosquitoes that had fed on patients with mild attacks of the disease. These experiments had tragic consequences. Some volunteers, instead of getting mild cases of the disease, became severely ill. One, Clara Maass, a twenty-five-year-old nurse from New Jersey, died on August 24, 1901; her death led to a public outcry against conducting further such human experiments.[97]

The findings of the Reed commission were used to begin an all-out attack against yellow fever. In 1901 Dr. William C. Gorgas, chief health officer of Havana, who had been at the bedsides of Lazear and Carroll, led a campaign that through improved sanitation measures and quarantine not only wiped out yellow fever in Havana but also almost entirely rid the area of malaria. The latter was an added benefit, accomplished by the elimination of standing fresh water where the insects bred. Ironically, Gorgas had been one of the most outspoken skeptics of the mosquito-yellow fever theory. Even as late as Reed's preliminary report given at the American Public Health Association meeting in Indianapolis, Gorgas had said he was not impressed with the mosquito theory. It was the later experiments that changed his mind—and quickly.[98]

Gorgas went on to Panama, where he applied the same measures he had used to clear yellow fever from Cuba to make the isthmus safe for canal workers. The last case of yellow fever in Panama occurred in 1906, one year after the disease disappeared from the United States.[99]

Gorgas predicted in his scientific report that "the next generation will look on yellow fever as an extinct disease having only historic interest" and that there was no possibility the disease would reappear on earth.[100] But his prediction was too optimistic. While yellow fever is now rare in the world, scientists have learned from epidemics in South America that different breeds of mosquitoes can transmit the disease to humans from jungle monkeys, which are a permanent reservoir of the yellow fever virus.[101] Today, jungle yellow fever is the principal source of yellow fever in the world, and it cannot be eradicated short of wholesale extermination of monkeys or mosquitoes. As long as the virus circulates anywhere, there is the very small chance that cases could reappear in the United States.

On Reed's final return to Washington, he was credited with being the mastermind of the yellow fever experiments in Cuba and was well on his way to becoming a public hero. Honorary degrees came from Harvard and the University of Michigan. Sternberg was retiring, and Reed's friends campaigned for his succession as surgeon general of the army. They also campaigned to secure a Nobel Prize for the yellow fever researchers. They failed on both counts.

In 1902, the second year of the Nobel Prizes, the award for Physiology or Medicine went to Ronald Ross for his work on mosquitoes and malaria. Reed died that year, losing his chance for the award; under the terms of Alfred Nobel's will, the prize is not awarded posthumously. Medical journals carried on the campaign for the surviving yellow fever principals. In 1906, for example, the *British Medical Journal,* the official publication of the British Medical Association, called the elimination of yellow fever from Panama and Cuba a feat "incalculable to mankind" and proposed that Carroll and Agramonte, the two Yellow Fever Commission survivors, share the Nobel Prize. "Their work is of far greater importance than that of several to whom the prize has been awarded in the past few years," the *Journal* said.[102]

But it would be another forty-five years before a Nobel Prize would be awarded for research in yellow fever. In 1951 it went to the South African–born Dr. Max Theiler, who worked at the Rockefeller Institute in New York, where he developed the vaccine that is still used to protect against the disease. In their pioneering research, Theiler and his coworkers took the first doses of their laboratory-made vaccine.[103]

Reed died from appendicitis in 1902, at a time when surgeons were just beginning to learn how to diagnose the condition and to do appendectomies. When Reed took sick, his surgeon, Dr. William C. Borden, vacillated about operating for several days; by the time he did, deadly peritonitis had set in. Borden, who was chief surgeon and commanding officer of the Washington army hospital, had ambitions of developing a huge army medical center at a time when all but two of the several hospitals built for the Spanish-American War had been closed. (The army hospital in San Francisco was the only other one still open.) Borden had gotten nowhere in submitting his plan to Sternberg. But he continued to lobby for a medical center, gaining valuable tips from influential patients about the workings of Congress and the government. Eventually he succeeded.[104] Though records do not make it clear why the army chose Reed's name for the hospital, presumably Borden had something to do with it. Thus Reed's fame endures: We are reminded of him each time a president or other government leader enters for medical care.

Walter Reed merited his image in some ways. His group of medical researchers was the first to formalize covenants between medical investigators and human volunteers. The commission members spoke to the ethical responsibility of the investigators to serve as the first human guinea pigs; they pledged to do it. The conduct of the yellow fever experiments was the forerunner of the current practice of informed consent and was cited in the formulation of the Nuremberg Code and in many other discussions about the ethics of human experimentation.

Yet it is one of the greatest ironies in medical history that Reed, almost alone, remains the hero of this extraordinary scientific discovery. Reed wrote few papers, but he had a first-rate scientific mind. Unquestionably he was a leading epidemiologist and bacteriologist who capped a distinguished career with the typhoid fever and yellow fever investigations. And though he did not self-experiment, he clearly offered valuable scientific insights into the conduct of the yellow fever experiments. Nevertheless, in that research, Reed's role was more that of an administrator, and in some ways a poorly prepared one.

Though the commission members promptly and formally reported their findings to medical colleagues and wrote many letters to relatives and friends that elaborated on their work, modern historians are still handicapped because many records were either lost or not kept and because no journalists were present to witness and record what happened. So far as is known, Reed kept no diary of the Yellow Fever Board meetings, as would have been expected from a top-notch scientist, and this oversight is a prime source of the feuding that went on after his death.

No one will know the true circumstances under which Lazear developed yellow fever, and no one will know why Reed failed to live up to his pledge to self-experiment unless more records are found.

Lazear's notebook, which Reed kept in his desk in Washington, disappeared after Reed's death. If Lazear's diary is ever found, it might help explain the circumstances of his experiment. It probably would not clarify why Reed left the morning after agreeing to self-experiment and why he ultimately failed to live up to his pledge.

Reed's most recent biographer, Dr. William B. Bean, suggests that Reed was advised or ordered not to experiment on himself because of his age: forty-eight. For that reason, Bean said, Reed would not use subjects over the age of forty in his future yellow fever experiments. "Had Carroll died as a result of his risky and frivolous auto-experimentation it would have put an end to the experiments and prevented verification of the preliminary studies," Bean wrote. "Indeed the death of any volunteer would most certainly have ended the experiments."[105]

However, this explanation is inadequate, first because Lazear's death did *not* stop the Commission's experiments, second because more volunteers were recruited and age seemed not to be a major criterion. Reed could certainly have been one of them. But he was not.

# Chapter Seven

# TAMING THE GREATEST KILLERS

Those of us who live in developed countries tend to think of parasitic diseases as a historical problem, one that no longer threatens humans because of improved sanitation and other public health measures. In fact, scores of parasites still sap the strength of millions of people, and while these parasites are found predominantly in developing countries, their existence is by no means limited to these areas. In the United States, there are at least six major parasitic infections which, at one time or another, have afflicted over half the population. Virtually every parasitic disease has been diagnosed in recent years in developed countries, and some victims have died because their doctors did not make the correct diagnosis in time. In a list of the top ten worst diseases worldwide, parasitic infections would rank among the top five. As yet we have no vaccines against any of them.[1]

But we are close. There is a real prospect that by the end of this century a vaccine will exist to control the greatest killer of them all—malaria. The groundwork that makes this a possibility was laid by a self-experimenter named David F. Clyde.

In the nineteenth century, eighty-five percent of Europeans who ventured into tropical West Africa died of malaria or suffered permanent complications from it. The risk was so high that life insurance policies were canceled for anyone traveling to that region.[2] The opening of Africa and other malarious areas of the world to exploration, development, and world trade might not have occurred as readily without the introduction of quinine and antimalaria drugs, as well as the discovery of ways to prevent transmission of the disease. Despite these scientific advances, the incidence of malaria is again soaring, partly because malaria parasites, transmitted to humans via the female *Anopheles* mosquito, are becoming increasingly resistant to the antimalaria drugs. This resistance is spreading relentlessly through the developing countries of the world. At least three hundred million people will suffer attacks of malaria this year, and in Africa alone more than one million children will die from this parasitic disease.[3]

The need for a vaccine against resistant malaria is imperative, and in the early 1970s, physician and parasitologist David Clyde took some of the early steps toward developing one.

The technique Clyde planned to use in his vaccine experiment was ingenious. Dissecting the infective malaria parasites from the mosquito and injecting them into humans might not only be ineffective for vaccination purposes, but also dangerous because the injected material would contain bits of mosquito tissue. Humans injected with such material might contract nonmalarial infections, die from allergic reactions, or be subjected to other unacceptable risks. Also, there was the possibility that tiny pieces of mosquito tissue would clog arteries, stopping the supply of vital oxygenated blood and causing a paralyzing or dementing stroke or destroying other organs.

Therefore, Clyde decided to use a technique recently developed for immunizing animals. He would expose infected mosquitoes to a dose of X rays sufficient to weaken the parasites inside them but not to kill the mosquitoes. His intention was that this irradiation method would weaken the ability of the malaria parasites to cause infection but still permit them to act as antigens that would stimulate the recipient to produce protective antibodies.

David F. Clyde was born in India and subsequently began his research on malaria in Africa. Later he moved to Baltimore to continue his research investigations at the University of Maryland. Clyde's malaria vaccine experiments in Maryland were funded by the U.S. Army and were done in cooperation with a New York University parasitologist, Dr. Harry Most, whose team of research workers led by Dr. Ruth Nussenzweig had already been experimenting with a vaccine against rodent malaria.[4] The human experiments were to take place from 1971 to 1975 among prisoner-volunteers in Maryland and elsewhere in the United States. Before the experiments at Maryland began, the necessary approval was obtained from the university's institutional review board, which governs the ethics of the research done by its faculty. In addition, Clyde's team explained the nature and risks of the experiments to the prisoners. All of them voluntarily signed so-called "informed consent" forms before participating.

But these reviews and safeguards came at a time when there were heated debates over the ethics of human experimentation and widespread attacks on the American prison system, including the practice of performing medical experiments on prisoners. Critics argued that the very fact someone was a prisoner made it impossible for him or her to volunteer freely without implied duress.

Clyde himself maintained that it was critical for at least one scientist to share the experimental process with the prisoners; there was never any doubt in his mind as to who that scientist would be. For more than twenty years Clyde had tested on himself each antimalarial drug he had used in his everyday practice and research in Africa. Testing the drugs he prescribed for his patients was as much a matter of curiosity as principle. He wanted to find out "about any side-effects such as lingering taste, nausea, insomnia which, being subjective, were difficult to elicit by questioning others."

In 1974 Clyde began a self-experiment to discover whether malaria parasites from infected irradiated mosquitoes could immunize against two types of malaria, *Plasmodium falciparum,* the most serious type, and *Plasmodium vivax.* The addition of the vivax form was important and necessary for two reasons. First, researchers did not know if immunization against one form would protect against another. Second, vivax is a major cause of malaria in many parts of the world, and any vaccine would have to protect against this form as well.

It was critical to his experiment that Clyde be susceptible to malaria. He presumed that he was, and tests indicated he had never been infected, but he could not be absolutely sure. He had, after all, been exposed to malaria parasites for much of his professional life and could have inadvertently acquired a mild infection. Because of this unlikely possibility, Clyde allowed nonirradiated mosquitoes that were infected with the two types of malaria (*P. falciparum* and *P. vivax*) to bite him. Indeed, Clyde had no immunity to malaria; he developed both types of the disease.

The first attack began when Clyde's body shook from a chill. As he described it: "You shake like anything. You are very cold. You have a high temperature and a splitting headache. Then you start vomiting, and that is the most awful part of it. You have about four hours of absolute misery and then it gradually lets off for about another twelve hours. Then it starts again." Clyde allowed himself to go through two fever cycles, in order to be absolutely sure that the blood tests would document malaria infection. Then he took mefloquine, an experimental drug, which promptly cured the infection before immunity developed.[5]

The second phase of the experiment took more than one and a half years. Clyde tested a variety of strains of malaria parasites collected in different areas of the world to see whether they had important immunologic differences. Researchers know that strains of microorganisms vary greatly in their ability to produce antibodies in humans, i.e., to immunize. Therefore, it is customary to test several strains of a species before selecting one for use in an experimental vaccine. In the Maryland experiment, Clyde followed that policy; he tested the capability of the several strains of malaria to produce enough antibodies by allowing infected irradiated mosquitoes to bite him. He did it again and again. Each time, he received scores of bites. "It was a damn nuisance and very unpleasant to have six cages of three hundred fifty mosquitoes hanging on you, but that's part of it," Clyde said. The welts from the bites itched. Clyde applied cortisone ointment for relief, but still he wanted to scratch his swollen arms and legs. By the end of the experiment, Clyde had received more than two thousand seven hundred mosquito bites.

Why so many? "Mosquitoes will bite you only every second or third day," Clyde explained, "and it is very difficult to get them infected with malaria in heavy densities. We had to apply large numbers of mosquitoes to a malaria patient willing to be bitten, then wait for those mosquitoes to become infectious. The infections in the mosquitoes all matured at the same time; but then the infectious stage of the parasite, the sporozoites, remained for several days in the mosquito's salivary glands, during which time they could be injected into the volunteer. To immunize the volunteer, we figured we had to allow at least three hundred fifty mosquitoes to be fed every second or third day on three occasions for a total of about one thousand mosquitoes. The problem was getting enough antigen into the volunteer to produce sufficient antibody to protect. Although you can get infected with the inoculation of just one parasite from just one mosquito, it is impossible to get protection from only one because one does not have enough antigen to produce antibodies."

Then, to test the efficacy of the immunization, at specified points throughout the experiment Clyde accepted the challenge of becoming sick from another malaria attack. On these occasions, the mosquitoes that bit Clyde were not irradiated—they were capable of causing infection. But Clyde escaped malaria, and the absence of infection meant that the antibodies that had developed in his blood from the vaccine had killed the parasites. Clyde had proved his technique would immunize humans. Still, he was only one subject; the experiments had to be done on more volunteers. Clyde repeated them on prisoner-volunteers in Maryland, and other researchers performed similar experiments on prisoner-volunteers in Illinois. The vaccine protected.

Unfortunately, however, the duration of protection was short. In the case of *P. falciparum* the benefits of the vaccine lasted no longer than three months. In the case of *P. vivax* immunity lasted from three to six months. Nevertheless, it was a key experiment that spurred interest in developing a malaria vaccine.

In the end, Clyde's irradiation method did not lead to a practical malaria vaccine because there was no way enough mosquitoes could be infected and irradiated to produce a vaccine for use on tens of millions of people. But scientists are trying to mass-produce antigens using the sophisticated molecular biological and gene-splicing techniques that have been developed in recent years.[6] In 1986 scientists began testing two types of experimental malaria vaccine on human volunteers, one gene-spliced into the common colon bacillus and the other a synthetic chemical product (the latter at the University of Maryland's Center for Vaccine Development, with Clyde's participation). But several years will pass before any can be used as a standard prevention; if one is, the world will owe much to the self-experiments of David Clyde, which the World Health Organization called "heroic" in awarding him the Darling Foundation prize in 1986.

Hookworm is another deadly parasitic disease and one that has not disappeared from the United States. It infects up to 15 percent of children and young adults now living in some rural areas of the South, although many may not suffer symptoms. Hookworm derives its name from the toothlike "hooks" in the mouth of the parasite, hooks the parasite uses to attach itself to the wall of the bowel, where individual worms have been known to survive for as long as fourteen years. The usual lifetime, however, is about two years, and all the time the hookworms are there, they suck blood, sapping the body of large numbers of oxygen-carrying red blood cells. If enough iron is stored or provided by the individual's daily dietary intake, the parasite's effect is a relatively harmless infection with few or no symptoms and therefore no need for treatment. But if the hookworms remove red cells more rapidly than they can be formed, anemia develops. In most cases the anemia produces chronic symptoms. It can also kill. The disease is usually spread when larvae from human excreta in the soil come into contact with a person's skin. Once the larvae enter the body, they are swept by the lymph and blood systems to the lungs; as they develop further, they travel to the windpipe and then into the small intestine. There they attach their hooks into the bowel.

Although hookworm was known in ancient times, and was probably the cause of the pallid appearance of miners described by Lucretius in 50 B.C., the first specific account of human infection was not reported in a medical journal until 1843, when Dr. Angelo Dubini, an Italian, found the worm in the intestines of a woman who died of pneumonia in Milan.[7] Later Dubini made a systematic study of hookworms and found them in about 20 percent of autopsies. In many of these cases, death had been caused by conditions other than hookworm.

Almost four decades after Dubini's discovery of hookworms in humans, Dr. Edoardo Perroncito, a pathologist at a veterinary school in Turin, began a lonely battle to provide convincing evidence that there was a connection between hookworms and the anemia he saw in many people. In 1880 he performed a number of autopsies on patients who had had suspicious symptoms in an attempt to prove that hookworm caused disease. In one patient he detected one thousand five hundred hookworms![8] Today the diagnosis of anemia is aided by standard blood tests. In Perroncito's time, it was usually judged by a much cruder method—looking for the degree of pallor in a patient's face.

Perroncito's research led to the first effective therapy for hookworm, aspidium, an extract from the male fern plant. But doses of aspidium can be unpredictably toxic and dangerous, affecting the heart, lungs, and central nervous system. Its use in the treatment of hookworm was eventually replaced by thymol, derived from the oils of *Thymus vulgaris* and other plants. But thymol, like aspidium, had negative side effects. It often caused headaches, nausea, and stomachaches. Further, each time thymol was administered, the patient had to take a purge to rid the bowel of the drug to prevent it from becoming absorbed into the body, where it could cause severe symptoms, even death. In time, thymol and other compounds gave way to a cheaper substance that needed no purge; it was carbon tetrachloride, often used as a cleaning solvent and fire extinguisher.

The discovery of carbon tetrachloride's effectiveness in the treatment of hookworm came in 1921 from an observation made by a veterinarian, Dr. Maurice C. Hall, who worked for the U.S. Bureau of Animal Industry. In experiments with the compound, Hall noted that it cleaned out hookworms from infected dogs without being toxic to the dogs. The forty-year-old Hall then tested the drug on himself by swallowing three capsules three hours after he had eaten a light breakfast and smoked a cigar. He did not have a hookworm infection; all he was testing was the safety of one dose of the drug on himself. Seven minutes later he belched and momentarily felt a mild burning sensation in his stomach. He carried on a normal day's activities, eating, working, and smoking cigars as was his custom. Other than a mild laxative effect, Hall noticed nothing else untoward about his experience. After the drug was tested further in animals, it was used to treat hookworm infection in thousands of humans.

Eventually, however, doctors abandoned carbon tetrachloride when they found that though effective in treating hookworm, it could cause liver damage. Hall continued his research, and in 1925 he found that a similar compound called tetrachloroethylene was about as effective against hookworm, and safer. Again, Hall tested the drug on himself without ill effect. By 1929 tetrachloroethylene had become the drug of choice for hookworm and remained so for several decades.[9]

All this, however, was unknown in the 1800s, when throughout Europe and other temperate areas hookworm was killing so many miners and construction workers that their malady became known as "miner's anemia" or "brickmaker's anemia." These laborers often worked in places where they would step barefoot on or touch their skin to moist soil that was contaminated with larvae from human excreta. Unaware of the dangers because they did not know the parasite's life cycle, they continued to spread the disease as they went from job to job.

Probably the worst recorded outbreak of hookworm occurred in the 1880s among the predominantly Italian workers who built the St. Gotthard tunnel connecting Italy and Switzerland through the Alps.[10] When the tunnel was completed in 1882, hookworm-infested workers scattered throughout Europe, and hookworm became a common condition wherever they went. Outbreaks occurred in coal mines throughout the continent, the sulfur mines of Sicily, the tin mines of England, the gold and silver mines of Hungary, and the lead mines of Spain. By 1903 hookworm was such a major problem in German mines that health officials started a control campaign. Sanitary conveniences were installed and new workers suspected of having the infection were excluded from underground work until therapy with aspidium, thymol, or carbon tetrachloride reduced the severity of their infections.

In the last century, public health measures to control parasitic diseases were virtually nonexistent because knowledge of specific parasitic infections was so primitive. With the discovery that a person infected with hookworm could pass thousands of eggs in the feces each day, doctors naturally assumed that the infection was spread by touching the mouth with unwashed hands or by swallowing water, foods, dust, and other items that had been contaminated with the hookworm eggs. Health measures were aimed at keeping a mine or construction area clean. But hookworm continued to affect large numbers of miners and other people. What doctors did not understand was that the chief means of transmitting the parasite was through the skin. Had they understood this, they would have recognized, for example, that the introduction of one safety measure in the coal mines had inadvertently created another public health menace. To prevent coal-dust explosions, mines were required to water down every working shaft. The unintended result was that the protective moisture aggravated the hookworm problem by helping to spread the eggs.

Control of hookworm became a reality only through an accident and later a deliberate self-experiment performed in 1898 by Arthur Looss in Cairo, Egypt.[11] A manufacturer's son who was born in Saxony in 1861, Looss was an enthusiastic and energetic researcher who paid great attention to detail and was able to make extremely accurate drawings to illustrate his descriptions of parasites.[12] Looss went to Egypt because of the wealth of opportunity for studying parasitic diseases there. He had visited Egypt briefly in 1893 and returned in 1896; this time he stayed for eighteen years, teaching at the Government School of Medicine, where the Egyptian colonial administration had created a special professorship for him.

It was as a thirty-seven-year-old researcher in 1898 that Looss first reported his research findings on the hookworm parasite. In fact, he made the discovery accidentally while doing an experiment with an organism called *Strongyloides stercoralis,* which causes an intestinal infection but has no connection with hookworm. Looss swallowed larvae of the strongyloides parasite, but when he tested his stools after an appropriate interval to determine the time required for the strongyloides parasite to pass through further stages of development in its complicated life cycle, he was surprised to find hookworm eggs. (Looss's records give us no way of knowing what happened to the strongyloides parasite.) Looss quickly understood that he must have become accidentally infected with hookworm in the laboratory. "Up to this point," he wrote, "I had had no idea that I was suffering from ancylostomiasis [hookworm]; although for weeks I had often felt rather exhausted and indisposed, I had nevertheless blamed this on the unusual heat of the Egyptian summer. A laboratory infection was not considered."[13]

In seeking to solve the mystery of how he had become infected with hookworm, Looss recalled that during earlier experiments with *Ancylostoma duodenale* [hookworm], he had dropped cultures of the young larval forms into the mouths of guinea pigs. On one occasion a few drops had accidentally fallen on the back of his hand. Looss said that he "paid no attention to this moist spot which dried by itself after a few minutes. But at the same time, I felt there was intense burning . . . and the spot became extremely red."[14] In recounting the episode and his carelessness, Looss said he was not concerned because he always maintained good hygiene; he kept his contaminated hands away from his mouth and thoroughly washed his hands with soap and alcohol before eating. Believing as he did at the time that the oral route of transmission was the only possible one, he felt these precautions were adequate to protect him from infection.

Looss could have dismissed his laboratory accident as simply an occupational hazard of working with dangerous organisms. Instead he asked: What did all this mean? To find out, he decided to repeat what he hypothesized had happened accidentally, this time as a deliberate experiment on himself. First, he poured plain water on his hands. Nothing happened. Then he cleaned the back of his hand and dropped hookworm larvae on it, spreading them lightly with the shaft of a scalpel. "Even before the liquid had entirely dried up, the reddening of the skin and the burning sensation started exactly as before," he wrote. "I then scraped off the last moisture residue from the epidermis [outer layer of skin] with the edge of a scalpel and put it under the microscope. The ancylostoma larvae previously present in such abundance had disappeared except for a very few indolent ones; in their place among the scraped-off epidermal cells were found numerous empty worm skins! The larvae themselves could only have penetrated the skin. Immediate pricks with a disinfected needle into the formerly moist spot on the skin failed to indicate the whereabouts of the larvae; none could be detected in the blood which oozed out."[15]

Thymol was available to Looss, and he "undertook two expulsive cures within a week. An examination of the stools undertaken about four weeks after the last cure showed a significant reduction in the number of eggs. Besides, my general state of health had improved so much that I no longer felt any discomfort."[16] But about three months later, feeling tired and occasionally depressed, he found that there were a considerable number of hookworm eggs still in his stools. Although he repeated the expulsion cures with thymol three times, he did not become entirely free of the parasite.

To confirm his hypothesis that the ancylostoma larvae had entered his body through his skin, Looss repeated his experiment on an eighteen-year-old boy whose leg was about to be amputated.[17] An hour before the operation, Looss applied larvae to the skin of the boy's leg. Following removal of the limb, Looss determined that most of the larvae had entered the skin through the hair follicles. He established further certainty of the importance of his finding by repeating the experiment on an otherwise unidentified Egyptian volunteer.

Looss recognized that he had made a revolutionary discovery and called it "an event which, until then, was without analogy in the history of parasites. . . . There was no known case at that time in which intestinal worms were able to penetrate into the bowel from the skin of the host."[18]

Looss's discovery explained why miners were so commonly afflicted with hookworm and why the existing public health control measures were inadequate. Larvae thrived in moist soil and could rapidly enter the body after touching the skin. Miners could become infected by contact with the soil, and people who went barefoot or whose skin was exposed to contaminated soil were also easily infected. Unfortunately, Looss's findings were not immediately accepted because other scientists, including J. S. Haldane (See Chapter Ten: Lifetimes of Self-experimenting) failed when they tried to replicate Looss's experiments. In 1904 Haldane, then a young medical investigator at Oxford, reported a study with Dr. Arthur E. Boycott, a senior researcher at Oxford, in which Boycott repeatedly tried to infect himself "by smearing cultures of larvae on the arm, where they were allowed to remain (bandaged up in a moist condition) for as long as twelve hours."[19] The experiments were repeated through October 1903 "but always with negative results," the two scientists said. The reason why Boycott could not immediately confirm Looss's findings is not known. Nevertheless, seven years later, in 1911, Boycott reported that he had finally succeeded in confirming Looss's work by infecting another colleague.[20]

Meanwhile, Looss, the ever-curious scientist, was troubled by another question: What became of the larvae in the body? By 1904, through experiments on dogs, he could report that the hookworm larvae migrated from the skin through the lymphatic system to the lungs and windpipe, from which they were coughed up and then swallowed into the intestines, where they finally settled.[21]

The next big boost in the fight against hookworm came from a philanthropist who wanted to pay society back for the billions of dollars he had made in oil. The philanthropist was John D. Rockefeller, and in 1909 he created the Rockefeller Sanitary Commission. Its first step was to make a thorough survey of hookworm to determine just where it occurred and how often. Researchers working for the commission in Puerto Rico estimated that the parasite was causing or contributing to about one third of all deaths there at the time.[22] In the southern United States, hookworm sapped the strength of so many schoolchildren—up to ninety percent in some areas—that it may have been responsible for the myth of southern lethargy. Several state boards of health, aided by the Rockefeller Foundation, began antihookworm campaigns. By that time doctors knew the cause of hookworm infection. More important, they had learned how to prevent and cure it.

When the Rockefeller commission began working on hookworm, thymol was the leading treatment. The commission planned to use it to eradicate the disease from the South. Belief in the possibility of eradication was based on the theory that treatment of everyone who was infected would rid them of the worms. The organisms would still, of course, be in the soil, ready to reinfect the same person or to infect more people, but it was thought that reinfection or new cases could be prevented by educating people on the need for sanitary latrines and wearing shoes.

When the Rockefeller Sanitary Commission was merged with the Rockefeller Foundation in 1913, the new organization embarked on a bold plan to put this concept into practice on a global scale—to eradicate hookworm from the entire world. The campaign that had begun in the southern American states was extended to fifty-two countries on six continents.

The successes were dramatic, but literal eradication proved impossible. Health workers learned that not every case of hookworm disease could be eliminated and that people who harbored even a small number of worms were still dangerous because they could spread the infection to others. Nevertheless, the foundation's hookworm program had a major impact on public health. The improved sanitation that resulted from the educational aspects of the campaign not only prevented hookworm infection but also many cases of typhoid fever and diarrheal diseases. Moreover, probably for the first time, communities in the United States were encouraged to fund and to organize public health programs.[23] And the Rockefeller Foundation went on to tackle other parasitic diseases and public health problems by supporting the research of scientists working on these diseases in laboratories around the world.

Among the scientists whom the Rockefeller Foundation supported from the 1920s through the mid-1940s was Dr. Claude Heman Barlow, who performed two daring self-experiments, each on a different continent at a different time in his life.[24] Born in 1876 in Lyons, Michigan, this tall, strong man with angular features went to China in 1908 as a Baptist medical missionary. He worked in Shaoshing, Chekiang Province, which is about 160 miles southwest of Shanghai. There, when Barlow was not treating patients, he learned to write Chinese with a brush. By 1911, his interest had turned to a parasitic disease caused by an inch-long fluke called *Fasciolopsis buski* that lives in the small intestine. This parasite was a major public health problem in China. Up to 50 percent of the patients at Barlow's hospital had evidence of the infection, and in some villages it attacked everyone. In Chekiang Province, one and a half million people were at risk of getting the infection. Barlow considered the disease such a problem that in 1914 he interrupted his stay in China to study it at the London School of Tropical Medicine. One year later he returned to China with a grant from the Rockefeller Foundation to study *Fasciolopsis buski.*

Barlow was a blunt, persistent individual who would not let etiquette stand in the way of getting things done. He was an excellent observational biologist, differing from the new breed of experimental scientists who try to understand the workings of the cell by manipulating the biochemistry and molecular biology within it.

Within a few years Barlow was able to describe the life cycle of *Fasciolopsis buski* and to alert public health workers to the role of water chestnuts, a staple of the Chinese diet, in spreading the disease. He found that the larval form of the parasite contaminates the outer layer, or skin, of the water chestnut. People living in Barlow's region traditionally used their teeth to peel the chestnut before eating it. Barlow discovered that the incidence of fasciolopsis infection fell drastically simply by educating people not to use their teeth for this purpose. Much of Barlow's knowledge came from experiments that he did on himself.[25]

On February 16, 1920, after fasting for a few hours to keep his stomach empty, he swallowed two adult *Fasciolopsis buski* flukes that he had collected from infected Chinese patients. He tested his stools for several days, and when he found no evidence of infection in himself, he deemed the experiment unsuccessful, attributing the failure to the possibility that the flukes had been digested in the stomach before passing into the intestines.

To determine whether the presence of food in the stomach would alter his susceptibility to infection, he repeated the experiment on himself three more times from March 5 to May 13, 1920. He drank bicarbonate of soda and condensed milk, swallowed the parasites, and had lunch. On each of these occasions, he swallowed a progressively larger number of flukes—from three to fifteen. "The swallowing of these flukes was indeed a nauseating process even though the experimenter went into a dark room to take them," Barlow wrote.[26] Still, he did not come down with a heavy infection, experiencing only mild symptoms. But he found eggs in his stool continuously for one year until he took beta-naphthol and magnesium sulfate to expel the adult fluke.[27]

In 1929 Barlow moved to Cairo to work on a Rockefeller Foundation program to control hookworm and schistosomiasis. This meant that for the first time Barlow would be working with the schistosome, another member of the fluke group of parasitic flatworms. Without question, schistosomiasis was then, as it is now, the second most common disease in the world, behind malaria. It occurs in seventy countries and infects at least 125 million people.[28] Moreover, at least one billion people live in areas where they are at daily risk of getting schistosomiasis every time they deposit their excreta and use the same water supply to do their daily chores. Africans in at least twenty-five countries, chiefly in the central and southern areas of the continent, risk getting schistosomiasis each time they dip their hands into water to do their laundry or to catch fish.

The parasites that cause schistosomiasis were first described in 1852 by Theodor Bilharz, a German doctor living in Cairo, and today, in many of the seventy countries where schistosomiasis is a health hazard, the disease often goes by the name bilharziasis.[29] The schistosome flatworm is about an inch in length. The three species that most commonly infect humans—*Schistosoma hematobium, S. japonicum,* and *S. mansoni*—each cause a different form of infection in different areas of the body.[30] The parasite has an extremely complicated life cycle, and to complete it, certain forms of the organism must live for a period in certain species of freshwater snails, giving the disease a third name—snail fever.

Schistosome larvae have suckers by which they attach themselves to their victim's skin. Within a few minutes after an individual touches contaminated water, the larvae bore through the skin, and the young parasites migrate through the circulatory system to the lungs and the liver to their final dwelling place. *S. japonicum* and *S. mansoni* settle in the blood vessels of the intestines; *S. hematobium* ends up in the urinary bladder. The young parasites mature into adult worms that usually thrive unmolested by the body's normal immunological defense mechanisms.[31]

In Cairo Barlow worked with another parasitologist, Dr. J. Allen Scott, to investigate schistosomiasis. Through his studies Barlow devised a plan to control the disease in Egypt by sustained efforts to clear the canals of snails.[32]

In 1944 the sixty-seven-year-old Barlow, now at an age when most people retire, embarked on another bold self-experiment—this one even more daring than his first. World War II was being fought, and Barlow feared that servicemen who had been infected with schistosomiasis during the war might pass the parasite on to previously uninfected snails on their return to the United States. He became determined to find out if the schistosome parasite could develop in any species of snail native to the United States. To do this, he needed a supply of schistosomes. This presented a problem: Scientists had been unable to grow in the laboratory the species of snail that carried the parasite. The snails were too fussy; they could not, like mice, be kept alive artificially. Some experts felt that even if the snails could be grown, they could not be infected under laboratory conditions. Several researchers, Barlow among them, had tried infecting animals in a country where the disease was common and sending them to laboratories in countries where the disease did not occur. But the animals usually died in transit. Further, the animal models were of limited utility for schistosomiasis research: Barlow knew from hours spent observing snails and other life in their natural habitat that the schistosome did not behave the same way in laboratory models as it did in the wild. But Barlow had an idea of how to solve his dilemma. He would import the schistosomiasis infection to the United States in his own body. He would give the infection to himself.[33]

In addition to Barlow's ethical belief that he should go first, just as he had in his first self-experiment in China, he had another reason for self-experimenting; it was the easiest way he knew to bring the infection into the United States. No permit was needed.[34]

It was the first recorded voluntary schistosomiasis infection in medical literature. It was also a controversial experiment, and Barlow did it against the advice of at least one colleague, Dr. Julius M. Amberson, then head of the U.S. Navy's preventive medicine unit in Egypt.[35] Amberson warned Barlow that the life-threatening risks of the infection were too great for anyone to try to acquire it voluntarily. Barlow disagreed. So did Horace W. Stunkard, a parasitologist who would work with Barlow in the United States and who had been assigned by the surgeon general to do a three-year study to determine whether native snails could transmit the parasite. Stunkard told me he had supported Barlow's position, citing a scientific paper in which he had stated: "The possible establishment of schistosomiasis in North America is more than an academic postulate." Moreover, Stunkard explained that the snails could not have been easily sent from the United States to Egypt for purposes of the experiment. Even if they had been sent, there was not much chance they would have survived. In fact, Stunkard said, Barlow had sent him many snails from Egypt and most of them had died in transit.

Barlow began his self-experiment with schistosomiasis in Egypt on May 31, 1944. On four occasions over a three-week period, he applied specific numbers of *S. hematobium* parasites, the type that produces an infection affecting the bladder, to the skin over his left forearm and to his navel. At the same time Barlow also infected a baboon with exactly the same number of parasites. His purpose was to study the natural course of the disease in parallel species—in a human, himself, and in an animal.

On July 4, 1944, twenty days after his principal exposure to the parasites, Barlow flew to the United States, accompanied by the infected baboon. He named him Billy—short for bilharzia. On the flight from Cairo to New York, Billy escaped from the flimsy cage Barlow had made for him, and while Barlow slept, Billy wandered down the aisle, scaring several passengers. The commotion awoke Barlow, who immediately called out, "Here, Billy. Come, Billy." The animal scampered back to Barlow's seat, hugged him, returned to his cage, and stayed there for the rest of the flight.

Barlow also brought along an infected hedgehog and two fat-tailed jerboas, but these animals did not live long once they arrived in the United States.

Barlow's report indicates that he felt well at the time, although Amberson later wrote in a medical journal that before Barlow left Egypt he had experienced "giddy, dizzy, nervous spells, aching muscles, some sweating, a decreased appetite, and irritability."[36]

Once in the United States, Barlow said he remained without symptoms for almost two months and could not be certain he was infected. The first important symptom occurred on October 31, when he experienced itching of his scrotum. Scratching produced four or five spots from which serum oozed. One spot was the size of a pea. From the discharge Barlow identified schistosomiasis eggs. The skin lesions were a highly unusual finding in this type of schistosomiasis.

On November 10, at New York University, Barlow told Dr. Henry E. Meleney that he needed a surgeon to take a biopsy of the skin so that he could look for the worms that were passing the eggs. The eggs were too large to pass through the capillaries that connect arteries and veins. Barlow, apparently puzzled as to how the eggs had reached the skin from the blood vessels, presumed that adult worms were present nearby. He insisted that the biopsy be done immediately. "What impressed me was how well he had learned to control pain from his experience in the Orient," Dr. Dominic DeGiusti, a parasitologist who worked with Barlow, remembered. "As soon as he got up on the table, he ordered the surgeon to start. Barlow refused to take a local anesthetic because he believed the injection might disturb the worms and ruin the experiment. He lay still and did not even grimace as the surgeon cut a piece of skin about one by two inches all the way down to the layer of fat beneath the skin. After the surgeon sewed him up, I told him that I would take him to a taxi so he could go to a station to go home to New Jersey. He said, 'What do you mean taxi? We'll walk.' He walked the pants off me even though he had had that biopsy."

The experiment was a success. The biopsy revealed a pair of adult schistosome worms.

Meanwhile, Barlow periodically observed Billy, who was being cared for by Dr. Stunkard in the animal quarters of the Department of Biology at New York University. Perhaps appreciating that the baboon was experiencing the same symptoms, Barlow would sit and talk to Billy and rub his stomach. Billy and Barlow seemed to understand each other. According to Dr. DeGiusti, "Barlow had such compassion for the animal that when the baboon finally succumbed to the schistosomiasis, he attributed his death to loneliness, not the parasitic disease. However, we did an autopsy and found that the baboon had died from schistosomiasis."

By December, the seventh month of the experiment, Barlow's own symptoms became severe. His temperature rose to 103.6 degrees Fahrenheit at night. When it fell to normal in the morning, he experienced drenching sweats. Blood and mucus appeared regularly in his urine and stools. He urinated frequently, and each time he had difficulty voiding because of the severe pain in his bladder. His rectum also hurt. He could sleep only with the aid of sedatives.

Barlow, the hardy desert nomad, was so sick he could not leave his bed. On December 30, 1944, seven months into his experiment, he wrote Amberson: "For the past two weeks I have almost more pain than I can take, fever, and great bladder distress. It all followed the two biopsies. Worms must have been disturbed and migrated en masse to the urinary plexus bringing with them fever and intoxication. . . . I am glad to be alive."[37]

On January 9, 1945, Barlow noted: "I have been in bed since 16 December. I have had rather a close call and rough sledding. I had a fever up to 104.2 Fahrenheit and great pain. Urinations every twenty minutes for three weeks and but little sleep during that time. Now things are settling down and the case has become chronic. No more fever, urinations free and spaced about two or three hourly, day and night. I sleep fairly well and life looks brighter again. . . . I do hope it has not all been in vain because I have suffered a lot."[38]

Despite his pain, Barlow continued to be the diligent scientist. He frequently examined his own specimens and kept an almost daily record of his clinical and laboratory observations.[39] He tested semen from his ejaculate. In tests of his urine he found he was passing up to twelve thousand eggs in each day's twenty-four-hour urine specimen.

By February he was still a sick man. ". . . it is not a light infestation. I have blood all the time in the urine and a good deal of bladder discomfort. It was a close call and I will not be sorry to cure it up."[40]

Barlow gave no indication to his colleagues of how long the experiment would last. He was reluctant to be treated with any medication, even aspirin, lest it possibly interfere with the course of the research. But by April 1945, ten months after he had infected himself, he was so sick that he finally consented to injections of a drug called Fouadin.[41] Five days later, Barlow flew back to Cairo because his home leave had expired and he had to return to work.

By the end of June, which was now more than one year after his initial exposure to the schistosome parasites, Barlow was still passing eggs in his urine. Fouadin treatment was repeated over a nineteen-day period, but the drug caused fever and painful urination and defecation. Furthermore, in October, three months after completion of the second course of drug therapy, eggs still appeared in his urine. (In retrospect, Barlow attributed the failure of the cure to the fact that the dosage had been calibrated for Egyptian patients. Barlow, at 180 pounds, weighed about fifty percent more than most Egyptian adults.)

On November 20 he was admitted to a Cairo hospital that specialized in treating schistosomiasis. He received injections of antimony, a drug so toxic that it has to be administered in small doses into the veins; any leaks into the tissues during the injection can cause damage that may necessitate amputation. The treatment was painful. Barlow's mouth watered. He vomited. His head ached. He was dizzy. His muscles cramped. He had poor coordination, particularly of his legs. He lost some hearing. His teeth ached. His heart beat erratically. By January 1946 an electrocardiogram showed damage to his heart, presumably from a toxic complication of the drug. But the antimony treatment successfully cleared Barlow's infection, and by December 1945, eighteen months after the initial exposure, he stopped shedding eggs. Later he looked back on his experience:

"If anybody ever tells you that the treatment is not too bad, advise them to take only one injection and report later. It is filthy . . . I used to sit with my watch in hand checking the injection. As soon as it was made it took from five to seven seconds before I began to salivate and then but a few minutes before I began to cough or to vomit. All that day I was fearfully nauseated. On the following day the nausea began to subside, only to come back in full force on the subsequent day of injection. No wonder the little boys and girls run away from it. No wonder that the men and women go only halfway through with the treatment."[42]

Although President Truman awarded the Medal of Merit to Barlow in 1948, some experts believe he risked too much for too little. Even his critics conceded, however, that Barlow's was the first chronicle of the natural course of schistosomiasis infection. He made continual observations on the course of the infection from the time of exposure to ultimate cure and provided material for teaching and research in the United States. His experiment conclusively proved that *S. hematobium* could cause sores on the skin and that from these sores eggs could be passed out of the body. Hitherto, doctors had believed that the eggs came out of either the urine or feces. Barlow had shown that they could also emerge from the skin and could theoretically infect snails.

Barlow had hoped that he could conduct field experiments to learn whether he could pass the parasites to American snails, but he had become so sick from his experimental infection that he had been forced to abandon this goal. Stunkard continued his studies in this area but was unable to infect any of the twenty-five native species with the *S. hematobium* parasite. Nevertheless, despite his three-year study, Stunkard said he had tested too few specimens to conclude that schistosomiasis could *not* be established in snails in the United States.

Today victims of schistosomiasis no longer need suffer the toxic and painfully prolonged treatment that Barlow went through. His case and those of many others spurred researchers to find less toxic and more effective drugs (oxyamniquine and praziquantel).

Claude Heman Barlow died in 1969 of causes unrelated to parasites. He was ninety-three.

Clyde, Looss, and Barlow contributed immeasurably to our knowledge of parasitic diseases. However, despite the advances made from their self-experiments and despite the introduction of new, more effective drugs, parasitic diseases are making a comeback. They are a growing problem in the areas of the world where a majority of people live. In Egypt, for example, schistosomiasis has spread over much of the country as a result of the building of the Aswan Dam; the spreading waters gave the snail a larger breeding area and with a sharply rising population in the region, more people have become infected.

The spread of parasitic diseases is also due to their neglect by international research.[43] One reason why scientists may not be attracted to parasitological research is quite simply a matter of money. In 1981, for example, American taxpayers spent $1 billion on cancer research whereas just $80 million was spent by all countries combined on research in tropical diseases. According to the World Health Organization, 97 percent of the world financing for biomedical research is spent on health problems occurring in developed countries, compared with only three percent for diseases that are the scourge of people in the Third World. Now that the World Health Organization is leading an intensified program aimed at stimulating researchers in the developed countries to tackle the major parasitic diseases, we can expect that other scientists will join David Clyde, Arthur Looss, and Claude Barlow in the fight against parasites and that these scientists, too, will add to our knowledge of these widespread and devastating killers by daring to go first.

# Chapter Eight

# TOXIC SHOCKS

Over the North Pole one day in November 1975, ham and cheese omelets were being served to 344 soft drink salesmen aboard a Japan Air Lines 747. The plane was more than an hour from Copenhagen, its last scheduled fuel stop on a flight from Tokyo to Paris via Anchorage. As the plane descended toward Copenhagen, some of the passengers in the forward section grabbed the paper bags from the pockets in the seat in front of them and vomited; they thought they were airsick. They were unaware that they were the first victims of what would turn out to be the largest food poisoning outbreak ever to occur aboard a commercial airliner. They were also unaware that if their pilots had eaten the same meal, all might have died in a crash.[1]

As the soft drink salesmen disembarked, an epidemic of vomiting and diarrhea struck in the airport lounge. Dozens of passengers lay prostrate with cramps; 144 were admitted to hospital. Scores of others less severely affected were treated in makeshift emergency rooms. Because none of the doctors understood Japanese and few victims spoke either English or Danish, Japanese-speaking waiters and chefs were summoned from Copenhagen restaurants to act as interpreters.

As the salesmen began to recover, public health workers in Alaska and Denmark, who had teamed up to do the laboratory and epidemiologic studies, traced the epidemic to a food handler in Anchorage, where omelets had been prepared by the airline's catering service. The food handler had sores on his fingers—infections caused by the staphylococcal bacterium, which is commonly called "staph"—but he had regarded the sores as trivial and had not reported the infection to his superior. As a result, he had inadvertently transferred staph from his infected fingers to slices of ham during the few seconds that he had touched them while preparing the omelets. In the ensuing hours the staph multiplied and produced large amounts of a heat-resistant toxin, a poison that was not destroyed when the stewardesses cooked the omelets aboard the jet and served them. Fortunately, the pilots' biological clocks had been set to Alaskan, not European, time; preferring supper to breakfast, they had eaten steaks instead of omelets.

Within three days, laboratory workers in the United States and Denmark, using a method called "phage typing" to identify subgroups of staphylococci, found the same types of organisms in the leftover food, the patients' vomitus, and the food handler's sores.[2] Several days later, as the last Japanese salesman left the hospital, the head of the Japan Air Lines catering service in Anchorage committed suicide. He was the only fatality of the outbreak.

Staphylococci are among the most versatile of bacteria.[3] They are the commonest cause of infections acquired in hospitals; they cause pimples, boils, carbuncles, and other more serious skin infections. Staph can invade the soft tissues below the skin to form abscesses. They can infect the bone, causing osteomyelitis, or spread through the circulatory system as blood poisoning. Sometimes they infect the lining and valves of the heart. Less often, they form abscesses in the brain. And, as the unfortunate salesmen aboard the Japan Air Lines 747 discovered, staphylococci can cause food poisoning.

No one knows when staphylococci emerged as a major cause of disease. Some bacteriologists believe they may have caused osteomyelitis in certain dinosaurs.[4] Even if this is true, the role of staphylococci in human disease was not recognized until the late nineteenth century. The famous German scientist Dr. Robert Koch, who identified and did pioneering experiments with the bacteria that cause anthrax, cholera, and tuberculosis and who won the Nobel Prize for his pioneering work in bacteriology, may have seen what we now know as staph bacteria in specimens he made from human pus in 1878. Two years later, Louis Pasteur succeeded in growing staphylococci in broth, though he did not recognize the diseases that they cause. While Pasteur worked in France, Alexander Ogston, a thirty-six-year-old Scottish surgeon, carried out independent studies using chemical staining and other laboratory techniques pioneered by Koch.[5] Ogston is credited with having discovered that staphylococci are an independent species that can cause disease. From microscopic studies of the pus obtained from eighty-two human abscesses, he identified clusters of a certain bacterium. Ogston named the newly discovered bacterium "staphylococcus" from a derivative of the Greek word "staphyle," meaning a bunch of grapes.

Bacteria are single-cell organisms. Each divides into two other cells asexually by a technique that biologists call binary fission. In staphylococci, the cell divisions occur at angles so that three-dimensional clusters are formed, giving them the grapelike look seen by Ogston. But staphylococci can also appear singly or as chains of fewer than four organisms. They are very hardy and more resistant than most other bacteria to disinfectants. They can be cultured from dried pus after as long as three months. Furthermore, they are found virtually everywhere—in dust, air, food, mammals, birds, and humans. No one can escape them. Newborn babies enter the world free of staphylococci, but soon thereafter they harbor them. From the first week of life, staphylococci become part of the harmless and often valuable sea of microorganisms known as "the normal flora" that live on the outside of the human body and in the intestines. By adulthood, about one third of healthy people harbor staphylococcal bacteria in the nostrils or on the surface of the skin without evidence of staphylococcal disease. On occasion, another one third of people harbor these bacteria without becoming ill. But staphylococci can be dangerous.

In 1881 Ogston injected staphylococci into animals and produced experimental infections in the laboratory. He thereby linked staphylococci to the serious, often fatal, infections then called "hospital sepsis" which frequently followed surgical operations, particularly amputations. His reports to the German Surgical Society, medical journals, and the British Medical Association stirred the scientific community to undertake a series of bacteriologic investigations that contributed to a late-nineteenth-century revolution in pathology, the branch of medicine that determines the cause of disease through microscopic and toxicologic studies of the body's organs. These investigations, many of them involving self-experimentation, taught us about the ability of staphylococci to cause infection and outbreaks of food poisoning such as the one that occurred on the Japan Airlines flight.

Staphylococcal food poisoning is so common that most of us have suffered from it, often without even knowing it. It is rarely fatal, but the symptoms can sometimes be briefly dire. Recognition of the role of staphylococci in causing food poisoning came about through a series of self-experiments. The first was in 1884, three years after Ogston's discovery. In that year Dr. Victor C. Vaughan, a physician who became one of the leading public health researchers of his day (see Chapter Six: The Myth of Walter Reed), investigated a series of outbreaks of illness attributed to cheeses produced by a manufacturer in Michigan. After he found that feeding the contaminated cheese to animals produced no ill effect, Vaughan ate the cheese himself. "There was considerable nausea," he reported, "and I could readily believe that a larger amount would have caused vomiting."[6] Over the next quarter of a century, other doctors in Europe and the United States identified staphylococci in contaminated food, but they could not reproduce the illness in experiments on animals.

In 1913 Dr. Marshall A. Barber, an employee of the American government in the biological laboratory at Manila in the Philippines, learned of repeated outbreaks of "milk poisoning" on a farm in Luzon.[7] Barber made several visits to the Luzon farm and discovered a seasonal pattern to the outbreaks; most occurred during the hot, dry period of the year. He himself had been the victim of stomach upsets three times. He noted that he remained healthy as long as he drank fresh milk. But when he swallowed a sample of cow's milk that had remained at room temperature for a day, stomach and intestinal symptoms came on quickly. Barber may have been the first to describe bovine mastitis, the staphylococcal infection of cows that contaminates milk.

Other volunteers who swallowed the suspect milk confirmed Barber's findings. Barber continued to experiment on himself. He added samples of the staphylococcal bacteria grown from the milk in the laboratory to refrigerated fresh milk and drank it. He developed violent symptoms and concluded that the illness was due to a poison formed by the staphylococcus in the milk. "The fresh milk was harmless," Barber wrote, "and the toxin was produced in effective quantities only after the milk had stood some hours at room temperature." Barber observed that whereas individuals who drank the milk continuously seemed to have developed some tolerance to the toxin, he had not. "In my own case, four acute attacks, three of them severe, afforded no protection against a subsequent fifth dose."[8]

Despite Barber's experiments, his findings were not appreciated for another fifteen years. During that interval, most staphylococcal food poisoning outbreaks were ascribed to other causes. When, for example, two thousand German soldiers in World War I suffered gastrointestinal symptoms typical of staph food poisoning and investigators found in the sausage they ate large numbers of two bacteria —staphylococci and *Proteus vulgaris*—the symptoms were wrongly attributed to proteus, which we now know to be a harmless organism found in the bowel. Staph food poisoning went unrecognized and therefore uncontrolled.

The rediscovery of staphylococcus as a cause of food poisoning came in 1929 after a lengthy investigation in Chicago, where eleven people had become violently ill from eating Italian Christmas cakes.[9] They were three-layered sponge cakes held together by a custard sauce and decorated with chopped pistachio nuts and maraschino cherries. The cakes had been delivered as presents to the homes of two doctors who, after the illness struck, sent the remainder to three University of Chicago scientists who were interested in food poisoning: Dr. Gail M. Dack, Dr. William E. Cary, and Dr. Edwin O. Jordan. Dack, through several scientific studies, had helped dispel the widely popular idea that food poisoning was caused by ptomaines, substances formed by bacteria in the decomposition of food and that until then were believed to be the principal cause of food poisoning.[10]

The three scientists fed samples of the cake to mice, rabbits, and monkeys, but nothing untoward occurred. Then they separated each component of the cake and prepared specimens to test on themselves. One ate a sample of the custard. Nothing happened. Another ate the frosting. Again, no symptoms developed. They went on to the nuts and cherries. Still, no one who ate the samples got sick.

By mid-January 1930, the sponge part of the cake was all that was left to test. It was Dr. Dack's turn, and he ate the sample at home, just after lunch. Later, as he was about to sit down for supper, he suddenly ran from the table to spend an hour in the bathroom. His wife heard him say, between paroxysms of vomiting and diarrhea, "Oh, this is wonderful." But Mrs. Dack thought otherwise. Believing that her husband was about to die, she summoned his partner, William Cary, who came but could offer little comfort other than staying by Dack's bedside until he recovered.

Dack's team now prepared a solution derived from the staphylococci found in the sponge layer and fed it to three additional researchers. They also became sick. Despite the University of Chicago team's findings, widespread skepticism remained about the role of staphylococci in food poisoning. When veterinarians examined cows that were the source of milk incriminated in outbreaks, they found no evidence of infection; they did not realize that a cow could spread staphylococci without showing symptoms of disease. When staphylococci were identified in cultures from samples involved in food poisoning outbreaks, the organisms were often regarded as irrelevant contaminants. Although the existence of staphylococcal toxins had been suspected since the beginning of the century, the rudimentary knowledge of biochemistry made their actual detection impossible.

The earliest recognized incident involving these toxins, and one of the few fatal outbreaks, did not involve food poisoning at all. In Bundaberg, Australia, in 1928, twelve children died following injections to prevent diphtheria. Medical investigators, among them Sir Frank Macfarlane Burnet, who later shared a Nobel Prize for his studies in immunology, found that the deaths were due to a powerful exotoxin that had been produced by staph bacteria.[11] In the Bundaberg Disaster, as it came to be known, the exotoxin had formed by accident. When the first set of diphtheria injections had been given, staphylococci from the skin of the injected children were transferred to the rubber-capped vial of diphtheria immunization material. The vial had been left unrefrigerated for a week in the subtropical heat, and during that time the staphylococci produced exotoxin. When the doctors used the vial to give the next set of diphtheria shots, more than half of the children who were inoculated with it died. The children who survived suffered severe skin infections.[12]

The Bundaberg Disaster stimulated some bacteriologists to study staphylococcal toxins, and one scientist who joined these investigations was Dr. Claude E. Dolman. In 1929, when Dolman first began to study staphylococci, he was twenty-five years old and had just graduated from St. Mary's Hospital Medical School in London, where Dr. Alexander Fleming, who discovered penicillin, and Dr. Almroth E. Wright, a self-experimenting pioneer in the development of vaccines (See Chapter Five: The Pasteurian Club) were among his teachers. The scientific report of the Bundaberg Disaster had just been published, and Fleming encouraged Dolman to experiment with staphylococcal toxins. In one experiment, Dolman shocked his colleagues when he duplicated the conditions of the Bundaberg Disaster and prepared a toxin so potent that it killed a rabbit during Dolman's short lunch break.

Dolman moved to Canada in 1931 and continued his research on staphylococcal toxins, trying to learn, among other things, what substance within the staphylococcus was responsible for producing the symptoms of food poisoning. Although he now knew that injections of exotoxin could kill, he also found out that large amounts of the same substance had no adverse effect when fed by mouth to animals.

The next logical step was to ask human volunteers to swallow the staphylococcal exotoxin.

First Dolman himself ate different preparations of staph toxin, and then he sought additional volunteers among his colleagues by putting up notices on the bulletin boards of the laboratory. His own signature was soon followed by that of the director and then by those of forty other colleagues. Dolman found among Canadian researchers the same willingness to volunteer for each other's experiments as he had known in England. Years later, when I talked with him about it, he explained that though willing, the volunteers were also cautious. "You certainly wanted to know the credentials of the person who was propositioning you," he said, "because you would not do it for everybody. Some were a little wilder than others."[13]

On 110 occasions, Dolman and his volunteers swallowed staphylococcal toxin similar to the type produced in the Bundaberg Disaster; nothing happened to any of them.[14] Clearly, the staphylococcal exotoxin was not identical to the one responsible for food poisoning.

The discovery raised a fundamental question: Did staphylococcal food poisoning exist at all? The University of Chicago group's self-experiments had implied that it did, yet medical leaders in England and elsewhere scoffed at the notion. Dolman studied more than two hundred strains of staphylococci. He passed each of them through a filter to collect the fluid that contained the staphylococcal toxin. In addition, the University of Chicago researchers sent him samples of strains of staphylococci that had been isolated from outbreaks of food poisoning.

It took enormous willpower for Dolman and his volunteers to swallow the samples. Because the experiments were so unpleasant, often leading to vomiting and diarrhea, Dolman developed tests that he could do on animals instead. Monkeys were too expensive and too difficult to work with. Dogs were prone to vomit too readily. So Dolman chose cats and developed what became known as the Dolman "kitten test" for staphylococcal toxins. Samples of food from incriminated outbreaks were injected through a needle that pierced the kitten's skin over the abdomen and went into the peritoneum covering the intestines, or directly into the veins. The test for staphylococcal food poisoning was positive if the kitten vomited after the injections. However, as scientific controversy about its value mounted, the kitten test was replaced by other laboratory techniques.

Dolman's laboratory studies helped show that the staphylococcal-produced enterotoxins are distinct from the lethal exotoxins. (It is believed that enterotoxins act on the centers of the nervous system that control the intestines and thus produce symptoms indirectly.) Dolman also showed that only a few strains of staphylococci produce the toxins responsible for food poisoning. Further self-experiments suggested to him that the enterotoxin of staphylococci acted specifically on the cells that lined the intestines.

During World War II Dolman experimented on himself and other volunteers with several additional forms of food poisoning. One of the volunteers in these experiments was a graduate student who later became a physician and his wife. The experiments required fortitude more than bravery; the risks in reality were not great.

In some of these experiments, Dolman squirted a small, measured amount of the test solution through the crust of a meat pie or into a sausage. He let the pies sit at room temperature for eight hours to mimic the condition of a food poisoning outbreak and to allow the organisms injected to grow—and, if they could, produce toxin. Then Dolman and his volunteers ate the meat pies or sausages.

Their symptoms varied according to the type of food poisoning under study, and the severity varied according to the dose involved. In the case of staphylococcal food poisoning, the symptoms usually developed abruptly, with an uncontrollable bout of vomiting from one to five hours after eating the test material. Then there was a great sense of relief as the vomiting, severe abdominal cramps, and diarrhea abated. However, any sense of relief disappeared quickly; it took only a few minutes for the symptoms to come back. Dolman and his volunteers experienced as many as sixteen paroxysms in a twelve-hour period. Often they developed a pinched, shocked appearance due to dehydration. The pulse would speed up and the volunteers would sweat, often profusely. Sometimes they were left with little desire to eat for several days. Other times, their appetite returned very quickly. There were many occasions when, even though they knew they would survive, they still felt they were about to die. But no one did. In reporting these findings to his colleagues, Dolman wrote:

"The ordeal can perhaps be compared to pregnancy, in that it may have been light-heartedly enough embarked upon the first time, but is not so willingly repeated; and in its being made bearable, as the situation moves toward a climax, only by the reflection that deliverance is bound to come. In one or two instances, a degree of exhaustion set in which bordered on collapse."[15]

From these experiments, Dolman proved that many—but not all—strains of staphylococci produce the enterotoxin that causes food poisoning. Once he had established that fact, he set out in another series of self-experiments to determine the ability of those toxins to produce immunity. Among the questions he asked were: Would repeated episodes of staphylococcal food poisoning confer immunity against further attacks? Could a vaccine be developed to prevent attacks?

Dolman devised a set of experiments that he performed on himself, his wife, and other volunteers. First he determined the minimal amount of enterotoxin that, when swallowed, would cause food poisoning in each volunteer. Then he gave a series of injections of this amount of staphylococcal enterotoxin in the upper arm of each volunteer over intervals of from four to seven days. Those injections often produced generalized temporary reactions characterized by symptoms of chills, fever to 103.6 degrees Fahrenheit, backache, loss of appetite, and general malaise. Last, within a few days of completing the series of immunization shots, each volunteer swallowed staphylococcal enterotoxin to challenge the potency of the vaccine by determining if there was any change in the volunteer's ability to withstand symptoms of staphylococcal food poisoning. For at least a seven-month period following the injections, Dolman maintained an immunity to more than four times the dosage that had previously caused him to suffer staphylococcal food poisoning. His self-experiments had shown that partial immunity could be produced, but that a vaccine was not a practical way to guard humans against staph food poisoning.

The upset stomachs that Dolman and his colleagues suffered made it clear that in most instances food poisoning is a misnomer, because although some foods are inherently poisonous, illness is more often due to contaminants, organisms, and toxins, and not to something in the food itself. Food is usually only the vehicle that carries disease-causing bacteria and toxins. Public health workers now know that many cases of food poisoning are due to staphylococci and that in general these bacteria affect high-protein foods such as milk, ice cream, cheese, custards, cream-filled pastries, ham, cured meats, chicken and meat salads, and sausages. Although many people believe that a food is safe for eating unless it smells or tastes spoiled, this is not the case; food contaminated with staphylococci often smells and tastes delicious. In many instances, symptoms produced by staphylococcal food poisoning may be falsely attributed to some other condition unless a fairly large cluster of cases such as the outbreak on the Japan Air Lines jumbo jet makes the diagnosis self-evident.

If staphylococcal food poisoning is rarely fatal, staphylococcal infections involving other body systems often are—and it took another daring series of self-experiments to convince doctors of their potential for harm.

Alexander Ogston's discovery of staphylococci was widely accepted, but until such infections could be deliberately produced in humans, and not just in animals, there were valid reasons for scientific skepticism about the ability of the bacteria to cause disease. Doctors in the late nineteenth century wondered if the same grape-like staphylococci could cause serious and painful infections such as osteomyelitis in bones, as well as superficial, minor infections such as boils—and if so, how? A century ago bacteriology was in its infancy, and it was hard for doctors to conceive of what we now take for granted—that the same organism can cause different clinical types of infections.

Some early answers to the questions about staphylococci came from the self-experiments of Dr. Carl Garré, a bacteriologist and surgeon in Basel, Switzerland.[16] Garré cultured staphylococci from bones diseased with osteomyelitis and from infections on and under the skin. When he tested the cultures from sixty-eight different sources with the methods then available, he could not detect any difference among the staphylococci. Could staphylococci isolated from a case of osteomyelitis, he wondered, cause an abscess if they were put into soft tissues beneath the skin? This question could only be answered with experimental proof. The Swiss surgeon designed such an experiment and performed it on himself because, as he said, he "lacked any other human volunteer."

On June 6, 1883, the twenty-six-year-old Garré scratched the outer edges of his nail bed with a platinum wire. On the wire were staphylococci freshly isolated from the blood of a thirty-nine-year-old man who suffered from osteomyelitis. For a few hours following the inoculation, Garré felt a light burning sensation. Because the scratch produced only a tiny red spot after twenty-four hours, he repeated the experiment a week later. On June 13, Garré rubbed staphylococci into three small scratches that he had made on another finger, also near the outer edges of the nail bed. This time, he probed a little deeper into the skin. "The redness was more intense and lasted longer," he reported. On the second day of the experiment, pus collected beneath the nail bed and the nail edges. He identified staphylococci in a sample, thus confirming that the bacterium was the cause of the inflammation.

Garré experimented again on June 17. First he examined his arms to make certain there were no pimples or staphylococcal infections that he might have acquired naturally. There were none. Then he cleaned the skin below the elbows with distilled water and made a scratch in each arm. He took staphylococci that he had isolated from a patient and "rubbed the staph culture in the manner of an ointment" on his left forearm. As a scientific control, he then rubbed gelatin into the wound on the other arm.

For about one hour both forearms felt warm. But six hours later, the staphylococcal wound began to burn in an "increasingly unpleasant and intensive" way which "felt very much like after contact with nettles—red and swollen." During the evening, more than twenty pinpoint pustules began enlarging around the bases of the hair on his forearm. By the following morning, the burning sensation became a stabbing pain which spread over the entire left forearm as the skin became swollen and painful even to a light touch. In what surely must have been an understatement, he reported that "the whole thing began to be unpleasant."

On the fourth day the pustules started to merge into one large carbuncle. About a week after the experiment began, Garré became quite ill with pain, fever, sleeplessness, and swollen lymph nodes in his armpit. Though he may not have realized it, the seeds of a fatal infection were there. He treated himself with the only method available then—hot compresses. It is a method still recommended today, along with antibiotics, which, of course, were not available to Garré. He was lucky. On the eighth day, when the carbuncle broke and discharged pus, he cultured it and identified the same clusters of spherical staphylococci that he had rubbed into his arm. The wound healed naturally over a three-week period but left his arm permanently scarred.

Garré's daring experiments proved conclusively that fatal osteomyelitis as well as simple skin abscesses could be caused by the same staphylococcus, and his report circulated widely. One reader, Dr. Max Bockhardt, a bacteriologist in Wiesbaden, Germany, decided to carry staphylococcal research a step further.[17] At that time, three skin conditions—impetigo, furunculosis, and barber's rash—were thought to be unrelated diseases, but Bockhardt suspected that each was caused by the same staphylococcus. He had tried to prove his theory in experiments on animals but had failed. Influenced by Garré's reports, he decided the only way to prove his point was to inoculate the organism into a human; he used Garré's technique.

On April 14, 1886, Bockhardt cleaned his left forearm with disinfectant, scraped off the top layer of skin with a scalpel blade, and inoculated himself with staphylococci obtained from a patient whose condition was not reported. Six hours later, a painful red pustule began to form. By sunrise the following morning, he could identify twenty-five pinhead-sized pustules, most of which had formed around a hair follicle. Some of the pustules were itchy, and others had bled under the skin; a biopsy showed the staph in the hair follicles. A week later, the pustules healed without scarring.

On April 25, Bockhardt decided to experiment again. He cleaned his left forearm and right hand with a disinfectant. Then, with his right index finger, he scratched the cleansed area, dipped his finger into the staph culture, and swabbed the area that had been scratched. By breakfast the following morning, thirty-five pustules of varying sizes had developed, and a day later twenty-five more appeared, for a total of sixty. Again he noted that most of the pustules were penetrated by a single strand of hair arising from a follicle. Bacteriological tests on ten of the sixty pustules identified them as staphylococci. A week later, the pustules dried and healed without leaving scars. Bockhardt's observation that the staphylococcal infections tended to develop around hair follicles still puzzles doctors. They wonder whether some endocrine factor in the secretions of the sweat gland or the hair follicle enhances the free growth of staphylococci.

Bockhardt, like Garré, was risking his life with these experiments, because the pustules could break down and become a fatal infection. Nevertheless, on May 10, 1886, in an expression of what can only be called German scientific thoroughness, Bockhardt carried out the self-experiment again, this time using a different anatomical area. He injected staphylococci into the nail bed of his left index finger and identified the same organisms from cultures of the lentil-sized abscess that developed forty-eight hours later. He produced what is called a paronychia, an infection of the nail bed, which doctors distinguish from a boil. Bockhardt concluded from these experiments that staph had caused the three infections. We now know he was correct, but his scientific evidence was weak because he never specified the source of the staphylococci for each of his self-experiments.

Meanwhile, a second physician, Dr. Ernst Bumm, a German gynecologist, had confirmed Garré's self-experiments.[18] Bumm told colleagues attending a scientific meeting in Wurzburg in 1885 that he had taken staphylococci from a breast abscess, injected it under his own skin as well as the skin of two other people, and produced abscesses in all three individuals.

These experiments showed that staphylococci could produce infection; it was not until World War II, however, and the discovery of penicillin, that doctors at last had a weapon to help the body kill the staph bacteria. But the weapon proved to be a double-edged sword. Humans and staphylococci had coexisted in a continuing process of mutual evolution and adaptation for millions of years. Widespread use of penicillin upset that evolutionary process. Penicillin killed off many susceptible staphylococci, but it also allowed a greater number of resistant strains to proliferate. By the mid-1950s, epidemics of infections, caused by strains of staphylococci that were resistant to penicillin and other antibiotics, began to occur after operations.

So scientists again began asking questions about staphylococci and hotly debated their viewpoints. Was there any difference in virulence among the strains of staphylococci, they wondered, that could account for the outbreaks? Was there some special circumstance in the process of a surgical operation that increased the chances for infection?

One scientist who believed that certain as-yet-to-be-detected special circumstances were important in causing staphylococcal infections was Dr. Stephen D. Elek. I met Dr. Elek, a native of Hungary who had emigrated to England at the age of twenty-one, on several occasions.[19] He is a short, witty man whose English carries a trace of a Middle-European accent. After taking a fling at business he settled on medicine, eventually becoming a professor of bacteriology at the University of London. In his spare time he was a sculptor, but his working hours were spent at St. George's Hospital, one of the oldest in England and the hospital where John Hunter and Edward Jenner had also practiced. There Elek had already earned an international reputation for discovering a laboratory test to detect the bacterium that causes diphtheria.

But his primary research interest was in staphylococci and wound infections. As a bacteriologist, he preferred to do test tube experiments instead of experiments on animals or humans; test tubes, he felt, reduced test conditions to fewer variables and offered a simpler means of answering scientific questions. But Elek knew that test tube conditions were not always adequate substitutes for living systems. He also knew that results of experiments performed on one species of animal could not necessarily be extrapolated to other species or to humans. In the case of staphylococci Elek doubted that the results obtained from experiments on rabbits and other animals could be validly extrapolated to humans. He pointed out: "Adult birds are known to be highly resistant to human staphylococci, but susceptible to bird-pathogenic [disease-causing] strains. No reliable information can be deduced about the virulence of staphylococci in man from experiments carried out solely on animals."[20]

In 1956, when outbreaks of staphylococcal surgical wound infections had become increasingly frequent in hospitals, Elek realized that the answer would have to come from experiments on humans. His first goal was to compare the ability of various strains to produce disease in humans. Would he find a difference between randomly selected strains of staphylococci taken from the noses of carriers and strains from naturally occurring human infections that were presumed to be more virulent?

In designing such an experiment, he found that no one knew how few staphylococci—the minimum infecting dose—it took to produce disease in humans. The reason was that the earlier experiments by Garré, Bockhardt, and Bumm, among others, did not provide quantifiable information. Accordingly, Elek decided to inject known numbers of pus-forming strains of staphylococci into the skin of humans to determine the minimum infecting dose. He would start with a very small number of bacteria and gradually work his way up to the dose that caused a pustule, or small boil.[21]

Elek discussed plans for the experiment with his partner, Dr. Patrick E. Conen. "We made absolutely sure that the staphylococci would be sensitive to penicillin so that we would improve the chance of cure by using the antibiotic in the event a serious infection developed," Elek remembered. The availability of penicillin was clearly an important factor in Elek's decision to experiment on himself and later on others. As he said: "I'm not particularly brave, and my curiosity is tempered very much by the situation. In the pre-antibiotic era, I would not have regarded it as a riskless experiment. I would not have done it." But even with penicillin the danger was great. "We had to do it to ourselves before we did it on others," Elek said, "because we were venturing into the unknown." Elek had very strong feelings on the subject of human experimentation, and he abhorred the notion held by some that the lives of scientists were too valuable to risk in experiments and that it was wiser to use derelicts as volunteers. "If anything goes wrong and the skid row bum dies, and the experimenter has not done the experiment on himself, he is liable for murder. It's as simple as that. A man is entitled to risk his own life. He is not entitled to risk somebody else's.

"Even if the experimenter thinks the risk is negligible he should not experiment on someone else without doing it on himself first. You can only accurately assess known risks, never unknown ones. In our staphylococcal self-experiments we did not know whether we would create very mild lesions or severe lesions, although we were careful to have penicillin ready to deal with anything that might have gotten out of hand."

Elek did not discuss the experiment with his wife for fear of alarming her. "I did not get clearance from an ethics committee beforehand because there was no such requirement in those days," he said. "We proceeded on the basis of our own code of ethics. Once we decided to do it on ourselves, we just embarked on the project."

Elek and Conen prepared cultures of penicillin-sensitive staphylococci that had been obtained from a patient with a staph infection. Then they measured the number of staphylococcal bacteria in specified amounts of fluid so that they knew how many organisms they would be injecting into themselves. It was a standard technique known as "serial dilution." They planned to start by injecting a small amount of fluid containing about ten staphylococci, and then to increase the dose tenfold each time, from ten to one hundred to one thousand and so on, until they produced an infection.

One evening after they had done their day's work and the technicians had gone home, Conen injected Elek's forearm, putting about ten staphylococci into the skin. Elek did the same to Conen. "I was apprehensive," Elek remembered. The possibility of blood poisoning, or septicemia, haunted him. "I thought of writing a will," he said, "but I didn't because I didn't have anything to leave."

To the surprise of the researchers, nothing had happened when they awakened the next day. Or the following day. Their skin was normal, and the needle marks had disappeared. Elek was still apprehensive, but he went ahead according to schedule. A few evenings later, they injected each other with the next larger dose, about one hundred staphylococci. Again no boils developed.

They tried a third time, injecting each other with about one thousand staphylococci. Still nothing happened. Now Elek became anxious about another problem. "I began to suspect that something was going wrong with the experiment. I was sure the injections would lead to a boil. The only question was: At what dose?"

On the sixth try they injected themselves with one million staphylococci. This time tiny pustules developed on their arms. Elek and Conen considered it inconceivable that the enormous doses of staphylococci that they had shown to be necessary to create an experimental infection would find their way into wounds made in the nearly sterile environment of operating rooms. The experiment seemed to confirm Elek's suspicion that a special set of circumstances must exist to cause infection: scratches in the skin, perhaps, or the presence of a foreign body such as a suture. To prove this thesis, Elek and Conen continued their research by putting sutures into the skin of volunteers. The stitches were purposely contaminated with staphylococci. Some were tied tightly, others loosely; sometimes Elek and Conen made incisions in the skin before threading the stitches, sometimes not.[22]

The experiments showed that there was a drastic reduction—by a factor of at least ten thousand—of the minimum dose required for staphylococci to produce pus when the suture was present.

Elek's study forced scientists to radically change their understanding of how staphylococcal infections occurred. "The concept of staphylococci was altogether wrong," he said. "The staphylococcus is not a pathogen in the same class as the spirochete that causes syphilis. The staphylococcus is an organism with a very low virulence for humans and it requires advantageous situations—a concatenation of circumstances—to set up infection. In other words, it is opportunistic."

Or, as Dr. David E. Rogers, an expert on staphylococcal infections, expressed it to me years later: "Staphylococci are the hyenas of the microbial world because they are unable to initiate infection in a healthy person but are quick to take advantage of breaks in the skin, the normal barrier against invasion of microorganisms, to start infections."[23]

The results of Elek's and Conen's experiments helped explain why so many patients got staphylococcal infections just after surgery and emphasized the importance of sterilized conditions during operations. Dust impregnated with staphylococci can be a factor; so can the surgeon who is not meticulous in handling tissue while operating. The untidy surgeon can leave behind in the body small pieces of devitalized tissue that are cut off from the blood supply, making it harder for the body's scavenger cells and immunological defense mechanisms to attack them. Bacteria thrive on the tiny bits of tissue, and the sutured wounds create an environment that is prone to staphylococcal infections.

In 1980 an extraordinary event once again thrust staphylococci into the news. That year, the United States witnessed an epidemic of a condition known as toxic shock syndrome, which is characterized by fever, headache, mental confusion, muscle pains and weakness, vomiting, and diarrhea—non-specific symptoms that accompany myriad illnesses. But toxic shock syndrome is also characterized by other, more specific symptoms. A skin rash can last several days and then fade, to be followed by peeling of the skin, particularly of the palms and soles of the feet. Worse, lethal complications can occur: potentially fatal heart rhythm abnormalities, fluid in the lungs, kidney failure, and gangrene. At any time the blood pressure may drop suddenly, and if it remains low enough for a long enough period, circulatory collapse, producing shock, can result.

Toxic shock syndrome made headlines after it was linked in epidemiologic studies to the use of tampons, largely Rely Tampons, in menstruating women, many of them adolescents. The illness was attributed to the effects of a toxin produced by staphylococci. In the wake of epidemiologic reports and in the belief that the characteristics of superabsorbent tampons promote the growth of staphylococci, Procter and Gamble stopped marketing its Rely Tampons. But cases continued to appear: from 1979 to July 1986 more than 2800 cases from all fifty states. About four percent of them were fatal. Although the preponderance of cases was among menstruating women, about fifteen percent of them occurred among nonmenstruating females—and males. Scientists considered toxic shock syndrome to be "a unique new syndrome."

Yet it was neither unique nor new. Rather, it was a new twist to an old problem—a new version of the Bundaberg Disaster and a resurfacing of an old disease: scarlet fever.

In all the research on toxic shock syndrome, apparently only one experiment was performed on a human; it was a self-experiment conducted in 1973 by Dr. Richard V. McCloskey, an infectious disease expert who was then working in San Antonio, Texas.[24] McCloskey was curious about a staphylococcal infection in the leg of a twenty-three-year-old female patient known in the scientific literature as D.S. The infection was so severe that it actually ate away the skin and the fibrous tissue of the woman's leg. Antibiotics could not stop the gangrenous process, and doctors were forced to amputate the leg in a desperate attempt to save her life. They did. McCloskey diagnosed D.S.'s illness as an unusual case of scarlet fever; whereas most cases of the condition are caused by streptococcal bacteria, hers was caused by a staphylococcus. Scarlet fever takes its name from the red rash that comes from a toxin produced by both these bacteria.

The staphylococcal form of scarlet fever had become quite rare in the United States by the early 1970s, so McCloskey was anxious to learn all he could about D.S.'s infection. He decided to experiment by injecting rabbits with samples derived from the staphylococci isolated from his patient's blood and skin infection. The animals developed an illness resembling scarlet fever. Now McCloskey went a step further. He wanted to be sure that scarlet fever in a human could also be due to the toxin produced by the staphylococcal bacteria that had caused his patient to lose her leg, as well as the traditionally recognized strep bacteria. This was not idle curiosity on McCloskey's part. He wanted to make an important therapeutic point to his colleagues. Most physicians would almost reflexively prescribe penicillin for scarlet fever on the presumption the rash was due to a toxin produced by streptococcal bacteria. During the first few years of the use of penicillin, the drug did cure both the staphylococcal and the streptococcal forms of scarlet fever, so the choice of antibiotic was not important. But by the 1970s many staphylococci had become resistant to penicillin; the one that caused D.S. to lose her leg was resistant to penicillin and two other antiobiotics, though it was susceptible to another. Thus, the choice of antibiotic could be a matter of life or death.

Therefore McCloskey wanted to make physicians aware of the importance of diagnosing precisely the organism causing the scarlet fever symptoms. He needed to find someone susceptible to scarlet fever and inject that person with samples derived from the staphylococci that had caused D.S.'s infection.

McCloskey tested several volunteers and found none who were susceptible—except himself. So for reasons that were more pragmatic than ethical, he volunteered for his own experiment after he had done a preliminary experiment on rabbits. He and his technician, William Jackson, prepared a staphylococcal solution diluted with saltwater, one part bacteria to forty parts water. Jackson told McCloskey that the dose was far too strong. But McCloskey disagreed, saying: "Oh, no, I am sure I am right." Jackson went ahead reluctantly, injecting the solution into McCloskey's forearm.

Within two hours McCloskey was sick, much sicker than he had expected to be. His muscles began to ache. He developed a fever of 101 degrees Fahrenheit. A six-inch area of skin around the injection site became hot, swollen, and bright red. The pain limited motion of his arm. When McCloskey put pressure on the bright red skin with his finger, it turned white; the reaction was indistinguishable from that of scarlet fever.

McCloskey was very sick. "I don't know what I've done to myself," he told another physician. The six-inch area of reddened skin, as small as it was, was the reason for the drop in his blood pressure, dehydration, and a general toxic reaction.

Jackson, the technician, had been correct. The dose had been excessive. McCloskey, the infectious disease expert, had been wrong. "I had made a serious miscalculation in the dose," he admitted later, "but I was correct in choosing the only animal—a human—on whom the experiment could be done."

McCloskey had learned what a generation of doctors had forgotten: that staphylococcal scarlet fever was a serious, potentially lethal condition. He had given himself a classic case of staphylococcal scarlet fever. His experiment proved, apparently for the first time, that staphylococci as well as streptococci can make a toxin that produces scarlet fever.

McCloskey published a paper describing the results of his experiment in the Annals of Internal Medicine with a dramatic photograph showing the white handprint in his reddened skin. But he had almost forgotten about the scientific paper when, on a hot summer night nine years later in Gladwyne, Pennsylvania (he had moved there from San Antonio), he was summoned from a swimming pool to take a telephone call from Dr. Bruce B. Dan, an epidemiologist at the Centers for Disease Control (CDC) in Atlanta. Dan was thinking about doing on himself a self-experiment similar to the one McCloskey had carried out. "I think you described a case of toxic shock syndrome and didn't know it," Dan told McCloskey.

Dan asked if there were samples of blood from either the woman or McCloskey still in a freezer. There were none. So the next day a technician withdrew a sample of blood from McCloskey's vein and mailed it to CDC researchers in Atlanta. The test results, completed several weeks later, showed that McCloskey's blood contained antibodies to the staphylococcal toxin. Comparative results of antibody tests of blood samples taken before the experiment were necessary to give ironclad scientific proof. But there was no sample from before his self-experiment. Also, because some people have such antibodies without any history of having had toxic shock, it was impossible to prove that the antibodies had formed as a result of the experiment.

Nevertheless, the CDC researchers made some important deductions from the experiment. They assumed that the bacteria in the patient's leg had manufactured a substance, a toxin, which when injected into McCloskey produced the same symptoms. "That was strong enough evidence to support our assumption that you did not need the staph bacteria to produce toxic shock syndrome," Dr. Dan said. It was logical to presume that McCloskey's patient had had toxic shock syndrome and that the physician had given it to himself. Staphylococcal scarlet fever and toxic shock syndrome were the same disease.

But Dan wanted to be sure, so he proposed doing an experiment on himself to conclusively prove the thesis. However, officials at the CDC told him he could not. The reason: A monkey had died in less than a day after it was injected with a biological sample prepared in the laboratory from staphylococci that had been isolated from the vagina of a woman who had toxic shock syndrome. In the years since toxic shock syndrome was first described (the term was first used in a report in 1978, when a group of American researchers linked seven cases of an illness in children to a toxin produced by certain staphylococci) scientists have published hundreds of papers in scientific journals.[25] No one has repeated McCloskey's self-experiment; the results were strong enough to make further confirmation unnecessary. "I wouldn't want anyone to repeat it!" McCloskey said emphatically.

It is now clear that the increased use of tampons was one of the reasons for the rise in the number of staphylococcal scarlet fever or toxic shock syndrome cases. Not only did staphylococci find a favorable place to grow, but in addition the toxin they produced was quickly absorbed through the vagina. But tampons are not the only way people get toxic shock syndrome. Anyone at any age can be struck by this condition. It is a reminder that the method by which many disease-causing microorganisms enter the body is what often determines the symptoms and type of infection. If someone swallows food that is contaminated with staphylococcal toxin, the victim gets food poisoning. If someone has a wound and staphylococci gain access to it, the bacteria will invade the body. Stephen Elek's description—"opportunistic"—is a good one. They are always lurking, waiting for the opportune set of circumstances that will allow them to strike out at their victim. Through the self-experiments of scientists like Elek, Claude Dolman, Richard McCloskey, and others, we understand a great deal more about these ubiquitous, opportunistic bacteria. We know that one type of microscopic bacteria can produce different toxic molecules, each of which can produce different symptoms, and that those symptoms can occur even in the absence of bacteria. We are better able to control the staphylococci, and though the battle between humans and staphylococci is far from over, thanks to these scientists we are keeping more than even.

# Chapter Nine

## FUNGI—INFECTING AND HALLUCINATING

There are at least seventy-five thousand primitive plants that lack leaves, roots, and stems and exist as yeasts, molds, and other forms in air, water, and soil and on animals or other plants. They are the fungi. Some are poisons, others are beneficial as drugs or food, and still others, in a manner similar to the staphylococcal bacteria, are "opportunistic," becoming dangerous to humans under certain specific circumstances.

On the whole, fungi probably do more good than bad. Lacking chlorophyll, they cannot make their own food as green plants do, and so they derive nourishment from other organisms, living or dead. Fungi play crucial and beneficial roles in nature by recycling chemicals from decaying material and thus help to prevent the world from being overrun with the remains of dead plants and animals. They have a nutritional value beyond the mushrooms we add to salads and gravies: They form the molds that ripen cheese. They also produce penicillin, they are also being used increasingly in biochemical research. The red bread mold formed by fungi is helpful to geneticists studying hereditary patterns.

But many fungi are harmful. One caused the potato blight that devastated Ireland in the mid-nineteenth century.[1] Another causes Dutch elm disease, which has killed millions of elm trees and forever changed the look of areas like New England.[2] Still other fungi kill salmon and trout.

Human fungal infections, which are called mycoses, are often confined to the skin, nails, and hair, causing nuisance disorders such as ringworm, athlete's foot, barber's itch, and jock itch. Sometimes, however, human fungal infections can be much more than a nuisance; they can be fatal. They can, for instance, cause opportunistic infections, taking advantage of immune defenses that have been weakened by drugs used to treat cancer or to help prevent rejection of transplanted organs. And they often infect people whose immune system has been knocked out by the newly recognized disease, acquired immune deficiency syndrome (AIDS).[3]

Two of the most notable self-experiments with fungi in recent years produced effects so diverse that it is hard to believe fungi were at the center of both. In one study, the researcher experimented with an organism that can cause fatal infections in humans; in the other, the experimental substance was literally mindbending. Yet *Candida albicans* and lysergic acid diethylamide (LSD) are related, and both are something of a scientific mystery.

*Candida albicans* is one of the most puzzling of the fungi. It can be present in the human body without causing any symptoms, or it can cause rather mild infections, such as thrush, characterized by creamy white patches in the mouth or gullet. (The white patches explain the name of the fungus: "Candida," derived from the Latin, means glowing white.) *C. albicans* can also cause potentially fatal infections when the fungi travel through the blood to settle in the liver, kidneys, heart, or brain. There these organisms can form multiple abscesses that damage the organs and cause generalized toxic reactions and high fevers. Certain conditions such as diabetes and disorders of the immunologic system can, for unknown reasons, predispose some patients to this systemic candidiasis, and it is one of the common infections that kill AIDS victims.

Ironically, candidiasis is mostly a disease of medical progress. It is most often triggered by the use or overuse of antibiotics. In addition to attacking the disease-causing organisms for which they were prescribed, antibiotics also kill large numbers of harmless bacteria—what doctors call the "intestinal flora"—that dwell in the bowel. This allows other organisms, such as fungi, that are not affected by the antibiotic to quickly multiply in the intestines. It does not take long for *C. albicans* to spread into areas of the bowel formerly dominated by other microorganisms. Sometimes so many grow that they overwhelm the body and kill the patient.[4]

In 1968 a doctor in Kassel, West Germany, found himself in a harrowing battle with the *C. albicans* organism. Over a period of several months, half a dozen elderly male patients of Dr. Wolfgang

Krause died. The men had succumbed to candidiasis six to ten days after the doctor had operated on them to repair a broken hip. Krause was deeply disturbed by the deaths of his patients and would perform a daring self-experiment in an attempt to find out how the men had acquired candidiasis and why they had died from it.

I first heard of Krause in 1969, after reading an account of his self-experiment in the *Lancet*, one of the oldest and most prestigious medical journals.[5] Krause had reported a new bit of physiological information, which I brought to the attention of my colleagues at the University of Washington Hospital in Seattle. It became the talk of our group of infectious disease specialists.

Later I went to Kassel, an industrial town near the East German border, to interview Krause. This doctor was neither a laboratory scientist nor a physician intent on devoting his career to scientific investigation.[6] He was a hard-working orthopedic surgeon who had been deeply disturbed by the unexplained deaths of six patients.

Medicine was a natural choice for Krause; there were already three doctors in his family. He had moved to Kassel at age thirty and had become a general assistant in orthopedic surgery at the Orthopädische Landesklinik. Later he was made chief of orthopedic surgery. The choice of specialty was also a natural one. As an adolescent Krause had been one of Germany's top fifty skiers, but an accident had broken his back and he had become a bone specialist instead of a skier.

As a surgeon, Krause was more interested in caring for patients than in doing laboratory research. He considered himself a careful surgeon who took all the customary precautions before, during, and after operating. He could not understand why six of his patients had died. He had prescribed antibiotics to ward off any infection that might have affected them after surgery. They had been fed intravenously, and nurses had been careful to prevent contamination of the tubing that connected the bottles containing saltwater, other fluids, and nourishment with the needle that had been inserted in their arms.

The men had developed slight fevers a day or so after their hip operations, and their temperatures had risen just a bit each day thereafter. Blaming the fever on an undetected infection, Krause had prescribed additional antibiotics. The fevers had gotten worse. The patients' condition had deteriorated slowly; six to ten days after surgery, they had died. That antibiotics had not checked the infections made Krause and his colleagues suspect that the cause was a virus, not a bacterium. Autopsies showed that, in fact, they had died from candida infections of their lungs, kidneys, and other organs.

Deaths of the elderly after surgery were not unusual, and no one blamed Krause. His colleagues assumed that the deaths resulted from contamination of some equipment. But Krause himself was not satisfied. He wanted to make sure that he had not somehow unwittingly contributed to the deaths. He took cultures at various sites in the operating rooms, in the hospital wards, and from the unused intravenous fluids and equipment, but he detected only a few candida organisms—a finding that might have been made in any hospital. He was puzzled, and the more he read about candida, the more puzzled he became. He could find no explanation of how the fungus had entered the patients' bodies. He began to suspect that the antibiotics he had routinely prescribed before surgery had led to an opportunistic infection. And he feared not only that this standard practice might have hidden dangers, but also that with increased use of antibiotics, fungal infections might become an increasingly serious problem.

Medical dogma at that time held that fungi could cause infection within the intestines but could not be absorbed into the body through the walls of the healthy bowel. They could invade other organs only if the bowel were damaged by an ulcer or wound. If the fungi were found in the blood, for example, doctors believed they must have entered through a cut, hole, or tube, not through the intestines. The bowel was thought to act as a protective barrier against most infectious agents.

Krause was not convinced. He wondered whether the fungi could have passed through the wall of some part of the intestines, entered the bloodstream and traveled to various organs of the body. Krause consulted German scientists, who assured him that this was impossible. A person could even swallow large quantities of fungi without consequence. The fungi would simply pass out of the body in the stool.

Then Krause learned that Dr. Gunther Volkheimer at Humboldt University in West Berlin had published articles showing that solid, undissolved food particles passed from the bowel into the body as a secondary aspect of the normal digestive process. Volkheimer's team showed that starch granules and particles as large as ten microns, or 0.00039 inches, could pass from the intestine into the body through a mechanism which the Berlin doctors called "persorption."[7] Krause wondered whether the phenomenon of persorption—if, in fact, it existed—might explain how candida passed from the bowel into the body to cause runaway infection. He consulted a friend, Dr. Horst Matheis, a dermatologist in Kassel who knew Volkheimer. Matheis then spoke to Volkheimer, who told him that the phenomenon of persorption could indeed account for the passage of fungi from the bowel into the body; in fact, he said, it had already been demonstrated in experiments on animals.

Theory and animal experiments were all well and good, Krause reasoned, but documentation that persorption could happen in humans was another matter. He and Matheis decided that the only way to prove the theory would be to swallow enormous numbers of *C. albicans* and see what happened. Krause obtained a special rare strain of the organism from experts in Hamburg to avoid possible confusion with any *C. albicans* that might have found its way naturally into his body without causing symptoms. He chose himself as the volunteer. "I could have asked a patient, but I did not believe anyone would be willing," he explained. "Man is not an animal. The patient could have died. There was this small risk." He did not think, however, that he would be seriously harmed. Unlike the sick, bedridden old men who had died after their hip operations, Krause was young, healthy, and active. Furthermore, he had not taken any antibiotics.

There were also practical considerations. Krause was just beginning his practice. If he asked a patient to volunteer and anything went wrong, he would be risking the lucrative career that was virtually guaranteed him. Undeniably, too, the horrendous experiments practiced by Nazi physicians had left their imprints on postwar German medicine. "In Germany," Krause said, "doctors would have considered this experiment on another man a moral crime. Perhaps doctors of another nationality might have had a different attitude—but not then in Germany."

Volkheimer, who was an expert in bowel physiology, told Krause he considered such an experiment too dangerous. If the fungi did pass through the bowel walls into the body, systemic infection too overwhelming to be stopped by antifungal drugs might develop. Krause disagreed. He believed the experimental candidiasis infection might make a human sick for a short period, but not dangerously so. "After months of discussion," he told me, "there comes a moment when you say, 'I want to know the answer—I want to do the experiment.' And you go ahead."

Krause did not change the will he had made when he had married, but he did buy a life insurance policy for half a million Deutschemarks ($125,000) to cover the period of the experiment. He told his wife what he was going to do but did not share his few doubts about the experiment's safety with her; he wanted to avoid the possibility that she might try to talk him out of it.

Krause considered himself in excellent health. He played soccer and rode horses every day. He had not missed a day's work in years. He had escaped even mild infections for at least three years and had not taken antibiotics for ten. Nevertheless, he had a thorough medical checkup before the experiment. It included routine tests and X rays to exclude the possibility that he had a silent ulcer or undetected bowel disease. Without these tests, any unfavorable experimental results might be criticized.

A week before the experiment, Matheis rubbed swabs over several areas of Krause's skin to pick up any fungi present and then did culture tests in the laboratory to detect the organisms. He also took cultures of Krause's blood, urine, and stool to exclude the possibility that he harbored *C. albicans* organisms. There were none.

On the morning of the experiment, Krause kissed his wife goodbye, saying only that he would be staying at the hospital for three days, as he often did when he was facing a series of difficult operations. That evening, after finishing his work at the Orthopädische Landesklinik, he and Matheis went to the operating room, where everything needed for the experiment, including emergency resuscitation equipment, was waiting. In the room with them were a young surgeon whom Krause had asked to help with the experiment and a nurse.

While Matheis attended to the *C. albicans* samples, the surgeon swabbed Krause's skin. The culture tests were repeated because of the remote chance that Krause had somehow become infected with candida during the week. He had not.

The young surgeon then injected a local anesthetic to deaden the skin over a vein in Krause's left elbow crease and picked up the scalpel to do a procedure he had done many times before. This time he could not bring himself to cut. He was too nervous.

Krause, miffed, did it himself. "I picked up the scalpel, cut my vein, and put the catheter inside myself," he recalled. He pushed the tube several inches up the vein in his arm so that it would stay in place. Samples of blood flowing through the tube were collected at that point and several additional times during the course of the experiment.

By then it was six in the evening. Krause swallowed a brew of white liquid that Matheis had readied. It weighed eighty grams and contained about a billion *C. albicans* organisms. They had been grown earlier in four hundred culture plates in the laboratory. The brew was the size of about two steins of beer. "No problem," Krause said, "for a former German medical student!" During the next hour, Krause drank another stein's worth of mineral water to wash down any fungi that might have stayed in his mouth.

If Krause's theory was correct, the fungi would pass through the bowel wall and enter his blood, causing some sort of reaction. He could not know what that reaction would be. About eight o'clock—two hours after he had swallowed the fungi—Krause suddenly felt ill. He was astonished at how quickly the feeling came on. Over the next seven hours he shivered and his head ached. His temperature rose to 101 degrees Fahrenheit. He felt miserable. But there was a certain elation. He had proved his theory. He was sure that in a few days the repeated cultures Matheis was taking from his blood and urine, among other tests, would confirm that he was suffering from a toxic reaction to *C. albicans.* In the meantime, what would the organism do to his body? He continued to think it would not seriously harm him.

Krause took two doses of Epsom salts to produce diarrhea and speed up the passage of the candida out of his body. And Matheis, after taking several more blood samples, injected a standard dose of Nystatin, an antifungal drug, through the tube into Krause's veins as a precaution. Krause would continue taking Nystatin pills for five more days.

For the first two nights after the experiment, Matheis stayed with Krause at the hospital as a further precaution. Krause continued to feel queasy and did not eat until the second day, when he had tea and biscuits. A specialist in internal medicine examined him periodically and was available at all times by telephone, just in case something went wrong. Nothing did. The self-experiment was over. By documenting that fungi can go through the bowel, enter the blood, and spread to any organ of the body, Krause added one more piece to the giant medical jigsaw puzzle.

Wolfgang Krause did no further self-experimenting. "That was it," he said, "I had proved my point. After the scientific papers were published, I was finished with the experiment and I went on with orthopedics."

As candida infections continue to rise because of the wider use of drugs that suppress the immune system, as well as because of the appearance of AIDS, Krause's experiment may take on added significance. "In that event," he said, "my satisfaction will be knowing that I made the discovery and that, long after I'm dead, someone not only may remember my name, but I may also save someone's life."

On Monday, April 19, 1943, Dr. Albert Hofmann, a chemist at Sandoz Pharmaceuticals in Basel, Switzerland, bicycled home from his laboratory with his assistant, Susan Ramstein. He had asked her to accompany him because he was not feeling at all himself. At 4:20 that afternoon he had swallowed a tiny dose of synthesized lysergic acid diethylamide. By 5:00 P.M. he had begun to feel dizzy and anxious. Paralysis took hold. He hallucinated. He wanted to laugh. He struggled to make his speech understood by others in the laboratory. It was then that he had asked his assistant to accompany him home. It was "a horrible and famous bicycle trip," Hofmann told me many years later.[8] As he pedaled through the streets, Hofmann felt he was peering through a curved mirror. He thought he was stuck, standing. Miss Ramstein had to keep reassuring him that such was not the case; they were bicycling along rapidly.

After he reached his home Hofmann had brief moments of lucidity. He asked Miss Ramstein to summon the family physician. Then the hallucinations swept over him again. His body felt so heavy that he seemed filled with lead. He felt he was choking. Everything was spinning. He was so dizzy he had to rest on the sofa. Familiar pieces of furniture became threatening objects. Perhaps milk was the antidote he needed. He opened the refrigerator, but the usual fresh supply was not there. His wife had left on a holiday with the children, and he had stopped deliveries. A neighbor was summoned, but when she arrived, Hofmann perceived her as a witch wearing a colored mask. He jumped up and screamed, trying to free himself from this invading demon he believed had come to control his body, mind, and soul. At that moment he thought he was going insane. He felt that his mind had drifted out of his body, and he wondered whether he was dying.

It may seem incredible that the mind-altering lysergic acid taken by Albert Hofmann could in any way be related to the *C. albicans* that killed Wolfgang Krause's patients, but it is a fact. Lysergic acid is the core of all ergot compounds, and ergot is produced by a fungus that grows on rye and other grasses. Ergot, which causes blood vessels to constrict, diminishing the vital blood supply to the tissues, can kill by causing gangrene, and epidemics of ergot poisoning have sickened tens of thousands in this way. However, it was these toxic effects that led some doctors to recognize ergot's potential for medicinal purposes, and it was prescribed to precipitate childbirth, to relieve headaches, and to treat many other conditions, sometimes doing more harm than good because at first doctors used it nonspecifically and indiscriminately.

Sandoz Pharmaceuticals, where Albert Hofmann was a chemist, was a pioneer in the marketing of ergot drugs. Hofmann had set out to synthesize the basic components of ergot in hopes of developing new compounds that might be useful in other fields of medicine. One of his chief aims was to develop a stimulant to the circulatory and respiratory systems.

Hofmann had chosen chemistry because he wanted to know the structure of the world, and he felt that studying the active components of medicinal plants and animals would give him insights into the essence of matter. His initial research involved the study of the constituents of Mediterranean squill (the bulb of the sea onion) for potential use in treating heart disease. One of these squill compounds, called scillaren, is a chemical cousin of digitalis and was marketed in Europe to help patients with failing hearts until recently, when newer, much more potent drugs replaced it.

In 1936 Hofmann turned his attention to lysergic acid, hoping that it might prove to be the respiratory and circulatory stimulant he was looking for. Two years later, he was the first to synthesize lysergic acid and to create a compound that later became known as lysergic acid diethylamide, or LSD. It was originally called LSD-25 because it was the twenty-fifth in a series of derivatives of lysergic acid that he and his colleagues had synthesized in the laboratories at Sandoz. (Another in this series of twenty-five compounds was Methergine, which, because of its powers to make the muscles in the uterus contract, is commonly used to stop bleeding after childbirth.) For five more years, Hofmann busied himself preparing other ergot compounds. In addition to Methergine, his work led to the introduction of a drug called Hydergine, which is used to help those with impaired circulation and those suffering from the memory problems of aging.

But Hofmann was still nagged by a desire to develop a circulatory and respiratory stimulant, and he continued to think that lysergic acid might be the candidate drug. So in 1943, with the approval of his superiors, Hofmann prepared a fresh batch of LSD-25. In the midst of the final steps of synthesizing the compound, he was suddenly overwhelmed by extraordinary sensations, which he described in a report he later sent to one of his superiors: "Last Friday, April 16, 1943, I was forced to interrupt my work in the laboratory in the middle of the afternoon and proceed home, being affected by a remarkable restlessness, combined with a slight dizziness. At home I lay down and sank into a not unpleasant intoxicated-like state, with eyes closed (I found the daylight to be unpleasantly glaring), I perceived an uninterrupted stream of fantastic pictures, extraordinary shapes with intense, kaleidoscopic play of colors. After some two hours this condition faded away."[9]

This bizarre reaction was not the result of a deliberate self-experiment; it was totally unforeseen, and Hofmann was baffled. Could he have inhaled and then absorbed some of the LSD-25? Had he accidentally spilled some on his fingertips and unwittingly licked them? He did not think so; finger-licking at best is a bad habit for any chemist. Furthermore, Hofmann was well aware that even small amounts of ergot preparations can be dangerous; he had been extremely careful and meticulous. He considered the slim possibility that he had absorbed a tiny amount of LSD solution through his skin.

The nature of good research is to take advantage of the unexpected. So, for Hofmann, there was only one thing to do: repeat the process, this time as an experiment to verify that his hallucinations were due to the compound he was synthesizing. Animal tests were out: How could he know what is going on in the mind of an animal? He was also driven by curiosity. Was there a compound that affected the mind with greater potency than hitherto known? He resolved to find out. Sandoz did not officially permit self-experimentation, but Hofmann believed scientists must do their own pioneering work. "I did not ask permission," he later told me. "It was simply unethical to think that someone else should be first."

He feared that the psychic reactions from a self-experiment with LSD-25 might be even more bizarre than those he had accidentally experienced in the laboratory. If such a tiny amount had warped his mind that much, could it harm other parts of the body? By his own description "a very, very cautious man," Hofmann chose the smallest dose he believed would produce an effect: one quarter of a milligram of LSD-25 added to a small glass of water. He arrived at that amount by extrapolating from the doses of ergot that had already been used on women during childbirth and older people with poor circulation. Nevertheless, this amount would turn out to be about five times the average effective dose.

The hallucinations Hofmann experienced that Monday in April 1943 lasted until he fell asleep about one in the morning, nearly nine hours after he had taken the LSD-25. His doctor had arrived earlier in the evening but could detect nothing wrong with him, other than a weak pulse, and when Hofmann got up the next morning, he felt fine. He had difficulty explaining to others just what had happened, however. "My doctor and my neighbors presumed that I had tried suicide," he remembered. "To their way of thinking, if I had done what I did voluntarily, it *must* be suicide."

Hofmann reported the experiment to Dr. Ernst Rothlin, Sandoz' chief pharmacologist, who at first doubted that such a minute amount of any substance could so affect the mind. To verify Hofmann's experiment, Rothlin agreed to repeat it on himself and two other researchers at Sandoz. Prudently, they chose about one-quarter the dose that Hofmann had taken. It seemed almost infinitesimally small, but the results were similar and clear-cut—everyone had hallucinations. "Rothlin believed it then," Hofmann recalled.

LSD-25 became part of the Sandoz pharmacological arsenal, and it was hoped it might provide crucial insights into schizophrenia and other mental disorders and help in the study of the functions of the brain and central nervous system. Dr. Werner A. Stoll of the University of Zurich, the son of Arthur Stoll, the Sandoz scientist who led the work on ergot chemistry, became the first psychiatrist to test LSD on healthy volunteers and on schizophrenics. Before doing these studies, Werner Stoll carried on the tradition of self-experimentation by testing on himself one-quarter the dose that Hofmann had taken.

Nearly fifty years after his harrowing self-experiment with LSD-25, Hofmann and I talked in the living room of his spacious home on a mountaintop in Burg-i.-Leimental, on the border between France and Switzerland. It was a home built in part from rewards earned from the drugs he had helped develop. In addition to Hydergine and Methergine, there was Sansert (methysergide), a drug used to prevent migraine headaches. But Hofmann never did succeed in his goal to develop a circulatory and respiratory stimulant.

As our interview progressed, I mentioned that his discovery was part of a long line of self-experiments with hallucinogens. Hemp, the resin extracted from the *Cannabis sativa* plant, for example, was known to Indians and Asians as hashish and had long been taken for its mental exaltations. In the mid-nineteenth century, many doctors in western countries prescribed it to relieve pain and spasms, but they soon stopped using it because the extracts available in apothecaries varied so greatly in strength and were therefore too unpredictable.

In 1869 Dr. Horatio C. Wood, Jr., a physician and professor of botany at the University of Pennsylvania, won an American Philosophical Society prize for his essay describing his reaction to different doses of extracts from the hemp plant.[10] Wood had tested extracts prepared in Philadelphia from hemp grown in Lexington, Kentucky. At midafternoon one day, he took a dose that a druggist estimated at twenty to thirty grains. Because he did not experience any immediate symptoms, he forgot about it when he was summoned after dinner to make a house call. By the time he had examined and treated the patient, he was in a trance, unaware of the passage of time. "Whilst writing the prescription, I became perfectly oblivious to surrounding objects but went on writing, without any check to or deviation from the ordinary series of mental acts, connected with the process," Wood said in his prize essay.

Upon returning home he had a feeling of hilarity and well-being. His mind leaped from one idea to another, but he had no visions or hallucinations. About four hours after taking the dose, Wood's heart rate sped up to 120 beats per minute (compared with the usual seventy to eighty or so), and his legs felt like "waxen pillars." A physician friend whom Wood called reported that he appeared to be drunk and noted that he had "a constant and overwhelming dread of impending death, which no amount of assurance could relieve for more than an instant." Wood said he felt numb and, when pinched, felt no pain. Despite his reaction, Wood repeated the experiment with smaller doses, experiencing milder symptoms.

Because animals can communicate little about what they see or feel or what is on their minds, research on hallucinogens is largely restricted to humans. The self-experiments of Hofmann and Wood provided important information on hallucinogens that could not have been obtained in any other way.

In 1896 Dr. S. Weir Mitchell, the pioneering American neurologist, began a self-experiment that resulted in the first complete and instructive description of the effects of another hallucinogen—mescaline, or peyote.[11] Mescaline, which is derived from mescal buttons, or the dried, hairy tops of a cactus plant *(Anhalonium lewinii)*, has been used over the centuries by many American Indian tribes for religious purposes. Mitchell wanted to know exactly what the effect of the strange drug was. At noon on a busy day he took the equivalent of one and a half mescal buttons, and another button an hour later.

By midafternoon his face was flushed. He felt physically vigorous, but his stomach ached, he had a headache, and he thought he was in "the land where it is always afternoon." Still, he said he was "more competent in mind than in my every-day moods." With an elated sense of superiority, he wrote a letter of advice regarding a doubtful diagnosis and did complicated arithmetic; the results, he later noted, were no better than his normal recommendations. With his eyes closed he saw tiny points of light like silver stars or fireflies, then fragments of stained glass windows, coming into view and fading. Next came floating films of purples and pinks, followed by a "rush of countless points of white light swept across the field of view, as if the unseen millions of the Milky Way were to flow a sparkling river before the eye."

There was an endless display of richly finished Gothic towers, statues, spinning hoops laden with jewels, and other marvels that Mitchell could see only if he kept his eyes closed. When he opened them, the hallucinations vanished. He closed them; the magic moments began again. This time he saw an array of green, orange, purple, and red, but never clear yellow and never blue. It all stopped after dinner.

Mitchell's reports of his experience stimulated Havelock Ellis, the famous British psychologist, to do a similar self-experiment a year later.[12]

The self-experiments of Mitchell and Ellis provided some of the first reliable descriptive accounts of hallucinogens in the scientific literature.

Among those who perpetuated the tradition of self-experimentation with hallucinogens after Hofmann's LSD experience was the Canadian-born psychiatrist Dr. Humphrey Osmond, a trained observer who had already experimented on himself with amphetamine, mescaline, and other drugs. In 1954, while working at the Saskatchewan Hospital in Weyburn, he took ololiuqui, the ancient Aztec narcotic. In the presence of a psychologist colleague, he worked up to a dose of one hundred seeds, which he had obtained from a botanical garden. Osmond hoped his self-experiment would lead to valuable insights into the acute phases of schizophrenia.[13] Usually a very energetic and talkative man. Osmond became lethargic and uncommunicative after swallowing the hard ololiuqui seeds, which he had ground with a mortar and pestle so that they would not damage his teeth.

Hofmann got up and walked with me to his library, which houses perhaps the world's largest collection of books on psychoactive drugs. He told me that he, too, had studied the ololiuqui seed and had been astonished to find that its active components were substances very similar to LSD. The major difference was in the dose: a much larger amount of ololiuqui was needed to produce effects similar to those of LSD.

Hofmann continued to experiment on himself, expanding his research to other psychoactive substances. In one self-experiment, he ate thirty-two dried specimens of a mushroom called *Psilocybe mexicana,* which corresponded to the average dose taken by members of some Mexican Indian religious sects. His goal was to discover the active ingredient. He and his research colleagues succeeded in isolating psilocybin and psilocin, two hitherto unknown substances.

Meanwhile, there was a virtual epidemic of "experimentation" with LSD and other psychedelic drugs by college professors and students. Sandoz, which had made the drug available free of charge to medical investigators, now stopped distributing it to anyone. It was simply too potent and too unpredictable.[14] Nevertheless, chemists who wanted to make LSD in the laboratory could do so with ease, and the illicit recreational use of the drug continued. LSD, which had been Hofmann's great discovery and one with so much promise, became what he called "my problem child."

Today LSD research has come to a virtual standstill, its promise largely unfulfilled. Its discoverers, however, were certainly not responsible for its abuse, and Hofmann has no regrets. The contributions of LSD as an adjunct to research in biochemistry and neuropsychology have been valuable. The compound, for the time being, is simply beyond control. Hofmann might have realized that the day he saw his neighbor turn into a witch.

# Chapter Ten

# LIFETIMES OF SELF-EXPERIMENTING

Most self-experimenters perform a limited number of experiments on themselves, confined to a particular period of time and usually in a specific field or for a particular purpose. Werner Forssmann, for example, won a Nobel Prize for the self-experiments he did by catheterizing his heart numerous times over a two-year period. Wolfgang Krause temporarily turned from his role as a practitioner to that of a researcher for a very specific purpose. He self-experimented in an attempt to learn the cause of death of his patients. Once he had achieved his goal, he returned to his orthopedics practice, never experimenting on himself again. Scientific investigation was of secondary interest to him, and he did not pursue further research. A few self-experimenters, like Frederick Prescott, for example, might have continued to experiment on themselves had they not been traumatized by a bad experience. Prescott, you may remember, had been near panic when, after self-experimenting with curare, he had been unable to communicate with his colleagues.

There are, however, some researchers who have made self-experimentation a continuing theme throughout their careers. In this chapter we will meet four scientists who spent a lifetime self-experimenting, who were members of the British scientific establishment, and who earned international acclaim for their contributions to medical science. They used self-experimentation as a basic tool in their scientific studies, and almost every step of their research followed logically from the one before, demonstrating a well-known dictum of scientific investigation—you never know where a finding will lead.

. . .

Not all scientists are white-clad individuals shut up in laboratories. Some consider the world itself a laboratory and experiment in virtually every sort of environment. Of these, few drew as much on nature and the world for experiments as did Dr. John Scott Haldane. Born in Edinburgh, Scotland, in 1860, to an old and financially comfortable family, Haldane was self-assured, compulsive, aristocratic, sometimes intolerant of those whose intellectual capabilities did not match his own, and nearly always impatient with superficialities. He rose late, worked until the small hours of the morning, rarely took a holiday, and seldom missed his afternoon tea. His mind was vigorous and constantly alert, and he had uncanny powers of observation as well as a flair for creating imaginative experimental methodologies. His experiments would have been worthless without precise measurements, and though the instruments he devised may seem crude today, his results remain accurate. Haldane was not in the Royal Navy, yet he contributed more to naval medicine than teams of navy doctors. He was not an engineer, yet his studies in occupational safety and industrial hygiene led him to a lifelong association with the mining profession and a professorship of mining at the University of Birmingham; his chief source of income was from his job as a gas "referee," arbitrating disputes dealing with safety in the mines and other workplaces.

Virtually all of Haldane's experiments were conducted with human rather than animal subjects, and in most Haldane himself served as his own volunteer. Years later, Haldane's son, John B. S. Haldane, commenting on his father's dislike for experimenting on animals, said that J.S. had "preferred to work on himself or other human beings who were sufficiently interested in the work to ignore pain or fear."[1] The son's comments might make it seem that Haldane's self-experiments were a tribute to the family motto—"Suffer." However, the younger Haldane explained that his father's "object was not to achieve this state [of pain or fear] but to achieve knowledge which could save other men's lives. His attitude was much more like a good soldier who will risk his life and endure wounds in order to gain victory than that of an ascetic who deliberately undergoes pain. The soldier does not get himself wounded deliberately, and my father did not seek pain in his work, though he greeted a pain which would have made some people writhe or groan, with laughter . . ."[2]

When J. S. Haldane began his scientific career in the Scottish port of Dundee, he made the town's dwellings and schools his laboratory.

There he studied the composition of the air in an effort to disprove the then widely held hypothesis that typhoid fever and other diseases we now know to be infectious were caused by "bad air."[3] He aimed to answer simple questions: What is bad air? What makes air dangerous to breathe? And how can the dangers be prevented?

During the course of his research he found that the air in the Dundee sewers, as well as in the sewers under the Houses of Parliament in London, was relatively free of microorganisms, making scientists suspicious of the prevailing opinions about the health hazards of sewer gas. Furthermore, in collecting samples for these experiments, Haldane spent hours at a time in the sewers, yet he never felt ill. He discovered, among other things, that the air of sewers was in "very much better condition than that of naturally ventilated schools" and "that the sewer air contained a much smaller number of microorganisms than any class of house."[4]

These studies in Dundee and in London foreshadowed Haldane's great work on the physiology of respiration, which he began in 1887 when he moved to Oxford, where his uncle, Sir John Burdon Sanderson, was professor of physiology. According to a general belief of the time, people exhaled nonodorous, volatile, potentially fatal substances in addition to carbon dioxide. The amount of carbon dioxide, in turn, was supposedly an index of the amount of the poisonous impurities included in the exhaled air. Haldane experimented on rabbits and found that when water condensed from breath was injected into those animals, it was no more poisonous than distilled water. Haldane showed that any fatalities attributed to inhalation of exhaled air had to be due to contamination from some other toxic substance, because carbon dioxide was the only volatile substance present in exhaled air.

Haldane believed that much prior work on respiration was flawed because it had been done on anesthetized or experimentally altered animals. So he emphasized the need to do the studies under normal conditions on humans. To destroy any arguments from scientific doubters, Haldane and his colleague Dr. J. Lorrain Smith performed further experiments on themselves. They remained for up to eight hours in a large, airtight wooden box about six feet square that they called "the coffin," panting twice as fast as normal and rebreathing their own expired breath, until the air became impure.[5] From these experiments Haldane and Smith concluded that "the air of ordinary close rooms is only injurious in so far as it is offensive to the sense of smell."[6]

Haldane continued his respiration studies on himself and others, determining the amount of carbon dioxide in the body in various situations and under varying degrees of atmospheric pressure and measuring the effect of physical activity on breathing. At times he and the other subjects turned blue from lack of oxygen and became mentally confused. From these experiments Haldane deduced that breathing was chiefly regulated by nerves in the respiratory center of the brain and that this center was sensitive to any change in the amount of carbon dioxide that reached the brain from the lungs in the arterial blood. The carbon dioxide acted on the respiratory center by virtue of its acidic properties on the blood. Haldane's results clearly established the importance of carbon dioxide as the chemical stimulus to respiration; as long as there was enough oxygen, it was the carbon dioxide in the respiratory center that determined the rate of breathing.[7]

These studies were later called Haldane's "most fundamental and far-reaching contribution to physiology."[8] They were revolutionary because they explained how breathing automatically changed in accordance with muscular and other body activity; they were startling because they implied that the nervous system was under the influence of components of the blood. It was the first scientific insight into the way that precise chemical changes in the blood correlate specifically with activities of different organs. Haldane's findings remain the basis for the principles on which physicians act in treating patients who have difficulty in breathing as well as in resuscitating those whose breathing has stopped.

Haldane did not think of these self-experiments as risky, because he considered the then reigning theories to be myths. However, when he turned to the study of industrial hygiene, particularly the effects of suffocating gases, his self-experiments involved considerable risks, and he knew it.

In 1895 Haldane's attention was drawn to a puzzling accident in the East Ham Sewage Works in London, where five men had died from poisonous gases.[9] The first victim had become ill while working at the bottom of a twenty-seven-foot-deep well. He had tried to return to the surface but had been overcome by fumes and had fallen, drowning in the sewage. Three of his coworkers had gone down the ladder to rescue him, but all three had also been overpowered by the fumes. Two of them had plunged directly to the bottom of the well, but one had landed on a screen. The engineer in charge had watched in horror, and when he had seen the man caught on the screen, he had immediately descended the ladder, hoping this man, at least, might still be alive. But the engineer, too, had fallen off the ladder and dropped to the bottom of the well. None of the men had survived.

Haldane reasoned that some unknown gas must have overpowered the men. He witnessed the autopsies on the victims and then descended the well himself to obtain samples of the air. He was protected by a rope, but he risked being poisoned by the same gas that had killed the sewer workers. Nevertheless, he reported, "I was unable to detect in myself any unusual symptoms," and in fact his tests showed that the sewer air differed very little from normal air.[10]

What, then, had made the men fall?

The solution to the puzzle came from a sample of the sewage that Haldane had collected from the well. He filled about a quarter of a bottle with the sample and shook it. Then he put a mouse in the upper part of the jar; almost immediately, the animal became unconscious, its breathing rate dropping drastically from the usual 140 breaths per minute to twenty. Haldane reasoned that the men had been overpowered by a high concentration of a poisonous gas liberated by sewage that irritated the lungs and hampered breathing. He identified it as "sulphuretted hydrogen," which is now known as hydrogen sulfide or sewer gas. The gas had dissipated after the accident as the amount of sewage and weather conditions changed.

Haldane's investigations led to safety measures—aerating sewers to avoid the production of the lethal gas, for example, and attaching safety ropes to workers.

Turning his research efforts from sewers to coal mines, Haldane determined to find the cause of colliery explosions and the resulting "afterdamp," a deadly mixture chiefly of carbon monoxide, carbon dioxide, and nitrogen. No one knew whether deaths in explosions from afterdamp were due to physical violence, to suffocation from the lack of oxygen, or to the direct effects of carbon monoxide. To find out, in 1896 Haldane investigated a colliery explosion in South Wales that had killed fifty-seven men and thirty horses. He found that only five men had been killed by the force of the explosion; fifty-two had died from carbon monoxide poisoning.

Haldane then tested the physiological action of carbon monoxide on animals and found that tiny amounts of the gas were fatal to mice. Next, he breathed carbon monoxide himself, at considerable risk, suffering from such problems as uncoordinated movements, staggering gait, and visual difficulties. His daughter, Naomi Mitchison, later recalled that her father often suffered from blurred vision and other effects of carbon monoxide poisoning. "My father would go off to any mine disaster wearing his mine clothes," she said. "Then there would be a series of telegrams saying 'All safe' and so on." Though some, she remembered, seemed suspiciously garbled.[11]

Haldane's laboratory notes on his self-experiments with carbon monoxide make fascinating reading, particularly his account of how he became partners with a mouse. Haldane and the mouse were together in the laboratory, each breathing carbon monoxide. After about a half hour, the mouse suddenly flopped on its back. Haldane, still alert, tested his blood and found it had the strong pink color indicative of carbon monoxide poisoning. "Stopped the experiment," he wrote. "Ran upstairs (twenty-four steps) once. A little later became giddy, much out of breath, had palpitations and could not see so well as usual. On standing for two or three minutes felt all right again. Vision cleared, and hyperpnea [rapid breathing] disappeared. Afterwards singing in ears."[12]

Mice or other small animals have higher metabolic rates than humans and are therefore affected by carbon monoxide faster than humans are. After his experience with the mouse, Haldane pointed out the value of the small creature as an index of danger in the coal mines. "A miner usually trusts to his lamp to give him indications of the presence of dangerous gases in a mine," he wrote. "A lamp is, however, of no service in detecting small quantities of carbonic oxide in air. It is this fact which makes after-damp, smoke, etc. so dangerous to men who attempt to penetrate them while trusting to a lamp to give warning of any danger."[13] Later, Haldane found that small birds, which breathed even faster than mice, reacted still quicker and were more useful as sentinels of poisonous gas.

Haldane's experiments, beyond their enormous practical value, provided explanations of the basic physiology of carbon monoxide. He found that the poisonous effects of the gas were due entirely to its chemical attraction to hemoglobin, the oxygen-carrying substance in red blood cells, an attraction about three hundred times stronger than that of oxygen. It is this vast difference that keeps the oxygen out of the red blood cells when carbon monoxide is breathed.

Haldane devoted much of his basic research to carbon monoxide and other gases largely because he was so keen to make the mines safer. He visited collieries and breathed poisonous gases variously called "blackdamp," "chokedamp," and "bottom gas" and compared their effects with those produced by toxic amounts of other gases. The effects were often quick and dramatic. In one experiment Haldane breathed from a pipe, turned blue, and felt his heart pound faster. "Within about thirty seconds I felt that I was becoming confused, and did not push the observations further," he wrote. "Two or three seconds after I had ceased to breathe from the pipe the blueness was seen suddenly to disappear from my face and lips and to be replaced by the natural color. The feelings which I experienced after the first fifteen or twenty seconds in breathing the black-damp were distinctly such as are produced by breathing air very poor in oxygen. The experiment of breathing the black-damp was repeated twice in order to leave no doubt."[14]

After breathing the gases in another coal mine experiment, Haldane reported, "My respirations rapidly became deeper and more frequent, so that after a short time I was panting violently. The panting, however, did not increase beyond a certain point, and was not distinctly accompanied by the peculiar feelings characteristic of distress from want of oxygen."[15]

During his numerous experiments over the years, Haldane developed imaginative methods to determine the amounts of various gases in the blood. For instance, he diluted a sample of blood, divided it into portions, mixed a known amount of carbon monoxide into one portion to make it turn pink, and then added measured amounts of carmine red dye to the untreated sample until it turned the exact shade of pink as the sample mixed with carbon monoxide. By determining the amount of carmine dye needed, he could accurately measure the capacity of hemoglobin to unite with oxygen or carbon monoxide. The less carbon monoxide the treated sample contained, the less carmine dye was needed.

But Haldane's genius was not only in the area of methodology. He also created forerunners to tools that are indispensable to physicians today: the hemoglobinometer and blood gas analyzer. These are used to do standard tests during routine checkups, to test patients with anemia or low red blood cell counts, and in the everyday care of patients with breathing difficulties from emphysema and other lung conditions.[16]

The studies established Haldane as the recognized authority on industrial hygiene; his contributions had already been significant enough to gain him lasting fame. But a further contribution, as significant as any he had yet made, was still to come.

Haldane now set about to develop a way to prevent the dreaded and debilitating condition called the bends, or, as it was better known in Haldane's time, caisson disease. Bends are also known as decompression sickness, and Haldane's contribution toward preventing this sometimes fatal disorder was the development of the concept of decompression by stages.

This concept, which allowed deep-sea divers to work longer and more safely, grew out of experiments that Paul Bert, the great French physiologist who made his name in politics as well as science, performed in 1878. Bert did 670 laboratory experiments, many on himself, to study the effects of changing atmospheric pressure on the body. From studies on himself in a pressure chamber, Bert learned that the effects of changes in barometric pressure were at the root of problems encountered by balloonists, mountain climbers, and deep-sea divers.[17]

The bends cause a variety of symptoms such as nausea, vomiting, dizziness, and pain in the joints and abdomen. The symptoms are painful but temporary if the condition is relieved. More important, they forewarn of far more serious and permanent consequences such as paralysis and other nervous system damage, shock, and ultimately death. Bert showed that the painful symptoms of the bends resulted from bubbles of nitrogen that blocked the circulation when they were released in the body during rapid ascent. He also showed that the symptoms could be avoided by means of very slow decompression, but his experiments did not provide enough data to determine the safety and rate of decompression.

J. S. Haldane advanced Bert's work. Haldane began his experiments with animals—particularly goats, because they were the largest animals that could conveniently be used in an experimental diving chamber.

"Goats," Haldane explained, "while they are not perhaps such delicate indicators as monkeys or dogs, and though they are somewhat stupid and definitely insensitive to pain, are capable of entering into emotional relationships with their surroundings, animate and inanimate, of a kind sufficiently nice to enable those who are familiar with them to detect slight abnormalities with a fair degree of certainty."[18] He had noticed, for example, that when a goat developed the bends, it would often hold up a foreleg, evidently because it was loath to bear weight on it.

Haldane placed the goats in a seven-foot-square steel chamber at the Lister Institute in London and observed them under varying degrees of air pressure. Then, in order to develop a precise decompression schedule for humans, he and his colleagues spent hours in the same pressure chamber as well as in deep-sea dives off a vessel called "The Spanker." From the data obtained in these experiments, Haldane calculated elaborate tables that accounted for the depths to which a diver descended as well as the time spent in deep water. Haldane's experiments showed that staged decompression was safer than the slow decompression then advised by the British and other navies. The compression and decompression schedules published in current diving manuals are based on Haldane's self-experiments.

Haldane continued his work in the mines, and the terrible conditions he encountered there, including excessively high heat, led him, in 1905, to study, once again through self-experiments, the influence of high temperatures on the body. These self-experiments of Haldane's advanced the knowledge gained from self-experiments conducted in 1775 by Charles Blagden, an English physician and secretary of the Royal Society. Blagden and his coworkers had observed their physiological reactions when, fully clothed, they remained for varying periods, sometimes up to forty-five minutes, in a room heated to 250 degrees Fahrenheit, or thirty-eight degrees above the boiling point of water, without being seriously inconvenienced. Under the same circumstances, however, a beefsteak was baked hard in thirteen minutes.[19] Blagden and his colleagues proved that for short periods humans could withstand extremely high temperatures, provided the air is dry. They demonstrated the importance of perspiration in maintaining the constancy of body temperature; they could not bear very high temperatures in moist air, because it prevented evaporation from the skin. The reason humans did not cook like the meat is because breathing, blood flow, and sweating control the temperature of living tissue by evaporative heat loss.

Haldane wanted to obtain information about the exact upper limits of air temperature and humidity that humans could endure without serious physiological disturbance. This would help determine the limits under which humans could work and live normally when exposed to abnormally high temperatures in mines and outdoors.

To gain this information, Haldane descended into Dolcoath Mine, the deepest and richest copper and tin mine in Cornwall, and subjected himself and a few of his colleagues to varying degrees of high temperatures and humidity by piping steam into a room and sitting in Turkish baths. Haldane, his son said, "could stand dry air to about three hundred degrees Fahrenheit, but if he moved about too much his hair began to singe."[20] Haldane concluded that "in still and warm air what matters to the persons present is . . . the temperature shown by the wet-bulb thermometer (a device that measures humidity). If this exceeds a certain point (about 78 degrees F. or 25.5 degrees C.) continuous hard work becomes impracticable; and beyond about 88 degrees F. or 31 degrees C. it becomes impracticable for ordinary persons even to stay for long periods in such air, although practice may increase to some extent the limit which can be tolerated."[21]

Haldane's research shed light on the physiological mechanism of heatstroke and led to improved ventilation in mines, mills, engine rooms of steamers, and other workplaces. As a further consequence of these experiments, he became known as the "father of the salt tablet" because he advised its use to replace salt lost in severe sweating.

Haldane then moved his laboratory to the top of a mountain. In 1911 he and several colleagues climbed Pike's Peak in Colorado and spent six weeks at the 14,019-foot summit in order to determine how oxygen is absorbed into the lungs and to learn how the body acclimatizes to high altitudes.[22] Haldane and his colleagues studied changes in their own bodies as they climbed from sea level to the summit. They measured the blood volume, or total amount of blood in the body, the concentration of red cells in the blood, and the change in the amount of production of the blood pigment or hemoglobin. They studied the effects of low barometric pressure and how lowering of the bicarbonate in the plasma (fluid portion of the blood) permitted increased breathing. Their studies challenged existing ideas about how we breathe, and they led to safer and more convenient means by which aviators and balloonists could reach high altitudes.

The results of these studies further convinced Haldane that the lung could function as a gland to secrete oxygen into the blood. This was a controversial theory. Another school of researchers, led by an equally famous scientist and self-experimenter, Joseph Barcroft, who was sometimes a research partner of Haldane, argued that oxygen passed from air to blood by diffusion. The distinction between the active secretion and the passive diffusion theories was scientifically important. Though Haldane's theory was later proved wrong, his studies stimulated further physiologic investigations of the composition of the fluid and chemicals excreted by the kidney and of cardiac output (the amount of blood the heart pumps in a minute).[23] Haldane provided some of the earliest evidence that the regulation of blood circulation was as delicate and precise as he had shown the regulation of breathing to be.

Haldane was a leader in scientific philosophy, and although he spoke in a halting manner, his students knew he quickly got to the root of a problem. One listener recalled how Haldane would often make the crucial point in his argument following a lengthy pause and accompanied by a short laugh and winsome smile. As testimony, the published version of his lectures on respiration in 1916 at Yale has become a classic.

During World War I the British government sent Haldane to France to advise on protecting troops from the chlorine and phosgene used in poison gas. In a series of brief and drastic experiments on himself as well as on his son, J.B.S. Haldane, and a few colleagues, Haldane showed that although there was no primary treatment to prevent eventual scarring of the lungs from the poisonous gas, the victim would survive if the lungs could heal during the acute phase of the poisoning. It was during this acute phase that many victims of poison gas died, either from lack of oxygen or, in the days before there were antibiotics, from secondary infections. Haldane devised a crude respirator which administered oxygen continuously until nature took over, healing the lungs with scar tissue. His studies contributed to the improved therapeutic use of oxygen in everyday medical practice.[24]

Haldane's lifetime of self-experimentation had little ill effect on his health. There is no evidence that he suffered any permanent damage at all. He remained actively involved with his work until his death in 1936 at age seventy-six following a visit to Persia and Iraq, where he had gone to do additional research on heatstroke. At the time of his death he was described not only as a champion of the worker but also as the greatest physiologist.

Parent-child teams are exceptional in science, as in the arts, because talent is so variably inherited. The Haldanes are all the more exceptional because John Burdon Sanderson Haldane, the son, never received a scientific degree; nevertheless, he achieved a scientific reputation that rivaled his father's and helped make the Haldanes one of the most famous families in the history of science. J. S. Haldane, the father, made his reputation as a physiologist, Haldane junior as a geneticist. J.B.S. Haldane's major contribution was in uniting the evolutionary theories advanced by Charles Darwin with the fundamental laws of genetics developed by Gregor Mendel.

J.B.S. Haldane was born in 1892 at a time when his father was breathing foul air and upsetting scientific dogmas. When the boy reached an age at which most other children were content to play games, he was helping his father record experimental data. On becoming his father's research assistant, Jack (as his parents called him) donated his own blood and took blood samples from his schoolmates for J. S. Haldane's experiments. Over the years J.B.S. Haldane, gifted with a prodigious memory, also acquired his father's ability to simplify complex systems, a talent that proved crucial to his study of genetics. In a brief autobiography, written while he lived in India in the late 1950s and early 1960s, the younger Haldane said: "I owe my success very largely to my father. . . . I suppose my scientific career began at the age of about two, when I used to play on the floor of his laboratory and watch him playing a complicated game called 'experiments'—the rules I did not understand, but he clearly enjoyed it."[25]

In addition to a talent for science, J. S. Haldane passed on the tradition of self-experimentation to his son. As a youth, Jack took deep-sea dives with his father, descended into mines, and climbed Pike's Peak. He recalled one event in a pit in North Staffordshire: "After a while we got to a place where the roof [of the mine] was about eight feet high and a man could stand up. . . . To demonstrate the effects of breathing firedamp my father told me to stand up and recite Mark Antony's speech from Shakespeare's *Julius Caesar*, beginning: 'Friends, Romans, countrymen.' I soon began to pant, and somewhere about 'the noble Brutus' my legs gave way and I collapsed on to the floor, where, of course, the air was all right. In this way I learnt that firedamp is lighter than air."[26] (The air near the roof was full of methane, or firedamp, which is a gas lighter than air, so the air on the floor was not dangerous.)

J.B.S. Haldane, like his father, accepted the risks of experimenting on himself, and said that "of the biochemical experiments which I have done on myself, perhaps two-thirds have had the results for which I was looking. But every one has also had unexpected, and many of them unpleasant, effects" including "lost consciousness from blows on the head, from fever, anesthetics, want of oxygen and other causes."[27]

Jack Haldane's unusual upbringing gave him a head start as a scientist, but it created problems in school. He was short-tempered and intellectually arrogant. As a result, he had to put up with more than the usual amount of bullying that characterized English school life. He overcame the problems, in part through his large physical size and his aggressiveness, but undoubtedly these childhood experiences contributed to his somewhat eccentric behavior as an adult. He developed a taste for politics and joined the Communist party, a move that at least one colleague, Dr. E. Martin Case, believed reflected his disdain for conventionally accepted behavior. Case described him as a cantankerous, unconventional man who very much enjoyed the role of showman. "He had a persecution complex and a chip on both shoulders," Case said. "He despised all the respectable things because they were the 'done' things. He liked people who did not like the 'done' things either." Case underlined this point when he said he had the feeling that "if everyone had been a Communist, J.B.S. Haldane would have become a Tory."[28]

Others described the bushy-eyebrowed Jack Haldane as a "cuddly cactus" because of his reputation as an extremely rude man with a soft heart.

J.B.S. Haldane, determined to educate the masses about the value of the research for which they paid, became one of the first and most effective researchers to popularize science. Moreover, he was one of the very few self-experimenters to record precise opinions on the subject of human experimentation. In an essay, "On Being One's Own Rabbit—The Story of a Skirmish in the War on Disease," he told why he experimented on himself: "For rough experiments one uses an animal, and it is really only when accurate observations are needed that a human being is preferable."[29] Also, he observed that "it is difficult to be sure how a rabbit feels at any time. Indeed, many rabbits make no serious attempt to cooperate with one."[30]

There was another reason why Haldane preferred experimenting on himself instead of animals. "The experimental pathologist is apt to miss the less obtrusive symptoms when working on other animals, and in the long run he is driven to use his own body as an instrument of research."[31]

J.B.S. Haldane continually expressed his sympathy for animals and raised a provocative question regarding the relationship of animal experimentation to self-experimentation. "I have seen numerous experiments on animals," he wrote, "but I have never seen an animal undergoing pain which I would not have been willing to undergo myself for the same object. Why, then, it may be asked, should not all painful experiments be done on human volunteers?"[32]

Although J.B.S. Haldane's scientific reputation was based chiefly on genetics research, which did not involve experiments on humans, he shared his father's interest in physiology, and some of his self-experiments in this area became landmark studies. In one series he learned that the fastest means of regulating the body's delicately balanced internal chemical environment was through breathing. Along with his colleagues, he hyperventilated as fast and as deeply as he could for up to three minutes. At times, he turned blue. Sometimes he stopped breathing completely, then resumed after his lungs reflexively blew out the excess carbon dioxide that had accumulated in his body. According to his description, he and his colleagues "were more worried than interested by certain extra effects which they noticed. After about half a minute they felt violent 'pins and needles' in the hands, feet, and face; and after three or four their hands became curiously stiff, and sometimes their wrists bent involuntarily."[33] Once, the symptoms lasted for ninety minutes, and Haldane noted that his nerves were more irritable for about two weeks after the experiment. He learned later that the symptoms were due to tetany, a condition that can be caused by a temporary respiratory disturbance or by an imbalance in the regulation of calcium or the body's balance of acid and alkali.

In later experiments he and a colleague, by overbreathing and eating up to three ounces of bicarbonate of soda, changed the acid-base balance of their bodies' biochemistry so it was more alkaline (basic).[34] Jack Haldane said it had taken three months of practice before they were able to master the laboratory methods needed to do the experiment in which they tested the minute changes in amounts of vital chemicals in their blood and urine. They also made the fluid composition of their bodies more acid by drinking ammonium chloride several times, sometimes for as long as a week. They had to dilute the chemical in about forty parts of water; otherwise it would have caused them to vomit. Also, they sat in an airtight room and breathed air that contained a high concentration of carbon dioxide. Once again they analyzed samples of their blood and urine and correlated the results with the changes that occurred. The acidic effect induced by the chemicals, J.B.S. Haldane said, "makes one breathe as if one had just completed a boat race, and also gives one a rather violent headache."[35] But the symptoms disappeared as soon as the body corrected the acid imbalance.

Haldane extended his father's experiments on survival in high temperatures by staying in saturated air at 120 degrees Fahrenheit. "It was terrible," Haldane said. "Every breath heated my throat and lungs."[36]

Like his father, J.B.S. Haldane was driven to reduce occupational hazards. In 1939 the Amalgamated Engineering Union and the Electrical Trades Union asked him to find out why the crew had not escaped in the sinking of the submarine *Thetis* off Liverpool, which had cost the lives of nearly one hundred men. Although it was not possible to raise the submarine to determine the cause of the sinking, Haldane knew one important factor was that the air pressure inside an area of the ship had to equal that of the water outside before a human could escape. He pointed out that the navy, in designing the submarine, had not considered certain physical factors which, in an emergency, would allow the crew to escape.

Haldane then carried out a series of high-pressure experiments in a steel chamber at Siebe Gorman and Company in south London to elucidate the effects of water pressure and temperature on the human body and thereby help prevent future tragedies. The chamber measured eight feet by four feet and accommodated two human volunteers at a time, three in a pinch. Haldane, who was then forty-seven years old, asked colleague Martin Case, age thirty-five, and twenty other volunteers, including Juan Negrin, a forty-eight-year-old physiologist who was a former prime minister of Loyalist Spain, to join him in the experiments.

There was no telephone in the chamber, so the volunteers communicated by tapping coded signals, by placing messages against a window, and by shouting. Before each experiment the volunteers were asked to perform tests to determine their manual and intellectual abilities. They did four-figure multiplications (e.g., 9,746 × 4,956) and placed steel balls in three holes, first using a forceps, then a scoop, and lastly finger and thumb. After the experiments these tests were repeated. The research was designed to study a variety of factors such as intoxication from carbon dioxide, nitrogen gas (which not only forms bubbles but is a narcotic at high pressures), and oxygen (which at high pressures can cause violent convulsions to come on suddenly without warning), as well as the combined effects of these gases and high atmospheric pressure on thinking. Any one of these factors would be fatal if they occurred while someone was trying to escape from a sinking ship, and the chief physiologic problem Haldane had to tackle was learning how to steer his experimental ship between the bends, nitrogen poisoning, and oxygen toxicity.

Other experiments were designed to test the effects of cold, both alone and in combination with carbon dioxide and high pressures under diving conditions. Haldane, wearing only a shirt and trousers, and Case, wearing a sweater instead of a shirt, submerged themselves in a bath containing water and large amounts of cracked ice. They stayed there, inside the pressure chamber, for periods of up to one-half hour, while they breathed carbon dioxide under increasing atmospheric pressure. Their teeth chattered. They shivered violently. They recited the words of a fairly lengthy song, making a few mistakes. Haldane erred but Case did not when they did multiplications in their heads. They concluded that cold somewhat enhanced the combined effects of carbon dioxide and high pressure.

Haldane also described a specific experience in the chamber under high atmospheric pressure: "Why cannot my companion behave himself? He is making silly jokes and trying to sing. His lips are rather purple, the color of hemoglobin when uncombined with oxygen. I feel quite unaffected; in fact, I have just thought of a very funny story. It is true I can't stand without some support. My companion suggests some oxygen from the cylinder which we have with us. To humor him I take a few breaths. The result is startling. The electric light becomes so much brighter that I fear the fuse may melt. The noise of the pumping engine increases four-fold. My notebook, which should have contained records of my pulse-rate, turns out to be filled with the often repeated but seldom legible statement that I am feeling *much* better, and remarks about my colleague, of which the least libelous is that he is drunk. I put down the oxygen tube and relapse into a not unpleasant state of mental confusion. An hour later, in spite of our indignant protests, the engine is stopped, and we return to normal pressure, no worse off except for a slight and transitory headache. For longer experiments a mountain is desired."[37]

The experiments were painful and dangerous. Haldane and his partners suffered the bends, bouts of unconsciousness, convulsions, pain in the ears and sinuses, and serious complications. During one experiment a volunteer whom Haldane and Case described as "very depressed" seized Case's hand and said, "I'm going to die. I'm going to die, I tell you." Another volunteer required surgery to repair a partially collapsed lung, and Haldane himself broke a vertebra in his back and injured his spinal cord. He was never again entirely free from pain.

The spinal cord injury occurred in 1940, when Haldane and Martin Case breathed a mixture of 85 percent helium and 15 percent oxygen for eleven minutes at high pressure to investigate a claim made by many that this combination prevented the bends. After he was decompressed according to plan, Haldane said he developed "severe pain in the right hip and both shoulders, becoming worse on moving; and itching of the back. An hour later there was also severe pain in the buttocks, and a burning pain in the skin of the left scrotum and thighs, later spreading to the calves."[38] The pain was assumed to be due to a bubble of helium that had settled in the tip of his spinal cord, damaging it and thereby affecting the pain sensations carried to and from the skin in the areas served by the fourth and fifth sacral nerves. "Even after seven months I prefer a cushion to a hard chair, and may perhaps be excused for skepticism of the alleged prophylactic value of helium."[39]

As an incidental finding of these experiments, Haldane and Case discovered that oxygen had a peculiar taste when breathed at high pressures. They described it as similar to dilute ginger beer or dilute ink with a little sugar. "It is clearly inaccurate," they reported, "to describe a gas as inodorous and tasteless. On the contrary, most or all gases may be expected to display these properties at sufficiently high pressures, just as they liquefy at sufficiently low temperatures. Whether men can survive the pressure under which, say, hydrogen develops a taste or smell is, of course, as yet unknown."[40]

J.B.S. Haldane's career of self-experimentation, like his father's, was fraught with dangers that many, if not most, other researchers would be unwilling to take. But Haldane saw it otherwise. "It might be thought that experiments such as I have described were dangerous," he wrote. "This is not the case if they are done with intelligence. Naturally one only drinks or breathes substances whose probable effects are fairly well understood, and which are known not to be fatal to animals in small quantities. One works up only gradually to the size of dose which produces striking symptoms. Experiments in which one stakes one's life on the correctness of one's biochemistry are far safer than those of an airplane designer who is prepared to fall a thousand feet if his aerodynamics are incorrect. They are also perhaps more likely to be of benefit to humanity in general. . . .

"Of course, it is occasionally necessary to make experiments which one knows are dangerous, for example, in determining how a disease is transmitted. A number of people have died in this way, and it is to my mind the ideal way of dying. Others make experiments which are apparently risky, but really perfectly safe provided the theory on which they are based is sound. I have occasionally made experiments of this kind, and if I had died in the course of one I should, while dying, have regarded myself not as a martyr but as a fool."[41]

To Haldane, death was an occupational risk, but one that he had weighed carefully.

The Haldanes worked at a time when the increasing complexities of science made it difficult for one researcher to know everything and to carry out experiments alone. The Haldanes, as well as many other researchers of the period, collaborated with other scientists, changing partners according to the time and type of project. They also taught younger researchers. Dr. Robert A. McCance was both a student and colleague of J.B.S. Haldane. He was a physician who devoted his career to clinical research, becoming one of the foremost experts in nutrition and kidney physiology. McCance, in contrast to the Haldanes, who worked with many sets of partners, formed a principal scientific partnership with just one researcher, Dr. Elsie M. Widdowson. Their collaboration, which lasted for more than half a century, was strictly professional, and all the more unusual in that Widdowson was one of the few female scientists of her era. McCance and Widdowson almost always experimented on themselves before repeating the experiments on other humans.

The two scientists had tremendously versatile and flexible careers. I first met them in 1973 in Cambridge, England.[42] McCance was then seventy and had become a legendary figure among his scientific peers. He seemed a caricature of a British professor. He would bicycle around Cambridge dressed in tweeds, carrying an old tan canvas World War II gas mask case filled with books on his back beneath a macintosh. His habit of not eating lunch left him skinny. Widdowson, a hefty woman, was operating on a pig when I was introduced to her.

McCance had been a pilot in the Royal Navy in World War I, and when it was over, he spent six months working at a model farm in his native Northern Ireland before going to Cambridge, where he studied natural science with the intention of returning home to join the Department of Agriculture. But the Anglo-Irish War upset his plans. After completing his studies, he did research for three years and then went to Kings College Hospital in London to complete his medical education.

He began self-experimenting in 1928 when he swallowed sugars called pentoses and injected them into his veins, partly in hopes of developing a test to measure kidney function and malfunction.[43] These experiments did not produce the intended result, but they increased McCance's interested in determining the body's rate of absorption of other forms of sugar from the intestines.

McCance and Widdowson first met in 1933 in the kitchen of Kings College Hospital in London. She had just finished her Ph.D. thesis in London on the carbohydrate content of ripening apples and was training as a dietitian at Kings College Hospital.

At the time McCance was conducting studies designed to provide accurate figures for the calories, carbohydrates, proteins, fat, and minerals in cooked food. Insulin had recently been introduced as a lifesaving therapy for diabetics, and this precise information on diet was crucial to their care.

Elsie Widdowson spent most of her day in the hospital kitchen, and she would often notice a thin white-coated man come in, put food in the oven or steamer, disappear for a while, and then return to take the food away. She wondered who he was and what he was doing. The cook identified him as "McCance, a researcher on cooking." Intrigued, Widdowson overcame her shyness, and spoke to this "researcher on cooking," who immediately invited her to visit his tiny laboratory. There McCance described his work. Widdowson, having recently completed her Ph.D. thesis for which she had tested the sugar content of apples, recognized that many of McCance's results were inaccurate because he had used a method that destroyed some of the sugar in the process of testing. "Your answers are all wrong," the dietitian told the physician. And he answered, "You had better come and put them right."

Thus began their first cooperative venture, which was to result in ten thousand separate determinations for water, protein, fat, carbohydrate, and eight minerals in foods. Their findings were published in a book that became the Bible in the field of nutrition. The fact that about half the values in that book are still listed in current editions testifies to the meticulous methods they used.[44]

The introduction of insulin stimulated physicians like McCance to learn more about general human physiology and biochemistry. Many of the diabetics whom he treated came to the hospital in a coma. McCance studied these patients carefully, testing their urine for substances other than sugar, and in the process discovered a curious absence of salt. The urine of healthy people usually contains salt that is excreted by the kidneys. McCance knew that patients with another disorder—a hormone deficiency of the adrenal glands called Addison's disease—had too little salt in their blood serum. He decided to study the mechanism of these disorders of salt metabolism by making himself and some healthy volunteers salt deficient.[45]

McCance, Widdowson, and the other volunteers ate foods that had been prepared without salt. To lose some of the salt that was already in their bodies, they sweated in a hot-air bath, keeping their body temperature at 100 to 101 degrees Fahrenheit for two hours each afternoon. Then they lay naked beneath a set of radiant lamps for about two and a half hours each session while up to three quarts of water either evaporated or ran off them and collected on a rubber sheet underneath. The sweat was analyzed and the water loss measured by determining the weight lost. Physiological recovery was quick following resumption of drinking the normal amount of fluids.

McCance and Widdowson performed the pilot studies on themselves. They went through all the steps and collected the sweat samples, but because it was only a test run, they did not do biochemical tests on those samples. The first full experiment was done with a female medical student volunteer, but the test was not a technical success. Biochemical analyses showed that she had not lost enough sweat to become salt deficient. A puzzled McCance repeated the experiment on himself the following day, losing copious amounts of salt. Then Widdowson took a turn, but, like the student, she could not sweat out enough salt to become salt deficient. The sex difference in the ability to lose salt by sweating, which they confirmed later, was an interesting observation in itself. From then on most of the studies were made on men.

It took up to a week of this regime to make all the salt disappear from the urine. Strangely, during this period, McCance had neither a craving for salt nor a feeling of hunger, although he noticed, for unknown reasons, a peculiar sensation akin to thirst.

McCance then wondered whether he could take the experiment a step further and, by overbreathing, produce urine that was without sodium. This was a technique he had learned from J.B.S. Haldane. "I sat in a chair and leaned over a sink with the hot water faucet running to keep my throat moist," he said. Then he breathed in and out as deeply and as rapidly as he could for forty-five minutes until the relative lack of carbon dioxide in his body made his blood more alkaline than normal.

As a safety precaution, Widdowson stood by while he was overbreathing, but when he had finished and was sitting comfortably in a chair, she went out for a moment. Suddenly something went wrong. McCance's body had become so alkaline from the loss of the carbon dioxide that no signal was being sent to the respiratory center in his brain to stimulate breathing. When Widdowson returned, she found that McCance was blue. "It was frightening," she said. "He just passed out. So I ran for expert help and when I got back McCance was just recovering. The first thing he said was 'give me my bottle' so he could donate a sample of urine."

McCance had been unconscious for several minutes and remained weak for several hours thereafter. He was lucky. He could have suffered permanent damage to his brain or other organs. Recalling the episode, McCance remarked, laughing, "I still have quite a good brain."

These self-experiments helped doctors appreciate the important role of fluids and sodium. Today, maintaining fluid and chemical balance is a standard part of the treatment of patients with diabetic coma, kidney disorders, and heart attacks and of those who experience episodes of severe vomiting and fever, as well as after surgery.

An interesting side result of these studies came when Dr. Winifred Young, one of McCance's students, went to work in a hospital in Birmingham. While working with McCance, Young had become so accustomed to testing urine for salt that in her new job she automatically tested the urine of newly born children. To her astonishment, she could not detect any salt. She and McCance set about to learn why the urine of normal newborn infants, unlike that of normal adults, contained no salt. They found that it was a normal variation —that infants were not just little adults but creatures with a composition and physiology all their own, an important but heretofore unrealized fact.[46]

In 1937 the interests of McCance and Widdowson turned in a new direction because of one of McCance's patients, a Mrs. Harris, whose body was producing an excessive number of red cells as well as hemoglobin from a condition called polycythemia rubra vera.[47] Her case led McCance and Widdowson to one of their major contributions—a fundamental discovery about the metabolism of iron—and it was made through experiments on themselves.[48]

Doctors then believed that iron was absorbed in the upper part of the small bowel and that the body shed excess iron through the large bowel into the stools. McCance and Widdowson treated Mrs. Harris with phenylhydrazine, a drug that leads to the breakdown of red blood cells and, in turn, to the release of iron contained in the hemoglobin portion of the red cells. They calculated that before her treatment Mrs. Harris had ten grams of iron in her body, or about twice the normal amount. In keeping with the prevailing opinion, they assumed that the excess iron released from her red blood cells would appear in her urine and feces, and they were astonished when tests showed this was not the case. There was virtually no excess iron. Mrs. Harris had retained all the iron set free from the red blood cells in her body. Was there something about iron metabolism that doctors had missed?

McCance and Widdowson questioned whether the body excreted surplus iron at all; they theorized that the body lost iron only through bleeding. To test the hypothesis, they did a series of experiments on themselves and other volunteers. For several weeks, the volunteers took very large quantities of iron, either by mouth or injected intravenously. They ate all their meals in the laboratory and kept duplicate portions of the food for chemical testing. Meanwhile, they collected all their body wastes for chemical analysis. The results proved that iron was not excreted from the body and that the bowel had no regulatory power over the amount of iron lost.

These findings did not help Mrs. Harris, who lived on for several years with her chronic ailment. But by showing that the body loses iron only when it is in certain chemical forms, they had an important bearing on the understanding of anemia and other disorders of the blood system. Furthermore, they led McCance and Widdowson to question the way the body handled other compounds such as calcium and magnesium. "It seemed a pity only to study iron," Widdowson said, "so we injected a calcium salt and a magnesium salt as well." They found that most of the injected calcium and magnesium, unlike iron, was excreted in the urine and, like iron, little if any appeared in the feces.[49]

What McCance and Widdowson had done, as they said, was to

"shake to its foundations" the widely held belief that the bowel regulated the excretion of iron, calcium, and magnesium.

Next they studied the element strontium, better known for its use in flares and fireworks. Strontium is one of the so-called "trace elements," chemicals that exist in minute amounts in the body. It resembles calcium, but while doctors knew a considerable amount about calcium's role in the body, they knew very little about the role of strontium. The element had been used medicinally for a long time for a variety of disorders, but although an understanding of how it is excreted is fundamental to its proper use in humans, few studies had been made. One of these had been conducted by J.B.S. Haldane, who drank a strong solution of strontium and reported that it caused a violent diarrhea, slight headache, and malaise lasting for several days.[50]

McCance and Widdowson designed a strontium experiment to determine how the element was excreted from the body. They would inject strontium into each other's veins each day for a week and then measure the amount in their stools and urine. This time they encountered the kind of unpredictable accident that can occur in any human experiment.

They started on a Monday with McCance injecting the strontium into a vein in Widdowson's arm. Nothing happened after twenty-four hours, so they decided to double the dose for each of them to forty-seven milligrams. On Tuesday McCance took his first dose. For the next five days they carried out their scheme without problems. But by Friday they had used up the entire original batch and had to sterilize some more strontium from the original solution.[51]

At eleven on Saturday morning, the sixth day of the experiment, they injected the prescribed dose into each other's arms. They had become overconfident, one of the biggest hazards of self-experimentation. During the week someone had always stood by, but because nothing had happened, they carried out this extension of the experiment alone. Less than an hour later, they began to feel ill. They suffered intense headaches and teeth-chattering chills. Their backs and thighs hurt. Widdowson, who was the sicker of the two, said: "We felt dreadful. We did not know what had gone wrong, and we were apprehensive."

Fortunately, someone came by and called John Ryle, a Kings College professor, who rushed to the laboratory. After realizing that their lives were not in immediate danger, Ryle took the two sick scientists home with him, where he and his wife could observe them. By this time about four hours had passed, and both McCance and Widdowson had developed fevers of about 102 degrees Fahrenheit. Yet they were so disciplined that, despite feeling ill, they still managed to collect the samples they needed. Later analysis of these samples showed that substances known as pyrogens, also called endotoxins and due to bacterial contamination, were present in the second batch of strontium. They had suffered a pyrogen reaction, which occurred much more commonly then than now because purification techniques were cruder.

McCance and Widdowson recovered quickly but gave themselves no further injections of strontium. The results of this experiment showed that the body rids itself of strontium slowly and that about 90 percent of the excretion is through the kidney—not the bowel.

It was now 1938, and McCance believed that England was heading for war. He was determined to get his wife and two children out of London before it began. Fortuitously, he was offered a position at Cambridge University. The salary was lower, but he accepted it. Elsie Widdowson went as well. One year later the war began.

In order to help the war effort, McCance and Widdowson turned their attention to nutrition. Their chief concern was to ensure that, if rationing were imposed, the English people should continue to have a nutritious diet.[52] In devising such a diet, they made several assumptions—that the principles of rationing in force in World War I would apply again; that the importation of foodstuffs would be curtailed; and that although England would have to import some wheat and animal feed, it could grow enough of nearly everything else.

To verify that the diet was a healthy one, McCance and Widdowson, along with six other people, lived on it for three and one-half months. Their weekly rations were limited to sixteen ounces of meat, offal, poultry, bacon, and fish. Not more than two ounces could be bacon and not more than four ounces fish. They fixed the egg ration at one per person per week and the milk ration at a quarter of a pint per person per day. Butter and cooking fats were excluded. The ration for margarine and cheese was four ounces for each person per week. The weekly five-ounce sugar portion per person per week could be mixed with tea or coffee or used in jam, marmalade, syrup, or honey, according to the wishes of each volunteer. The amounts of coffee and tea were unlimited because of their psychological appeal. The volunteers were limited to six ounces of homegrown fruit and three ounces of dried vegetables, but there was no limit to the amount of potatoes. The volunteers weighed their portions on spring balances, and a seven-day supply of some foods such as margarine was apportioned to each person at the beginning of the week.

For most of the volunteers this regimen meant sudden, drastic changes in their diet. At first breakfast tended to be a dull meal of toast or plain bread, with perhaps a scrape of jam or margarine. Then by trial and error the volunteers found that reheated vegetable mixtures made breakfast more appetizing. At least three lunches each week consisted of large helpings of "vegetable soup," which was merely vegetables cooked in water and flavored variously. Sometimes the soup doubled as gravy for the potatoes or vegetable dishes that made up the other four lunches in the week, or it was served with dry bread to make it more palatable. Dinner was usually a single course containing the daily meat, fish, or cheese ration. Although the amount of cheese was small, it was enough to make a large dish of potatoes, rice, or vegetables tasty. Moderate amounts of curry, herbs, vinegar, and spices also proved valuable adjuncts. The volunteers' only dessert was an occasional baked apple. The food was so dry and bulky that it took more than an hour to eat most meals.

Just after Christmas 1939, four of the volunteers went to the Lake District of England for an additional two weeks. Wanting a vacation, they combined work with pleasure. They tested their physical fitness with very strenuous exercise while still living on the diet. McCance and another member of the party cycled over two hundred miles from Cambridge to the Lake District, the last one hundred miles over snowy roads. Widdowson came by car and brought sacks of potatoes, flour, and the other items in the diet; she did the cooking in a rented cottage.

At the end of the three-and-a-half month experimental period, the volunteers were in good health and physically fit, and most had acquired a taste for their new regime.

The experiment ended just as rationing went into effect in the United Kingdom, and the British government relied on the lengthy scientific report that McCance and Widdowson had written to set rations. The government regarded their work as so secret that it delayed official publication of the report until after the war.

On returning to Cambridge, McCance and Widdowson continued

their nutritional studies. Laboratory tests suggested that some volunteers were losing more calcium from their bodies than they were taking in, a trend that would be dangerous if it persisted. So in the spring of 1940 the two scientists expanded their research to investigate the absorption and excretion of calcium, magnesium, potassium, and phosphorus with diets containing a great deal of bread and very little milk or cheese. They also investigated the effect of taking additional vitamin D.

In the era before plastic bags, a certain amount of organization and forethought was necessary to carry out these experiments. When, for example, McCance and Widdowson traveled to London to give lectures, attend meetings, or discuss the progress of the research, they would carry their own bottles for collecting their urine. "You got used to the inconvenience," McCance said. When the volunteers were invited to a party, they carried along their bottles and special meals. They explained the reasons to their hosts. If someone objected, Widdowson said, "I was quite happy to let them think I was crazy."

As a direct result of these experiments, which lasted more than a year, manufacturers were required to modify the flour used for making bread during World War II; calcium carbonate was added to bread by law because the foods high in calcium such as milk and cheese were so drastically reduced in the wartime diet. The law still stands, although McCance and Widdowson believe it is now unnecessary.

Robert McCance and Elsie Widdowson, like the two Haldanes, spent most of their professional life investigating how the body works, and, like the Haldanes, they relied over and over again on the methodology of self-experimentation. Their experiments were more laborious than heroic, more grueling than dramatic. But this is often the case in science. Their contributions to medical knowledge were immense. The results of their dietary self-experiments, for example, not only helped the British maintain their health during the grim days of World War II but also contributed to the recognition of nutrition as an independent scientific discipline.

In the next chapter we will take a closer look at this relatively new area of science, and we will see how the self-experiments of two men in particular, one a Hungarian immigrant in New York City, the other the son of a Boston grocer, were crucial in helping science understand the role and importance of vitamins.

## Chapter Eleven

# DIETARY DEPRIVATIONS

Dr. Joseph Goldberger sat in his office at the U.S. Public Health Service and pondered the mysterious, itchy skin condition known as Schamberg's disease that was invading the city of Philadelphia. The disease had been named after an internationally known dermatologist who had first reported it in 1901, but Dr. Schamberg had been unable to determine its cause. Now, in 1909, Schamberg's disease, characterized by violent itching, a chicken poxlike rash, and sometimes fever and malaise, was nearing epidemic proportions in Philadelphia, keeping people from work and even threatening to close a fashionable hotel near the city.

As a quarantine physician and epidemiologist for the U.S. Public Health Service, it was Goldberger's task to discover the cause of Schamberg's disease, and quickly. He did. He had the answer in just two days.

Joseph Goldberger was born in Hungary in 1874. As a young boy he emigrated with his family to New York City, where he grew up with the ambition of becoming a mining engineer. However, when a friend took him to hear a lecture by a prominent physician, Goldberger was so impressed that he immediately changed his career plans. After interning at New York's Bellevue Hospital, Goldberger practiced general medicine for a short while before beginning a lifelong career with the U.S. Public Health Service in 1899, at the age of twenty-five.

Goldberger's methods of investigation were as thorough as those of the most skilled detective. Faced now with the mystery of Schamberg's disease, he meticulously set out to find clues. He examined patients, mapped out the distribution of the disease, and discovered a common thread: Each patient had slept on, or had been in contact with, a new straw mattress. Further sleuthing led to the discovery that the straw for these mattresses had come from a common source in New Jersey which, Goldberger hypothesized, must be infested with insects.[1]

To obtain conclusive proof, Goldberger kept his bare left arm and shoulder extended between two of the suspected straw mattresses for an hour. Sixteen hours later, the characteristic itching eruption appeared on the arm. Three other volunteers slept on the mattresses for one night; the next day, they, too, had the condition.

Next Goldberger took straw from a mattress implicated in a case of Schamberg's disease and sifted it through a fine flour sieve. He collected a boxful of the siftings and took it to a laboratory in Washington, where he divided the siftings into two dishes. He exposed one dish to chloroform fumes to kill any living organisms, but he did not disturb the other. Then he taped one dish to each side of his chest and left them there for several hours. After removal, the side with the dish that had been exposed to chloroform fumes was clear; the other side itched. Using a magnifying glass and a needle, Goldberger picked out from the straw tiny insects that were less than a hundredth of an inch long. An expert later identified them as a wheat-infesting mite called *Pediculoides ventricosus.* Thereafter, mattress manufacturers searched for this tiny troublemaker whenever they bought straw.

For the next five years Goldberger continued his medical detective work, becoming an authority on infectious diseases and earning a reputation as a gifted scientist and investigative genius. During this time, he contracted yellow fever, dengue fever, and a near-fatal case of typhus. Then in 1914 the surgeon general of the U.S. Public Health Service assigned Goldberger to his most challenging task. The dread disease pellagra, thought to be infectious, was spreading like an epidemic throughout the United States. Major outbreaks had occurred in orphanages, insane asylums, and rural villages, mostly in the southern part of the country. Congress responded by creating a Pellagra Commission; Dr. Joseph Goldberger was placed in charge.

We know today that pellagra is a dietary deprivation disease. Its name is derived from the Italian words for "rough skin," and it came to be known to doctors as a disease of the "three D's"—dermatitis, dementia, and diarrhea. Pellagra damages the skin in a variety of ways. In some individuals it reddens it like a sunburn, later producing scales and crusts that fall off or that become secondarily infected by bacteria and fungi. In others, the skin thickens, loses its elasticity, and turns brown. Sores develop in the mouth and the tongue becomes swollen and turns a scarlet red. Ulcers appear under the tongue and on the lip. More ulcers appear in the bowel, contributing to nausea, vomiting, and bloody diarrhea. Pellagra victims become confused and disoriented. They confabulate, fluently reciting fictitious events to cover up gaps in their memory. Some are depressed, others manic, and still others paranoid. Many become psychotic, sometimes permanently.

The first documented case of pellagra in the United States was reported in 1864, but it was in 1906 that the first large outbreak occurred.[2] That year about 150 cases appeared at the Mount Vernon Insane Hospital in Alabama. The death rate was as high as 63 percent, and in many cases it made people who were already mad even more insane.[3] Suddenly a "new" disease was spreading fear more rapidly than it was spreading itself.[4]

At the time medical opinion held that pellagra was an infectious disease caused by some unknown microorganism. Fear of transmission led many to adopt isolation, quarantine, and other drastic measures to "control" the disease. A commission supported the infectious concept, concluding in a report in the *Journal of the American Medical Association* that "pellagra is in all probability a specific infectious disease communicable from person-to-person by means at present unknown."[5]

Some scientists supported the belief that pellagra was an insect-borne disease like yellow fever and malaria. Louis Sambon of the London School of Tropical Medicine and Hygiene proposed that pellagra was transmitted by an insect, probably some species of the buffalo gnat.[6] This expert opinion was offered despite the fact that all previous attempts to transmit the disease by inoculating people with material from affected victims had failed.

Goldberger knew nothing about pellagra when he was ordered to head the commission; he had never even seen a case.[7] He observed sufferers in dirty dresses and grimy shirts living near garbage heaps amid flies and insects, and he considered the possibility that the disease was due to poor hygiene. But he was swayed from this when he read reports from the first pellagra conference, held in 1909. Though the disease was prevalent among residents of institutions, he noted, the nurses, doctors, and various other employees of the same institution had escaped it. He asked himself a simple question: How could an infectious organism affect one group and not another in the same environment? His answer: It could not. Goldberger was struck by another fact: Well-to-do people seemed exempt from the disease. Then, when he learned of the futility of several attempts to infect rhesus monkeys with pellagra, he discarded the theory of infectivity, and theorized that pellagra somehow resulted from an improper diet, not from an infection.[8]

To prove it, he began a series of experiments. He cured the disease in one ward of an orphanage in Mississippi by supplementing diets with milk, eggs, beans, peas, oatmeal, and meat. Pellagra continued in another ward of the orphanage, among a second group that was not given any dietary supplements. Next, by putting volunteers on a six-month diet that was low in protein but otherwise nutritious, he produced symptoms of pellagra in six of eleven prisoners at Mississippi's Rankin prison farm, where the disease had never been known to occur. Goldberger thought he had the answer now but he still could not be sure.

He brought his research to a climax with a series of experiments which he performed on himself, his wife, and about a dozen other doctors in four different areas of the United States. The experiments were designed to test every conceivable method of transmitting the disease in order to prove conclusively that it could *not* be transmitted.[9]

Goldberger's first self-experiment began on April 25, 1916, in Spartanburg, South Carolina. About a fifth of an ounce of blood drawn from a patient with a moderately acute first attack of pellagra was injected into the forty-two-year-old doctor's left shoulder and into the shoulder of another volunteer, Dr. George A. Wheeler. Wheeler then rubbed secretions taken from the nose and mouth of the pellagra patient into Goldberger's nose and mouth. Goldberger returned the favor. Nothing untoward happened.

Three days later, in Columbia, South Carolina, Goldberger swallowed capsules containing urine, feces, and skin taken from patients with severe cases of pellagra. A half hour before, and again after, the experiment, Goldberger swallowed a large amount of sodium bicarbonate to reduce the amount of acid in his stomach—a precaution taken to increase his chances of acquiring the disease. If a causative organism were present, the sodium bicarbonate would neutralize the acidic gastric juices that might kill it. Goldberger experienced a bout of diarrhea lasting a week after the experiment ended, but no pellagra.

On May 7, again in Spartanburg, he repeated the swallowing experiment on himself and five other volunteers, including his wife, Mary, the mother of their four children, who had insisted on the privilege of representing women as a volunteer in the experiments.[10] Mary Goldberger described her experience: "The men would not consent to my swallowing the pills, but I was given by hypodermic in the abdomen an injection of the blood of a woman dying of pellagra. This was an act of faith; it took no courage."[11] None of the volunteers developed pellagra.

A month later, in the fourth self-experiment in the series, Goldberger and four other volunteers swallowed more specimens taken from patients at the Washington Asylum Hospital in the nation's capital. During the next three weeks, Goldberger volunteered for three final experiments, bringing the total to seven in what he called the "filth parties." On June 25 Goldberger wrote: "We had our final 'filth party'—Wheeler, Sydenstricker [another researcher] and I—this noon. If anyone can get pellagra that way, we three should certainly have it good and hard. It's the last time. Never again."[12]

He and his colleagues remained healthy, proving conclusively that pellagra is not an infectious disease. But Goldberger's work was not done. Although he was certain that pellagra could be prevented by improving the diet, he had not yet identified its specific cause. Then in 1917 researchers at Yale showed that a canine disease called blacktongue was the equivalent of pellagra in man, and Goldberger began working with dogs.[13] His team eventually learned that brewer's yeast was an excellent pellagra preventive. But just what it was in the yeast that prevented the disease was still unknown. It was not until 1937 that other scientists learned that pellagra was caused by a deficiency of a B complex vitamin called nicotinic acid, or niacin.[14]

Goldberger's self-experiments were masterpieces of research and classics in epidemiology. Although he did not identify the vitamin, his pellagra studies had immediate impact, saving the lives of tens of thousands of people who now ate improved diets. Experts thought the research worthy of the Nobel Prize, but although he was nominated five times, Goldberger never did win medicine's highest award.[15] Many consider it one of the great injustices in the history of the prize.

In retrospect it can be seen that the long epidemic of pellagra in the United States had its origin in social causes. In the south, where the disease was most prevalent, an agricultural depression had been more or less constant since the 1890s. Wages were low, food prices high. The very poor ate a diet consisting largely of corn. But it was a change in the milling processes of grain that caused the spread of the disease to cities. Millers began producing fine-grain meal instead of whole-grain meal, and the new process removed the nicotinic acid.[16] It was a seemingly harmless change, but it created one of the most devastating epidemics in American history.

Understanding that the absence of certain substances from the diet can sicken or kill us was a monumental medical advance that had its roots in centuries of observation and experimentation. The ancient Egyptians, for example, used ox and fish liver to treat night blindness; today we know they were successful because liver is a rich source of vitamin A.

Over the years researchers have identified thirteen vitamins: A, C, D, E, K, B-6, B-12, biotin, folic acid, nicotinic acid (niacin), pantothenic acid, riboflavin, and B-1 (thiamine). These chemical substances control biochemical reactions by serving as partners with enzymes to accelerate chemical reactions, yet they are not consumed or permanently changed in the process. They are usually produced by plants, less often by animals. Vitamin research has passed through three phases: first, the recognition that vitamins are distinct from foods; second, the isolation of specific vitamins responsible for specific deficiencies; and third, the understanding of physiological and biochemical processes as well as the recognition that many vitamins are essential to normal growth and development.[17]

A crucial step in the discovery of vitamins occurred in the late 1800s, when a Dutch army doctor, Christiaan Eijkman, working at a military hospital in the Dutch East Indies, accidentally disproved the long-held medical assumption that beriberi, a disorder that begins with loss of appetite and moves on to paralysis, mental confusion, congestive heart failure, and, ultimately, death, was an infectious disease.[18]

Eijkman was observing the chickens in his courtyard when he noticed their wings drooped and they had the same upward-moving paralysis and bizarre gait of people with beriberi. Intrigued, Eijkman decided to investigate why. He learned that the chickens were fed garbage from the wards of the military hospital and that this garbage consisted chiefly of boiled polished rice (instead of the usual raw husked rice). After several experiments in which he tried unsuccessfully to transmit the disease from chicken to chicken, Eijkman eventually deduced that it was the polished rice itself that was causing a condition of the nervous system in the chickens. The condition is called polyneuritis, and it is the fowl equivalent of beriberi. Eijkman did not know that polished rice lacked vitamin B-1, or thiamine, so he attributed the disorder to a toxin. Today we know that, as in the case of pellagra, the milling method was the villain; it removed the vitamin from the protective outer coating of the rice.

Eijkman's discovery won him a Nobel Prize, which he shared in 1929 with Sir Frederick Gowland Hopkins, a British biochemist who, in 1912, described the substances we now call vitamins as "accessory factors of the diet."[19]

Meanwhile, Dr. Casimir Funk, a Polish-born biochemist working in England, isolated a crystalline substance from rice bran that could cure a type of beriberi that he had experimentally induced in pigeons.[20] He also found the same substance in yeast, and in 1911 he isolated small amounts of another substance that would later prove so elusive to Joseph Goldberger in his search for the specific cause of pellagra, nicotinic acid, or niacin. In 1912, the same year Hopkins wrote about "accessory factors," Funk named these substances "vitamines," short for vital amine, in the erroneous belief that they contained a nitrogen component called an amine. Later, when it was discovered that not all vitamins contained nitrogen, meaning not all were amines, the word was retained, but shortened to "vitamin."

The two decades it took from Goldberger's landmark studies to the discovery that the lack of niacin caused pellagra was a short time compared to the nearly two *centuries* that passed between the recognition that fresh fruits and vegetables could prevent and cure another dietary deprivation disease, scurvy, and the discovery that the specific cause of the disease was a lack of ascorbic acid, or vitamin C. The history of scurvy is one of discoveries being made and ignored, then having to be made again. Meanwhile, thousands of people, including a self-experimenter, died.

Scurvy attacks the body's connective tissues, weakening the support of bones and loosening the walls around the capillaries, the tiny blood vessels that connect arteries and veins. As a result, bleeding in the bones makes walking excruciatingly painful. The gums bleed. Minute hemorrhages develop in the skin around hair follicles and under the fingernails. Muscles and joints ache. Wounds heal poorly and break open easily. The personality changes. A scorbutic (vitamin C deficient) individual is easily exhausted and finds it increasingly difficult to do routine chores. Bleeding within the heart can cause sudden death. Scurvy decimated populations in medieval England, where diets were rich in beer, bread, dried peas and beans, salted meat, and cheese, but lacked vitamin C. It contributed to military defeats and disrupted explorations. In 1535 Jacques Cartier lost twenty-six men from scurvy in an expedition to the St. Lawrence River before the Indians came to his rescue by offering a cure—pine needles—which we now know contain vitamin C.[21]

We do not know who first learned the value of fresh fruits and vegetables in preventing and curing scurvy, but it was a British ship physician, Dr. James Lind, who made the first scientific documentation of the disease. He published "A Treatise on Scurvy" in 1753 after six years of study on board the H.M.S. *Salisbury.*[22] Incredibly, many knowledgeable people refused to accept his simple prescription—citrus fruits and vegetables. For several decades after Lind's discovery, his observations were ignored and scurvy continued to kill.[23] There were those who chose to believe that the cold, or salt air—not a lack of citrus fruit—caused scurvy, and Lind himself, while certain of the value of citrus fruit, continued to hold to meteorological beliefs, blaming the damp sea air. This may have been a factor in why his proposal for fresh food supplies on ships was rejected out of hand by British officials. At any rate, the failure to apply his findings has been called one of the most flagrant examples of administrative apathy in history.[24] It took forty-two years after publication of his treatise before government officials ordered navy ships to carry compulsory rations of lemon juice.[25]

The lack of immediate enthusiasm for Lind's findings partly explains why one of the earliest recorded nutritional experiments ended so tragically. In 1769, sixteen years after Lind published his treatise, Dr. William Stark, a twenty-nine-year-old physician in London, carried out a series of seemingly harmless dietary experiments on himself.[26] He kept superb records of his experiments and carefully documented their purpose: "Although air is more immediately necessary to life than food, the knowledge of the latter seems of more importance. . . . If possibly it could be pointed out to mankind that some articles used as food were hurtful, whilst others were in their nature innocent, and that the latter were numerous, various and pleasant, they might, perhaps, from a regard to their health, be induced to forego those which were hurtful, and confine themselves to those which were innocent. To establish such a distinction as this, from experiment and observation, is the chief object of my enquiry . . ."[27]

Stark was a friend of Dr. John Hunter, whose own self-experiment had such unforeseen consequences (see Prologue), and it was Hunter who helped him gain appointment to St. George's Hospital in London. Stark was also a frequent visitor to Benjamin Franklin's lodgings when the American lived in London as a representative of the Commonwealth of Pennsylvania. Franklin suggested the benefits of simple diets to Stark, and it was partly at his urging and that of Sir John Pringle, a leading London physician, that Stark began his self-experiments. His curiosity was particularly aroused by Franklin's description of how, as a journeyman printer, he had lived on a diet of bread and water for two weeks and had managed to remain well.

Stark, a well-built man who stood six feet tall, decided to determine by direct experiments whether such simple diets were, in fact, healthy. He lived on bread and water, sometimes supplemented with sugar and olive oil, for ten weeks. Then for another period of time, he ate flour and oils, bread and honey, and lean or fat meat such as roast goose or stewed or boiled beef. Among the questions he was trying to answer was: Which was more nutritious, the fat or the lean part of meat?

It was a change of schedule in his dietary experiments at a time when he was developing symptoms of scurvy that cost Stark his life. He had originally planned to investigate the effects of greens and fresh fruits next. Had he done so, his scurvy would have been cured, and most likely he would have been in better condition to withstand the intestinal infection that he also developed. Instead, he decided to test the food value of honey pudding and Cheshire cheese.

Possibly because Stark suspected his illness was scurvy, he consulted Pringle, who had considerable experience with the disease. Two editions of Lind's treatise had already appeared, but Pringle could not have been strongly influenced by Lind's observations. Instead of advising Stark to add fruits and vegetables to his diet, he recommended that Stark merely abstain from salt. Stark died on February 23, 1770, less than nine months after beginning his self-experiments. His friends attributed his death to "the impudent zeal with which he prosecuted" his investigations.[28]

One hundred forty-four years after Lind's documentation that oranges and lemons can cure and prevent scurvy, two Norwegian researchers, Dr. Axel Holst and Dr. Theodor Frölich, accidentally discovered an animal model for scurvy. In 1907, at the University of Christiana, the two researchers set out to repeat Eijkman's chicken-paralyzing experiment on guinea pigs, but when they fed the guinea pigs various types of grain, groats, and bread, the animals died of a disease that corresponded to scurvy rather than beriberi. Thus, guinea pigs became the test animals used to determine which foods protected against scurvy. Holst and Frölich found that scurvy did not develop in the guinea pigs when the animals were fed fresh cabbage or fresh potatoes, whereas it did appear when they ate dried potatoes. Additionally, the researchers found that boiled cabbage lost its power to prevent scurvy. By varying the amounts of fresh and stored foods, the scientists learned that dried material was generally useless in preventing scurvy and that the protective effect came largely from fresh foods. These experiments showed that the substance in scurvy-producing food was much less stable than the substance that protected against beriberi, for example.[29]

The existence of an animal model for scurvy moved scientists an important step closer to discovering vitamin C, but the observations were still crude because investigators lacked a source of the pure scurvy-preventing substance. Without that, they could not determine what symptoms were specifically due to a lack of that substance and not another, and how long it took for such a deficiency to develop. Another quarter of a century would pass before Albert Szent-Györgyi, a Hungarian chemist, would identify ascorbic acid, or vitamin C. His discovery helped to clarify the chemical structure of the vitamin and paved the way for the production of synthetic vitamin C. It also earned Szent-Györgyi a Nobel Prize in 1937.[30]

In the late 1930s, just after scientists had developed the biochemical techniques to isolate pure vitamin C, doctors began studying the role of the vitamin in the healing of surgical scars.[31] Surgeons had long known that previously well-healed wounds would break down in patients with scurvy. They were also keenly aware that surgical incisions and wounds from injuries among poorly nourished patients were slow to heal.

When tests to measure vitamin C first became available, doctors arbitrarily decided that an amount below 0.4 milligrams in every hundred milliliters of blood was abnormal. The results of these new vitamin C tests often showed very low figures, sometimes even zero, among patients whose surgical incisions would not heal quickly. Many surgeons assumed that low vitamin C levels indicated the presence of scurvy and that any coexisting anemia also was due to a lack of the vitamin. Yet doctors were puzzled because the tests measured no vitamin C among some patients whose surgical incisions healed quickly.

Dr. Charles C. Lund, a surgeon at the Boston City Hospital, headed a team of medical investigators who set out to answer some very basic questions: What was the normal amount of vitamin C in the blood? What did a low test result mean? How did blood test results for vitamin C correlate with the normal healing of a surgical wound? How much vitamin C must be lost before a wound would not heal properly? How much was poor wound healing due to a deficiency of this substance and not to other vitamins? Once scurvy was treated, how long would it take for proper tissue healing? Did lack of vitamin C itself produce anemia, or was anemia due to other nutritional deficiencies?[32]

Dr. John H. Crandon, an assistant surgical resident two years out of medical school, was a member of Lund's team. Crandon had been born poor, the son of a grocer, but when he was five, his mother divorced his father in order to marry a prominent doctor, the chief surgeon at the Boston City Hospital. The boy took his stepfather's name and followed his career, first to Harvard Medical School, then to the Boston City Hospital, where he trained under Lund. Lund's own father had, in fact, forced Crandon's stepfather to quit as chief surgeon because of a squabble involving medical politics. The sons of the two adversaries nevertheless became friends.

Crandon's mother, a woman with little education, became a well-known psychic who went by the name of Margery.[33] Crandon remembered witnessing one séance where his mother went into a trance and wrote several pages in Chinese, a language she did not know. A Chinese laundryman could not interpret the writing, but an expert at Harvard identified it as early Confucian Chinese. "It was hard for me to believe she didn't have a gift," Crandon told me years later. "But the pressures got too great and as her fame spread, my mother became less and less careful about what she did."[34]

Margery was a friend of Sir Arthur Conan Doyle, and although the respected Sherlock Holmes's author defended her supernormal powers, others, including the magician Houdini, were skeptical. In time some of Margery's feats were exposed as frauds, greatly embarrassing her son. As a result, the young Crandon became even more determined to become a success in his chosen career. As assistant surgical resident, he worked all day every day in the operating room and on the hospital wards. In addition, he took calls all night every other night.

Crandon was especially interested in the biochemistry of vitamin C and its relationship to surgical wound healing. With Lund's approval and the assistance of nutritionists at the Thorndike Research Laboratory at the Boston City Hospital, Crandon designed an experiment to determine how well and how quickly surgical wounds would heal in patients on a vitamin C-deficient diet. In the experiment, volunteers would eat foods with no vitamin C until scurvy developed. Then a series of deep incisions would be made through the skin and into the muscles, followed by periodic biopsies to determine how the wounds were healing.

Before the experiment could begin, Crandon had to learn the precise vitamin C content of various foods, as well as how practical it would be for a person to stay on such a diet for weeks, and what vitamin supplements the volunteer would need to prevent other dietary deficiencies.

Crandon planned to conduct the experiment on three people, on the presumption that data from three would have more scientific value than from just one. Without question, he himself would be one of the three. "I wouldn't think of experimenting on someone else until I had done the thing on myself," Crandon told me nearly forty years later, when he was still practicing medicine near Boston. "I wouldn't want to take the chance of killing anybody. I didn't expect to die because there was a good deal known about scurvy. People had gotten scurvy and had not died. But at the same time, I didn't feel it was morally correct to experimentally give scurvy to someone else unless I did it to myself."

Federal grants for such clinical experiments, standard now, were virtually unheard of in those days. Experimenting on himself would not require a special budget, but the two other volunteers would have to be paid for their cooperation. That was customary.

Crandon's aunt, Clara Stinson, a missionary, decided to help him by hiring two teenagers whom she knew from her work. Crandon was careful to explain to them exactly what was involved. Reliability was key. The volunteer had to studiously avoid vitamin C in his diet each day. Just one unintentional slipup could ruin the experiment. The teenagers were from poor families, and the fifty dollars per week they were paid for participating in the study was excellent money in those days. But three weeks after beginning the experiment, they quit after others observed the two drinking orange juice in a nearby cafeteria. They explained that they could not continue living on such a diet. Crandon carried on alone, living on a diet that, as he explained, "came down pretty much to cheese and crackers."

Crandon had begun his experiment on October 16, 1939, and for the first two months his diet consisted of well-cooked meat, butter, cake (containing no fruit or fruit flavoring), polished rice, and coffee. For the next six weeks, he ate Swiss and American cheeses, crackers, eggs, black coffee, beer, and a semisweet chocolate candy bar. He supplemented this with all the vitamins except C. "I never ate anyplace during the six months except at the Boston City Hospital and a delicatessen near the hospital called Bernstein's," Crandon told me. "I spent a lot of money in Bernstein's when I found I couldn't get the proper food in the dining hall. I had to be very careful of what I ate, but Bernstein understood because I had discussed it with him."

On the forty-first day of the experiment, vitamin C was no longer detectable in Crandon's blood. But because he had no evidence of scurvy, the experiment continued.

"At the end of three months, I thought for sure I must have scurvy," Crandon remembered. "We made a three-inch-long surgical incision down the right side of my back. Ten days later, a biopsy was taken to study the process of healing. Much to my horror, when the pathologists looked at small pieces of tissue under the microscope, they found evidence of good healing." Such a pathologic report would have pleased any other patient, but not Crandon.

Could it be that despite his diligence, he had somehow slipped up and eaten foods containing vitamin C? The answer was negative. To preclude just such a possibility Crandon had arranged for a technician to take a sample of his blood each morning to measure the level of ascorbic acid. Had he eaten any vitamin C, the blood test would have revealed it.

Crandon had been selling his blood to help defray the costs of his frequent meals at Bernstein's, and now, after the last blood donation, his blood pressure suddenly fell about thirty points. Furthermore, he began to let his work slip. He took afternoon naps in his room instead of caring for patients. "Fatigue was the overriding factor," he recalled. "I would get calls in the middle of the night that I should have answered by going over to the ward. Instead, I would ask someone else to do it because I was just too darn tired to get up."

Crandon's self-experiment drew a variety of reactions from his Boston City Hospital colleagues. Some began to wonder out loud what it would prove, and they accused him of "goofing off." A former secretary at the hospital recalled how a practical joker "paid a waitress at Bernstein's to put a large glass of orange juice in front of Crandon when he and others from the hospital were there on a coffee break."[35] The director of the experimental laboratory began to worry that Crandon would eventually kill himself. "But nobody told me I couldn't do the experiment," Crandon said.

Then, in late March, 132 days after the experiment had begun, Crandon happened to scratch his buttocks and calves and noted the skin was unusually rough. He spotted several bleeding spots at the point where the hair roots emerged from the skin. His first thought was that it was due to vitamin A deficiency. But an expert said no. Only in retrospect did Crandon realize that the tiny bleeding spots represented the first sign of scurvy. Meanwhile, he continued his monotonous diet of cheese and crackers. Before clear clinical manifestations of scurvy would become evident, Crandon would undergo an unforeseen and dramatic experience.

As a peripheral part of his experiment, Crandon had agreed to cooperate in a study designed to learn more about fatigue. The study was being conducted at the Harvard Business School by a team headed by Dr. David B. Dill.[36] Crandon had thought his vitamin experiment was without risk; now he discovered this was not the case. "They put me on a treadmill," he said, "and told me to run as fast as I could. I had not realized how weak I was. I had run just a little while when suddenly I had a feeling of impending death. My heart rate went up to one hundred ninety beats per minute, and I blacked out. The next thing I remembered was waking up on a cot in a small room, with someone hovering over me."

Crandon was lucky; he made a quick recovery.[37] Lind, the eighteenth-century scurvy pioneer, had described sudden deaths among people with scurvy, presumably from bleeding into their heart walls.[38] And Crandon most definitely had scurvy. The clinical evidence was clear when a surgical incision that had been made years earlier suddenly broke down. "I had had an appendectomy at age eight that my father had performed," Crandon told me. "One day, in the late stages of this experiment, I looked down and noticed a little black spot in my appendectomy scar. It was a silk stitch that my father had put in there. This wound was actually beginning to disintegrate." At last it was time to study scurvy's effect on the healing of fresh surgical wounds.

Exactly six months after the experiment had begun, Lund injected Crandon with a local anesthetic and prepared to make another long surgical incision down Crandon's back. Lund discussed the procedure in great detail before making the cut because he was apprehensive; he did not want to create a large wound. "Look, Charlie," Crandon said, "we've gone this far. I'm not going to have just a little skin wound and have the experiment loused up." He wanted Lund to make a true surgical wound to determine what happened in the deep layer of tissue between the skin and muscle known as the fascia.

Lund operated. He made an incision on the left side of Crandon's back, right down to the muscle. After ten days, the doctors did another biopsy. This time, in striking contrast to the results three months before, pathologists could see no evidence of healing.

Crandon remained on the vitamin C-free diet, but was given a gram of ascorbic acid each day for one week by intravenous injection. It was a step to assure the scientific validity of the findings, since some vitamin C taken by mouth can be destroyed by alkali in other foods. By getting the vitamin C by vein, Crandon could be certain he received the full dose. During that week, additional tests of his blood and urine were made for comparative purposes. All his wounds—the new and old ones—now healed quickly.

Crandon, who had started the experiment weighing 158 pounds, lost thirty-one pounds during the six months. "It did not take very long to regain the weight," he said. "At the end of the experiment my technician and I went over to Schrafft's in Harvard Square. I ordered roast beef and potatoes, and I ate and ate and ate."

What did the experiment prove?

First, it showed that a value of less than 0.4 milligrams of vitamin C per hundred milliliters of blood, the figure that doctors had arbitrarily selected as abnormal, was not necessarily dangerously low. Crandon and Lund, in their report of the study, explained that a very low amount of vitamin C in the blood "does not necessarily mean the presence of scurvy or even of a vitamin deficiency that is close to clinical scurvy, or that such a level indicates any necessary interference in wound healing."[39] Normal wound healing was slowed down, but Crandon could not determine precisely when, except that it occurred sometime between the third and sixth month after the experiment began. Crandon's experiment also showed that scurvy did not produce anemia, at least in the first six months, as some believed.

Lund, not Crandon, was the senior author of the scientific paper reporting the experiment, and Lund was quick, some say too quick, to broadcast the results at medical meetings. Crandon was upset, but as a young resident he had neither the administrative clout nor the willingness to protest. Nevertheless, he recalled the experiment with satisfaction: "The most important thing I proved," he told me, "was that vitamin C deficiency, if severe enough, would prevent wound healing in humans." It was one of the most cost-effective experiments ever done. "After all," he added with a chuckle, "just cheese and crackers!"

# Chapter Twelve

# THE RED CELL RIDDLE

Thirteen years before John Crandon began his vitamin C-free diet at the Boston City Hospital, another Harvard Medical School graduate was training at the hospital's Thorndike Memorial Laboratory to become a specialist in internal medicine. William Castle was to become a model for Crandon and others, one of the most admired professors at Harvard Medical School and a world-famous medical figure. But then, in 1926, he was a young doctor studying a serious illness called pernicious anemia, and, each morning, as part of his investigation, he was making himself sick.

Pernicious anemia is appropriately named because, until the early part of the twentieth century, it was deadly, usually killing a victim within two years of the diagnosis.[1] It is a disease that seems to be hereditary, though the precise pattern of inheritance is not known, and for unknown reasons it strikes more women than men, usually in middle age or later. In its initial stages pernicious anemia causes the tongue to become smooth and the mouth sore. Fruits and spicy foods burn, and appetite lessens. Personality changes can occur, with the patient becoming progressively more confused about simple matters. Eventually the disease can damage the nerve fibers in the spinal cord. The patient becomes clumsy, unable to perform the fine movements involved in writing, sewing, or turning the pages of a book. In its most severe form, pernicious anemia can cripple and ultimately kill. Moreover, it has been linked with stomach cancer.

The vast array of symptoms can easily lead to misdiagnoses—even admission to a mental institution—unless the doctor takes a careful medical history, does a thorough physical and neurological examination, and orders tests. In the mid-1920s, just before Castle began his experiments, pernicious anemia was killing about six thousand Americans and tens of thousands of people elsewhere around the world every year.[2] Yet all that doctors could offer as a remedy were large doses of arsenic. It was a distasteful and ineffectual treatment and potentially as dangerous as the disease it was supposed to cure.[3]

There are several types of anemia, each with a different cause and each requiring a different therapy, but all due to a lack of red blood cells, essential because they carry vital oxygen throughout the body. Red blood cells are produced in the bone marrow, and each of us has about twenty-five trillion of them circulating through our blood vessels. In their youngest form, red cells are known as reticulocytes. As a reticulocyte develops, its nucleus disappears and with it the ability to reproduce. Then, as the normal red blood cells age (their life span is about 120 days), the body begins to treat them as foreign objects, destroying them in much the same manner as it would invading bacteria. Their graveyard is the spleen, the organ wedged into the upper left quadrant of the abdomen. Here the dying red cells are broken down and the iron released is carried in the blood to the marrow for the formation of new red cells. The process goes on constantly; each day about 1 percent of the red cells are replenished. Anemia occurs when something in this process breaks down, causing a shortage of red blood cells; it is one of the most common conditions in the world.

Pernicious anemia is one of two megaloblastic anemias, so called because the mother cells (called stem cells) that form the red cells are unusually large and the marrow red cells they produce have an underdeveloped and abnormally large nucleus. William Castle's experiments would lead to a greater understanding of pernicious anemia and to dramatically improved treatment for victims of the disease. Castle would prove that without a certain substance, the reticulocytes of patients with pernicious anemia do not mature, resulting in an inadequate supply of functioning red cells. His work was to profoundly change medical concepts about anemia.

Historically, at least from the mid-nineteenth century, some doctors had observed, without proof, that dietary therapies could relieve the symptoms of pernicious anemia.[4] However, these observations failed to convince most doctors because they did not believe that diet could influence the formation of blood cells.

But in 1917 attitudes began to change and the outlook for pernicious anemia patients to brighten as a result of experiments on dogs performed by Dr. George H. Whipple, working first in San Francisco and later in Rochester, New York, where he was dean of the medical school for thirty-two years. Whipple and his associates made the dogs anemic by draining blood from their veins to remove red cells. After feeding a variety of dietary items to the animals, Whipple was able to establish that eating cooked liver could speed up the formation of hemoglobin and the regeneration of blood in the anemic dogs.[5]

The results of these studies led two Boston physicians, Dr. George R. Minot and Dr. William P. Murphy, to investigate the effect of liver on pernicious anemia. The occasionally beneficial results led them to make a serious therapeutic trial in 1925 that exceeded all their expectations.[6] Liver therapy actually saved a few patients, because it caused the production of mature red cells to begin within a few days. Some of their patients were so near death that the liver had to be forced through a stomach tube inserted in the nostril. The research led to a Nobel Prize in Physiology or Medicine in 1934 for Whipple, Minot, and Murphy, and helped make the study of blood diseases (hematology) a specialty of medicine. Furthermore, their work stimulated widespread interest in anemia. One physician who was particularly excited by the new liver therapy was Castle at the Thorndike Memorial Laboratory, a pioneering institution that had been formed by officials at Harvard and the Boston City Hospital to learn more about the physiological and biological aspects of disease and to train physicians in research and patient care.

William B. Castle was the son of a famous Harvard zoology professor and geneticist, so it was not surprising that he entered Harvard Medical School. At least one of his professors, however, must have been surprised when Castle went on to make major discoveries in the field of blood disorders and anemia, for in 1919 Castle failed a medical school course in blood diseases and had to repeat the final examination. Questions asked during the second examination stimulated his interest in studying disorders of the blood. Now, in 1926, the new therapy for pernicious anemia excited Castle, but it also puzzled him. Why did it work? Specifically, Castle wanted to learn why people who ate meat only occasionally, and then in cooked form, did not need to eat liver each day to avoid pernicious anemia. He began to ask himself how he might be able to find out.

The answer came one day while Castle was riding in an elevator on his way to hear Minot lecture on liver therapy. A hallmark of the disease was a scientific mystery—the absence of hydrochloric acid in the stomach. Castle wondered why patients who dramatically improved after eating liver still did not produce hydrochloric acid in their stomachs like other normal people. As he got off the elevator, he decided he would talk with Minot, so after the lecture, Castle went up to the podium and began to describe the thought that had just occurred to him. Perhaps, Castle told Minot, the patient with pernicious anemia had to eat liver because it contained a special substance, something curative that was created by the action of normal stomach juices on beef, a substance the pernicious anemia stomach lacked. Minot thought the theory had merit and encouraged Castle to design an experiment.

Castle was an extremely practical and frugal man, and he was very good at fixing things. He always kept a set of tools by his medical bag, and whenever a sink or faucet leaked in one of the old buildings that made up the Boston City Hospital complex, he would drop his research to fix it. His practical nature was very evident in the research design he developed for his experiment. The protocol was so simple that it required little more equipment than a meat chopper, a ten-inch yellow mixing bowl, an eggbeater, a tea strainer, a tablespoon, and a microscope. His intention was to feed a pernicious anemia patient 200 grams (a little less than half a pound) of rare hamburger meat each day for ten days to determine whether that amount would stimulate the body to form new red cells. If it did not, he would go on to a second step. He would feed a like amount of rare hamburger to himself, let the meat partially digest, then recover it from his stomach by self-induced vomiting. He would then concentrate and liquefy this material by incubation and insert it through a small flexible tube into the stomach of a pernicious anemia patient.

Castle would test the blood of the anemic patient every day for the presence of reticulocytes. If the youngest red blood cells were absent before the experiment but developed as a consequence of the feeding, then surely the results would point to something in the normal stomach that, acting on or in combination with a substance in the beef, stimulated production of red cells. Moreover, if the substitute digestion worked, it would imply that some previously undetected natural stomach substance was lacking in the pernicious anemia stomach.

Castle wanted to show that two factors existed. The one in the stomach he called "intrinsic factor" because it was naturally present in the body. The other, which was outside the body and something specifically present in meat, he called "extrinsic factor." In some way the "intrinsic factor" assisted in the absorption of the "extrinsic factor."

Castle did not explain the source of the material he inserted into the stomachs of his patients; any objection, he felt, would be esthetic, not biological. He acted with the approval of the senior Harvard physicians at the Thorndike, and he had a medical checkup before beginning to ensure that his own stomach juices would not spread a disease to anyone.

The initial part of the experiment progressed without incident. Castle fed a patient with pernicious anemia two hundred grams of rare beef hamburger daily for ten days. There was no change in the patient's reticulocyte count. Clearly, beef was of no curative benefit. It was time for the second phase of the experiment.

Castle began eating three hundred grams (about two thirds of a pound) of finely ground hamburger every morning. And each morning, an hour after his breakfast, he would throw up, recovering the partially digested stomach contents. Then, he would incubate the meat in the laboratory for three to four hours, sometimes adding pepsin (an enzyme produced by the stomach that chemically breaks down protein) and hydrochloric acid to make it more liquid. He would then pass the material through a fine wire strainer and eat some himself before feeding it to a patient through a stomach tube.

For purposes of the experiment, the patients ate a diet containing no beef, liver, or kidneys, and they fasted six hours before receiving Castle's concentrated material, to avoid complicating the experiment with possible effects from other food or digestive actions. "Reticulocyte tests were made daily," Castle told me many years later. "On the sixth day, there was evidence of a rise that was followed by further increases, giving an effect similar to the feeding of modest amounts of liver."[7]

Castle continued the experiments for about a month, sleeping in a room next to the Thorndike ward so he could care for the pernicious anemia patients himself. There was a progressive rise in their red cell counts as the days passed.

Castle was elated. There had to be something in his own stomach —intrinsic factor—that was lacking in the stomachs of pernicious anemia patients. Castle's stomach was the human factory that supplied the missing ingredient.

Next Castle tested the effects of pure stomach juice alone to make sure that, by itself, stomach juice was not the crucial missing substance. The results proved that stomach juice alone produces no rise in the number of new red cells in pernicious anemia patients. In another step, the human stomach juice was incubated with beefsteak in glass beakers in the laboratory before it was fed to patients. Several Harvard Medical School students were paid $15 a week to insert a tube through their nose and then swallow it into the stomach to supply 150 cubic centimeters of their stomach juice each day for Castle's experiments. Their stomach acid was used to treat the meat before it was then fed to the patients. Results confirmed the validity of Castle's scientific hunch; there was an increase in the red cell count of the pernicious anemia patients.

By showing that there was a substance, or factor, missing in the stomach of some people that led them to become anemic, Castle linked the stomach with the bone marrow, the main site of red cell production. Previously, doctors had known that one gland could affect other areas of the body, but this was the first time the stomach had been included in such a scheme. Castle was now ready to report the findings to his scientific peers. He appeared before a Washington meeting of the American Society for Clinical Investigation; at twenty-nine, he was an unknown researcher, and he was extremely nervous. "I sat up all night in Boston preparing my ten-minute talk," he recalled. "The next morning, while shaving, I could have sworn that my hair had turned gray at the temples."

At the meeting Castle's report stirred little immediate enthusiasm, and some participants even criticized his findings. As much as a decade later, one of Castle's critics published results of experiments that he believed disproved Castle's "extrinsic factor." The critic disputed Castle's interpretation of his findings because his theory was "complicated and seemed to present no analogy to any known biologic mechanism and to resemble no known deficiency state."[8]

Castle plunged into a further set of experiments that he hoped would meet the objections. This time the process would take not months but years. He and other researchers developed techniques to increase the concentration and reduce the volume of meat extract needed to treat pernicious anemia. Drug companies developed oral preparations of liver extract and of dried, ground-up hog stomach. They learned that liver was more potent than beef but they did not know why. It took more than two decades before investigators in the United States and England, partly inspired by Castle's self-experiment, were able to identify his extrinsic factor as vitamin B-12.[9] A few years later, Dorothy Hodgkin at Oxford University in England determined the detailed structure of vitamin B-12 by a process called X-ray crystallography. "The molecule that appears is very beautifully composed," she reported, "not far from spherical in form, with all the more chemically reactive groups on its surface." Hodgkin was awarded the Nobel Prize in Chemistry in 1964 for this and related major discoveries.[10]

Doctors now understood that because liver is so rich a source of vitamin B-12, someone who lacks intrinsic factor can absorb a tiny amount of the vitamin by eating liver and the amount will be enough to prevent pernicious anemia. Because beef contains much less vitamin B-12, the same pernicious anemia victim cannot absorb enough to prevent or treat the disease. Finally, it was clear that what intrinsic factor did was sharply enhance the absorbency of the small amounts of B-12 present in most animal foods. Intrinsic factor, we now know, is a protein in stomach juice. The presence of the protein permits absorption of about 70 percent of the vitamin B-12 consumed; in its absence, only about two percent of the vitamin is absorbed from the diet. Castle's experiments thus set the foundation for further discoveries relating to the absorption of foods and drugs into the body and the relationship of this absorption to both intrinsic and extrinsic factors.

Today death from pernicious anemia is rare. The stomach defect is not curable, but the disease can be kept in total remission by regular injections of vitamin B-12; only if the injections stop will the symptoms of pernicious anemia gradually return.

Castle continued to investigate blood disorders and anemia, and as subsequent research obliterated the criticism of his initial experiments, he became a world-famous medical figure. In 1931 and 1932, in studies in Puerto Rico for the Rockefeller Foundation, Castle and his colleagues found that iron supplements could correct a different type of anemia that was associated with infection from the hookworm parasite, even without removing the parasite. And just over a decade later, it was William Castle who stimulated Dr. Linus Pauling to investigate another form of anemia—sickle-cell anemia, a disorder that primarily affects blacks and people of Mediterranean origin.

Pauling's interest in sickle-cell anemia began during a scientific "bull session" that Pauling, a chemist, and Castle held in the club car of an express train as they were returning from a committee meeting in Denver in 1945.[11] The two scientists were discussing results of earlier sickle-cell research when Castle said he thought the molecular alignment of the sickled red cell might intrigue Pauling. The chemist followed up on the lead and in 1949 reported the evidence that sickle-cell anemia was a molecular disease, an abnormality due to the replacement of just a single amino acid in the complex hemoglobin molecule with the wrong one. It was the first time anyone had recognized that such a disorder was due to molecular derangement. This and other Pauling feats won him the Nobel Prize in Chemistry in 1954.

Such accomplishments might have made Castle a rich man, but he followed the Harvard policy of the time: No discovery or contribution to medical science or to the welfare of patients could be privately patented. For years he drove a 1929 Ford Model A roadster. Then, in 1953, he bought a secondhand 1936 Plymouth. In 1960, when the graduating medical class at Harvard, as an amusing gesture of appreciation, formally presented him with another old Plymouth bedecked with crimson ribbons, Castle promptly declined it. "If I had not," he said, "my apparent affluence of transport might suggest to the new medical alumni that there was no further need for contributions to the support of their Alma Mater!"

From the 1920s until he retired in the late 1960s, no professor at Harvard Medical School was more admired than Castle. He did research. He treated patients. He trained younger researchers. To work with Castle at the Thorndike was one of the most valued research opportunities in the world.

On a spring day in 1959, a young doctor walked into the Thorndike Memorial Laboratory building for the first time and noticed a tall man working on the wiring in the corridor, a toolbox by his side. The young doctor had arrived to discuss a research position that Dr. Castle had offered him, and, assuming the man was a janitor, he asked directions to Dr. Castle's office. The man paused in his work and directed the visitor to his appointment. Several minutes later, the "janitor," toolbox in hand, returned to his office and shook hands with the stunned young physician. His name was Victor D. Herbert, and he, too, would make a dramatic discovery about anemia.[12]

Victor Herbert, a namesake of the famous operetta composer who was his father's cousin, was a thirty-two-year-old hematologist when he met Castle, who was sixty-two. Herbert's father, a military man who composed marches and popular songs of lesser note than his cousin's, had joined the Lincoln Brigade and had been killed in the Spanish Civil War when Victor was just ten years old. Herbert's mother, who was a lawyer, died three years later after a long battle with breast cancer.

Herbert drifted from the Brooklyn Hebrew Orphan Asylum to a succession of foster homes and then lived at the Boys' Club on Manhattan's Lower East Side. After two years of college financed by scholarships and a stint in the army as a paratrooper, he settled down to study chemistry. But the memory of his mother's fight against cancer tugged at him, and his thoughts turned to medical school, despite the fact that it was well beyond his financial means. In 1948, when he applied to the Columbia University College of Physicians and Surgeons, prospective students were required to have guaranteed tuition funding and to list their sources of financial support. "I told them on my application that I had $25,000 in the bank, and various other lies like that," Herbert recalled. Columbia accepted him, and Herbert helped pay his tuition by selling life insurance policies to his teachers. On learning of his activities, the medical school dean was enraged. "He wanted to have me kicked out for lying on my application for admission," Herbert remembered.

But other faculty members supported him, and Herbert remained at Columbia. Following graduation, he interned at the Walter Reed Army Medical Center in Washington and then spent another tour of duty in the army, this time as a medical officer in Germany. He returned to New York to embark on a career as a research biochemist in the field of nutrition and blood disorders at the Albert Einstein College of Medicine in the Bronx. In 1958 he developed an interest in megaloblastic folic acid deficiency anemia, which, like pernicious anemia, produces red cells with large, underdeveloped nuclei. He moved to Mount Sinai Medical School in Manhattan to do research in that field, and, with another colleague there, Herbert developed the first practical laboratory test for measuring folic acid in human blood.[13] The test was based on the fact that bacteria called *Lactobacillus casei* need folic acid to grow. Folic acid, also called folate, is a vitamin that takes its name from the Latin word for leaf, a reflection of folate's abundance in green leafy vegetables. It is also plentiful in yeast, liver, and mushrooms. Folate is present in most foods, but it is destroyed by cooking and other processing.

Today, we know that a deficiency of folate can produce such symptoms as sore tongue, sore throat, difficulty in swallowing, diarrhea, gas pains, ulcers around the anus, and other gastrointestinal problems. Among those most susceptible to dietary folic acid deficiency are alcoholics, because they often eat poorly and because alcohol can interfere with the metabolism of folate; the elderly, those who live on marginal subsistence diets such as canned goods; and anyone whose diet consists entirely of cooked food.

In Herbert's day folic acid deficiency was considered a rare condition, and most doctors thought that when it did occur, there was usually a complicating disorder such as alcoholism, another blood disease, or an impairment of digestion that explained the folate deficiency. Herbert disagreed. He had treated several patients who had folic acid deficiency but who had no detectable intestinal malabsorption disorder or other complications. He believed a poor diet alone could produce folate deficiency.

Experience with a single patient often influences a researcher's career. For Herbert, the pivotal case was that of a retired engineer in the Boston subway system who had a combination of scurvy and folate-deficient megaloblastic anemia. Herbert learned that his patient, who was on a very tight budget, ate all his meals at a chain of fast-food hamburger stands in Boston. The practice of this particular chain was to make very thin hamburgers on a steam table in a central kitchen early in the morning, then ship them to various stands around the city, where the hamburgers continued to steam until served. Herbert determined that by the time the burgers were eaten, virtually all the vitamin C and folate had been steamed out.

"After a diet of such fifteen-cent hamburgers, donuts and coffee for five years," Herbert said, "my patient developed scurvy as well as a megaloblastic anemia, which I believed was due to folate deficiency."

The link between diet and megaloblastic anemia was clear in Herbert's mind. But, the subway engineer's case notwithstanding, it was still just a hunch. The only way to clarify the issue was to perform an experiment to determine whether an individual with dietary folic acid deficiency could develop megaloblastic anemia. This was a step that Herbert, now part of Castle's research team at the Thorndike, decided to take.

He set out to do the experiment on an informed colleague. "I thought I might be a more objective observer of someone other than myself," he told me. "I felt that if I used myself, various emotional things would be more likely to creep into the experiment and I might make a wrong judgment, such as terminating the study prematurely because I might think that the outcome was hopeless and that I would never develop megaloblastic anemia." In a customary research practice, Herbert proposed to one of the younger investigators training under him that he take on the project, both as the volunteer and as the senior author of the subsequent research paper.

But the young doctor, Louis W. Sullivan, declined. Sullivan's main interest at the time was in trying to determine the mechanism of action of Castle's intrinsic factor. "It was my first year as a fellow," Sullivan, who is now president of Morehouse School of Medicine in Atlanta, recalled, "and in my professional naiveté I did not recognize the significance of the study. Victor was asking an interesting question, but I did not recognize the magnitude of its importance. I was not enamored of going through a study whose length was unknown and whose potential payoff, in terms of importance, was not clear. I was happy to help out but not to do it myself."[14]

Sullivan's refusal did not offend Herbert, who told me later that he had really wanted to be the volunteer himself. He had come to believe that his original premise was wrong. Reliability was crucial to his experiment. "You have full responsibility and control over yourself," he explained, "but not over others. If I did the experiment on myself, I would know exactly what the subject did at all times." Furthermore, the risks were unknown and while Herbert did not think there was any real danger, he could not be certain. "If anything went wrong with someone else I would not want it on my conscience."

A final factor influenced his decision to perform the experiment on himself. "I greatly admired Dr. Castle," Herbert said, "and I respected him for the crucial and world-famous experiment he had performed on himself." He also knew that John Crandon had given himself experimental scurvy at the same hospital. "I wanted to be part of that courage, to be included in that company," Herbert said.[15]

Elaborate preparations had to be made before Herbert could begin the experiment. First, with the help of his technicians who used the bacteriologic test that he had developed, he determined the folate content of a variety of foods. The foods were tested raw and then boiled once, twice, and even three times to make certain that no folate remained.

When the experiment began in October 1961, Herbert had no idea how long it would take for him to develop anemia. He was prepared to stay on his special diet for six months, even a year, if necessary. He began eating most of his meals in the hospital kitchen, where dieticians prepared his food according to the research protocol. For weekends and travel, the meals were put in cellophane bags that Herbert took with him. This occasionally led to unusual and amusing situations. "At Thanksgiving," he recalled, "I pulled out my outrageous cellophane bag of finely diced and thrice-boiled chicken, poured it on an empty plate, and ate it instead of turkey and the trimmings."

And so Herbert, like Crandon before him, purposely set out to give himself a disease through a meticulously followed diet. For breakfast, he had unlimited cups of sugared black coffee. For lunch he ate a slice of chicken or a frankfurter, plus rice or diced potato with margarine. He would vary this with Maine sardines in soybean oil or a casserole of beef hamburger, potato, rice, onions, and egg white. Desserts included flavored gelatin, cornstarch pudding, and thrice-boiled applesauce. Beverages included colas, ginger ale, and Seven-Up. He avoided anything fresh, anything uncooked.

Despite the copious use of salt, pepper, lemon extract, Worcestershire sauce, and monosodium glutamate, the diet was so unpalatable that Herbert sought ways to make it tastier. Lobster was a delicacy that he particularly missed, and suspecting that lobsters did not contain much folate, he tested one. To his surprise, its folate level was high. When a physician friend told him that some lobsters were caught close to shore and others farther out, Herbert tested one from deep waters. Its folate level was extremely low. The difference, he learned, was that those lobsters caught closer to shore had scavenged human refuse. Lobsterman friends began supplying the experimenter with an occasional lobster caught far offshore.

Herbert continued to carry his full research and teaching load at the hospital during the experiment, and colleagues would often stop and ask, "How's it going?" He sensed they admired him for it, although there was one person who strongly disapproved of any self-experimentation. "He said I was committing a social wrong," Herbert said, "because doctors should not experiment on themselves. It smacked of Frankenstein's monster to him."

Castle, of course, approved, but he was extremely busy, and there were times when it was hard for him to discuss experiments in progress with his younger researchers. Herbert, however, knew how to get in touch with his boss, by appealing to the Mr. Fixit in him. "I kept a few bad washers around," he told me with a broad grin. "Whenever I had to discuss something urgently with him, I would replace the good washers in the faucet with bad ones. Then I would call him to fix it. He would come immediately, and while he made the repairs, we discussed the research problems."

Meanwhile, each day doctors stuck a needle into a vein in Herbert's arm to take blood samples. The blood was then analyzed to determine the amount of folic acid and to measure the production of new red blood cells. Periodically, a bone marrow test was done to see whether megaloblastic anemia had developed. This is a momentarily painful procedure because a needle must be inserted into the soft part of the hip or breastbone to withdraw a sample of the marrow that produces red blood cells. Sullivan, the younger researcher who had declined to be the volunteer, performed the test on Herbert. "There's always a fear in the back of your mind that the guy with the needle is going to press too hard and go through the back wall of your breastbone and into your heart," Herbert said. "That's a frightening thought. I knew Lou Sullivan was skilled with the bone marrow needle, and I knew that it wouldn't happen. Still, there was that fear." Nine times during the experiment, Herbert went to the treatment room at the Thorndike Memorial Laboratory for the bone marrow test. Each time his hands were sweaty, reflecting his anxiety. To partly relieve his fear, he would hold hands during the procedure with a pretty technician, Brenda Conti. "I used to kid Victor that holding hands with Brenda was the reason he had so many bone marrow tests," Sullivan recalled with a laugh.

As the days and weeks passed and Herbert's body became depleted of its stores of folic acid, he became forgetful. When he went to drive home after work one day, he could not remember where he had parked his car. According to his wife, he got "very skinny and very, very irritable."

Fall turned into winter, and the experiment continued. On Christmas Eve, Herbert went to bed feeling a little weak. In recent days, he had not been quite up to par. He decided to sleep late on Christmas morning. His wife got up early and went out with the children. She wanted to give her husband a few extra hours of sleep. When Herbert awoke and tried to get out of bed, his legs were so weak they seemed paralyzed. "I was quite frightened," he remembered. "My first thought was: Could I have gotten polio? I was pretty scared until I calmed down and started to assess what was going on."

There was then a belief among some physicians that folic acid deficiency could damage nerves in a manner similar to pernicious anemia. Herbert had never agreed with the notion, but as he lay motionless on his bed that Christmas morning, he considered that he might have proved himself wrong. Could he have developed a permanent paralysis from folic acid deficiency? Then he thought of another possibility.

"It suddenly dawned on me," he explained, "that the elaborate preparations of my food might have removed much of the potassium. I had recently read an article about paralysis resulting from potassium depletion. Drug companies would send me samples every day, and my custom was to throw them in the drawer of an end table next to the bed. That morning, I reached over and opened the drawer. Luckily, amid the drug samples I found some that contained potassium iodide. I took them, and after a short while I was able to swing my legs off the side of the bed. I was pretty weak but able to walk."

Herbert dressed and drove to the Thorndike. "I had a standard shift car, and it was difficult to depress the clutch."

The physician on duty was Dr. Ronald Arky, now a professor at Harvard and chief of medicine at the Mount Auburn Hospital in Cambridge, Massachusetts. When Arky arrived at the hospital on Christmas morning to attend to a research project of his own, he saw Herbert weakly trying to open the elevator door.[16]

"What's the trouble?" Arky asked. Herbert did not know. He could move his arms and legs, but he had difficulty raising his feet. It might be potassium deficiency. Arky got a wheelchair and took Herbert up to the second floor to examine him. It is hard for people now to imagine that the extensive blood tests given so routinely today were not always routine, nor were they automated. "In 1961," Arky told me, "the test for potassium was not in wide use, and it had to be done by hand by someone competent in the technique known as flame photometry. At the Boston City Hospital, this test was not done on holidays, so I had to get one of the kidney experts to do it as a favor. The results came back: 2.77."

That was an extremely low value, much lower than the number recorded at the beginning of the study. Presumably, the amount of potassium had been even lower before Herbert had swallowed the potassium-containing medicine at home. Herbert was in danger of sudden death. Within the day, however, after receiving more potassium, his condition improved dramatically. With sufficient amounts of potassium in his body, the paralysis disappeared. For the remainder of the experiment, potassium tablets were added to his boiled food, and the weakness never returned.

A frightened Herbert had diagnosed his own condition, and in doing so had demonstrated the value of self-experimentation by a trained researcher. "Had I been a layman volunteer," he said, "I would not have made the association between the diet, potassium deficiency, and paralysis. I probably would have called my family physician, not the researcher doing the experiment. It was Christmas morning, and even if the doctor had seen me he might have dismissed the weakness as psychological, or, more likely, he would have admitted me to a hospital with the diagnosis of polio. In the hospital I would have eaten a regular diet containing more than enough potassium to correct the paralysis. The gradual improvement would have been attributed to recovery from polio."

A few critics recently have suggested that Herbert jeopardized his life by working alone and not regularly testing his body chemicals throughout the experiment. However, Castle and the entire Thorndike research team reviewed Herbert's and each other's projects at weekly meetings, welcoming suggestions from anyone. In fact, the team that looked in on Herbert's folate experiment included an expert in potassium abnormalities, and he had not recommended routine potassium tests.

Herbert underwent tests to ensure that his bowel was functioning normally so that if a megaloblastic anemia developed he could prove to any critics that it was not due to any anatomical or biochemical abnormality. For one of these tests a biopsy of his small intestine was to be taken. Dr. Lansing C. Hoskins, a colleague, inserted a tube device called the Crosby-Kugler capsule, through Herbert's mouth.[17] When an X ray showed the tip had reached Herbert's small intestine, Hoskins attached a syringe to the end sticking out of Herbert's mouth and pulled the syringe plunger back to create negative pressure. The suctioning triggered a second plunger and knife at the tip that acted as a guillotine to snare a tiny piece of Herbert's small intestine. Hoskins then began to pull the tube back through Herbert's body, but Herbert screamed at him to stop. "I had the distinct feeling my guts were being turned inside out," Herbert recalled, "until the plunger was released."

Hoskins, a specialist in gastroenterology (disorders of the intestinal tract) at the Veterans Administration Hospital and a professor of medicine at Case Western Reserve University in Cleveland, recalled the incident. "The thing got stuck coming out. It was sort of a tug of war. His intestine was on one end and I was pulling on the other. It is a complication that no longer occurs because of improvements in the device."

Eventually, Hoskins was able to retrieve the tiny piece of Herbert's intestine, and test results showed no abnormalities.

Herbert continued on the diet, and for four and a half months he detected no anemia. Then, after 133 days, and a total weight loss of twenty-six pounds, he developed a case of the megaloblastic form—the one he had predicted would occur. His hematocrit (the percentage of red cells in the blood) dropped from 48 to 42 percent. It was a mild anemia. At that point he stopped the experiment. There was nothing to be gained by developing a more severe anemia. He had proved his point.

When he delivered his scientific report at a medical meeting in Atlantic City, Herbert did not mention that he himself had been the volunteer. During the discussion Dr. Arnold D. Welch, who was head of the pharmacology department at Yale and who had worked with Castle, congratulated Herbert for "a fine piece of work that has been needed for many years." Welch knew Herbert had done the experiment on himself because Castle had told him. Yet when Welch spoke, he showed the same reluctance many investigators have to discuss self-experimentation in public. "I don't know whether the secret of who the subject was should be mentioned," Welch said. "Perhaps I should say only that there is courage here, as well as scientific brilliance."[18]

Herbert's self-experiment had an important impact on the practice of medicine. He proved conclusively that there was such a condition as diet-induced folic acid deficiency anemia, a disease now recognized to be widespread throughout the world. From the hundreds of laboratory tests that Herbert had done on samples of his blood and other materials collected from his body while he lived on the folate-free diet, the Thorndike team was able to reconstruct the sequence of biochemical, physiological, and pathological events that occur in the body as folate deficiency develops. Now doctors can interpret the results of blood tests to determine whether a patient has early, moderate, or advanced megaloblastic anemia due to folic acid deficiency. Further, Herbert's self-experiment led to the knowledge that the anemia that often develops among pregnant women was due to folic acid deficiency. Today women routinely take folic acid during pregnancy to compensate for the additional folic acid requirements imposed by the growing fetus.

Following the experiment, Herbert did additional studies to determine the minimum daily requirement of folic acid. These helped establish official dietary recommendations for this vitamin.[19]

Dr. Herbert is now chief of the hematology and nutrition research laboratory at the Bronx Veterans Administration Medical Center and a professor of medicine at Mount Sinai Medical Center in New York.[20] He told me that his self-experiment has had another positive benefit; it has made it easier for him to communicate with patients who need bone marrow aspirations. "When patients tell me, 'Doc, you don't know what this feels like,' I say, 'Yes I do. I have had nine of them and I know exactly what they feel like. I know they're scary and uncomfortable as hell, but I can tell you with complete candor that they are completely safe.' "

# Chapter Thirteen

# BLACK AND BLUE AT THE FLICK OF A FEATHER

Late on an April night in 1945, a seventeen-year-old girl was rushed to the Cambridge City Hospital across the Charles River from Boston. She was bleeding profusely from her womb. The resident doctor on call promptly accused her of having had an illegal abortion, which the young woman vigorously and tearfully denied, both to the resident and to her horrified parents.

William J. Harrington, a student from Tufts Medical School in Boston, who was helping to pay his tuition by working nights at the hospital, believed her story.[1] Indeed, the tests he did showed that her massive bleeding had been caused not by an abortion but by an unusual condition called idiopathic thrombocytopenic purpura, or ITP, a blood disorder that leads to a lack of platelets, blood cells essential to clotting.

There is no cure for ITP, and at the time of the girl's illness there was only one treatment—surgical removal of the spleen, which is the graveyard of the body's red blood cells and platelets. Removing this organ allows the platelets to function a little longer, sometimes providing enough time to help the patient with ITP.[2]

The girl died after the operation, not from ITP, but from atrocious surgery. The surgeon failed to tie the knot securely around the stump of the artery that once had fed the spleen. When the suture slipped off, she bled to death.

Harrington was so horrified by the whole episode—the boorish resident, the erroneous diagnosis, the atrocious surgery, and finally the inability of medicine to help the girl—that he changed his career plans. He had been training to become a pediatrician; now he determined to specialize in hematology. He would go on to develop a particular expertise in ITP, and he would follow in the footsteps of William Castle and join a number of contemporary researchers in making valuable contributions to medical knowledge of blood disorders through a special research methodology—self-experimentation.

Harrington was an Irish-American from a humble background, the son of a steamfitter, beloved by the neighborhood kids, and a mother whose vision for her children demanded hard work and learning. Some time after his graduation from Tufts Medical School, he went to St. Louis for postspecialty training with Dr. Carl V. Moore, a leading expert in blood disease, who headed the Department of Internal Medicine at Washington University Medical School.[3]

When in 1950, at the age of twenty-seven, Harrington applied to work with Moore, he was one of two candidates for the single hematology fellowship available there; it was funded by the National Institutes of Health. His competition was Dr. James W. Hollingsworth, whose main interest was in the study of antibodies. Instead of choosing one of the two and paying the winner a full salary, Moore hired both men, paying each a half-salary, or $1,800 a year for a seven-day work week. It was a pittance even in 1950, but Harrington and Hollingsworth were able to live comfortably, thanks to an aunt of one of the doctors who worked with them. She went to Europe for some months and allowed four young doctors, including Harrington and Hollingsworth, to take care of her mansion.

Moore was an inspiring teacher. When he learned of Harrington's interest in ITP, he encouraged the young doctor to think of experiments he could do to discover more about the mysterious disorder.

Idiopathic thrombocytopenic purpura is aptly named. "Idiopathic" is from the Greek, and means "of unknown cause"; "thrombocyte" is the technical name for a platelet; "-penia" is the suffix doctors add to denote a deficiency, and "purpura" is from the Latin for purple, describing the leakage of blood into the skin to form black and blue marks. These marks appear for no apparent reason and can be caused by a touch as light as the flick of a feather.[4]

ITP, though a frightening and potentially dangerous disease, is not painful. It can strike at any age. In children it may follow swiftly in the wake of a viral infection such as rubella (German measles), and it is usually temporary; most children recover completely. In adults, however, ITP's onset is completely unpredictable and it may last many years, waxing and waning for a decade or longer before it disappears. It often does not disappear at all. Whatever the age of the patient, ITP produces showers of pinpoint-sized bleeding points (petechiae) in the skin that cluster to form larger black and blue marks (purpura).[5] The severity of the disease, the amount of damage created by platelet destruction, is unrelated to the intensity of the purpura, or purple color.

ITP, which for unknown reasons strikes women more frequently than men, can also make its presence known in other ways. It may mean repeated bouts of nosebleeds or excessive bleeding from the gums or vagina, in the stool or the vomitus. Occasionally death occurs from internal bleeding. When the bleeding is in the brain, ITP can result in a stroke.

Over the years physicians have learned that certain drugs, toxins, chemicals, foods, organisms, and other factors can sometimes produce ITP in susceptible people. If a specific factor is laid to the disorder, "idiopathic" is dropped, and the diagnosis becomes thrombocytopenia purpura (TP) secondary to the offending drug or agent. The treatment then is to isolate the offending substance and avoid it. For some, it may be a seemingly harmless substance such as the quinine in tonic water, for others it appears as a reaction to insect bites. For still others, the agent may be a medication such as "water pills" (the diuretics that make the body lose water and that are common in treating high blood pressure), sulfa drugs, or Dilantin (the drug taken by many epileptics).

Nevertheless, despite exhaustive medical detective work, physicians are stymied most of the time: ITP is still much more prevalent than TP.

The lack of platelets in the blood of ITP patients caused some doctors to hypothesize that the large platelet-producing cells in the bone marrow called megakaryocytes simply did not mature and make platelets. Others believed that the bone marrow functioned normally but the spleen destroyed normally produced platelets at an abnormally rapid rate.

William Harrington was tantalized by an idea that had occurred to him after reading a report that some mothers with ITP had given birth to babies with too few platelets. The platelet destruction theory suggested to him that some factor in the plasma portion of the blood had penetrated the placenta and harmed the platelets of the fetus. Now, he sought a way to prove it.[6]

Perhaps, Harrington thought, he could determine what caused the platelet destruction by taking plasma from a patient with ITP (animals were not known to be susceptible), injecting it into another person who did not have the condition, and then measuring the platelet count. If the active substance in the plasma caused a failure of the megakaryocytes to produce platelets in the bone marrow, he could expect to see a gradual decrease of platelets over five or six days, as they died off during the period then considered to be their normal life span. If, as Harrington suspected, the plasma contained a substance that destroyed platelets after their production, he could expect to see evidence of platelet destruction almost immediately. All Harrington needed to conduct his experiment was a patient with active ITP who was willing to cooperate.

One summer Sunday, a middle-aged woman with ITP was admitted to the hospital in St. Louis. A few weeks earlier her spleen had been removed, but the illness had persisted and grown worse, so she had returned to the hospital. She was an ideal candidate for Harrington's experiment and when he asked for her cooperation, she agreed. It was as simple as that.

"It was a different era," Harrington told me. "There were no human experimentation committees from which advance approval had to be obtained, as is the case today. There were no informed consent forms to sign. If we needed a blood sample, we took it from someone else in the laboratory. It was—and still is—customary to stick a colleague's finger for a few drops of blood or to put a needle in his vein to fill a syringe. Another day, that person would return the favor. I didn't see anything strange about the practice. It was the easiest and the least costly way of doing things."

Harrington designed the experiment and enlisted Hollingsworth's help; one of the two researchers would be the "other person" to get the ITP patient's plasma. They could not know in advance which of them it would be, because the choice depended on the results of a standard blood test. "Whoever had the correct blood type would get a unit of her blood and would give one back to her in an exchange transfusion," explained Hollingsworth, who is now a professor of medicine at the University of California Medical School in San Diego.[7]

The blood test showed that the patient had O positive blood; so did Harrington. Harrington became the volunteer.[8] Neither researcher informed Moore of the experiment; the senior physician was away.

The transfusion was not done directly; rather, a pint of blood was removed from both Harrington and the patient. Both pints were then sent to the laboratory so the blood could be tested first. They measured Harrington's platelets and those of the patient. Her platelet count was a mere 5,000 per cubic milliliter of blood; Harrington's was in the normal range, about 250,000. The two researchers had already tested the patient's bone marrow to confirm that her illness was not due to some other condition that would nullify the experiment and might endanger Harrington's life. Now it was Harrington's turn. He knew, just as Victor Herbert had known, that the bone marrow test could be intensely painful for a few seconds when the doctor pulled back on the syringe to aspirate a sample of the marrow. (See Chapter Twelve: The Red Cell Riddle.) Hollingsworth painted the skin over Harrington's chest with iodine, injected some procaine to help lessen the pain, and waited a few moments. Then he inserted a needle into the center of Harrington's breastbone. Hollingsworth pulled on the syringe, but Harrington did not flinch. He was so excited about the experiment that he hardly noticed the pain.

Following the bone marrow test, Hollingsworth began the exchange transfusions. As the patient rested in her hospital bed, Hollingsworth put a needle into her vein and watched as Harrington's blood began to flow. Then Hollingsworth returned to the laboratory and put a needle in Harrington's arm. As a pint of the woman's diseased blood trickled into his vein, Harrington sat quietly in a chair, reading a medical journal. The decision to choose one pint as the amount transfused was simply a matter of convenience; containers of that size were on hand in the blood bank.

"I didn't feel well soon after taking the stuff," Harrington said. "Nothing specific. I felt rather light-headed, with muscle aches—like the flu. No chills. Nothing to suggest a transfusion reaction. We readied the laboratory to do more platelet counts. Three hours after the transfusion, it was clear I didn't have too many platelets left. And I kidded Holly about not knowing how to count them. After we grabbed a bite to eat in the cafeteria, I lay on the table waiting for Holly to take the second bone marrow test. After it was done I said, 'I really don't feel very well. I think I am going to pass out.' "

Whereupon Harrington's muscles stiffened and twitched violently. He fell unconscious. Hollingsworth, his back turned, thought his partner was joking, but when he glanced at Harrington on the table, he knew immediately that something was wrong. Harrington's ear was blue, and he was twitching.

Harrington regained consciousness to find Hollingsworth shaking him. The two doctors were alone, and Hollingsworth, a Southerner, was yelling: "Come on, godammit, Yank. Stop fooling. We have lots of platelets to count."

Harrington got up and went back to counting platelets. There were very few in his own blood—but the patient's count had not risen. Harrington's mind was focused on the experiment. He was so enthusiastic that he was oblivious to any danger from another fainting spell. "Maybe," he said in retrospect, "I was too dumb to be worried!"

Finally, finished for the night, the two doctors walked the several blocks from the hospital to their mansion and went to bed. Only in the morning did they begin to speculate on what might have happened. Hollingsworth was convinced that his partner had not simply fainted. He believed Harrington had had a grand mal seizure, the type that affects many epileptics. Harrington had never had one before and even now no one knows precisely what caused it.

"My God," Hollingsworth thought to himself that morning. "What would have happened if he had dropped dead in that little room? I began to realize how dangerous this really was. Neither of us had considered that before." For the moment, at least, Harrington remained unconcerned.

In the early morning, they returned to the hospital to examine the woman with ITP and they learned that Moore had returned. When formal rounds began they told him about the ITP patient but not about the experiment. Moore examined the patient and was very pessimistic about her recovery. "After he had seen her," Harrington recalled, "he just shook his head and said, 'Well, this is bad. The lady has not responded to splenectomy. You are giving her cortisone [a then newly available steroid drug]. Still no response. These patients usually don't live.' I didn't quite know what to say. I just laughed. He turned, looked at me, and remarked how unprofessional it was for a doctor to laugh when he saw a patient in that condition."

So Harrington and Hollingsworth told Moore what they had done.

By now eighteen hours had elapsed since the experiment. Moore examined Harrington and found a few bleeding patches around his ankles. He had his technician verify Harrington's very low platelet count. Though producing just a few spots, the bleeding was enough to make Moore, who had had much more experience in treating ITP than Harrington, decide to admit Harrington to Barnes Hospital, the university's teaching hospital. Up to this point, Harrington had not been worried. Now, Moore's concern began to rub off, particularly when Moore mentioned the possibility of stroke.

"I decided that if I were going to get any more petechiae, they were not going to be upstairs in my head!" Harrington said. "I was determined to sleep upright [to counteract gravity and to minimize the blood flow to the brain]. There was a fair amount of kidding about that. Some doctors elsewhere in the hospital—not in the hematology group—felt I had probably lost what good sense I had anyhow during the seizure."

A clumsy examination by a younger colleague only added to Harrington's anxiety. Doctors, in examining a patient, routinely use their hands to check the size of the spleen; it is a diagnostic technique known as palpation. "In the hospital, a good-hearted but terribly rough intern palpated for my spleen," Harrington recalled. "I was getting rather bruised by someone who should have been a football player, and I told him to lay off. By that time I had some bruises from ITP on my legs, some petechiae on my lower legs, some bleeding from my gums and some blood in my stools." It was one of the most anxious moments in the most memorable week of Harrington's life. His concern was that his spleen would rupture from the physician's poking and that he would bleed to death or require emergency surgery. The intern seemed oblivious to this danger.

Harrington spent his first day at the hospital—as he would the rest of the week—sitting upright in bed, propped up by a pile of pillows. He was sure his platelets would return to normal in a few days' time. But every so often he wondered for a fleeting second: What if they do not?

Five days later the ordeal was over. His platelets were back to normal and the experiment was a spectacular success. Harrington had transformed theory into fact; not only had he developed the physical symptoms of ITP but he had also obtained scientific documentation from the bone marrow tests, which showed that the platelet production in his bone marrow was normal. The destruction, therefore, had to come from elsewhere; ITP was due to some factor in the blood that destroyed the platelets, not to a failure of the megakaryocytes to produce platelets in the bone marrow.

Harrington's success was reinforced by the reaction of the woman's body to his blood. Her platelet count did not rise. This lack of response to Harrington's normal blood in her body backed the theory that something in her own blood destroyed her platelets. For several weeks after the experiment, the woman had a very hard time, suffering massive internal bleeding. "She had fifty-six transfusions," Harrington remembered, "which is an enormous amount of blood. She was in her mid-fifties and obviously concerned that we had not been successful in treating her. Then she recovered for reasons we could never explain."

Harrington was thrilled by the contribution his experiment would make to knowledge about ITP. He was a bachelor at the time, and his concern about experimenting on himself was less than it might have been if he had had a wife and family. However, Hollingsworth recalled that Harrington, a devout Catholic, had become deeply concerned that some people might raise the issue of suicide if he were to die from the experimentally induced ITP and that at some point during the experiment Harrington had discussed the matter with church officials. Harrington denied it. "Holly's confused," he told me. "Someone called my family and told them I was in the hospital and they called my brother's classmate who had become a priest and who was at St. Louis University. Naturally, my brother's priest friend came to see me. But we did not discuss suicide."

When Harrington was a medical student in Boston, his mentor had been Dr. William C. Moloney of the Peter Bent Brigham Hospital. Moloney recalls that Moore called him after Harrington had carried out his experiment to explain the facts to Harrington's family, but Moloney denied to me knowledge of any such discussions with religious officials.[9]

Moore now repeated Harrington's experiment on himself. His blood group was also O positive. Taking another sample of blood from the same patient, he had it injected into his arm vein—in doses of fifty cubic centimeters, or about one-tenth of a pint. With that smaller amount, Moore's reaction was not as severe as Harrington's, but the results were demonstrably similar.[10]

For Harrington, the research on ITP was just beginning. He and his group of researchers now wanted to find out the nature of the substance in the plasma that had caused the reaction. Harrington repeated his self-experiment as many as thirty-five times during the next two years, and he was joined by virtually everyone in the laboratory—technicians, secretaries and colleagues. No volunteer developed permanent ITP.

These studies confirmed that ITP plasma contained an antiplatelet factor, a fact that contributed substantially to the understanding of the mechanism that produces the disorder. The discovery did not result in any specific therapy, but, by giving physicians a better understanding of what goes wrong in the physiology of an ITP patient's body, it helped them make better judgments about treatment. That, in turn, stimulated further research that now suggests that ITP results from an immunologic disturbance in which the body makes antibodies that destroy its own platelets.

Furthermore, Harrington's research helped establish that the platelet's normal life span is nine days, not five or six, as originally thought. This is not a trivial difference. Platelets are needed in the treatment of cancers such as leukemia as well as other diseases, and collecting them is technically difficult and costly. With the knowledge that platelets can live for three or four days longer than was previously realized, fewer transfusions are needed.

Today Harrington's work stands out as a classic experiment in hematology. As well as helping to clarify the function of platelets, it opened up new avenues of scientific investigation by advancing the concept of autoimmune disease, a condition in which the body damages itself. Humans do not ordinarily destroy their own tissues because the body recognizes the cells as its own and protects itself. However, the body is quick to recognize foreign substances such as invading microorganisms or transplanted tissue. Such foreign substances trigger the production of protective antibodies that destroy the invaders. According to the concept of autoimmune disorders, an individual's body regards some of its own cells as if they were from someone else. It begins to destroy itself by making antibodies against its own tissues. Precisely how a healthy body distinguishes between its own tissues and foreign ones is not known, nor is it known why autoimmunity develops.

Harrington, and then other researchers, provided evidence that ITP is caused in part by antibodies produced against a normal component of one's own platelets. Although the triggering agent could be a foreign substance, it could also be something within one's own body.

Autoimmune disorders had been suspected before Harrington's experiment was performed, but because scientific evidence was lacking, there was heated debate about their existence. Now Harrington had provided considerable evidence; ITP was the first documented autoimmune disease based on experiments in a living person. Additional research has since identified other autoimmune disorders, among them rheumatoid arthritis and lupus erythematosus, as well as some types of thyroid disease and anemia.

Harrington's research led indirectly to a Nobel Prize, won not by him but by Professor Jean Dausset of Paris. After Harrington's experiment, Dausset spent several years investigating the antibodies against platelets produced in ITP and other diseases. Then he began research into the immunology of white blood cells. He shared the Nobel Prize in 1980 for his studies that demonstrated the existence of HLA (histocompatability locus antigens, or, more popularly, the so-called "transplantation" antigens) in human cells. "Reading Harrington's work pushed me to try my experiments," Dausset said.[11] Dausset also told me that he had experimented on himself. Six skin grafts from other volunteers had been put on his forearms as part of his own immunological studies.[12]

Harrington went on to head up the Department of Internal Medicine at the University of Miami. He upheld a tradition of self-experimentation at Washington University Medical School in St. Louis that had begun well before him and would continue long after. Its use as a research tool at this particular university was so frequent and had gone on for so many years that some scientists—especially those who had never self-experimented themselves and perhaps did not understand the reasons for it—nicknamed the University "The Kamikaze School of Medicine."[13] It was a tradition that would continue at the same school even more dramatically—with cancer self-experiments.

# Chapter Fourteen

# CANCER: CAN YOU GIVE IT TO YOURSELF?

Dr. Carl Moore of Washington University in St. Louis was spending the Thanksgiving weekend of 1953 as a patient in Barnes Hospital, where he was head of medicine. His nose was oozing blood, and he sat in bed propped up by pillows to prevent damage to his brain. But this severely bleeding physician might just as well have been sitting in his office a few doors away. Calmly, unflappably, he interviewed Dr. Thomas E. Brittingham III of New York, a young doctor who was hoping to earn a fellowship and work for Moore to learn the specialty of hematology.

"It was some way to get introduced," Brittingham recalled many years later.[1] In fact, with nurses frequently interrupting to check Moore's blood pressure and other vital signs, it was one of the oddest interviews in medical history.

Moore had wound up a patient after the latest in a series of self-experiments trying to pin down the nature of the blood disorder idiopathic thrombocytopenic purpura (ITP).[2] Two of Moore's older trainees, Dr. William Harrington and Dr. James Hollingsworth, had begun the research three years earlier. (See Chapter Thirteen: Black and Blue at the Flick of a Feather.)

Brittingham was mesmerized by Moore's personality, particularly his seeming self-possession. "He was totally calm, unflustered, and composed," Brittingham told me, "and he transmitted that feeling to those around him." When Moore offered the fellowship to Brittingham, he accepted without hesitation. The younger researcher had no idea that in time he, too, would be a patient in the same hospital, fighting for his life as a result of complications from his own self-experiment.

Thomas Brittingham was born in Cleveland, Ohio, the son of wealthy parents. His physician father died when the boy was just twelve, and soon thereafter young Thomas was sent away to boarding school. It was not a happy time for him; he missed his home and family. From boarding school, Brittingham went to Princeton, where he recalls being "a terrible student who got excellent grades." He quit after his sophomore year and joined the army. During his time in the service Brittingham was able to focus more clearly on his future, and he decided to become a physician, like his father. He entered Harvard Medical School and graduated in 1950. He was in his fourth year of training as a specialist in internal medicine at New York Hospital when he traveled to St. Louis to meet with Dr. Moore.

When Brittingham returned to St. Louis on September 1, 1954, to take up his new position, Moore assigned him a special project to find out whether white blood cells had other properties beyond their role in fighting infection. Moore challenged his student to explore other facets: Why, for instance, even when tests verified that blood groups were correctly matched, did some people have serious reactions to blood transfusions? The St. Louis researchers suspected that such reactions were due to white blood cell antibodies called leukoagglutinins, which the body sometimes forms to counter foreign substances contained on the surface of the donor's white cells, known as antigens, even when the red cell group was properly matched.

Brittingham accepted the challenge and began his study of white blood cells with ferocious determination. First he adapted a laboratory test to detect white cell antibodies that Dr. Jean Dausset, the immunologist, and his colleagues had developed in France a few years earlier.[3] Then he spent hours in the laboratory, examining the white cell antibodies in patients with white cell disorders. He began to notice an interesting correlation—the white cell antibodies seemed to be highest among those patients who had received the most blood transfusions. Were these antibodies an artifact (something seen in the laboratory that appeared to be real but was not) or a genuine phenomenon?

Brittingham believed they were real and that they were produced in response to injected white cells. He theorized that after a blood transfusion a recipient's body sometimes recognized a donor's white cells as foreign. This stimulated the production of antibodies, just as though a virus or other infectious organism had invaded the body; in this case the antibodies formed were directed against the donated white cells. If an individual got enough transfusions, Brittingham hypothesized, the white cell antibodies could cause the distressing, sometimes fatal reactions that complicated more than 1 percent of all transfusions. The theory was supported by clinical observations that the St. Louis team, among others, had made. They had found that strong white cell antibodies were present in the blood of most patients who had received several transfusions and who had histories of fever and other reactions to them. Laboratory tests showed that the white cell antibodies in such patients had no effect when mixed with the patient's own white cells but that they reacted in test tubes when they were mixed with white cells from other people (as occurs in a transfusion).

Brittingham carried his hypothesis a step further and theorized that the white cell antibodies might be beneficial in treating patients with leukemia and perhaps even other cancers. He knew that patients with leukemia produced an excessive number of white cells. White cell antibodies might inhibit the process. He could test this theory by taking some of the gamma globulin (the antibody-containing portion of the blood) formed in a person who had been immunized against white cell antigens and injecting it into a leukemic individual. Such an experiment would be risky, but it would offer hope to a person with a disease that was otherwise incurable.

But Brittingham had other questions and he wanted to take the experiment a step further. He believed there might be unknown differences between the characteristics of the antigens produced by normal cells and those of cancerous cells that proliferate wildly in leukemia. To test this hypothesis, he wanted to inject white cells from a leukemic patient into a person who was free of any form of cancer to determine whether the recipient reacted and, if so, whether the reactions were specific to leukemic cells or to that individual's biology. He did not think the risks of such an experiment were great, but he felt that for ethical reasons the investigator who designed such a study would have to do it on himself first. He was willing, even eager, to be the volunteer. He talked it over with his two bosses, Moore and Harrington, and the more he talked, the more his enthusiasm for the idea increased. He had an insatiable curiosity about the whole project.

Moore voiced no objections, but Harrington was skeptical. He told Brittingham that it was "silly" to take the chance of getting leukemia. Brittingham replied that he would do the experiment with or without Harrington's help, so Harrington, sympathetic to Brittingham's curiosity, agreed to cooperate. Harrington could well understand Brittingham's willingness as a scientist to put his life on the line for an experiment he believed in.[4] Furthermore, a few medical reports had shown that nothing untoward had happened to patients who had accidentally or inadvertently received blood transfusions from leukemics.[5] But both Harrington and Brittingham knew that too few experiments had been done to rule out the possibility that blood cancer could be transmitted. Brittingham believed that the possibility was "extremely unlikely," but he was willing to face the consequences if he was wrong. In fact, Harrington recalls Brittingham's enthusiasm about this prospect. "Wouldn't it be great," Brittingham told him, "if I could also prove that leukemia was a transmissible disease."

Brittingham, like Harrington and Moore, was anxious to make an impact on science and to advance it. "It was his way of serving humanity," said Dr. Seymour Reichlin, one of Brittingham's oldest professional colleagues and friends. "If an experiment ended in death," Reichlin told me, "Tom would not consider it a suicide, but the price one would have to pay."[6] Reichlin, as we shall see, did not share his friend's views on this subject.

As dangerous as Brittingham's proposed cancer experiment was, it was not the first. In 1777 Dr. James Nooth, surgeon to the Duke of Kent, a member of the Royal College of Surgeons, and a practitioner in Bath, England, inserted cancerous tissue into a small incision in his arm. Later he reported: "Two hours afterwards I felt the part uneasy, with a strong pulsation. On the following day, it was more uneasy, and much more inflammation appeared than generally attends so small a wound inflicted by a sharp instrument; on the third, it remained nearly in the same state; on the fourth day the wound became easier, and the inflammation and pulsation began to subside. A few days afterwards a large dry scab was formed, which I removed, and found the sore perfectly healed."[7] Not wanting to rely on a single experiment, Nooth repeated it several times; he did not become ill nor did he develop cancer.

Shortly thereafter, another set of self-experiments was done across the English Channel, and little more is known about them than about Nooth's. On October 17, 1808, Dr. Jean Louis Alibert, a French dermatologist who would become Louis XVIII's personal physician, permitted a colleague to inject him with a sample of liquid material from a woman who had cancer of the breast. The same material was also injected into a medical student and two of Alibert's colleagues. Except for an inflammatory reaction, none became ill. A week later, Alibert and another of his colleagues received a second injection of cancerous material; the records do not indicate whether it was from the same patient. Again, Alibert had nothing other than a mild inflammatory reaction; his colleague developed a more severe infection, which caused swelling of the lymph nodes in the armpit and in the neck. But he did not get cancer either.[8]

Then, in 1901, Dr. Nicholas Senn, a leading surgeon in Chicago, dared to implant cancerous tissue in his own body to demonstrate his belief that cancer was neither contagious nor communicable (transmitted by common sources such as food or insects). On May 4, after finishing an operation on a sixty-year-old man with cancer of the lip, Senn allowed a fragment of that patient's malignant cancerous lymph node to be put under the skin of his own forearm. A week later, a new nodule appeared at the site of the incision; it remained for about two weeks, then vanished. Seven weeks after the injection, the only visible evidence of Senn's self-experimentation was a thin red scar at the site of implantation.

In reporting his experiment in the *Journal of the American Medical Association,* Senn cited the vast amount of accumulated evidence that cancer was not caused by a microbe transmissible to humans. Furthermore, he noted that: "No well-authenticated case of inoculation carcinoma has occurred among surgeons who have frequently injured their fingers and hands during operations for carcinoma, while inoculation tuberculosis from the same cause has been frequently observed. The same can be said of persons who take care of carcinoma patients, or who live with them in the same room."[9] Despite Senn's experiment, many scientists continued to believe that cancer was a communicable disease.

Cancer self-experimentation also attracted a prominent German scientist, Dr. Gerhard Domagk, who sought a substance that would kill cancer cells without harming normal ones. Domagk, a microbiologist, had won the Nobel Prize in 1939 for his discovery of sulfa drugs. Now, in the last few years of his professional life, he focused his interests on cancer. In 1949, he reported that he had sterilized extracts of human cancers and that he had then injected them repeatedly into animals as well as into himself to learn whether he could use such extracts as a vaccine to protect cancer patients.[10] "I have proved the innocuousness of sterile extracts of human tumors by injecting myself on many occasions during the past ten years," Domagk said.[11]

Little more was heard about the immunization concept until recently. Now, in a variation of Domagk's theory, the World Health Organization and other groups are sponsoring research projects aimed at determining whether a vaccine can prevent a liver cancer called a hepatoma, one of the most common cancers in the world. The WHO strategy is not the direct one Domagk tried but an indirect one, based on the belief that a common liver infection called hepatitis B is often a precursor of hepatomas. The vaccine strategy is to prevent hepatomas by first preventing hepatitis B.

Cancer self-experiments remain, however, few and far between. Ethical considerations seem to preclude human experiments with this disease. The ideal way to discover whether leukemia can be transmitted between people is to inject leukemic blood into healthy individuals, as Brittingham proposed. But none dared do it. A few doctors did try to transmit leukemia to patients who were suffering from other kinds of cancers.[12] In these instances, none of the patients developed leukemia before they died from their original cancers. This did not in fact disprove the theory that the disease could be transmitted among humans, because the incubation period of leukemia might have exceeded the time left to such terminally ill patients.

Brittingham was unaware of this history of cancer self-experimentation, but he knew enough to be sure he wanted to proceed. He was thirty years old, married, and the father of three children with a fourth on the way. Even with these family responsibilities, he never considered doing the experiment on another person first. He sought to answer two questions: First, could he pass the cancer from one person to another? Second, would his body produce antibodies to the injected leukemic white cells? He designed an experiment that would allow him to answer both these questions in the same person—himself. He would inject white blood cells into his own body from someone with chronic myelogenous leukemia, a blood cancer in which the body produces from thirty to fifty times the usual number of white cells—about 150,000 to 250,000 per cubic milliliter. No other condition produces such an excess. He would then test his blood, first to determine whether he had developed the disease, second to see whether his body had produced antibodies to the injected white cells.

The injections, given by Harrington, began on December 1, 1954, and ended on April 14, 1955. Each time, Harrington would withdraw 100 milliliters of blood—enough to fill two large syringes—from the vein of a fifty-eight-year-old housewife who had chronic myelogenous leukemia. He would then inject the entire amount—within sixty seconds, to make certain the cells were fresh—into Brittingham's arm. The transfusions were given ten times—once a week for each of the first nine weeks and then once more, almost three months later. In all, Brittingham received a total direct transfer of about a quart of blood. Before each injection, Harrington or another doctor tested the blood from the leukemic woman for the number of white cells and also pricked Brittingham's fingertip for a few drops of blood to count his white cells. The laboratory tests were repeated six times during the first twelve hours after each transfusion. If Brittingham had developed leukemia, his white blood count would have risen dramatically. It did not.

By the sixth transfusion, Brittingham's body was becoming a human antibody factory, producing antibodies against the donor's white cells. By the ninth injection, Brittingham called the amount of those antibodies "striking." He was elated because not only had he proved that the white cell antibodies he had worked with in the laboratory were genuine (not artifacts), he had also confirmed his basic suspicion—that humans could be immunized against white cell antigens.

But the process was as painful as it was exciting. After the first six injections, Brittingham felt no effects, but following the seventh, his symptoms became severe. About ten minutes after the injection he felt flushed. His head felt full. The blood vessels over his temples swelled. He coughed. The symptoms disappeared within ten minutes; thirty minutes later, they were back. Now he had a more severe headache, nausea, back discomfort, and a shaking chill and fever. His teeth chattered constantly. One chill lasted thirty-seven minutes. For several hours, he was markedly fatigued. Yet during all this period he performed his own blood counts. Dr. Elmer Brown, then a fellow in Moore's department and now chief of blood diseases at Barnes Hospital, recalled how Brittingham, despite feeling so terrible, went to the microscope to test his own blood samples. "He wouldn't trust anyone else to do the blood tests after these injections," Brown said, "and it was a fantastic sight to watch him sit there at the microscope having shaking chills and almost getting black and blue around the eyes looking through the eyepiece of the microscope!"[13]

Brittingham's symptoms disappeared within twelve hours, just as they did in patients who had reactions to blood transfusions. The observation supported his hypothesis that white cells were responsible for the transfusion reaction, and it also suggested that white cells were more important than platelets as a cause of fevers and other reactions following transfusions.

At this point Brittingham, in an attempt to expand his view and to see the connection between various sorts of white cell disorders, began a series of experiments in which he injected himself with the blood of ten patients, each with different white-cell or other blood disorder, both cancerous and noncancerous. In doing so, he nearly killed himself.

For these experiments Brittingham was hampered by the same serious limitation that affects all researchers who investigate uncommon disorders—timing. The key experiments could only be done when he had the right patient. Since diseases in humans cannot be made to order, the planned series of ten experiments could run on for months. Every time patients with one of the uncommon disorders he was studying came into the hospital, Brittingham would perform another self-experiment. He had performed nine of them when the last patient in the series entered Barnes Hospital in late May 1956 for treatment of aplastic anemia, a disease in which there is a deficiency of both red and white cells in the blood. The condition was particularly relevant to Brittingham's cancer studies because it is occasionally linked to leukemia.[14]

Brittingham wanted to transfuse himself with 250 milliliters of the patient's plasma. Harrington, however, knowing that this particular patient had very strong white cell antibodies and having previously seen an adverse reaction to such a large dose, told Brittingham the amount was too large.[15] He persuaded Brittingham to settle on a fraction of that amount, just fifty milliliters.

At 2:45 P.M. on June 21, 1956, Brittingham received the injection of blood from the patient with aplastic anemia and immediately felt faint. That was not unusual; he had experienced a similar reaction before. But then, about fifteen minutes later, he was weak and short of breath. He turned pale. Forty-five minutes after the transfusion, he was vomiting, had diarrhea, and had developed shaking chills. His temperature increased rapidly; his blood pressure fell. Two hours after the transfusion, Harrington injected epinephrine, a potent hormone stimulant, to help Brittingham respond to the crisis. His blood pressure was low, 75/60; it was to drop still lower. A colleague put a needle in Brittingham's vein and started an intravenous drip as a means of giving him medications as well as the fluids needed to keep his circulation from collapsing altogether. Harrington and the other doctors preferred not to move him, so they converted the laboratory into a makeshift hospital room. More epinephrine was administered. He was given oxygen by face mask. At 5:30 P.M.—not quite three hours after the transfusion—Brittingham's blood pressure fell precipitously, to 60/0, a dangerously low level. He was probably in shock. He was breathing sixty times a minute instead of the usual sixteen to twenty times, and still he was short of breath. His skin turned blue from cyanosis—a lack of oxygenated blood. The tiny tubes that carried air to and from his lungs were so constricted by the reaction that they cut down on the amount of oxygen and carbon dioxide that his lungs could exchange. His lungs filled with fluid, a condition called pulmonary edema.

Almost eight hours later, as Brittingham's condition continued to deteriorate, his colleagues admitted him to the hospital. It was the same Barnes Hospital where Harrington had been treated for ITP after his own self-experiment and where Brittingham had had his interview with Moore three years before. Brittingham's electrocardiogram and chest X rays were alarming. "I thought Tom was going to die," Harrington told me.

At that point, Brittingham's wife, Dotsy, arrived at the hospital and, according to Elmer Brown, she "really tore into Carl Moore. Carl, who was ordinarily of a rather ruddy complexion, told me he really turned white after she had gotten through with him for allowing this experimentation to go on."

Mrs. Brittingham recalls that "they didn't call me; I called them. That was the thing that made me so mad. I phoned down there because Tom always called if he was coming home late for dinner and he hadn't called. I think I spoke to Bill Harrington, and he was very vague." She suspected that something was wrong and went to the hospital immediately. Sy Reichlin came over and told me that it was a subtle form of suicide, that Tom was trying to commit suicide, which really had me in a fit."[16]

Reflecting on the episode today, Reichlin, now a professor of medicine at Tufts University and chief endocrinologist at the New England Medical Center Hospitals in Boston, says, "In retrospect I am not sure Tom was trying to commit suicide. I am sure that I thought so at the time. For reasons mysterious to me, he thought himself to be a very unimportant being, dispensable to his family and to his friends."

Harrington continued the story: "We all were frightened. We gave him adrenaline and antihistamines, but nothing seemed to make any difference."

They had wisely chosen to start therapy with hydrocortisone, a steroid drug that reduces acute inflammation and aids the body when it is under stress, but in doing so they almost got off to a disastrous start. When Harrington asked a nurse to get some, she returned with a syringe of what was, presumably, hydrocortisone for intravenous use. But Harrington noticed it was milky, a telltale sign that it was not to be given intravenously. "I grabbed it from her just before she began to squirt it in the IV tubing," Harrington recalled. "I knew it couldn't be for intravenous use. Sure enough, it said: 'Hydrocortisone for intramuscular use only.' So I just took the syringe, walked out of the room in despair, and went to the nurse's station. There was only one person there, another doctor. I sat down and told him we had some of the brightest nurses in the country at Barnes Hospital and some of the dumbest. This nurse was the dumbest of the lot. When I asked who she was, he answered, 'My wife.' "

The intramuscular form contained tiny crystals that, if injected, could have killed Brittingham by damaging his lungs. The correct form was found, and Harrington injected it into one of Brittingham's veins. In addition, he was given other drugs to maintain his blood pressure and to prevent him from going deeper into shock.

Meanwhile, Brittingham had stopped producing urine, and the doctors were concerned that his kidneys might be damaged from a condition called acute tubular necrosis, which can be treated successfully now but that was often fatal then.

But the drugs worked. Within a few hours Brittingham was out of danger.

Moore visited his sick colleague at the hospital that night. As he was leaving he stopped to chat with Dr. Robert M. Heyssel, a resident who was at the desk at the time. "Tom looks like he's going to be all right," Moore said. "But you know, we had better stop this self-experimenting, or we are going to kill somebody." Heyssel agreed. But the tradition was too strong; self-experimentation at Washington University and Barnes Hospital continues to this day.[17]

Brittingham went home the next day, but he never fully recovered. His weakness did not go away, and his doctors thought it might be a psychological reaction. It was not. By Labor Day, his skin had turned yellow, and it became obvious he had developed serum hepatitis (now known as hepatitis B), presumably from the near-fatal transfusion. He eventually recovered from the hepatitis, but he was left with at least two permanent legacies from his experiment. A blood clot had formed in the external jugular vein in the right side of his neck; it was not a major problem because the body rapidly developed an alternative path for the blood to follow on the way back to his heart. And he could no longer tolerate alcohol. He had never drunk much, but the few beers he used to enjoy now were enough to make his liver ache and his sex drive disappear.

Brittingham is certain that Harrington saved his life, not only by caring for him in the crisis, but, more importantly, by urging him to use a much smaller dose of the donor's blood than he had originally planned.

Such a brush with death might be expected to have curtailed Brittingham's enthusiasm for self-experimenting. It did not. Even as he was recuperating, he began another set of self-experiments, the second phase of his original leukemia experiment. It was now twenty months since he had first injected himself with leukemic cells, and tests no longer detected the white cell antibodies in his blood. In this new set of self-experiments, Brittingham used normal white cells, not leukemic ones, and he obtained them from another physician, Dr. Robert T. S. Jim, then a fellow in the department and now a specialist in blood diseases in Honolulu.[18]

Jim's white cells were injected into Brittingham's veins eleven times between August and November 1956. One purpose of this phase of the experiment was to determine whether Brittingham's immune system would still recognize the antigens in the injected white cells, despite the disappearance of the white cell antibodies his body had once made against those very same antigens. A second purpose was to determine how rapidly his body could produce white cell antibodies similar to those that were produced in the original series of injections.

As part of the experiment, Brittingham underwent several painful and potentially dangerous bone marrow tests. "He didn't mind at all," Jim recalled. "He said go ahead and do it. It was part of the game to him."[19]

From the experiments, Brittingham found that the white cell antibodies did, in fact, reappear, and quickly, within a week of an injection of as little as one hundredth of what it took to produce them originally. "This meant that you were looking at a true anamnestic [booster] response and that the white cell antibodies worked in the same way a booster dose does in renewing protection against an infectious disease."

Brittingham now set out to test his most important hypothesis—that injection of leukemic white cell antibodies into leukemic patients might suppress the cancer by attacking the diseased white cells. As a pilot test, he carried out the experiment on himself.

He began these experiments on February 13, 1958, more than three years after he had first risked his life in the laboratory. Once again, Harrington repeatedly injected Brittingham with leukemic white cells to boost the amounts of white cell antibodies in his blood. The first donor with chronic myelogenous leukemia had died, so the cells were now obtained from a second patient with the same disease. The injections were given twenty-three times over an eight-month period, and they promptly restimulated production of the white cell antibodies. Brittingham cannot recall why he needed so many injections, but he clearly remembers how sick he became after most of them. The severity of the reaction generally correlated with the number of white cells transfused.

Brittingham's work involved a technique called plasmapheresis, in which his blood was removed and then separated into its plasma, or liquid portion, and red cell components. Brittingham then separated the plasma that was retained into component fractions and he and his colleagues prepared an antiserum by separating the gamma globulin fraction that contained the white cell antibodies. Later, they injected the antiserum made from Brittingham's blood into the chronic myelocytic leukemia patient who had donated the leukemic cells to Brittingham.

For a while it seemed that Brittingham's dream of developing an effective antileukemia therapy was at hand; the injection of the antiserum halted the rise in the patient's white cell count. But the dream vanished, because the effect was only temporary. The therapy worked for about two months by slightly increasing the rate of white cell destruction rather than by diminishing their production. It was a pioneering effort in cancer immunotherapy, a concept that is still alive today as researchers are trying to use an immunological technique known as monoclonal antibody testing in their fight against this devastating disease.[20]

In 1959 Moore put Brittingham in charge of the medical program at St. Louis City Hospital in a move perhaps intended to curtail Brittingham's self-experiments. If so, his efforts were unsuccessful. Brittingham persisted. From January through March 1960, he repeatedly took blood from a seventy-year-old woman with chronic lymphocytic leukemia and injected it into himself.[21] Nothing happened. He developed no symptoms, certainly none that resembled the reactions he had had earlier. He wondered if he had developed some immunity to leukemia and white cell reactions. So he repeated the experiments in April 1960, using blood from a third patient with chronic myelocytic leukemia. He did not develop leukemia but did develop the typical reaction of fever and malaise from the foreign white cells.[22]

But never in all his experiments did Brittingham get leukemia. If he had, it would have strongly pointed to the presence in the blood of some communicable agent of an infectious nature, such as a virus or a chemical, and would have been an extraordinarily valuable first step in stimulating researchers to isolate that transmissible agent. Brittingham checked his blood count frequently for many years, then stopped because it never gave a hint of leukemia. Nor was there evidence of leukemia when he died in the summer of 1986. His death was the result of cancer of the kidney; there is no reason to suspect it was in any way related to his self-experiments.

In the end, Brittingham's self-experiments made more of a contribution to hematology than to cancer research. They proved that leukagglutinins—the white cell antibodies—were real, not just a laboratory phenomenon, and they helped clarify the different types of reactions that can result from blood transfusions. One was the "buffy-coat" reaction that had nearly caused Brittingham's death in a self-experiment. Its name is derived from the color of the mixture of white cells and platelets that occurs at the place where the serum and red cells meet when blood is separated by centrifuge.

Some doctors belittle the experiments, believing that what Brittingham did was not only poor science but also self-destructive. Yet many others feel that Brittingham's self-experiments epitomize the spirit of medical progress. Brittingham himself, in retrospect, believes he was wrong to experiment on himself only because he overlooked his family obligations. "It isn't just you that's at risk," he said. "You are taking chances with your family. At the time I did not think my death would have been a disaster to my wife or children. Now that's a good example of making your thinking meet the circumstances! It wouldn't have bothered me to die then. But it would have bothered them a lot. I was awfully wrong from that standpoint, as I only came to understand later."

Nevertheless, Brittingham's self-experiments were a reflection of his personal belief in the importance of firsthand experience. In preparation for a speech to the 1986 Harvard Medical School graduating class, Dean Daniel Tosteson asked Brittingham, whom he called a "master internist," to cite the most essential skill for all physicians to share. Brittingham, Dean Tosteson said, "emphasized the capacity to elicit information during conversations with patients. . . . To observe in this setting," the dean added, "requires that the physician build with the patient a trust that allows for candor. Without such trust, there may be nothing to hear."[23] Brittingham's self-experiments not only enhanced his ability to observe his patients, they also earned him their trust.

Brittingham's willingness to risk his own life to advance medical knowledge contrasts with the attitudes of some other cancer researchers, specifically those who became involved in a major scandal in medical ethics in 1963. News accounts of that period described how scientists from the prestigious Sloan-Kettering Institute for Cancer Research (part of the Memorial Sloan-Kettering Cancer Center) in New York had injected live cancer cells into patients without their knowledge. The research team was led by Dr. Chester M. Southam and Dr. Emmanuel E. Mandel.[24]

The aim of the experiments was to learn what would happen when cancer cells were injected into humans. The study began in 1954, when the researchers inoculated fourteen patients at Memorial Hospital with cancer cells different from those that were already ravaging their bodies. The implanted cancer cells grew in the cancer patients, producing small nodules that enlarged over six weeks, then shrank spontaneously and completely without appearing to have any effect on the course of the patients' disease. The next step was to learn what happened when cancer cells were injected into healthy people.

In a news release on January 23, 1964, the cancer center said: "Initially, several members of our scientific staff implanted these cancer cells on their own arms and backs. Then they continued the study on other healthy volunteers."[25]

Some may have; the head of the team, Southam, did not. He did not do to himself first what he did later to others. An article in the journal *Science* described the events: "At this stage the doctors faced a choice that has confronted researchers since the beginning of experimental medicine: Should they use themselves as subjects?"[26] Southam told *Science* that, despite the lack of any theoretical likelihood that the injections would produce cancer, he was unwilling to inject himself or his colleagues. A group of normal volunteers at the Ohio Penitentiary were fully informed about the experiment and its possible risks, and were willing to participate in it. "I would not have hesitated," Southam said, "if it would have served a useful purpose." But, he continued, "to me it seemed like false heroism, like the old question whether the General should march behind or in front of his troops. I do not regard myself as indispensable—if I were not doing this work someone else would be—and I did not regard the experiment as dangerous. But, let's face it, there are relatively few skilled cancer researchers, and it seemed stupid to take even the little risk."

The experiments were of the highest scientific quality. When doctors lecture about them today, they can find little fault with their technical aspects.

The ethics are another matter. The fact that the patients at Memorial Hospital were never informed of the project horrified many people and led to new rules about the way research is conducted. Both Southam and Mandel were later "censured and reprimanded" for the unethical conduct of their experiments by the New York State Board of Regents, which governs medical licenses in that state. Today physicians are required to discuss the risks and benefits of any research project with a patient or volunteer and to obtain written consent before proceeding with an experiment. The Sloan-Kettering experiments became a notorious case in debates over the ethics of human experimentation.

# Chapter Fifteen

# CHOOSING THE RIGHT ANIMAL

If researchers had chosen guinea pigs instead of mice for the initial tests of penicillin during World War II, we might never have benefited from that wonder drug or the resultant antibiotic revolution. Tiny doses of penicillin kill guinea pigs—but only during the winter; at other times of the year, even huge doses of the drug are completely harmless.[1]

Penicillin's lethal effects are confined to this single animal species in a single season and, despite numerous experiments, no one understands why. The fact underscores not only the limitations of extrapolating results from one species to another but also the importance of choosing the right animal for particular medical experiments.

Research moves in logical steps, with numerous stops and starts, from test tube and other laboratory experiments to experiments on different species of animals, and when these show promise, investigators go on to do further tests on humans. But animals are not humans, and a considerable amount of luck is involved in evaluating the mountains of data obtained from animal experiments to predict whether similar experiments will be safe for humans.

Ultimately, man must face the crucial tests, for as Alexander Pope, the British poet and essayist, said in 1733, "The proper study of mankind is man."[2] More than two centuries later, Pope's statement takes on even greater meaning because federal laws and regulations mandate human experimentation for the overwhelming majority of medical research projects. Before a drug can be marketed in the United States, for example, it must pass through three stages of human experimentation. The first involves tests of toxicity and safety on just a few human volunteers. Then the studies are enlarged in scope and participation.

Though a substantial number of investigated drugs fail to advance to the later stages, the number of substances tested on humans is increasing because society is demanding more and more cures and preventions. Congress has enacted legislation to finance programs to conquer the major killers in the western world—cancer, heart disease, and stroke—as well as to help victims of many less common but serious disorders. These goals will be impossible to achieve without an enormous amount of further research. For as knowledgeable as doctors are today, they remain ignorant about the causes of most diseases. In short, medicine cannot progress without human experimentation.

Because experiments with humans are voyages into the unknown, an element of risk is always involved; the potential for death, injury, or illness can be reduced, but it cannot be eliminated. Clearly the risk varies from one experimental situation to another, depending on a number of factors, including the subject's age and state of health. Moreover, the risks of an experiment must be viewed in the context of the scientific knowledge of the era when it is done. What was considered a major risk only a few years ago may no longer be so because of knowledge gained in the interval. Conversely, the discovery of unexpected hidden dangers from further research may turn what was assumed to be a safe procedure yesterday into something known to be hazardous today.

A comparison can be drawn between the risks researchers take in human experimentation and those taken by pilots, mountaineers, astronauts, and others who choose dangerous occupations. What one person regards as safe another may think too risky. We see these judgments reflected in everyday life. Test pilots or workers who gingerly toe cables or hang suspended at great heights to build new bridges or skyscrapers adjust to the risks they willingly take in their jobs.

The ultimate risk, of course, is death. We have seen how Daniel Carrión, William Stark, and Jesse Lazear died from their self-experiments, but there must have been many more. Just how many is impossible to determine, because no registry for such events exists, and deaths from self-experiments are often not reported in the press or medical journals. Even when they are, they may not be accurate or complete because they are usually reported by colleagues who do not have all the details or who are constrained in some way from presenting them. In some cases, all the facts are simply impossible to ascertain. Consider, for example, the death of Dr. George R. Mines, a Canadian physiologist.

Mines was an important figure in the history of cardiac physiology who died from a self-experiment in Montreal on November 7, 1914. At age twenty-eight, Mines had just become head of physiology at McGill University and was considered the most promising young physiologist of his time. He did pioneering studies on the electrocardiogram as well as the effects of the body's basic chemicals, electrolytes, on the action of the heart and the role of the contraction of heart muscle fibers in pumping blood. Mines died on a Saturday when he was apparently working alone, trying to further experiments he had begun in his native England. He had found that muscarine and related drugs act on the heart's electrical system as well as on the pumping mechanism of the heart muscle itself, and he had suggested that scientists should study both reactions in order to understand how the heart works. He spent months at marine zoological stations studying ways to precisely record heart action in tortoises and other lower animals. Presumably he was working on some aspect of this problem the day he died.

Since no one is known to have witnessed Mines's last self-experiment, there is no exact account of what went wrong in the interval between the afternoon when he went to his laboratory and six o'clock in the evening, when a janitor found him unconscious. Mines died in a hospital without regaining consciousness, leaving a widow and three children.

An autopsy report showed that Mines appeared to be in excellent health. It also showed that he had injected himself intravenously with fluids; there were two incisions on his left arm and large amounts of fluid, as well as air in the arm. It is possible that doctors made the incisions while trying to resuscitate him in the hospital, but this is unlikely because at that time intravenous infusions were not routine. The presumption is that Mines injected the fluid into his veins under air pressure and that the needle slipped out, remaining beneath the skin as he lost consciousness. Whether Mines injected muscarine or other drugs with the fluid cannot be determined now. The morphine detected in Mines's urine may be attributable to his preparations for the experiment; he may have taken it to ease the pain of the cuts in his arm and the injection of fluids. The cause of death was attributed to "poisoning by an unknown poison."[3]

A device was found near Mines's unconscious body; it may have been a primitive electrocardiographic apparatus, or it may have been a tool to record his respirations. No one at the time was certain. If Mines made any such measurements, the records are not available. Mines may have invited a medical student or another scientist to witness or to join in the experiment. If so, that other person or persons never came forward, perhaps fearing implication in Mines's death. But if Mines experimented on himself without any assistance, then he was culpable of unwise research practice: Self-experiments must be done under the same conditions in which experiments are done on other volunteers.

It is doubtful that we will ever know exactly what it was that killed Mines that fateful Saturday, but his death, at least, was reported in the press and then in medical journals. There is no way to determine how often deaths known to result from self-experiments are not reported in medical journals. Consider the deaths of two self-experimenters in separate incidents in Milan, Italy.

Dr. Gianni Pauletta, a thirty-four-year-old microbiologist and the father of two young children, was the head of a research unit in an Italian drug company. In 1951 he had just returned to Italy from a visit to several research centers in the United States, where he had studied new antibiotics. One, chloramphenicol, had been discovered four years earlier, and Pauletta was trying to improve the injectable form by mixing chloramphenicol with small amounts of various other substances. He had already tested one, chloramphenicol succinate, on himself without any adverse effect.

A few weeks after his return home, Pauletta went on with the series of tests. A colleague injected him with the first dose of chloramphenicol glutarate. Within a few minutes Pauletta was dead. Quarts of fluid had accumulated in his lungs, apparently from anaphylactic shock—an acute and dangerous allergic reaction; Pauletta had actually drowned in his own body fluids. It was an unpredictable catastrophe, one that could happen to anyone after the injection of any drug, and an example of the unexpected dangers that always lurk in any experiment. At least for this particular one, Pauletta was the wrong animal.

The second fatal incident took place in 1970. Montedison, the Italian manufacturer of a fire extinguisher called Fluobrene that was being marketed in Italy and advertised for its value in squelching flaming racing cars at the Monza track, asked Dr. Gianmario Cavagna, a researcher at the Occupational Medicine Institute in

Milan, to study the chemical's effects on humans. Cavagna's chief interest was cardiology, and he tested the effects of Fluobrene on his heart and blood vessels. For the more complicated tests of central nervous system function, Cavagna sought the advice of a neurological colleague, Dr. Renato Gilioli, who outlined a standard set of tests. Gilioli insisted that, for ethical reasons, he himself should undergo the first set of these experiments. Cavagna agreed, for he had done the same thing with other aspects of the Fluobrene testing.

In the first experiment in the series, the two researchers sat in adjoining rooms. Through a window in the wall that separated them, Cavagna watched Gilioli perform the tests. For purposes of comparison, Gilioli would carry out the tests (computing mathematical calculations and moving blocks) in stages. First he would breathe room air and perform the tests, then he would repeat them several times while breathing predetermined amounts of fire extinguisher chemical that had been released into the room.

On the day of the experiment Gilioli first measured his baseline ability to perform the tests while breathing room air. Then he turned on a cylinder, allowed the determined amount of fire extinguisher gas to escape, took several whiffs, and began his mathematical calculations. Suddenly he slumped in his chair.

Cavagna ran to Gilioli's rescue. He opened the door to let in fresh air. Then he dragged Gilioli out of the room. But as soon as he had reached the corridor, Cavagna dropped to the floor. Others, hearing the commotion, came to the scene and immediately tried to resuscitate Cavagna, but without success. Meanwhile, as Gilioli was being taken to the institute's intensive care unit, he began to regain consciousness. He was discharged from the hospital two days later without organic injury. But his colleague was gone. An autopsy could establish no specific link between the chemical and the cause of Cavagna's death. Neither Pauletta's death nor Cavagna's was reported in any medical journal.[4]

Though it is clear that Cavagna died from the self-experiment, establishing a cause-and-effect relationship between his death and the self-experiment is difficult, if not impossible. This problem of cause and effect in fatalities from self-experiments was further exemplified by the death of Dr. Gary Leinbach in Seattle in 1972, at age thirty-nine.

Leinbach was a physician with whom I studied the specialty of internal medicine at the University of Washington. He was trying to develop a more reliable test to help diagnose a common disorder of fat metabolism called steatorrhea, and he swallowed a fatty substance that had been laced with radioactive iodine to trace its path through his body. Leinbach also swallowed a tube that contained a small knife so that he could cut out a tiny piece of the lining of his small intestine for examination under a microscope and in laboratory tests. He died within a few years of his experiment from a rare form of cancer that arose from his small intestine. None of the other volunteers whom Leinbach had subjected to the same procedures developed cancer. However, in a videotaped interview that was made for a course in death and dying, Leinbach said his cancer was the legacy of the self-experiment, a contention that was debated without resolution among other scientists at the University of Washington.[5]

Since risks accompany any experiment, why should healthy individuals take them when they have nothing directly to gain?

The reason is basic: Human experimentation cannot be limited to studies done on diseased and sick people. Researchers must know what is normal in order to appreciate what is abnormal, and what is normal can only be learned from studies on healthy individuals. Without such knowledge, doctors would have little understanding of what goes wrong in various diseases and disorders. Nor could researchers determine the body's normal response to interventions with new devices, techniques, drugs, or other treatments. The most common reasons doctors give for experimenting on themselves first are that it allows them to share the risk with a patient or volunteer and that it provides confidence to prospective subjects.

Furthermore, by subjecting themselves to the same processes as their volunteer subjects, medical investigators are able to scrutinize their plans more carefully, avoiding unnecessary tests and preventable discomfort to the participants. Such a step helps cut down on abuses—however few they may be—in human experimentation. It acts as a consciousness-raising experience, and it helps force investigators to clarify their thinking and improve the quality of their work.

The list of known self-experimenters exceeds the length of this book, and drawing a psychological profile of them is beyond its scope. Moreover, they are such a diverse lot that it is doubtful that even if a trained psychologist could examine them all, a consistent profile would emerge. However, in addition to sharing risk and providing confidence, self-experimenters have cited a long list of practical and ethical factors for going first, among them reliability, dependability, convenience, curiosity, perpetuating a tradition, and an ethical code reflecting the Golden Rule as applied to medical research. Let us take a look at some of these motivating factors.

*Reliability.* A paramount practical motivation for self-experimentation is the need for reliability. Some experiments last for long periods of time. A minor lapse of memory, a "slipup" of just a few minutes, can invalidate or distort the results. Recall the teenagers John Crandon hired who drank orange juice in a coffee shop when they were supposedly on a vitamin C-free diet. Imagine the erroneous conclusions that would have been reached if they had not been spotted and Crandon had continued to use them as experimental subjects.

Self-experimenters are more highly motivated to maintain rigidly prescribed diets, to avoid forbidden items, and to adhere to specific scientific blueprints. Two self-experimenters at the Lister Institute in London, Charles J. Martin and Robert Robison, explained why, when they studied the biologic value of various proteins for human nutrition. "This is inconvenient," they wrote in 1922, "but advantageous, for the experiments are exacting and necessitate constant supervision of one's actions if sources of error are to be avoided. The partial abandonment of the joys of life is to some extent compensated by interest in the results."[6]

*Dependability.* Physicians are valuable healthy volunteers because they are trained to be good, dependable observers—to be objective and aware of subtle clues that an ordinary individual might overlook. Recall, for example, how on Christmas morning Victor Herbert was able to diagnose his paralysis as due to a depletion of potassium.

Also, the trained observer can detect the unanticipated small problems in the scientific design—the inevitable difficulties that arise when a written protocol is first translated into the tamperings of the human body. Most of these problems are seemingly trivial, of the sort that can make the experience unpleasant. Yet if they are not caught, they are the very things that can adversely influence the experimental results, sometimes to the point of invalidating all the data from an expensive and time-consuming study. By going first, the experimenter can often iron out these problems as well as serve as a point of comparison, a control, for the experiments that follow on others.

Sometimes the problems are not trivial. Many self-experimenters believe that by going first and experiencing for themselves an adverse effect that might occur among volunteers or patients, they are in a better position to identify reactions that might occur in people with specific medical conditions and thus prevent possible hazardous consequences.

*Spirit of adventure.* Scientists are often motivated by a spirit of adventure, both intellectual and physical, that others can seldom appreciate because, as J.B.S. Haldane said, "Intellectual adventure is the hardest kind to share."[7]

It is the rare investigator who is not driven by curiosity, and satisfying it was a motivating factor for most of the self-experimenters cited in this book. Chance led many of them to a new observation they could not explain. And so, to answer their own questions, they chose to repeat purposely as an experiment on themselves what they had noted previously by accident. The itchy, red skin reaction that developed when Arthur Looss spilled a drop of water containing hookworm larvae on his hand led him to suspect the two events were cause and effect. He repeated the experiment to prove his deduction, and made a discovery that was of great epidemiologic importance.

That same curiosity can translate into the persistence and perseverance that is required of researchers who must overcome the doubts of others when they have a compelling but controversial theory they want to test. Discoverers often need strong mental courage. Remember the difficulties Werner Forssmann had to overcome and the penalties he subsequently paid for defying his superiors in carrying out heart catheterizations. Then remember how his experiments benefit us.

*Firsthand experience.* There is little question that people learn best from reactions they experience firsthand, which is one reason many senior investigators who have experimented on themselves urge their students to do the same. A leading tutor was Sir Thomas Lewis, a British physician who did pioneering studies in a number of areas, including pain and heart disease, in the first half of this century. Lewis insisted that anyone training in his London laboratory follow his example and do their experiments on themselves. Lewis and one of his students, Dr. Jonas H. Kellgren (who later became dean of the University of Manchester Medical School), made significant contributions in the area of human pain through a number of very painful self-experiments. They chose themselves because humans are the only possible subjects for experiments on sensation and pain.[8]

Kellgren and Lewis devised a scheme to produce pain by repeatedly injecting small amounts of chemical solutions into their own muscles, tendons, cartilages, and bones. The aim was to systematically map the patterns of referred pain—pain that originates in one part of the body but that is felt in another. They found that a concentrated salt solution was the best chemical for their experimental purposes because it produced severe, continuous pain lasting up to five minutes but left no aftereffects.

The observations were made over a period of years. During this time Kellgren and Lewis had more than a thousand painful shots of one sort or another—often up to five times in a single day. The two doctors even had needles thrust through the skin of their back to a depth of up to two and a half inches, until they reached the ligaments between the bones in their spine. In another experiment, Kellgren had a surgeon drive a wire through the tibia bone in his leg after the overlying skin and bone covering were anesthetized with novocaine. The purpose was to describe the pain felt within the bone itself. "While the wire was passing through the compact bone I experienced a sensation of pressure and vibration but no pain," Kellgren said, "but when the wire entered the soft cancellous [spongy] bone, diffuse pain was added to the sensation of vibration."[9]

Kellgren and Lewis observed that the continuous aching pain from ligaments was indistinguishable from pain produced from muscle. They also found that the pain arising from muscle was diffuse and that the segmental distribution of muscle pain was dependent on the architecture of the nerves as they branched out of the spinal cord. Further, they found that each anatomical structure gives rise to characteristic pain that often is felt at a distance from the source of provocation. For example, pain arising in muscle was often "referred" to the region of a joint, which meant that it could easily be confused with pain arising in the joint itself.

In the 1930s, when Lewis and Kellgren did these self-experiments, doctors had difficulty diagnosing many painful conditions, particularly of the limbs and back. But the findings from their research are now part of the everyday practice of medicine. When you feel pain in your hip, for example, the astute physician examines your knee as well as your hip because the pain may be due to a knee problem. When you feel pain in your little finger, the physician may check to determine if the pain is originating in the triceps muscle in the arm. Similarly, when you feel pain in the shoulder, the careful doctor looks for a potential source in the diaphragm, the muscle that separates the chest and the abdomen and that helps you breathe.

As a result, doctors now reflexively examine many anatomical areas for the source of a patient's pain, not just where it is felt. And doctors, in seeking a source of trouble, often inject a local anesthetic into a distant anatomical area to relieve the pain and thereby confirm its origin.

*Self-protection.* A researcher's selfish desire to protect his own health is another prime practical reason for self-experimenting. A classic example is the story of the vaccine against Rocky Mountain spotted fever, a tick-borne infection that is caused by a rickettsia (an organism classified between a virus and a bacterium).

In Montana, in 1924, Dr. Roscoe R. Spencer, a U.S. Public Health Service officer, and Dr. Ralph R. Parker, an entomologist, developed a vaccine against that often fatal disease. They made it by grinding up infected ticks and chemically treating them with an acid to modify their virulence. When the doctors found the vaccine safe and effective in tests on small animals in the laboratory, they bypassed similar experiments on primates because no monkeys were available to them and moved directly to humans. On the morning of May 19, 1924, Spencer rolled up his shirtsleeve to receive the first injection —a double dose. Paul de Kruif described Spencer's feelings in his fictionalized journalistic account of the event in *Men Against Death:* "Spencer (who is a most mild dreamy man) gets indignant at any hint that there might be anything of the heroic about this self-experimentation. 'Why, it would make me feel silly if anybody tried to make out there was anything really risky about it,' Spencer said.

"What didn't harm a measly guinea-pig couldn't hurt a full-grown man, at least Spencer was certain of it.

" 'Then again, you see, I was scared of this spotted fever,' Spencer said. 'Look at all that hot virus we were breeding, with all those ticks around here. Why shouldn't I have grabbed at *any* way to protect myself?' "[10]

Spencer experienced no harm from the brew he had made from the ticks. But there was risk to his experiment, as the pioneering polio vaccine researchers found out when they used virus that had not been completely killed. Also, a vaccine must contain a sufficient amount of antigen, the substance that stimulates production of antibodies, to make it an effective immunizing agent. If there is too little antigen, the substance does not protect but may sensitize, creating a potentially fatal allergic reaction if the individual is later exposed to the antigen again. Fortunately, Spencer used a large enough amount of antigen in the vaccine he tested.

The behavior of Spencer and Parker contrasts sharply with that of Dr. Hideyo Noguchi, a Japanese researcher who worked at the Rockefeller Institute in New York City with several strains of the microbe that he received from Parker for use in developing another spotted fever vaccine. Noguchi refused to take his own vaccine, but he gave it to a group of volunteers, several of whom became ill.[11]

*Convenience.* Another motivation to self-experiment is convenience; investigators become as frustrated as anyone else by obstacles that upset their daily plans or impede their progress. It is sometimes simply easier to do a self-experiment rather than wait until someone else can meet an appointment. Furthermore, because researchers are so familiar with their own projects, they often self-experiment without thinking much about it. Consider the donation of blood samples, something scientists do frequently in the laboratory. Because of their everyday experience in obtaining blood samples from patients, doctors shrug the procedure off as routine, looking upon it quite differently from those squeamish individuals who fear having their blood drawn or who will not give a sample.

It is now standard practice for researchers, once they have thought through the problems and risks involved in their experiments, to explain them to the prospective patients and volunteers as part of the "informed consent" process. Some self-experimenters save time by eliminating this step in the initial phase of research. They simply roll up their own sleeve to get a blood sample, or push a plastic tube through their nose and swallow it to get a sample of stomach fluid, or test their own breathing capacity by blowing into machines.

*Experience.* When the experiment involves greater degrees of risk, experience also plays a role. Many researchers are willing to self-experiment in an area in which they have had a great deal of experience, but would not do so in another. Dr. Robert A. McCance, who spent a lifetime doing physiological and nutritional experiments on himself, said he had little hesitancy in conducting tests where "with a little patience one can work up the dose on oneself or other normal people so gradually that the risk can be reduced to vanishing point." He could push experiments on salt deficiency or dehydration, for example, to the point where the effects were severe because he knew a remedy was always available.

On the other hand, McCance said he doubted he "would ever have had the temerity" to take the risk of injecting himself with an infectious agent because "once the inoculation had been made, I would have lost control."[12]

Despite its recognized contribution to medical knowledge, self-experimentation has its limitations and its critics. Some say the methodology is flawed because the self-experimenter may lose perspective and take unnecessary risks. Mentally unbalanced investigators may be tempted to do crazy things to themselves and then use the fact that they went first to rationalize repeating these things on others. Notwithstanding the special advantage that physician scientists have as trained observers, critics also have contended that the practice of self-experimentation is unwise because subjectivity can influence the investigator's judgment and self-experimenters may lack the ability to evaluate their results critically and objectively.

Loss of objectivity is of paramount importance in any kind of medical research whether it is an experiment done in test tubes, on animals, or with humans. Because a strong bias on the part of any investigator can discredit the results of his experiments, this sort of influence must be removed from all experiments—whether they are done by investigators on themselves or on other individuals. The issue here is not self-experimentation; it is the ability of the researcher to be a good trained observer and to be objective in doing any kind of research.

These criticisms are really caveats that can be overcome by taking them into account in the design of the study; many self-experimenters have carefully structured their experiments to exclude the possibility that as volunteers they might influence the results of the overall project.

Some self-experimenters, among them a British researcher, Dr. Kenneth Mellanby, have made it a practice to participate in any experiment at least once before asking a volunteer to follow suit. "But after that I have been the observer and not the guinea pig," Dr. Mellanby said.[13]

This approach works because the results of most studies are based on an analysis of a large group of subjects. Only rarely can valid results be based on an experiment involving just one volunteer—Werner Forssmann's heart catheterization is a noteworthy example. The validity of most studies is based on the pooled responses of a group of subjects. In this way, spurious individual variations are averaged out. If the bias of one subject—a self-experimenter or volunteer—can influence the outcome of the total study, then the design of the study is flawed.

There are, of course, situations in which self-experimentation cannot be used. Technical reasons, for example, may inhibit opportunities for a doctor to experiment on himself. Consider surgeons who wish to develop new operations. Even if a surgeon could carry out an experimental procedure on himself, to do so would be unwise or foolhardy. To be certain, a few doctors have operated on themselves by using mirrors to remove an appendix, for example, or a bladder stone. These efforts are not experiments. For some, the purpose was to relieve pain or other symptoms under emergency circumstances. For others, it was showmanship, a sort of medical circus act to prove that such a feat could be accomplished.[14]

There are other valid reasons why researchers should not or cannot go first. Although there are no limits to the age at which investigators can do experiments, advancing age itself may be a restricting factor for some contemplated self-experiments. If an experiment involves strenuous physical exertion, the risks to an older experimenter in poor health could exceed the potential benefits. Forssmann's heart catheterizations would have been much risker if he had done them in his sixties or seventies, when he had a serious heart condition, than in his twenties, when he did not.[15]

Even younger self-experimenters might endanger their lives if they had a serious medical condition such as diabetes. A diabetic physician or researcher faces no hazards from caring for patients or working at the laboratory bench. Yet, because diabetics often have more difficulty fighting infections than nondiabetics, the same individual could be at risk in a self-experiment if it posed the possibility of infection.

The cumulative effect of doing an experiment repetitively on oneself can also be hazardous, even if the researcher has done the experiment several times without incident. Performing a self-experiment just one additional time can provide the critical marginal factor that is harmful. In immunological studies, for example, the extra challenge to the immune system can impose hazards such as potentially fatal allergic reactions.

Sex differences can also impose critical limitations. I have met and heard about only a few women who self-experimented, which I suspect reflects, as much as anything, the statistical representation of women in medicine. Until recent years, women comprised only about 5 percent of the total number of doctors in the United States, and only a small percentage of women doctors went into research.[16] Female medical researchers could, however, be taking an undue risk if they experimented on themselves during pregnancy or at a time when they might become pregnant. It could be foolish for a woman of reproductive age to jeopardize her own health and the well-being of an unborn child by doing an experiment on herself.

For the male, too, the desire to father children could preclude self-experimentation in some types of research that might affect the male reproductive system.

And clearly the great hormonal differences between males and females may preclude an investigator of either sex from going first. Accordingly, male researchers cannot draw valid conclusions when testing the efficacy of something affecting female physiology on themselves, and vice versa. Still, the preliminary studies of safety and toxicity of a drug are among the things that can be tested with equal validity by researchers of either sex.

Before we leave this discussion of some of the limitations of self-experimentation, it is important to take a look at the subject of suicide. Over the years, some critics have voiced the opinion that occasionally researchers have deliberately exploited the risks of self-experimentation to commit suicide. Undoubtedly this has been the case in some instances, but it is extremely difficult to verify. Many such incidents, if they did occur, may never be known because they are kept secret by family and colleagues or not recognized as suicide.

In all my research, I found evidence of only one attempted suicidal self-experiment. It involved Elie Metchnikoff, a Nobel Prize–winning pioneer immunologist. (See Chapter One: An Overview.) In 1881, in a fit of depression, Metchnikoff chose to kill himself by giving himself an infectious disease called relapsing fever. He was thirty-six. (It was his second attempt at suicide; in 1873 he had taken morphine just after the death of his first wife.) According to his second wife, Olga, Metchnikoff decided to kill himself in a way that his death might benefit society.[17] However, Metchnikoff recovered from his attack of relapsing fever, and his experience provided further documentation of the transmissibility of this disease through blood. He went on to do another self-experiment with cholera in 1892 that was not believed to have been motivated by any morbid thoughts, and died of natural causes in 1916 at the age of seventy-one.

More systematic research and case-by-case analysis are needed before we can truly quantify risk in human experiments. The very fact that the risk cannot be measured accurately is all the more reason why much more attention should be devoted to the question of who goes first.

Should not researchers discuss fully with their spouse their decision to self-experiment? This and a number of other questions need to be considered not only for self-experimentation but also for human experimentation in general. For instance, what indemnity should be provided to the spouse of someone who is injured or who dies in a self-experiment? And who pays? Many important issues have not been clarified for human experimentation in general, let alone self-experimentation.

Scientists take pride in being independent thinkers and intellectual revolutionaries. Over the course of history some have made their discoveries in defiance of advice and of social authority. Modern anatomists and surgeons tell with some relish the stories of the pioneers in their fields who robbed graves to get cadavers to do the studies that have helped advance medicine. Some who were criminals in their own day are heroes in ours.

Consider, then, the defiant or "unethical" researcher whose experiments produce important data. Are physicians in violation of their institution's clinical investigation committee rules if they fail to gain advance clearance for their own self-experiment? Failing clearance, may the investigator still investigate? Do the same constraints that apply to the use of other human volunteers in clinical experiments also apply to the investigator who volunteers himself? What of those who disobey federal regulations and review board decisions? Would the Nobel Prize Committee be obligated to deny an award to the Forssmann of tomorrow who defies the decision of an ethics committee? If an assistant helped a self-experimenter and the latter died, would this be murder? Remember the saga of the doctor who helped Daniel Carrión. These are questions for which we have no clear answers.

If you are asked to volunteer for an experiment at some point in your life, you—the potential subject—should, in turn, ask the researcher: "Have you done the experiment on yourself?" With the assurance from an affirmative answer, you should proceed to question the researcher about the specifics of the project and the results of the self-experiment. But if the researcher says "No" and can provide no valid reason why he or she has declined to go first, then you would be wise to refuse participation unless you can satisfy yourself as to why you should assume a risk that the researcher was unwilling to take. The risk of an experiment can and has involved psychological damage, permanent disability, and even death. Why should a volunteer not connected with the research study go first and risk those consequences when the researcher has no valid justification for not having done so?

Several essays on human experimentation have emphasized the fact that the investigator must be willing to perform the experiment on himself, but the crucial issue seems to be in the actual performance of the experiment on oneself, not the mere willingness to do so. Sir George Pickering, who was Regius Professor of Medicine at Oxford in England, addressed himself to the issue. "The experimenter has one golden rule to guide him to whether the experiment is justifiable," Dr. Pickering said. "Is he prepared to submit himself to the procedure? If he is, and if the experiment is actually carried out on him, then it is probably justifiable. If he is not, then the experiment should not be done."[18]

The medical schools and medical centers where most research is done today could do much more to stimulate substantial improvements in the ethical climate and quality of research.[19] Before the federally mandated Institutional Review Boards (human experimentation committees) that exist in each medical center grant approval to scientific research protocols, their members should routinely ask themselves and the applicants: Who goes first? Medical schools should pay more attention to the process of human experimentation by offering courses on the subject to young investigators. If researchers were better prepared in the issues and procedures of human experimentation, then presumably the facts about the research project that these physician-investigators provide to their human volunteers would be clearer.[20]

Furthermore, increased attention to the subject of who goes first would improve the quality of the informed consent process that the Nuremberg Code has made mandatory. Dr. Eugene G. Laforet, a surgeon in Massachusetts, is among those who contend that no one can be fully informed about everything involved in such a complex thing as an experiment and that probably there is no truly informed consent. However, Laforet says, "Certainly the knowledge that the investigator is in their ranks should prove more reassuring to the subjects of any experiment than a properly executed and legally correct informed consent document."[21]

Dr. Rosalyn S. Yalow, a Bronx, New York, scientist who won a Nobel Prize in 1977 for the development of a technique known as the radioimmune assay that allows the measurement of tiny amounts of substances in the body, also defines the term "informed consent" in a narrow sense: "In our laboratory," she said, "we always used ourselves because we are the only ones who can give truly informed consent."[22]

While self-experimentation should ethically precede performing an experiment on other subjects, the fact that a researcher has first tried his experiment on himself does not in itself justify trying it on another.

The risk of performing an unethical human experiment is enormous. As Robert A. McCance, the British scientist, said: "Everyone working experimentally with normal human subjects or with patients must remember not only his responsibility to the subject or patient but also his responsibility to the discipline of experimental medicine. One irresponsible experimenter can do great harm to medical science."[23]

As science grows in its complexity and sophistication, the public has greater difficulty understanding it. Informed consent does not justify or validate an experiment that is poorly designed or improperly executed, but it forces researchers and volunteers to articulate better the points and principles involved in an experiment.

Who goes first is a prime ethical issue in human experimentation. Yet it is an issue that probably cannot be codified. Laws mandating self-experimentation by researchers might unnecessarily jeopardize their own lives or, on the other hand, discourage those whose health prevents them from self-experimenting, yet who are good scientists, from devoting careers to research. Short of legislation, a greater public awareness of the ethic of self-experimentation would force more researchers to apply the Golden Rule to medical research. Self-experimentation should become something every researcher and volunteer considers before undertaking an experiment.

The methodology of self-experimentation also has value in conventional medical education. There was a day when all medical students swallowed standard drugs to learn their function and did laboratory experiments on themselves to learn physiology and biochemistry. Dr. Edouard Brown-Séquard was a famous nineteenth-century physician whose self-experiments led to hormonal treatment. In 1886 Brown-Séquard, who taught in England, France, and the United States and who never hesitated to experiment on himself, told Harvard medical students: "You will never know fully the action of certain remedies, if you have not ascertained, on your own person, what effects they produce on the brain, the eye, the ear, the nerves, and the principal viscera."[24] That practice is now far less commonly carried on in medical school classes. If it were done more often, more physicians would have greater empathy with their patients in considering such factors as the timing of necessary but uncomfortable diagnostic tests.

Scientists have likened researchers to generals, and critics of self-experimentation have said that just as the lives of generals are too valuable to risk in leading troops into battle, so, too, are the lives of researchers too valuable to risk in any experiment. On both sides of many wars there have been generals who never saw the trenches and who had no feeling for what their men were going through.

One man's life is not more valuable than another's. The lives of nonresearchers are as valuable to their families and to society as are the lives of scientists. The argument advanced by opponents of self-experimentation, that the lives of researchers are too valuable to risk in experiments because of their specialized knowledge, opens up research to elitism of the worst kind. Furthermore, it allows unethical researchers to advance their careers by taking unnecessary risks on patients and volunteers while avoiding them themselves. If there is risk, why should someone other than the scientist himself take it first? If there is no risk, or it is ever so slight, what then is the scientist's objection to going first? When scientists say there is "little risk" to their experiment and do not go first, could it be that the "little risk" looms as a much larger one in their mind, a fear that they are unwilling to express to their subjects, their professional peers, and the public?

Scientists like to think of themselves as leaders, and the best way to lead is by example. There is an analogy to be drawn between scientific research and the affairs of state. The principle of enlightened responsibility over the lives and well-being of others is appropriately shared by the clinical investigator as well as the political leader. H. G. Wells, commenting on the responsibility of those leaders who willfully make war and promote international dissension, might well have been discussing human experimentation when he wrote: "It is not reasonable that those who gamble with men's lives should not stake their own."[25]

Self-experimentation, and the issues and questions the subject raises, will take on increasing significance as society's involvement in the ethics of medical care and medical research matures. More people will come to recognize that ultimately the right animal in experiments designed to advance our knowledge of human diseases must be human. And they will realize the obvious fact that someone must be the first volunteer. As the public learns more about human experimentation in general and self-experimentation in particular, and as doctors are taught more about the history of scientific research, undoubtedly many more medical investigators will decide to perpetuate the tradition of going first.

# Notes

## PROLOGUE

1. I first heard about Carrión in medical school, where we were taught that he deliberately set out to prove that both diseases were the same. But a few years later, when I worked as an epidemiologist at the Centers for Disease Control in Atlanta, a colleague, Dr. Myron G. Schultz, who knew of my interest in self-experimentation, told me the story was a myth—the link between the two diseases that Carrión had made was an accidental finding in his deliberate self-experiment. Schultz elaborated on that point later when he wrote the first detailed accounts in English of Carrión's research. (Refs.: C. Medina et al., *La verruga peruana y Daniel A. Carrión,* Lima: Imprenta del Estado, 1886. M. G. Schultz, "Daniel Carrión's Experiment," *New England Journal of Medicine,* 278: 1323–1326, 1968. M. G. Schultz, "A History of Bartonellosis [Carrión's Disease]," *American Journal of Tropical Medicine and Hygiene,* 17: 503–515, 1968.)

2. M. G. Schultz, "Daniel Carrión's Experiment," p. 1325.

3. The link between sandflies (phlebotomus) and verruga was made in 1912. (Ref.: C.H.T. Townsend, "Resumen de la labores en el Perú sobre el *Phlebotomus verrucarum* y su agencia en la transmisión de la verruga," *Anales de Zoología Aplicada* [Santiago], 1: 44–64, 1914, cited in M. G. Schultz, "History of Bartonellosis.")

4. M. Kuczynski-Godard, "La autoexpérience de professor Max Kuczynski-Godard," *La Reforma Medica* (Lima) 23: 758–778, 1937. D.

Mackehenie, "Un caso de verruga humana por autoinoculación experimental," *La Reforma Medica* (Lima) 23: 741–744, 1937.

5. A. L. Barton, "Descripción de elementos endoglobulares hallados en los enformos de fiebre verrucosa," *Crónica Médica* (Lima) 26: 7–10, 1909.

6. D. Hendin, *The Life Givers,* New York: Morrow, 1976, p. 211. L. McLaughlin, *The Pill, John Rock, and The Church,* Boston: Little, Brown, 1982. A key researcher in this study was Dr. John Rock. Many years later I learned from his daughter, Mrs. A-J Rock Levinson, that to her knowledge the patients had been properly informed.

7. J. Hunter, *A Treatise on the Venereal Disease,* Philadelphia: J. Webster, 1818, pp. 302–304.

8. A. Castiglioni, *A History of Medicine,* New York: Alfred A. Knopf, 1947, p. 598.

9. Ibid., p. 597. F. H. Garrison, *An Introduction to the History of Medicine,* Philadelphia and London: Saunders, 1929, p. 346. J. Kobler, *The Reluctant Surgeon. A Biography of John Hunter,* Garden City, N.Y.: Doubleday, 1960, pp. 154–155.

10. Even today, modern physicians often cannot detect syphilis without laboratory tests, and recent textbooks have said that gonorrhea and syphilis coexist in about 3 percent of cases. (Ref.: H. N. Beaty and R. G. Petersdorf, "Gonococcal Infections," in *Harrison's Principles of Internal Medicine,* sixth edition, M. M. Wintrobe, et al., eds., New York: McGraw-Hill, 1970, pp. 798–801.)

11. Over the years I have found just a few references that deal specifically with self-experimentation:

a. "The Changing Mores of Biomedical Research," *Annals of Internal Medicine* (Supplement 7) 67: 7, 1967.

b. E. F. Dach, "Sondernummer: Selbstversuche von Ärzten mit lebenden Krankheitserregern," *Ciba Zeitschrift,* 1: 143–176, 274–276, 305–309, 311–313, 1934; and 3: 955–963, 1936. Unreferenced self-experiments narrated in style similar to that of Glaser (see paragraph e). This essay was part of the Ciba Symposium collection, but it appeared only in the German series and was not translated into English.

c. "The Doctor as the Guinea-Pig," *Medical Journal of Australia,* 2: 65–66, July 12, 1969.

d. E. Ebstein, "Medical Men who Experimented upon Themselves: A Contribution to the Causes of Death in Physicians," *Medical Life,* 38: 216–218, 1931. The title is misleading because the article does not distinguish between those who risked illness from occupational hazards and those who faced risks from self-experiments.

e. H. Glaser, *The Drama of Medicine,* London: Lutterworth, 1959. The self-experiments described are based on medical journal accounts; they are not supplemented by interviews, and they are not referenced.

f. J.B.S. Haldane, "On Being One's Own Rabbit—The Story of a Skirmish in the War on Disease," in *Possible Worlds and Other Essays,* London: Chatto and Windus, 1927, pp. 107–119. One of the rare accounts by a researcher of the method of self-experimentation. The essay deals specifically with Haldane's description of how, by swallowing large doses of ammonium chloride, he had a role in the discovery of an improved method of treatment for a rather unimportant disease.

g. B. Karger-Decker, *Ärzte im Selbstversuch. Ein Kapitel heroischer Medizin,* third edition, Leipzig: Koehler & Amelang, 1969.

h. "Martyrs of Medicine," *Journal of the American Medical Association,* 90: 1712–1713, 1928.

i. Jon Franklin and John Sutherland, *Guinea Pig Doctors: The Drama of Medical Research Through Self-Experimentation,* New York: Morrow, 1984.

Among the anthologies on human experimentation that have been published since I began this project are:

a. "Ethical Aspects of Experimentation with Human Subjects," *Daedalus,* Spring 1969. Excellent essays on the overall subject. Several articles allude to self-experimentation; none, however, is specifically devoted to the topic.

b. J. Katz, A. Capron, and E. S. Glass, *Experimentation with Human Beings: The Authority of the Investigator, Subject, Professions and State in the Human Experimentation Process,* New York: Russell Sage Foundation, 1972. A huge tome whose value lies in the fact that it is based on excerpts from dozens of scientific papers. The discussion of self-experimentation is limited.

c. I. Ladimer and R. W. Newman, *Clinical Investigation in Medicine,* Boston: Law-Medicine Research Institute, Boston University, 1963. An anthology and a bibliography of five hundred of the earliest papers in the scientific literature on the ethics of human experimentation.

12. See, for example, A. C. Ivy, "The History and Ethics of the Use of Human Subjects in Medical Experiments," *Science,* 108: 1–5, 1948. This article has been treated as the authoritative paper on self-experimentation for more than three decades, but it cites only nine self-experimenters, none after 1903. Ivy confused two points: self-experimentation and what he called "random experiments," which might be better phrased as poor research. Others borrowed from Ivy's list without doing further research and thus perpetuated some myths and errors about these particular self-experiments.

13. Several times when I followed the leads and asked why the author had omitted references, I was told it was because he did not want to seem to be boasting.

14. For examples: Dr. Ralph E. Cutler, a specialist in glandular and kidney disorders, swallowed thyroid pills, thus making the gland in his neck overactive, or hyperthyroid, to study how that condition affected kidney function. Dr. Charles E. Pope II, a specialist in disorders of the bowel, studied the mechanics of swallowing by drinking acids and inserting a variety of tubes and other devices through his mouth. Dr. Robert A. Bruce, a cardiologist who pioneered in exercise testing, had monitoring tubes put in his heart in a procedure known as cardiac catheterization as part of the experiments his team did to develop the now standard exercise studies and stress tests that are used to help detect heart disease.

15. L. K. Altman, "Auto-Experimentation—An Unappreciated Tradition in Medical Science," *New England Journal of Medicine,* 286: 346–352, 1972.

Ingelfinger's strong encouragement in no small part reflected his own extensive experience in experimenting on himself. (Refs.: J. R. Bingham, F. J. Ingelfinger, and R. H. Smithwick, "Characteristics of Visceral Sensation in Man, as Observed in Normal Subjects and Patients with Unilateral Sympathectomy," *Journal of Clinical Investigation,* 28: 771–772, 1949. J. R. Bingham, F. J. Ingelfinger, and R. H. Smithwick, "The Effects of Sympathectomy on the Motility of the Human Gastrointestinal and Biliary Tracts," *Gastroenterology,* 15: 6–13, 1950. F. J. Ingelfinger and W. O. Abbott, "Intubation Studies of the Human Small Intestine: Diagnostic Significance of Motor Disturbances," *American Journal of Digestive Diseases,* 7: 468–474, 1940.)

16. Although the results of the research did not solve the mysteries of this disease, they did add to the knowledge of the pattern of inheritance. (Refs.: L. K. Altman et al., "Pseudoxanthoma Elasticum," *Archives of Internal Medicine,* 134: 1048–1054, 1974. R. Ross, P. J. Fialkow, and L. K. Altman, "The Morphogenesis of Elastic Fibers," *Advances in Experimental Medicine and Biology,* 79: 7–17, 1977.)

17. Interviews with Sir Douglas Black in London, January 31 and February 2, 1977.

## Chapter One: AN OVERVIEW

1. The first scientific journals were the *Philosophical Transactions,* which were published by the Royal Society of London in 1664–1665.

2. In ancient Persia, for example, it was the practice of the king to hand over condemned criminals for experimental purposes in science.

3. Oath of Hippocrates (fifth century B.C.), in J. Katz, *Experimentation with Human Beings,* New York: Russell Sage Foundation, 1972, p. 311.

4. J. Katz, "The Education of the Physician-Investigator," in "Ethical Aspects of Experimentation with Human Subjects," *Daedalus,* Spring 1969, p. 481.

5. J. W. Underwood, *The Aphorisms of Hippocrates,* London: privately printed, 1831, p. 75.

6. From Slater *v.* Baker and Stapleton. 2 Wils. K.B. 359 95 Eng. Rep. 860 (1767).

7. 21 R. C. L. 385, Sec. 29 (1918).

8. C. Bernard, *An Introduction to the Study of Experimental Medicine,* translated by Henry C. Green, New York: Dover Publications, 1957, p. 101.

9. Ibid., p. 102.

10. T. Taylor, in United States, Adjutant General's Department, *Trials of War Criminals Before the Nuremberg Military Tribunals, Vols. I and II, The Medical Case,* Washington, D.C.: U.S. Government Printing Office, 1948.

11. United States, Adjutant General's Department, *Trials of War Criminals Before Nuremberg Military Tribunals under Control Council Law No. 10 (October 1946–April 1949),* vol. 2, *The Medical Case,* Washington, D.C.: U.S. Government Printing Office, 1949, pp. 181–183.

12. Interview with Dr. Leo Alexander in West Newton, Massachusetts, January 24, 1978.

13. H. K. Beecher, *Experimentation in Man. The Authority of the Investigator, Subject, Professions, and State in the Human Experimentation Process,* Springfield, Ill.: Thomas, 1959. H. K. Beecher, *Research and the Individual: Human Studies,* Boston: Little, Brown, 1970.

14. H. K. Beecher, "Ethics and Clinical Research," *New England Journal of Medicine,* 274: 1354–1360, 1966. "Experimentation on Man," *New England Journal of Medicine,* 274: 1382–1383, 1966.

15. J. H. Jones, *Bad Blood. The Tuskegee Syphilis Experiment,* New York: Free Press, 1981.

16. "Senators Are Told of Test of a Gas Attack in Subway," *New York Times,* September 19, 1975, p. 14. "Feigned Germ War Admitted By

Army," *New York Times,* December 23, 1976, p. 12. "Army Tells of U.S. Germ War Tests; Safety of Simulated Agents at Issue," *New York Times,* March 9, 1977, p. A-1.

17. A second purpose of the memorandum was to "protect the process of human investigation in this time when the process has articulate critics. While this requirement for review is a limitation of freedom, it is the price we must pay to protect clinical investigation. If there were any accident leading to a death or permanent handicap, there would be a flurry of regulations involving all types of human investigation. The paperwork that we now have would seem trivial indeed, and there is a strong likelihood that much of the human investigation that we currently do would be outlawed." (Ref.: T. R. Hendrix, "Guidelines on Self Experimentation," Memorandum to the Faculty, Joint Committee on Clinical Investigation, The Johns Hopkins University School of Medicine and The Johns Hopkins Hospital, August 25, 1983.)

18. The regulation noted wisely "that an investigator who utilizes himself repeatedly may, by the sum of the investigations, do harm to himself that a single study would not do. Experience has shown that investigators tend to be less rigorous in providing themselves with the precautionary techniques they utilize with their subjects." (Ref.: "Self-Experimentation," Medical Board Minutes—National Institutes of Health/Clinical Center, December 12, 1967.) In addition, the Clinical Center's *Policy and Communications Bulletin* of February 1, 1977, said: "Investigators may serve as subjects for their own research projects without a referring physician or agency provided two criteria are satisfied: 1) The project must be written in protocol form and be approved by the ICRS, and the Director, Clinical Center. It must explicitly indicate that investigators may serve as subjects. 2) Before serving as a subject for his study, an investigator must be registered as a Clinical Center patient or volunteer, must be assigned to the care of a staff member other than himself, and standard medical record requirements must be complied with."

19. The American public spent an estimated $8 billion in 1986 for medical research, compared to $28 million in 1947. (Ref.: National Institutes of Health, Office of Program Planning and Evaluation.)

20. O. D. Ratnoff and M. F. Ratnoff, "Ethical Responsibilities in Clinical Investigation," *Perspectives in Biology and Medicine,* 11: 82–90, 1967.

21. S. Santorio, *Medicina Statica,* second edition, translated by John Quincy, M.D., London: W. and J. Newton, 1720, sect. 1, pp. 43–122.

22. A. Castiglioni, "Life and Work of Sanctorius," *Medical Life,* 38: 729–785, 1931, pp. 744–745.

23. Pettenkofer lived from 1818 to 1901. Today, an institute at the University of Munich is named for him. (Refs.: A. S. Evans, "Pettenkofer Revisited," *Yale Journal of Biology and Medicine,* 46: 161–176, 1973. N. Howard-Jones, "Robert Koch and the Cholera Vibrio: A Centenary," *British Medical Journal,* 288: 379–381, 1984. M. von Pettenkofer, "On Cholera, With Reference to the Recent Epidemic in Hamburg," *Lancet,* 2: 1182–1185, 1892.)

24. J. Snow, *Snow on Cholera. Being a Reprint of Two Papers by John Snow, M.D. Together with a Biographical Memoir by B. W. Richardson, M.D. and an Introduction by Wade Hampton Frost, M.D.* New York: Hafner, 1965.

25. M. von. Pettenkofer, *Untersuchungen und Beobachtungen über die Verbreitungsart der Cholera,"* Munich: Cotta, 1855, cited in N. Howard-Jones, "Gelsenkirchen Typhoid Epidemic of 1901, Robert Koch, and the Dead Hand of Max von Pettenkofer," *British Medical Journal,* 1: 103–105, 1973.

26. Edgar E. Hume, *Max von Pettenkofer,* New York: Hoeber, 1927, pp. 54–55.

27. C. von Voit, *Max von Pettenkofer zum Gedächtniss,* Munich, 1902, cited in Hume, *Max von Pettenkofer,* p. 56.

28. R. Emmerich, *Max Pettenkofer's Bodenlehre der Cholera Indica,* Munich, 1910, cited in Hume, *Max von Pettenkofer,* pp. 56–57. O. Metchnikoff, *Life of Elie Metchnikoff,* London: Constable, p. 155.

Pettenkofer's experiment attracted wide interest. Ten days later, on October 17, Dr. Rudolf Emmerich, one of Pettenkofer's assistants and a microbiologist who isolated the common colon bacterium and made other original contributions, repeated it on himself. He had to defecate almost hourly for two days. His stool, like that of his teacher, yielded pure cultures of cholera bacteria.

Somewhat later, at least three other pupils of Pettenkofer carried out the cholera self-experiment. One was Dr. Elie Metchnikoff, a French immunologist. (For further discussion of Metchnikoff, see Chapter Fifteen: Choosing the Right Animal.) A second was Dr. Jaime Ferrán y Clua, who was a colleague of Pasteur and who had developed a dangerous cholera vaccine in 1884. (See Chapter Five: The Pasteurian Club.) None of these self-experimenters died from cholera, but one had a severe case of diarrhea that was dismissed as not being cholera.

29. D. Zagury et al. "Immunization Against AIDS in Humans." *Nature,* 326: 249–50, 1987.

30. In 1958 Lovelace became head of the flight medicine and biology committee for the nation's space medicine program at the National Aeronautics and Space Administration (NASA). (Refs.: W. R. Lovelace II, "Physiologic Effects of Reduced Barometric Pressure," *Collected Papers of the Mayo Clinic,* 33: 25–26, 1941. "Army Flier Jumps From 40,200 Feet," *New York Times,* July 1, 1943, p. 9.)

31. Interviews with Dr. John P. Stapp in Alamogordo, New Mexico, June 22–23, 1980. J. P. Stapp, *Human Exposures to Linear Deceleration. I: Preliminary Survey of the Aft-facing Seated Position,* Air Force Technical Report no. 5915, June 1949. J. P. Stapp, *Human Exposures to Linear Deceleration. II: The Forward Facing Position and the Development of a Crash Harness,* Air Force Technical Report no. 5915, part 2, December 1951.

Stapp refused any compensation for injuries because he accepted them as part of the hazards for which he received flight pay and because he did not want to set a precedent for phony claims.

32. L. K. Altman, "Transplants Are Surging As Survival Rates Improve," *New York Times,* October 5, 1982, p. C-1. Interviews with Dr. Jean Borel in Basel, Switzerland, October 1, 1982, and August 15, 1983, and in New York City on February 20, 1984.

33. In 1840 Jakob Henle described a set of concepts that his student, Robert Koch, further described in lectures in 1884 and 1890. Since

then, they have served as a guide to determining cause and effect in disease, particularly infectious diseases. (Ref.: A. S. Evans, "Causation and Disease: The Henle-Koch Postulates Revisited," *Yale Journal of Biology and Medicine,* 49: 175–195, 1976.)

34. D. A. Robinson, "Infective Dose of *Campylobacter jejuni* in Milk," *British Medical Journal,* 282: 1584, 1981. Interview with Dr. Robinson in Geneva, Switzerland, February 8, 1984.

35. B. J. Marshall et al., "Attempt to Fulfill Koch's Postulates for Pyloric Campylobacter," *Medical Journal of Australia,* 142: 436–439, 1985. Interviews with Dr. Barry J. Marshall from Australia, July 24 and 27, 1984.

36. K. Landsteiner, "Ueber Agglutinationserscheinungen normalen menschlichen Blutes," *Wiener Klinische Wochenschrift,* 14: 1132–1134, 1901.

37. J. Goldstein et al., "Group B Erythrocytes Enzymatically Converted to Group O Survive Normally in A, B, and O Individuals," *Science,* 215: 168–170, 1982.

## Chapter Two: DON'T TOUCH THE HEART

1. Lung surgery in its simplest form, draining pus from the chest cavity, had been done in the days of Hippocrates in 400 B.C. However, the techniques were inexplicably lost over the centuries, and lung surgery was not performed because it was dangerous. Surgeons did not know how to prevent the complications from a pneumothorax, commonly known as a collapsed lung, when the chest cavity was opened.

During the nineteenth century, there were some attempts at heart surgery and even a few successes, but they were too isolated to be influential. Basically, these early operations were done on people who had been stabbed or wounded in the heart and who would have died without surgery. None of these were operations to correct heart disorders.

By the turn of the twentieth century, surgeons had sewn wounds of the heart. Doctors knew that, at least in theory, lung and heart disorders were correctable surgically. But doctors had yet to operate on a heart damaged by natural causes.

A few surgeons believed heart surgery would be beneficial and should be tried, but to express such beliefs publicly was to subject themselves to severe criticism. This held true even when surgeons did the first heart valve operations in the 1920s.

2. Although the electrocardiogram was invented in the late nineteenth century, it had not yet come into standard use. Its introduction into general medical practice in the United States began only in the late 1930s, according to George E. Burch and Nicholas P. DePasquale in *A History of Electrocardiography,* Chicago: Year Book Medical Publishers, 1964.

3. Billroth's warning was undoubtedly sound for his time, but coming from so powerful a man, it must have discouraged many surgeons from pursuing any interest they might have had in experimenting with the heart. Doctors educated in Germany early in the twentieth century interpreted Billroth's warning to mean that if they touched a living human heart they would be regarded as criminals. Precisely when and where Billroth issued his warning is a subject of controversy in the medical literature. (Refs.: R. Nissen, "Billroth and Cardiac Surgery," *Lancet,* 2: 250–251, 1963. K. L. Schober, "The Quotation about the Heart. Comments on Theodor Billroth's Attitude Towards Cardiac Surgery," *Thoracic and Cardiovascular Surgeon,* 29: 131–137, 1981.)

4. Paget's name is well known to modern physicians, who use it to describe two diseases that he first recognized—one a type of breast cancer, the other a benign bone condition. His remarks on heart surgery were published in S. Paget, *The Surgery of the Chest,* New York: Treat, 1897, p. 121, and S. Paget, *Surgery of the Chest,* London: Wright, 1896.

5. F. Sauerbruch, "Über die Ausschaltung der schadlichen Wirkung des Pneumothorax bei intrathorakalen Operationen," *Zentralblatt für Chirurgie,* 31: 146, 1904. F. Sauerbruch, *Die Chirurgie der Brustorgane,* Berlin: Springer, 1920–1925. F. Sauerbruch, "Zur Pathologie des offenen Pneumothorax und die Grundlagen meines Verfahrens zu seiner Ausschaltung," *Mitteilungen aus den Grenzgebieten der*

*Medizin und Chirurgie,* 13: 399, 1904. F. Sauerbruch and L. O'Shaughnessy, *Thoracic Surgery,* London: Arnold, 1937. J. Thorwald, *The Dismissal. The Last Days of Ferdinand Sauerbruch,* translated by Richard and Clara Winston, New York: Pantheon, 1962.

Sauerbruch is credited with being the first to peel off the pericardial layer around the heart in an operation he performed in 1913. But though Sauerbruch is considered a pioneer in chest surgery, he did not go on to develop cardiac surgery as a specialty. The reasons have never been clear.

Sauerbruch also devised a bizarre airtight chamber in which the pressure was kept lower than the atmosphere, at a level corresponding with that of the patient's lungs. The chamber was large enough to accommodate not only the patient's body but also the surgeon and his assistants. The patient's head, tightly sealed at the neck, extended outside the chamber, which, in reality, was a makeshift operating room. Although its usefulness in chest surgery was limited, it became the prototype for the iron lung that later kept many poliomyelitis patients alive. (Refs.: H. W. Meyer, "The History of the Development of the Negative Differential Pressure Chamber for Thoracic Surgery," *Journal of Thoracic Surgery,* 30: 114, 1955. R. Nissen, "Historical Development of Pulmonary Surgery," *American Journal of Surgery,* 89: 9–15, 1955.)

6. André Cournand, "Cardiac Catheterization. Development of the Technique, Its Contributions to Experimental Medicine, and Its Initial Applications in Man," *Acta Medica Scandinavica,* 579: 3–32, 1975. Tubes of glass or flexible material were guided into the hearts of animals through veins and arteries in their necks. The purpose was to record physiological data. In 1861 two French researchers, J.B.A. Chauveau, a professor of veterinary medicine in Lyon, and Etienne J. Marey, a Parisian scientist, inserted catheters into the hearts of animals to settle scientific disputes over the nature and timing of the heartbeat. Marey wrote: "One can be reassured of the innocuity of this method by examining the horse, who is scarcely disturbed, walks and eats as usual." It is not known why they did not go on to use the technique in humans. (Refs.: J. Bost, "Chauveau and Marey's Accomplishment: The First Intracardiac Pressure Records," pp. 7–9, and A. J. Dunning, "Interview with André Cournand at Leiden, November 1979," pp. 33–37, both in H. A. Snellen, A. J. Dunning, and A. C. Arntzenius, *History and Perspectives of Cardiology—Catheterization, Angiography, Surgery and Concepts of Circular Control,* The

Hague, Netherlands: Leiden University Press, 1981. J.B.A. Chauveau and E. J. Marey, "Appareils et expériences cardiographiques," *Mémoires de l'Académie Impériale de Médicine,* 26: 268–319, 1863. J.B.A. Chauveau and E. J. Marey, "Détermination graphique des rapports du choc du coeur avec les mouvements des oreillettes et des ventricules; Expérience faite à l'aide d'un appareil enregisteur (sphygmographe)," *Comptes Rendus Hebdomadaires des Séances de l'Académie des Sciences,* 53: 622–625, 1861.)

7. Even after Forssmann's experiments, the idea that drugs could be delivered directly to the heart through a tube was laughed at; recently his technique has been used to deliver a drug called streptokinase to dissolve clots in the coronary arteries and help stop heart attacks. That technique has led to experiments with another clot dissolver called tissue plasminogen activator, which is injected into the veins. Also, epinephrine and other drugs are delivered through catheters in some cases of cardiac arrest and cardiopulmonary resuscitation.

8. Interviews with Werner Forssmann in Wies Wambach, West Germany, and Basel, Switzerland, March 2, 3, and 4, 1973, November 4–5, 1975, December 3–4, 1975, and September 11, 1978. Forssmann lived in a hamlet in the Black Forest. In medical school I had heard several conflicting versions of his self-experiment—mostly unfavorable to Forssmann. Some professors described him as crazy, saying that he had done the experiment as a means of trying to commit suicide. They had heard such tales from German doctors who knew of him from their medical school days, before they fled to the United States from the Nazis. But none had talked to Forssmann directly. And in the 1960s, when I read translations of his papers, I found that his experiments, though flawed, were more sensible than I had been led to believe.

At the time of my first visit in 1973, Forssmann's autobiography was not available to me. It was published in the United States in 1974. (Ref.: Werner Forssmann, *Experiments on Myself. Memoirs of a Surgeon in Germany,* New York: St. Martin's Press, 1974.) To my surprise, Forssmann told me that I was the only person to have interviewed him extensively about any of his experiments. I returned several more times to clarify points that had arisen from previous interviews. The last time was in 1978, just after I had interviewed Dr. Rudolf Nissen in Basel. Nissen was Sauerbruch's chief resident and was the only physician I located who had known Forssmann during the years he was doing these experiments. Nissen was critical of Forssmann for reasons that struck me as reflections of a personality clash and jealousies that had developed over the years. After cross-checking the stories, I supported Forssmann's version, though I recognized it was told many years after the events.

9. I could not locate Gerda Ditzen to interview her for independent verification of this story.

10. Werner Forssmann, "Die Sondierung des rechten Herzens," *Klinische Wochenschrift,* 8: 2085–2087, 1929.

11. The aim was to introduce a drug called "collargol," and it was another example of self-experimentation. Bleichroeder said: "Before I used this method in human subjects, I further convinced myself by two very thorough experiments, performed on my own veins, of the safety of such procedures. My colleague, Dr. Unger, introduced a catheter through a slit into a vein of my forearm and advanced it up to the level of the axilla. Later he performed a similar experiment using a vein in my thigh and advanced the catheter into the vena cava [the main vein in the abdomen]." (Ref.: F. Bleichroeder, "Intraarterielle Therapie," *Berliner Klinische Wochenschrift,* 49: 1503–1505, 1912, translated in *Classic Descriptions in Diagnostic Radiology,* A. J. Bruwer, ed., vol. 1, Springfield, Ill.: Thomas, 1964, pp. 502–504.)

12. A. J. Benatt, "Cardiac Catheterization: A Historical Note," *Lancet,* 2: 746–747, 1949. Werner Forssmann, "Addendum," *Klinische Wochenschrift,* 8: 2287, 1929.

13. Schneider introduced Forssmann to Dr. Wilhelm His, a pioneer cardiologist, and to Dr. August Bier, a prominent German surgeon who developed spinal anesthesia through experiments on himself. (See Chapter Three: The Perilous Route to Painless Surgery.) However, Forssmann told me that neither His nor Bier could take him on because they were retiring. Bier suggested that Forssmann work with Sauerbruch, who had by then become one of the stars of German surgery.

14. Werner Forssmann, "Über Kontrastdarstellung der Hohlen des lebenden rechten Herzens und der Lungenschlagader," *Muenchener Medizinische Wochenschrift,* 78: 489–492, 1931.

15. When I interviewed Dr. Rufold Nissen in Basel, Switzerland, on September 9, 1978, he was very critical of Forssmann's scientific abilities and claims. I asked Nissen why, if that were the case, he and Sauerbruch as the leaders had not developed Forssmann's idea into a useful tool. Nissen gave an answer that revealed a certain and surprising amount of tunnel vision for a pioneering surgeon: "We were interested in the lungs, not the heart." Any doctor knows that the physiology of the two organs is inextricably related.

16. W. Forssmann, *Experiments on Myself,* p. 241.

17. A. Cournand and H. A. Ranges, "Catheterization of the Right Auricle in Man," *Proceedings of the Society for Experimental Biology and Medicine,* 46: 462–466, 1941.

18. A. Cournand, H. A. Ranges, and R. L. Riley, "Comparison of Results of the Normal Ballistocardiogram and Direct Fick Method in Measuring the Cardiac Output in Man," *Journal of Clinical Investigation,* 21: 287–293, 1942. D. W. Richards, Jr. et al., "Pressure of Blood in the Right Auricle, in Animals and in Man: Under Normal Conditions and in Right Heart Failure," *American Journal of Physiology,* 136: 115–123, 1942.

19. Interviews with Dr. Dickinson Richards in New York City, 1968, and with Dr. André Cournand in New York City, December 16, 1976.

20. G. Liljestrand, "Presentation Speech, 1956 Nobel Prize," *Nobel Lectures: Physiology or Medicine,* vol. 3, Amsterdam: Elsevier, 1964, p. 502.

21. J. Dieffenbach, "Physiological and Surgical Observations on Cholera Patients," cited in H. Sturzbecher, "Cholera. Dieffenbach und die Catheterisierung des Herzens, 1831," *Deutsches Medizinisches Journal,* 22: 470–471, 1971.

## Chapter Three: THE PERILOUS ROUTE TO PAINLESS SURGERY

1. W. Ayer, "Account of an Eye Witness," in *The Semi-Centennial of Anesthesia,* Boston: Massachusetts General Hospital, October 16, 1896, pp. 89–90.

2. "Hospital Record of the First Public Administration of Ether," Appendix, in *The Semi-Centennial of Anesthesia,* Boston: Massachusetts General Hospital, October 16, 1896, p. 88.

3. Ibid., p. 20.

4. Zachary Cope, *William Cheselden. 1688–1752,* Edinburgh and London: Livingstone, 1953.

5. F. W. Cock, "The First Operation Under Ether in Europe—The Story of Three Days," *University College Hospital Magazine,* 1: 127, 1911. A.H.M. Littlewood, "Robert Liston," *British Journal of Plastic Surgery,* 13: 97–101, 1960–1961. M.J.L. Patterson, "Robert Liston," *St. Bartholomew Hospital Journal,* 62: 135–141, 1958.

Liston was the first to do an operation under ether anesthesia in Europe. "We are going to try a Yankee dodge for making men insensible," Liston said before he did the operation, an amputation of a leg, in twenty-five seconds. When it was over, Liston said, "This Yankee dodge beats mesmerism hollow." (Ref.: Patterson, "Robert Liston," p. 139.)

6. Centuries ago, barbers were the surgeons; they filled both roles. Some, such as Ambroise Paré, achieved fame. Only since about the eighteenth century have surgeons come from the ranks of the medical profession. (Ref.: J. C. Krantz, Jr., *A Portrait of Medical History and Current Medical Problems,* Baltimore: Lucas, 1962, p. 51.)

7. J. Priestley, *Experiments and Observations on Different Kinds of Air,* London: J. Johnson, 1775, vol. 2, p. 102.

8. H. Davy, *Researches, Chiefly Concerning Nitrous Oxide,* vol. 3 of *The Collected Works of Sir Humphry Davy,* J. Davy, ed., London: Smith, Elder, 1839. H. Davy, *Relating to the Effects Produced by the*

*Respiration of Nitrous Oxide upon Different Individuals,* vol. 4 of *The Collected Works of Sir Humphry Davy,* J. Davy, ed., London: Smith, Elder, 1839. "Bicentenary of Nitrous Oxide," *British Medical Journal,* 2: 367–368, 1972.

9. H. Davy, *Researches,* vol. III, p. 271.

10. Ibid., p. 274.

11. H. Davy, *Researches, Chemical and Philosophical; Chiefly Concerning Nitrous Oxide, or Dephlogisticated Nitrous Air, and Its Respiration,* London: J. Johnson, 1800, p. 465.

12. Ibid., p. 556.

13. F. F. Cartwright, *The English Pioneers of Anesthesia (Beddoes, Davy, Hickman),* Bristol: Wright, 1952.

14. Letter cited in F. L. Taylor, *Crawford W. Long and the Discovery of Ether Anesthesia,* New York: Hoeber, 1928, pp. 63–64.

15. C. W. Long, "An Account of the First Use of Sulphuric Ether by Inhalation as an Anesthetic in Surgical Operations," *Southern Medical Journal* (new series), 5: 705–713, 1849. Taylor, *Crawford W. Long,* pp. 42–43.

According to one account, in Anderson, South Carolina, in 1839 a group of boys seized a black boy and forced him to inhale ether from a handkerchief that was held over his mouth and nose. Soon the boy became motionless and unconscious and was feared dead. But after an hour he revived, no worse for his alarming experience. Three years later, one of the actors in this affair told Long about the episode; the tale reportedly "added courage to" Long's meditations. (Ref.: H. M. Lyman, *Artificial Anaesthesia and Anaesthetics,* New York: Wood, 1881, p. 5.)

16. G. Q. Colton, letter to the *New York Times,* February 5, 1862, p. 3.

17. H. Wells, letter to the *Hartford Courant,* December 9, 1846.

18. Dr. Charles T. Jackson was a controversial figure. He had publicly proclaimed that he, not Samuel F. B. Morse, was the discoverer of telegraphy. Jackson claimed he had discussed new developments in electricity with Morse during an ocean crossing before Morse patented the telegraph in 1840. G. P. Merrill and J. F. Fulton state that regarding the electric telegraph, "It is known that Jackson had previously perfected a working model of such a device, but he thought lightly of the instrument and failed to realize its commercial value. In the controversy as to priority which followed the announcement of Morse's patent, Jackson claimed for himself the honors of the discovery." (Ref.: *Dictionary of American Biography,* New York: Scribner, 1932, p. 536.)

19. E. W. Morton, "The Discovery of Anesthesia. Dr. W.T.G. Morton and His Heroic Battle for a New Idea—How Painless Surgery Began Fifty Years Ago," *McClure's Magazine,* 7: 311–318, September 1896.

20. W.T.G. Morton, *Remarks on the Proper Mode of Administering Sulphuric Ether by Inhalation,* Boston: Dutton and Wentworth, 1847, pp. 43–44.

21. W.T.G. Morton, *A Memoir to the Academy of Sciences at Paris on a New Use of Sulphuric Ether,* New York: Schuman, 1946, pp. 8, 10.

22. Morton, "Discovery of Anesthesia," p. 313.

23. O. W. Holmes, letter to Morton, in E. Warren, *Some Account of the Letheon; or Who Was the Discoverer?* third edition, Boston: Dutton and Wentworth, 1847, pp. 84–85.

24. "Death of Dr. Horace Wells," *Boston Medical and Surgical Journal,* 38: 24–25, 1848.

25. Morton, "Discovery of Anesthesia," p. 318.

26. This version is told in R. Fulop-Miller, *Triumph Over Pain,* translated by Eden and Cedar Paul, New York: The Literary Guild of America, 1938, pp. 321–323.

Dr. Francis de Marneffe, general director of the McLean Hospital, said that as a matter of hospital policy in keeping the confidentiality of the medical records of all patients, even long after death, he could neither confirm nor deny that Jackson was a patient at McLean. (Ref.: F. de Marneffe, personal communication, March 1, 1983.)

27. J. Y. Simpson, "Account of a New Anesthetic Agent as a Substitute for Sulphuric Ether," Edinburgh, 1847, reprinted in L. Clendening, *Source Book of Medical History,* New York: Hoeber, 1942, pp. 373–377.

28. Simpson said that less chloroform was needed than ether because chloroform was a quicker-acting anesthetic and also was more pleasant. He said he tried chloroform "in order to avoid, if possible, some of the inconveniences and objections pertaining to sulphuric ether (particularly its disagreeable and very persistent smell, its occasional tendency to irritation of the bronchi during its first inspirations, and the large quantity of it occasionally required to be used, more especially in protracted cases of labour) . . ." (Ref.: Simpson, "New Anesthetic Agent," p. 374.)

29. Professor R. E. Kendall, dean of the Faculty of Medicine, University of Edinburgh Medical School, told me about the use of chloroform in the United Kingdom in an interview in November 1983 and in personal communications, December 1, 1983 and July 7, 1986.

30. It was a time when by Freud's own admission he was misdiagnosing neuroses as chronic meningitis. "I understood nothing about the neuroses. On one occasion I introduced to my audience a neurotic suffering from a persistent headache as a case of chronic meningitis; they quite rightly rose in revolt against me, and my premature activities as a teacher came to an end. By way of excuse I may add that this happened at a time when greater authorities than myself in Vienna were in the habit of diagnosing neurasthenia as cerebral tumor." (Ref.: S. Freud, *Autobiography,* New York: Norton, 1935, p. 20.)

31. The first substance isolated, in 1855, was called erythroxylon; most probably it was a mixture of alkaloids containing cocaine. In 1860 Albert Neimann of Gottingen, Germany, isolated the principal alkaloid from the leaves of Peruvian coca; he called his preparation cocaine.

32. Christison helped establish toxicology as a branch of medicine. His excellent reputation was based on his thorough research, largely done through self-experiments, sometimes at imminent risk to himself. He ate an ounce of the root of *Oenanthe crocata* to prove that in Scotland it did not have the toxic properties that were well known in England and countries further to the south. In another self-experiment, he ate a portion of a Calabar bean, a poisonous seed from tropical Africa. Christison's interest in the bean had been aroused when a missionary sent him one. He gave it to animals, then ate it himself. Just a small piece of the bean produced such alarming symptoms that, with the instinct of a toxicologist, Christison reached for the first emetic he could find—the water he had just used to shave. His experience led him to recommend the Calabar bean as a means of human executions. (Refs.: R. Christison, "Observations on the Effects of Cuca, or Coca, The Leaves of Erythroxylon Coca," *British Medical Journal,* 1: 527–531, 1876. R. Christison, "On the Properties of the Ordeal-Bean of Old Calabar, Western Africa," *Monthly Journal of Medicine,* 20: 193–204, 1855. "Obituary: Sir Robert Christison," *British Medical Journal,* 1: 249–252, 1882.)

From further experiments on the Calabar bean, two other doctors in Edinburgh, including Dr. Thomas R. Fraser, one of Christison's students, developed treatments for eye disorders and an antidote to curare. In 1863 Fraser isolated the active substance from the Calabar bean—called eserine or physostigmine—and became the first to observe the drug's ability to contract the pupil, his own. He recommended its use in ophthalmology. (Ref.: T. R. Fraser, "On the Characters, Actions and Therapeutical Uses of the Ordeal Bean of Calabar [*Physostigma venenosum,* Balfour]," *Edinburgh Medical Journal,* 9: 36–56, 123–132, 1863.) Also in the same year, Dr. Douglas Argyll Robertson, a leading ophthalmologist in Edinburgh, did controlled experiments with physostigmine on his own eyes and showed the pharmacological antagonism between it and medicinal extracts from the poisonous belladonna plant. Robertson suggested the use of physostigmine for the relief of eye pain and paralysis of one of the eye muscles. (Ref.: D. A. Robertson, "On the Calabar Bean as a New Agent in Ophthalmic Medicine," *Edinburgh Medical Journal,* 8: 815–820, 1863.) For a historical overview, see B. Holmstedt, "The Ordeal Bean of Old Calabar: The Pageant of *Physostigma venenosum* in Medicine," in T. Swain, ed., *Plants in the Development of*

*Modern Medicine,* Cambridge, Mass.: Harvard University Press, 1972.

33. L. Grinspoon and J. B. Bakalar, *Cocaine. A Drug and Its Social Evolution,* New York: Basic Books, 1976, p. 21.

34. P. Mantegazza, *Sulle virtu ingieniche e medicinali della coca,* Milan, 1859 (privately published).

35. T. Aschenbrandt, "Die physiologische Wirkung und Bedeutung des Cocainum muriaticum auf den menschlichen Organismus," *Deutsche Medizinische Wochenschrift.* 9: 730–732, 1883.

36. E. L. Freud, ed., *Letters of Sigmund Freud,* New York: Basic Books, 1960, letter 43, April 21, 1884.

37. South American Indian practitioners of folk medicine used cocaine as a local anesthetic long before the arrival of the Spaniards. By the end of the 1800s, a staggering number of doctors throughout the world described cocaine's local anesthetic effects but did not take the crucial step of applying this knowledge to clinical medicine. Most of these doctors experimented on themselves, noting such symptoms as a numbing and paralytic effect on the tongue. Others used it to soothe sore throats and to anesthetize the eyes of animals. A partial list of these doctors includes Scherzer, Gardeke, Samuel R. Percy, Paolo Mantegazza, Friedrich Wohler, Albert Neimann, Carl Schroff, Charles Fauvel, Thomas Moreno y Maiz, Alexander Bennett, B. von Anrep, Coupard, Borderau, and William A. Hammond (who became a surgeon general of the United States.)

38. S. Freud, *Cocaine Papers,* R. Byck, ed., New York: Stonehill, 1974, p. xx. According to Byck, "All of Freud's papers on cocaine can be said to be thorough in their review, accurate in their physiological and psychological experimentation, and almost prescient in their consideration of points which have become major issues in modern psychopharmacology."

39. Ibid., p. 98.

40. Ibid.

41. Ibid, p. 101.

42. Ibid, p. 104.

43. S. Freud, "Über Coca," *Centralblatt für die gesamte Therapie,* 2: 289–314, 1884. S. Freud, "Coca," translated by S. Pol, *St. Louis Medical and Surgical Journal,* 47: 502–550, 1884.

44. C. Koller, "Historical Notes on the Beginning of Local Anesthesia," *Journal of the American Medical Association,* 90: 1742–1743, 1928. C. Koller, "Über die Verwendung des Cocain zur Anästhesirung am Auge," *Wiener Medizinsche Wochenschrift,* 34: 1276–1278, 1309–1311, 1884.

45. J. Gaertner, "Die Entdeckung der Lokalanaesthesie," *Der Neue Tag,* Vienna, 1919, cited in H. Koller-Becker, "Carl Koller and Cocaine," *Psychoanalytic Quarterly,* 32: 309–373, 1963, p. 332.

46. Freud, *Cocaine Papers,* pp. xxxiii–xxxiv.

47. A. Wood, "New Method of Treating Neuralgia by the Direct Application of Opiates to the Painful Points," *Edinburgh Medical and Surgical Journal,* 82: 265–281, 1855.

48. F. Garrison, "Halsted," *American Mercury,* 7: 396–401, 1926. R. J. Hall, "Hydrochlorate of Cocaine," *New York Medical Journal,* 40: 643–644, 1884. W. G. MacCallum, *William Stewart Halsted: Surgeon,* Baltimore: Johns Hopkins, 1930. For further reading on Halsted, see W. Penfield, "Halsted of Johns Hopkins. The Man and His Problem as Described in the Secret Records of William Osler," *Journal of the American Medical Association,* 210: 2214–2218, 1969.

49. Hall, "Hydrochlorate of Cocaine," p. 644.

50. Today, the most commonly used local anesthetic drug is lidocaine (also known as xylocaine.) Its benefits, as well as those of some other commonly used local anesthetics, were discovered through further self-experiments in Sweden. At the University of Stockholm, two chemists, Nils Lofgren and Holger Erdtman, synthesized sixteen compounds in a systematic search for safe local anesthetics. They found that although these numbed the tongue, they had no local

anesthetic action when injected into the skin. However, success came in 1943, when Lofgren and Bengt Lundquist, another chemist at the university, synthesized lidocaine; they tested it first on animals and then on themselves. Lidocaine has found an even greater use as a heart drug than as a local anesthetic. It is now a standard drug in all coronary care units because it can prevent and suppress the formation of potentially fatal heartbeats called premature ventricular contractions, which often develop as a complication of heart attacks. (Ref.: N. Lofgren, *Studies on Local Anesthetics. Xylocaine. A New Synthetic Drug. Inaugural Dissertation.* Stockholm: Hoeggstroms, 1948.)

51. Penfield, "Halsted," p. 2216.

52. Ibid., p. 2217.

53. Credit for the discovery of the spinal tap is given to Dr. Heinrich Quincke. (Refs.: H. Quincke, "Die Lumbalpunction des Hydrocephalus," *Berliner Klinische Wochenschrift,* 28: 929–933, 1891. H. Quincke, "Zehnter Congress für innere Medicin Wiesbaden, No. 3," *Deutsche Medizinische Wochenschrift,* 17: 809, 1891.)

54. A. Bier, "Versuche über Cocainisierung des Rückenmarkes," *Deutsche Zeitschrift für Chirurgie,* 51: 361–369, 1899.

55. A. R. McIntyre, *Curare,* Chicago: University of Chicago Press, 1947. P. Smith, *Arrows of Mercy. The Story of Curare—From the "Flying Death" of the Amazon Jungle, to the Wonder Drug of Modern Anesthesiology,* New York: Doubleday, 1969.

56. B. C. Brodie, "Experiments and Observations on the Different Modes in Which Death Is Produced by Certain Vegetable Poisons," *Philosophical Transactions of the Royal Society of London,* 101: 178–208, 1811. B. C. Brodie, "Further Experiments and Observations on the Action of Poisons on the Animal System," *Philosophical Transactions of the Royal Society of London,* 102: 205–227, 1812. B. Brodie, "Letter to Flourens," *Union Médicale,* 4: 98, 1859.

57. W. C. Bowman, "Peripherally Acting Muscle Relaxants," in M. J. Parnham and J. Bruinvels, *Discoveries in Pharmacology,* vol. 1, Amsterdam: Elsevier, 1983, pp. 135–136.

58. A. E. Bennett, "Curare: A Preventive of Traumatic Complications in Convulsive Shock Therapy," *American Journal of Psychiatry,* 97: 1040–1060, 1941. A. E. Bennett, "Preventing Traumatic Complications in Convulsive Shock Therapy by Curare," *Journal of the American Medical Association,* 114: 322–324, 1940. McIntyre, *Curare.*

"Although Bennett was the first to report on the use of curare for softening convulsions in shock therapy, d-tubocurarine chloride, an alkaloid obtained from crude curare, was used at Woodside Hospital [in England] for a considerable time before the publication of this paper. Unfortunately the work was interrupted by the war and was not followed up." (Ref.: J. A. Hobson and F. Prescott, "Use of d-Tubocurarine Chloride and Thiopentone in Electro-Convulsion Therapy," *British Medical Journal,* 1: 445–448, 1947, p. 445.)

59. Interviews with Dr. Frederick Prescott in Churt, Surrey, England, August 28, 1973, December 15, 1975, February 15, 1977, and August 30, 1983, and in London, November 24, 1980, and November 1983. For Prescott's scientific papers, see J. A. Hobson and F. Prescott, "Use of d-Tubocurarine Chloride and Thiopentone in Electro-Convulsion Therapy," *British Medical Journal,* 2: 445–448, 1947. F. Prescott, "The Clinical Pharmacology and Uses of Curare," *Journal Belge de Neurologie et de Psychiatrie,* 47: 599–612, 1947. F. Prescott, "Discussion on Further Experiences with Curare," *Proceedings of the Royal Society of Medicine,* 40: 593–602, 1947. F. Prescott, G. Organe, and S. Rowbotham, "Tubocurarine Chloride as an Adjunct to an Anaesthesia," *Lancet,* 2: 80–84, 1946.

60. Interviews with Sir Geoffrey Organe in Seaton, Devonshire, England, February 2, 1977, and November 27, 1980.

61. Interviews with Dr. Scott M. Smith in Salt Lake City, Utah, July 29, 1976, and January 13 and 14 and November 6, 1983. Smith's key paper is S. M. Smith et al., "The Lack of Cerebral Effects of d-Tubocurarine," *Anesthesiology,* 8: 1–14, 1947.

62. Interviews with Dr. Louis Goodman in Salt Lake City, Utah, 1975, 1976, 1981, and January 14, 1983. Goodman's planning and involvement in Smith's experiment in part reflected his experience in an experiment he had done on himself with a drug called prostigmine

when he was working at Yale in 1936. Prostigmine was first used to treat patients with a life-threatening nervous system disease called myasthenia gravis that leads to muscle weakness. Goodman, who did not have the disease, tested the drug's effects on his own muscles by measuring his hand grip strength. However, the dose Goodman took produced an alarming reaction: While walking home from his laboratory, he experienced a runny nose, excess salivation, restlessness, a feeling of tremulousness, difficulty breathing, severe giddiness, faintness, and a fear of impending death. When Goodman arrived home, he called a physician friend to bring an antidote called atropine. A medical student who was a partner in the experiments suffered no adverse effects. (Ref.: L. S. Goodman and W. J. Bruckner, "The Therapeutics of Prostigmine. A Warning Concerning Its Oral Use Based on a Personal Experience," *Journal of the American Medical Association,* 108: 965–968, 1937.)

63. Smith's failure to forewarn his wife about his experiment would remain such a sore point that years later he asked me not to discuss it with her.

For an overview of anesthesia, see also:

H. J. Bigelow, *Surgical Anesthesia,* Boston: Little, Brown, 1900.

J. F. Fulton and M. E. Stanton, *Centennial of Surgical Anesthesia. An Annotated Catalogue of Books and Pamphlets Bearing on the Early History of Surgical Anesthesia,* New York: Schuman, 1946.

C. D. Leake, "Historical Development of Surgical Anesthesia," *Scientific Monthly,* 20: 304–328, 1925.

For further reading on specific anesthesia pioneers, see:

A. D. Aberbach, "Samuel Latham Mitchill: A Physician in the Early Days of the Republic," *Bulletin of The New York Academy of Medicine,* 40: 502–510, 1964.

W. H. Archer, "Chronological History of Horace Wells, Discoverer of Anesthesia," *Bulletin of the History of Medicine,* 7: 1140–1169, 1939.

W. H. Archer, "Life and Letters of Horace Wells, Discoverer of Anesthesia: Chronologically Arranged with an Appendix," *Journal of the American College of Dentistry,* 11: 81–210, 1944.

W. H. Archer, "The Discovery of Anesthesia," *Connecticut State*

*Medical Journal,* Horace Wells centenary number, 8: 756–759, November 1944.

H. W. Erving, "The Discoverer of Anesthesia: Dr. Horace Wells of Hartford," *Yale Journal of Biology and Medicine,* 5: 421–430, 1933.

C. R. Hall, *A Scientist in the Early Republic. Samuel Latham Mitchill,* New York: Columbia University Press, 1934.

C. W. Long, "First Surgical Operation under Ether," *Transactions Georgia Medical and Surgical Association,* 1853, in L. Clendening, *Source Book of Medical History,* New York: Hoeber, 1942, pp. 356–358.

W.T.G. Morton, Statements supported by evidence of William T. G. Morton, M.D., on his claim to the discovery of the anesthetic properties of ether, submitted to the honorable select committee appointed by the Senate of the United States, 32nd Congress, 2nd session, January 21st, 1853.

N. P. Rice, *Trials of a Public Benefactor,* New York: Pudney and Russell, 1859, chapter 4.

W.D.A. Smith, *Under the Influence,* London: Macmillan, 1982.

M. E. Soifer, "Historical Notes on Horace Wells," *Bulletin of the History of Medicine,* 9: 101–112, 1941.

C. J. Wells, "Horace Wells," *Current Researches in Anesthesia and Analgesia,* 14: 176–189, 216–224, July–August 1935.

H. W. Wells, *History of the Discovery of the Application of Nitrous Oxide Gas, Ether, and Other Vapors to Surgical Operations,* Hartford: Wells, 1847.

## Chapter Four: THE CASE OF THE QUEASY CHEMISTS

1. W. Osler, "Recent Advances in Medicine," *Science* 17: 170–171, 1891.

2. During Hippocrates' time in Greece (about 400 B.C.), diet, which included exercise and baths, was a mainstay of therapy. Yet drugs such as flax, dill, scammony, and other botanicals were prescribed, as were alum and other minerals. (Ref.: J. Stannard, "Hippocratic Pharmacology," *Bulletin of the History of Medicine,* 35: 497–518, 1961.)

3. N. Taylor, "The Pleasant Assassin: The Story of Marihuana," in D. Solomon, ed., *The Marihuana Papers,* Indianapolis: Bobbs-Merrill, 1966, p. 7.

4. A. Grollman and E. F. Grollman, *Pharmacology and Therapeutics,* sixth edition, Philadelphia: Lea and Febiger, 1965. R. R. Lingeman, *Drugs from A to Z. A Dictionary,* New York: McGraw-Hill, 1974.

5. Von Hohenheim took the nickname of Paracelsus in about 1529, but the precise reason for the choice is not known. According to Walter Pagel's sketch in the *Dictionary of Scientific Biography,* vol. 10, New York: Scribner's, 1974, Paracelsus may have denoted the following: surpassing Celsus; a latinization of Hohenheim; or possibly his authorship of "para(doxical)" works that overturned tradition. I could find no evidence that Paracelsus experimented on himself.

6. The first reports of the use of quinine as an antimalarial drug came from Ecuador in 1630; it was used in the form of the bark of the cinchona tree, which is indigenous to regions of South America. A physician used cinchona bark to successfully treat a countess for fever, then introduced it into Spain in 1638, and by 1640 use of the drug had spread through Europe. In 1820 quinine was identified as the active pharmacologic component. (Ref.: L. Goodman and A. Gilman, *The Pharmacological Basis of Therapeutics,* New York: Macmillan, 1941, p. 903.) Brazilians made preparations of dried roots of *Psychotria ipecacuanha* to treat diarrhea, and the therapy was introduced into Europe in 1658. Later, ipecac was identified as the active pharmacologic ingredient. (Ref.: Goodman and Gilman, *Pharmacological Basis,* p. 931.)

7. A. Storck, *An Essay on the Medicinal Nature of Hemlock,* London: J. Nourse, 1760.

8. Ibid., p. 3.

9. Ibid., p. 4.

10. In 1864 Alfred B. Garrod, a physician to Queen Victoria who made an important finding about gout, reported that hemlock was used most commonly to allay spasm because it was regarded as a powerful

sedative to the spinal cord. (Ref.: A. B. Garrod, "Lectures on The British Pharmacopoeia: Its Construction, Its Comparison with the London Pharmacopoeia, and the Value of Its New Remedies in the Treatment of Disease," *Medical Times and Gazette,* 1: 167–169, 1864.)

11. Storck, *Hemlock,* p. 9.

12. Though Serturner began his research in 1803 and first reported it in 1805, it had no impact until he published a more complete report in 1817. (Refs.: P. J. Hanzlik, "125th Anniversary of the Discovery of Morphine by Serturner," *Journal of the American Pharmaceutical Association,* 18: 375–384, 1929. D. I. Macht, "The History of Opium and Some of Its Preparations and Alkaloids," *Journal of the American Medical Association,* 64: 477–481, 1915. F. Serturner, Darstellung der reinen Mohnsäure [Opiumsäure] nebst einer chemischen Untersuchung des Opiums mit vorzüglicher Hinsicht auf einen darin neu entdeckten Stoff und die dahin gehörigen Bemerkungen. *Journal der Pharmacie für Ärtze Apotheker,* 14: 47–93, 1806. F.W.A. Serturner, "Über das Morphium, eine neue salzfähige Grundlage, und die Mekonsäure, als Hauptbestandtheile des Opiums," *Gilbert's Annalen der Physik* [Leipzig], 25: 56–89, 1817.)

13. F. Serturner, cited in J. C. Krantz, *Historical Medical Classics Involving New Drugs,* Baltimore: Williams and Wilkins, 1974, p. 8.

14. Ibid., p. 9.

15. E. Hale, *Boylston Medical Prize Dissertations for the Years 1819 and 1821. Experiments and Observations on the Communication Between the Stomach and the Urinary Organs and on the Propriety of Administering Medicine by Injection into the Veins,* Boston: Everett and Ingraham, 1821, p. 79.

16. It was Hale's second Boylston prize. Both awards were based on research he had done on himself. The first was for physiological observations on "the communication between the stomach and urinary organs." At that time, some doctors believed that there was a direct passage for fluids between the stomach and the kidneys. Hale undertook experiments to disprove that theory. The experiments themselves had no lasting value, but they provided insights into

Hale's thinking about the ethics of human experimentation. He said: "Experiments must be performed on living animals. But the difference in habits and character, between man and the smaller animals, is so great, as to give a great degree of uncertainty to the deductions from the results of experiments made on them. . . . Experiments on our own race can never be performed to any considerable extent. If they are hazardous in their nature, they of course are never to be attempted, even if subjects could be found who would be willing to undergo them. And when they are not so, none but professional men can estimate the degree of inconvenience or risk to which they may be subjected by submitting to them. To obviate these difficulties, I have in the first dissertation made myself the subject of my experiments."

17. Several twentieth-century writers, however, criticized Hale's experiment as unwise and foolhardy, apparently without having researched the circumstances of the experiment. One was Chicago researcher Andrew Ivy, who was critical of a number of self-experimenters. Ivy actively participated in the Nuremberg trials and wrote one of the earliest and most frequently cited papers on the ethics of research.

18. Hale, *Medical Prize Dissertations,* p. 115.

19. Ibid., p. 117.

20. Ibid., p. 119.

21. "Boylston Medical Prize Dissertations for the Years 1819 and 1821," *New England Journal of Medicine and Surgery,* 11: 163–175, 1822.

22. The physician and author Oliver Wendell Holmes, one of the leaders of American medicine, later praised Hale's experiments for their contribution to medical practice. He said that Hale's method had extended ether and other inhalation therapies to become "the most rapid and potent means of subduing pain and other forms of suffering." (Ref.: O. W. Holmes, *Addresses and Exercises at the One Hundredth Anniversary of the Foundation of the Medical School of Harvard University, October 17, 1883,* Cambridge, Mass.: John Wilson & Son, pp. 3–35.)

23. V. Kruta, *J. E. Purkyne (1787–1869), Physiologist. A Short Account of His Contributions to the Progress of Physiology with a Bibliography of His Works,* Prague: Academia, 1969. V. Kruta and M. Teich, *Jan Evangelista Purkyne,* translated by Samuel Kostomlatsky and Alice Teichova, Prague: State Medical Publishing House, 1962. J. E. Purkinje, translated by V. Kruta, *Ziva,* 6: 45, 1858. Interview with Dr. Vladislav Kruta in Brno, Czechoslovakia, December 5–8, 1975.

24. Goethe said: "It was remarkable to me how he rose from the abyss of clericalism relying on his own spiritual strength, a self-educated man, concentrating himself on his inner being, and undergoing voluntary martyrdom to acquire knowledge by studying his own self, in details and generally, thus to get to understand himself." (Ref.: Letter from Goethe to C.L.F. Schultz, September 12, 1882, cited in Kruta and Teich, *Jan Evangelista Purkyne,* p. 50.).

25. J. E. Purkyne, quoted in Z. Votava, "Purkyne's Pioneer Contribution to Neuro-Psychopharmacology," *Acta Facultatis Medicae Universitatis Brunensis,* 40: 47–56, 1971, p. 48.

26. J. E. Purkyne, cited in H. J. John, *Jan Evangelista Purkyne,* Philadelphia: American Philosophical Society, 1959, p. 56.

27. P. J. Hanzlik, "Jan Evangelista Purkyne (Purkinje) on Disturbances of the Vision by Digitalis, One Hundred Years Ago," *Journal of the American Medical Association,* 84: 2024–2025, 1925.

Dr. William Withering of Birmingham, England, is credited with having introduced digitalis, the dried leaf of the foxglove plant, into medical practice in 1775. He recognized it as the active ingredient of an old woman's secret formula. Presumably, digitalis was used for some time before Withering.

28. J. E. Purkyne, cited in B. Holmstedt and G. Liljestrand, *Readings in Pharmacology,* New York: Pergamon Press, 1963, p. 89.

29. Today, when nutmeg is used in small amounts as a flavoring agent, cases of poisoning are rare. But in the past, when nutmeg was used in medicine, toxic reactions were numerous. Doctors prescribed nutmeg as a narcotic, and other people abused it for its hallucinogenic effects. Many cases of poisoning resulted from its use to induce abortions.

30. In his early years, Purkyne amused himself by observing visual sensations in his eyes. He studied the images of a candle flame reflected in the refractive surfaces of the eye. Those observations formed the basis for the current practice whereby ophthalmologists measure the cornea as part of the standard eye examination. He also realized that certain sensations that occurred in the absence of adequate external cause, as well as some errors in visual perception, were not due to chance but rather were related to such factors as features in the structure or function of the eye and its nerve connections with the brain. For example, he showed that the shadows of one's own retinal vessels—Purkinje's figure or tree—could be seen when a spotlight light is focused on the white of the eye. It was Purkyne who discovered that colors could not be distinguished in the peripheral parts of the retina; his recommendations contributed to later development of the ophthalmoscope, which is now an indispensable medical tool. His observations of the furrows on the skin of his fingers led to the discovery of dermatoglyphics and the use of fingerprints.

31. By the time of his death in 1869, Purkinje was famous and had made many lasting contributions to medicine. Among his legacies are the cells that are situated in the heart and the cerebellum of the brain that now bear his name. (Ref.: Purkinje, *Ziva,* p. 45.)

32. W. Murrell, "Nitro-gylcerine as a Remedy for Angina Pectoris," *Lancet,* 1: 80–81, 113–115, 151–152, 225–227, 1879.

33. A. G. Field, "Nitro-Glycerine or Glonoine," *Medical Times and Gazette* (new series), 18: 339–340, 1859. A. G. Field, "On the Toxical and Medicinal Properties of Nitrate of Oxyde of Glycyl," *Medical Times and Gazette* (new series), 16: 291–292, 1858.

34. W. Murrell, "Nitro-glycerine," p. 81.

35. L. E. Holt, Jr., and P. H. Holz, "The Black Bottle. A Consideration of the Role of Charcoal in the Treatment of Poisoning in Children," *Journal of Pediatrics,* 63: 306–314, 1963.

36. M. Bertrand, quoted in B. H. Rand, "On Animal Charcoal as an Antidote," *Medical Examiner,* 4: 528–533, 1848. P. F. Touéry, quoted by Secheyron and Daunic: "Le Charbon animal ou végétal; antidote

général populaire, Congrès Français de Médicine, sixième session (Toulouse), *Comptes Rendus,* 2: 373, 1902. P. F. Touéry, quoted in L. Lichtwitz, "Die Bedeutung der Adsorption für die Therapie," *Therapie der Gegenwart,* 10: 542–546, 1908.

37. Interviews with Dr. Erik Jacobsen and Dr. Jens Hald in Copenhagen, Denmark, March 27–29, 1972. Interviews with Dr. Jacobsen, May 7–9, 1973, November 27, 1975, February 16, 1977, and September 20, 1978, and personal communications, August 1982.

Hald and Jacobsen's scientific papers are: E. Asmussen, J. Hald, E. Jacobsen, et al.: "Studies on the Effect of Tetraethylthiuramdisulphide (Antabuse) and Alcohol on Respiration and Circulation in Normal Human Subjects," *Acta Pharmacologica et Toxicologica* (Copenhagen), 4: 305–310, 1948. J. Hald and E. Jacobsen, "A Drug Sensitizing the Organism to Ethyl Alcohol," *Lancet,* 2: 1001–1004, 1948. J. Hald, E. Jacobsen, and V. Larsen, "The Sensitizing Effect of Tetraethylthiuramdisulphide (Antabuse) to Ethylalcohol," *Acta Pharmacologica et Toxicologica* (Copenhagen), 4: 285–296, 1948.

38. A possible link between disulfiram's chemical cousin, tetraethylthiuramdisulfide, and alcohol had been suggested earlier by an observant physician, Dr. E. E. Williams of Naugatuck, Connecticut. As a physician to a chemical company, Dr. Williams noticed that workers exposed to the chemical could not drink alcohol in any form and that they had "become involuntary total abstainers." He said: "One wonders whether one has discovered the cure for alcoholism." But his suggestion was ridiculed. (Ref.: E. E. Williams, "Effect of Alcohol on Workers with Carbon Disulfide," *Journal of the American Medical Association,* 109: 1472–1473, 1937.)

39. E. Jacobsen, *Omgang med alkohol,* Arnold Busck—Nyt Nordisk Forlag, 1944. "The book, which aimed to make people drink in a sensible way, was severely criticized by the temperance people, but generally accepted by the rest of the Danish population," said Jacobsen. (Ref.: E. Jacobsen, personal communication, August 27, 1982.)

40. Telephone interview with Dr. Tage Hansen, research director, Dumex, in Copenhagen, November 1978.

41. For example, Dr. Chauncey D. Leake of the University of California at San Francisco, one of the foremost pharmacologists of his time, told of the pain he suffered after testing a substance called furan, derived from wood tar, as a substitute for aspirin in the 1930s. Leake's team detected nothing unusual among the rats, rabbits, and dogs that received repeated doses of furan aspirin in the form of a white powder for up to two weeks. So Leake practiced what he believed: "Pharmacologists have a moral obligation to test drugs on themselves after appropriate clearance with experimental animals before using them experimentally on any other human being." When Leake suffered one of his frequent headaches, he tried furan. One dose afforded relief within fifteen minutes and produced no abnormal effects. When he had another headache the next day, he got relief from two doses of furan aspirin.

"A possible competitor to aspirin gave me visions of laboratory funds beyond anything I had dared to hope for," Leake said. "Details of patenting and marketing, could, I thought, easily be worked out."

To reassure himself, Leake took another furan aspirin the next day, though he had no headache. Two hours later, he took a second dose. The little tingling he noted on urination did not stop him from taking a third dose. Four hours later, the pain became so sharp that he avoided urinating for the rest of the day. The next morning, he consulted a urologist, who admitted Leake to the hospital and rigged up a bladder-flushing device to wash Leake's urinary system. Three days later, the pain stopped. Leake returned to the laboratory to continue the furan experiments on animals. When he killed them, he did what he and his colleagues had not done on the previous autopsies—he carefully examined their bladders. Leake's dream of a new aspirin vanished when he found what the rats could not have communicated to him: The furan aspirin had precipitated onto their bladder walls, causing a painful and unacceptable side effect. (Refs.: L. K. Altman, "Dr. Chauncey D. Leake Dies at 81; Pharmacologist and Administrator," *New York Times,* January 13, 1978, B-6. C. D. Leake, "Discussion of Technical Triumphs and Moral Muddles," *Annals of Internal Medicine,* 67 [Suppl. 7]: 43–56, 1967. C. D. Leake, "The Interesting Case of Furan Aspirin," *Texas Reports on Biology and Medicine,* 30: 105–107, 1972. Interviews with C. D. Leake in San Francisco and New York, 1963, 1970, 1971, 1977.)

For a general medical textbook reference to pharmacology, see: A. G. Goodman, L. S. Goodman, and A. E. Gilman, *The Pharmacological Basis of Therapeutics,* New York: Macmillan, 1980. The first edition, published in 1941, has a fine historical description of the older drugs.

## Chapter Five: THE PASTEURIAN CLUB

1. J. Baron, *The Life of Edward Jenner, M.D.,* London: Colburn, 1838. E. Jenner, "An Inquiry Into the Causes and Effects of the Variolae Vaccinae: A Disease Discovered in Some of the Western Counties of England, Particularly Gloucestershire, and Known by the Name of Cowpox," London: Low, 1798, p. 75. E. Mellanby, "Jenner and His Impact on Medical Science," *British Medical Journal,* 1: 921–926, 1949.

2. Letter from John Hunter to Edward Jenner, August 2, 1775. Reprinted in *Annals of the Royal College of Surgeons of England,* 54: 48, 1974.

3. J. H. Steele, "History of Rabies," in: G. M. Baer, ed., *The Natural History of Rabies,* New York: Academic, 1975, vol. I, pp. 1–29.

4. There may have been some merit in the technique. In 1831, at a time when there were extensive rabies outbreaks in Europe, about a dozen people were bitten by a rabid wolf in Arbois, France; several who were cauterized survived. (Ref.: R. J. Dubos, *Louis Pasteur. Free Lance of Science,* New York: Scribner's, 1976, p. 332.)

5. Ibid., p. 53.

6. L. Pasteur, C. Chamberland, and E. Roux, "Sur une maladie nouvelle provoquée par la salive d'un enfant mort de la rage." *Comptes Rendus Hebdomadaires des Séances de l'Académie des Sciences*, 92: 159–165, 1881.

7. Microbiology was in its infancy, and scientists then used the term "virus" loosely, generally to refer to organisms that could not be cultured in the laboratory. Only with the advent of the electron

microscope in the twentieth century did doctors see a virus for the first time. The year was 1939 and the virus the tobacco mosaic virus. (Ref.: G. A. Kausche, E. Pfankuch, and H. Ruska, "Die Sichtbarmachung von pflanzlichem Virus im Übermikroskop," *Naturwissenschaften,* 27: 292–299, 1939.) Electron microscopic pictures of the rabies virus were not obtained until the early 1960s, and then by several groups. (Ref.: F. A. Murphy, "Morphology and Morphogenesis," in G. Baer, *The Natural History of Rabies,* vol. 1, New York: Academic, 1975, pp. 33–61.)

8. R. Vallery-Radot, *The Life of Pasteur,* vol. 2, New York: McClure, Phillips, 1902, p. 222.

9. V. Galtier, "Les Injections de virus rabique dans le torrent circulatoire ne provoquent pas l'éclosion de la rage et semblent conférer l'immunité. La rage peut être transmise par l'ingestion de la matière rabique," *Comptes Rendus Hebdomadaires des Séances de l'Académie des Sciences,* 93: 284–285, 1881. V. Galtier, "Observations à l'occasion du procès-verbal," *Bulletin de l'Académie de Médicine,* ser. 2, 10: 90–94, 1881.

10. L. Pasteur et al., "Sur la rage," *Comptes Rendus Hebdomadaires des Séances de l'Académie des Sciences,* 92: 1259–1260, 1881. Vallery-Radot, *Life of Pasteur,* p. 224.

11. L. Pasteur et al., "Nouveaux faits pour servir à la connaissance de la rage," *Bulletin de l'Académie de Médicine,* ser. 2, 11: 1440–1445, 1882.

12. Some dogs, unlike humans, seem to abort rabies infections just as they appear to be developing the most severe symptoms; the reasons for the phenomenom are unknown. Pasteur observed that some dogs were spontaneously refractory to rabies, and that was a crucial factor in leading him to believe that it was possible to produce immunity to rabies. It was an additional factor in the need for control groups in the rabies animal experiments. (Refs.: Interviews with Dr. James H. Steele in New York City, July 19, 20, and 21, 1983. Interview with Dr. Gerald L. Geison in Princeton, New Jersey, August 23, 1983.)

13. L. Pasteur, M. M. Chamberland, and E. Roux, "Nouvelle communication sur la rage," *Comptes Rendus Hebdomadaires des Séances de l'Académie des Sciences,* 98: 457–463, 1884.

14. L. Pasteur, M. M. Chamberland, and E. Roux, "Sur la Rage," *Comptes Rendus Hebdomadaires des Séances de l'Académie des Sciences,* 98: 1229–1231, 1884.

15. L. Pasteur, "Microbes pathogènes et vaccins," *Semaine Médicale,* 4: 318–320, 1884.

16. P. Vallery-Radot, *Correspondance de Pasteur. 1840–1895,* vol. 3, Paris: Flammarion, 1951, pp. 438–439.

17. Vallery-Radot, *Correspondance de Pasteur,* vol. 3, pp. 445–446.

18. Ibid., vol. 4, pp. 14–15.

19. Ibid., vol. 3, p. 249. L. Pasteur, "Méthode pour prévenir la rage après morsure," *Comptes Rendus Hebdomadaires des Séances de l'Académie des Sciences,* 101: 765–772, 1885.

20. A. Loir, "Le Traitement de la rage après morsure," in "A l'Ombre de Pasteur," Paris, in: *Le Mouvement Sanitaire,* 14: 328–348, 1937.

21. In the first few years following the administration of the first doses of rabies vaccine to humans, several thousand people were immunized against rabies after having been bitten by animals that were suspected of being rabid. For comparison, in 1981 about three and one-half million people throughout the world received rabies vaccine; most of them were treated with vaccines that differed little from the one that Pasteur gave Joseph Meister. (Ref.: G. S. Turner, "Rabies Vaccines and Immunity to Rabies," in C. Kaplan, *Rabies. The Facts,* Oxford: Oxford University Press, 1977, pp. 104–113.)

22. L. Pasteur, "Résultats de l'application de la méthode pour prévenir la rage après morsure," *Comptes Rendus Hebdomadaires des Séances de l'Académie des Sciences,* 102: 459–466, 1886.

23. Among the critics was Georges Clemenceau, a physician who would become the French prime minister. He contended that Pas-

teur's vaccine, not rabies, had killed those who died after vaccination. (Ref.: Dubos, *Louis Pasteur,* pp. 347–348.)

24. C. Fermi, "Über die Immunisierung gegen Wutkrankheit," *Zeitschrift für Hygiene and Infektionskrankheiten,* 58: 233–276, 1908. C. Fermi, "Über die Virulenz des Speichels und der Speicheldrüsen wutkranker Tiere," *Zentralblatt für Bakteriologie, Parasitenkunde und Infektionskrankheiten,* 44: 26–27, 1907. D. Semple, "On the Nature of Rabies and Antirabic Treatment," *British Medical Journal,* 2: 333–336, 371–373, 1919. D. Semple, "The Preparation of a Safe and Efficient Antirabic Vaccine," *Scientific Memoirs by Officers of the Medical Sanitary Departments of the Government of India,* no. 44, 1911.

25. They were called neuroparalytic accidents, and the term was applied to an illness that developed during the course of antirabies treatment, generally about two weeks after it began.

26. C. N. Leach and H. A. Johnson, "Human Rabies, with Special Reference to Virus Distribution and Titer," *American Journal of Tropical Medicine,* 20: 335–340, 1940.

27. Nitsch's research is described in R. Nitsch, "Bemerkungen über die pasteursche Methode der Schutzimpfungen gegen Tollwut," *Wiener Klinische Wochenschrift,* 17: 959–966, 1904.

28. Koprowski went from Poland to South America because a Brazilian diplomat and piano-playing friend offered him a visa to his country. In Rio de Janiero, Koprowski was an unemployed doctor until he took a stroll one day and met a high school classmate from Poland, who was by then an epidemiologist for the Rockefeller Foundation. The epidemiologist invited Koprowski to join the Rockefeller group in Brazil, and for four years he worked on yellow fever, Japanese B encephalitis, and other viral diseases.

29. H. Koprowski and H. R. Cox, "Colorado Tick Fever. Studies on Chick Embryo Adapted Virus," *Journal of Immunology,* 57: 255–262, 1947. H. Koprowski et al., "Response of Man to Egg-Adapted Colorado Tick Fever Virus," *Proceedings of the Society for Experimental Biology and Medicine,* 74: 126–131, 1950.

30. H. Koprowski, "Biological Modification of Rabies Virus As a Result of Its Adaptation to Chicks and Developing Chick Embryos," *Bulletin of the World Health Organization,* 10: 709–724, 1954.

Around this time, doctors at Memorial Hospital in New York operated on a woman who had cancer of the cervix. When the surgeons made the incision, they found that her cancer had spread so extensively that there was nothing they could do for her. They immediately closed the incision, and she returned to her home in Yonkers, New York, to live out the few months the doctors thought she had left. Three years later, the Memorial Hospital doctors were startled to see the woman return for a checkup. When the doctors examined her, they found that her cancer had gone into remission. One thing she told them was that during the interval she had been bitten by a dog believed to have been rabid and had received a full course of rabies shots. Might her drastic improvement have been due to the vaccine? The answer could come only from experiments on humans. The doctors asked Koprowski for a supply of the still experimental LEP Flury rabies vaccine; Koprowski had not reached the one hundred eightieth passage in the chick eggs and thus did not yet have his HEP vaccine. The doctors injected the LEP vaccine into thirty-three other cancer patients at Memorial Hospital. Although the experiments indicated that the LEP rabies vaccine did not stop cancer —the woman's remission was strictly coincidental—they did show that the vaccine was safe for humans.

The case started a flurry of activity to use several vaccines to treat a wide variety of diseases. However, the attempts failed and they were not reported, largely because scientists do not often publish negative results. (Ref.: Interviews with Dr. Hilary Koprowski and Dr. James Steele in New York City, July 21, 1983.)

31. Interview with Dr. Martin M. Kaplan in Geneva, Switzerland, December 29–30, 1976.

32. T. J. Wiktor, S. A. Plotkin, and D. W. Grella, "Human Cell Culture Rabies Vaccine," *Journal of the American Medical Association,* 224: 1170–1171, 1973.

33. S. A. Plotkin et al., "Immunization Schedules for the New Human Diploid Cell Vaccine Against Rabies," *American Journal of Epidemiology,* 103: 75–80, 1976.

34. M. Bahmanyar et al., "Successful Protection of Humans Exposed to Rabies Infection," *Journal of the American Medical Association,* 236: 2751–2754, 1976.

35. Interview with Dr. Hilary Koprowski and Dr. Warren Cheston, Wistar Institute, in Philadelphia, August 23–24, 1983.

36. J. Ferrán, "Le Microbe de choléra; sa morphologie, son action pathogénique et prophylactique," *Gazette Hebdomadaire des Sciences Médicales de Montpellier,* 7: 265–270, 1885. J. Ferrán, "Nota sobre la profilaxis del colera por medio de inyecciones hipodermicas de cultivo puro del bacilo virgula," *El Siglo Médico,* 32: 480–481, 1885. J. Ferrán, "Sur la prophylaxie du choléra au moyen d'injections hypodermiques de cultures pures du bacille-virgule," *Comptes Rendus Hebdomadaires des Séances de l'Académie des Sciences,* 101: 147–149, 1885. J. Ferrán, "Sur une nouvelle fonction chimique du bacille-virgule du choléra asiatique," *Comptes Rendus Hebdomadaires des Séances de l'Académie des Sciences,* 115: 361–362, 1892. J. Ferrán and I. Pauli, "Le principe actif du koma-bacille, comme cause de mort and d'immunité," *Comptes Rendus Hebdomadaires des Séances de l'Académie des Sciences,* 102: 159–160, 1886. W. Kolle, "Die aktive Immunisierung des Menschen gegen Cholera nach Haffkines Verfahren in Indien," *Zentralblatt für Bakteriologie, Parasitenkunde, Infektionskrankheiten und Hygiene,* 19: 217–221, 1896. O. Voges, "Die Cholera-Immunität," *Zentralblatt für Bakteriologie, Parasitenkunde und Infektionskrankheiten,* 19: 325–341, 395–400, 444–470, 1896.

37. Ferrán did not disclose the details of his preparation, and there are no precise statistics available as to its results.

38. W. M. Haffkine, "Inoculation des vaccins anticholériques à l'homme," *Comptes Rendus Hebdomadaires des Séances et Mémoires de la Société de Biologie* (ser. 9), 4: 740–741, 1892. W. M. Haffkine, "Vaccination Against Asiatic Cholera," *Indian Medical Gazette,* 28: 97–101, 1893, p. 100.

39. B. Cvjetanovic, "Earlier Field Trials of the Effectiveness of Cholera Vaccines," in *Proceedings of the Cholera Research Symposium, Honolulu, 1965,* PHS Publication no. 1328, Washington, D.C.: U.S.

Government Printing Office, 1965, pp. 355–361. W. M. Haffkine, "A Lecture on Vaccination Against Cholera," *British Medical Journal,* 2: 1541–1544, 1895. S. A. Waksman, *The Brilliant and Tragic Life of W.M.W. Haffkine,* New Brunswick, N.J.: Rutgers University Press, 1964.

40. W. Bulloch, "Waldemar Mordecai Wolff Haffkine," *Journal of Pathology and Bacteriology,* 34: 125–129, 1931. B. B. Gaitonde, "Haffkine Institute," in *Haffkine Institute, Platinum Jubilee Commemoration Volume, 1899–1974,* Bombay: Haffkine Institute, 1974, p. 2. R. Pollitzer, *Cholera,* Geneva: World Health Organization, 1959. J. Taylor, "Haffkine's Plague Vaccine," *Indian Medical Research Memoirs,* no. 27, March 1933.

41. E. Lutzker, "Waldemar Mordecai Haffkine, C.I.E.," in *Haffkine Institute, Platinum Jubilee Commemoration Volume, 1899–1974,* pp. 11–19. Waksman, *W.M.W. Haffkine,* p. 35.

42. *Nature,* 58: 354, 1898.

43. J. Taylor, "Haffkine's Plague Vaccine," *Indian Medical Research Memoirs,* no. 27, March 1933, p. 17.

44. K. F. Meyer et al., "Plague Immunization. I. Past and Present Trends," *Journal of Infectious Diseases,* 129: S-13, 1974.

45. L. Colebrook, *Almroth Wright. Provocative Doctor and Thinker,* London: Heinemann, 1954. Z. Cope, *Almroth Wright. Founder of Modern Vaccine-Therapy,* London: Nelson, 1966.

46. A. E. Wright, "On the Association of Serous Hemorrhages with Conditions of Defective Blood Coagulability," *Lancet,* 2: 807–809, 1896. A. E. Wright, "On the Changes Effected by Anti-Typhoid Inoculation in the Bactericidal Power of the Blood; With Remarks on the Probable Significance of These Changes," *Lancet,* 2: 715–723, 1901.

Two German researchers, Pfeiffer and Kolle, probably established priority with another typhoid vaccine, which they discussed in a published report in 1896, the year Wright gave himself his vaccine. (Ref.: R. Pfeiffer and W. Kolle, "Experimentelle Untersuchungen zur

Frage der Schutzimpfung des Menschen gegen Typhus Abdominalis," *Deutsche Medizinische Wochenschrift,* 22: 972–973, 1896.)

47. A. E. Wright and D. Semple, "Remarks on Vaccination Against Typhoid Fever," *British Medical Journal,* 1: 256–259, 1897.

48. A. E. Wright and F. Smith, "On the Application of the Serum Test to the Differential Diagnosis of Typhoid and Malta Fever," *Lancet,* 1: 656–659, 1897.

49. C. Birt and G. Lamb, "Mediterranean or Malta Fever," *Lancet,* 2: 701–710, 1899.

50. Colebrook, *Almroth Wright,* p. 28.

51. M. Brodie, "Active Immunization Against Poliomyelitis," *American Journal of Public Health,* 25: 54–67, 1935. M. Brodie, "Active Immunization in Monkeys Against Poliomyelitis with Germicidally Inactivated Virus," *Science,* 79: 594–595, 1934. M. Brodie, "Active Immunization of Children Against Poliomyelitis with Formalin Inactivated Virus Suspension," *Proceedings of the Society of Experimental Medicine and Biology,* 32: 300–302, 1934. M. Brodie, "The Rate of Antibody Formation in Monkeys Actively Immunized with Poliomyelitis Virus," *Journal of Immunology,* 27: 395–405, 1934.

52. J. R. Paul, *A History of Poliomyelitis,* New Haven and London: Yale University Press, 1971, p. 256.

53. J. A. Kolmer and A. M. Rule, "A Successful Method for Vaccination Against Acute Anterior Poliomyelitis," *American Journal of Medical Sciences,* 188: 510–514, 1934, p. 512. See also: J. A. Kolmer, "Susceptibility and Immunity in Relation to Vaccination in Acute Anterior Poliomyelitis," *Journal of the American Medical Association,* 105: 1956–1961, 1935. J. A. Kolmer, G. F. Klugh, and A. M. Rule, "A Successful Method for Vaccination Against Acute Anterior Poliomyelitis. Further Report," *Journal of the American Medical Association,* 104: 456–460, 1935. J. A. Kolmer, and A. M. Rule, "Concerning Vaccination of Monkeys Against Acute Anterior Poliomyelitis," *Journal of Immunology,* 26: 505–515, 1934.

54. J. A. Kolmer, "Immunity and Vaccination in Infantile Paralysis," *American Journal of Nursing,* 35: 311–313, 1935, p. 312.

55. Paul, *History of Poliomyelitis,* p. 258.

56. J. P. Leake, "Poliomyelitis Following Vaccination Against This Disease," *Journal of the American Medical Association,* 105: 2152, 1935.

57. S. Benison, *Tom Rivers: Reflections on a Life in Medicine and Science,* Cambridge, Mass.: MIT Press, 1967, p. 189.

58. N. Nathanson and A. Langmuir, "The Cutter Incident. Poliomyelitis Following Formaldehyde-Inactivated Polio Virus Vaccination in the United States During the Spring of 1955," *American Journal of Hygiene,* 78: 16–81, 1963.

59. H. Koprowski, G. A. Jervis, and T. W. Norton, "Immune Responses in Human Volunteers upon Oral Administration of a Rodent-Adapted Strain of Poliomyelitis Virus," *American Journal of Hygiene,* 55: 108–126, 1952. Interview with Dr. Hilary Koprowski in Philadelphia, August 23–24, 1983.

60. Interview with Dr. Albert B. Sabin in Hamilton, Bermuda, May 25, 1979.

61. I received no reply from Salk when, while working at the University of Washington Hospital, I wrote him to ascertain the facts. In 1970 Al Kildow, the public relations officer of the Salk Institute, having come across the letter, called me at the *New York Times* and asked if I still wanted the information. I said I did and explained why. According to Kildow, Salk told him that he had not taken his own vaccine because it would serve no purpose; Salk already had antibodies to polio. At a lunch in 1976, I was seated across from Salk after we had participated in a symposium on vaccine development at the National Institutes of Health. Others who knew of my interest in self-experimentation brought up the subject. I asked Salk why he hadn't taken his own vaccine when he had given it to his children. Even though he had antibodies, I said, he could have tested the safety of the polio vaccine by taking it himself. Salk then insisted that he

had actually taken it. When I asked why he told Kildow a different version, Salk said it was because he did not know why the question was being asked.

For overviews on immunization:

L. K. Altman, "Vaccines: Building Defenses Against Illness," in *Encyclopaedia Britannica, Medicine and Health Annual,* 1979, pp. 113–124.

A. Chase, *Magic Shots,* New York: Morrow, 1982.

For overviews on rabies:

C. Kaplan, *Rabies. The Facts,* Oxford: Oxford University Press, 1977.

## Chapter Six: THE MYTH OF WALTER REED

1. "Yellow jack" was a popular nickname for yellow fever, but the choice of yellow for the flag apparently had no relationship to the yellowing of the skin that occurs with the disease. Since yellow stands for "Q" in the international flag code, the best guess is that it was therefore chosen to represent all quarantined diseases.

2. Although the first appearance of yellow fever cannot be dated with certainty—it was not described in ancient writings—the name was applied to an epidemic in Barbados as early as 1715. (Ref.: G. Hughes, "Natural History of Barbados," book 2, London: privately printed, 1750, p. 37.). The disease was an important public health problem in early North American history. (Ref.: C.-E. A. Winslow, *The Conquest of Epidemic Disease,* Princeton: Princeton University Press, 1943.) The first importation of yellow fever into the United States occurred in 1693. (Ref.: W. Reed and J. Carroll, "The Prevention of Yellow Fever," *Medical Record of New York,* 60: 641–649, 1901.) Interesting historical accounts of specific epidemics can be found in J. M. Keating, *History of the Yellow Fever Epidemic of 1878 in Memphis, Tennessee,* Memphis: printed for the Howard Association, 1879. R. La Roche, *Remarks on the Origin and Mode of Progression of Yellow Fever, in Philadelphia, Based on the Occurrence of the Disease in That City and at the Lazaretto, in the Months of July, August and*

*September, 1870* (extracted from the Report of the Board of Health for 1870), Philadelphia, 1871.

3. The epidemic of 1793 killed one person out of ten in Philadelphia and caused many government leaders to flee the then-capital of the United States. Benjamin Rush, one of the most famous physicians in Colonial America, recognized that mosquitoes were abundant during one epidemic, but he did not suspect them as disease carriers. Rush was a proponent of blood purging, which was then a popular therapy for a wide variety of diseases and one that, of course, hastened the demise of many patients. (Ref.: N. G. Goodman, *Benjamin Rush—Physician and Citizen,* Philadelphia: University of Pennsylvania Press, 1934, p. 186.)

4. Reed and Carroll, "Prevention of Yellow Fever," p. 641.

5. The *Washington Post* and *Baltimore News,* for example, reported that Reed had experimented on himself; others called him a Great Knight. (Refs.: "Causes Yellow Fever: The Mosquito Responsible for Spread of Disease," *Baltimore News,* April 24, 1901.) "Yellow Fever Germs," *Washington Post,* April 18, 1901.

6. Membership in the Walter Reed Society was by invitation, and the more than five hundred elected were scientists who had experimented on themselves. Dr. Max S. Sadove, a Chicago anesthesiologist who was organizing president of the society, told me that although he knew Reed had never experimented on himself the society memorialized his name because it embodied the spirit of research. The society is now defunct. (Ref.: Interview with Dr. Max S. Sadove in Chicago, November 2, 1976.)

7. Virtually all physicians and lay people with whom I discussed Reed thought he had experimented on himself, and many thought he had died of yellow fever. These independent observations were made as recently as 1982. (Ref.: W. H. Crosby and W. S. Haubrich, "The Death of Walter Reed," *Journal of the American Medical Association,* 248: 1342–1345, 1982.)

8. E. Harris, *New York State Marine Hospital at Quarantine, Staten Island. Annual Report,* Albany, 1857, pp. 1–64. W. Reed, "Examina-

tion Questions and Answers. February 8, 1875," in W. B. Bean, *Walter Reed,* Charlottesville: University of Virginia Press. 1982, pp. 21–22. W. Reed, "The Propagation of Yellow Fever. Observations Based on Recent Researches," *Medical Record,* 60: 201–209, 1901. T. F. Rochester, "Address in Practice of Medicine, Materia Medica, and Physiology," *Transactions of the American Medical Association,* 30: 127–146, 1879.

William Osler, the famous Johns Hopkins medical professor, too, was in error. In 1892 he wrote: "The epidemics are invariably due to the introduction of the poison either by patients affected with the disease or through infected articles. Unquestionably, the poison may be conveyed by fomites." (Ref.: W. Osler, *The Principles and Practice of Medicine. Designed for the Use of Practitioners and Students of Medicine,* New York: Appleton, 1892, p. 125.)

9. I. Cathrall, *A Medical Sketch of the Synochus Maligna or Malignant Contagious Fever as Appeared in the City of Philadelphia, to Which Is Added Some Account of the Morbid Appearance Observed After Death on Dissection, with an Appendix . . . , 1794,* Philadelphia: R. Folwell, 1796. I. Cathrall, *Memoir on the Analysis of the Black Vomit Ejected in the Last Stage of the Yellow Fever,* Philadelphia: Folwell, 1800, pp. 3, 4, 10, 19, 20.

10. S. Ffirth, *On Malignant Fever: With an Attempt to Prove Its Non-Contagious Nature, From Reason, Observation, and Experiment,* Philadelphia: B. Graves, 1804.

11. Ibid., p. 47.

12. Ibid., p. 53.

13. Ibid., preface.

14. Ibid., p. 50.

15. Ibid., p. 55.

16. Ibid., p. 56. Ffirth did not specify how he injected the material; presumably he used a quill, which doctors often used for injections before the advent of the hypodermic syringe.

17. Ibid., p. 57. Ffirth and Cathrall were by no means the only physicians to do yellow fever experiments on themselves. In 1816 N. Chervin of Pointe-à-Pitre (Antilles) drank large amounts of black vomit without any ill effect. In addition to those I have cited, E. H. Ackerknecht lists Dorsey, Govin, J. L. Guyon, Lavallee, Musgrave, O'Connor, Potter, Prost, and Pulschneider. (Ref.: E. H. Ackerknecht, "Anticontagionism Between 1821 and 1867," *Bulletin of the History of Medicine,* 22: 562–593, 1948, p. 568.)

18. J. Crawford, in: *The Observer and Repertory of Original and Selected Essays in Verse and Prose, on Topics of Polite Literature,* vols. 1, 2, 1807, cited in S. Peller, "Walter Reed, C. Finlay and their Predecessors Around 1800," *Bulletin of the History of Medicine,* 33: 195–211, 1959.

19. J. C. Nott, "Yellow Fever Contrasted with Bilious Fever—Reasons for Believing It a Disease Sui Generis—Its Mode of Propagation—Remote Cause—Probable Insect or Animalcular Origin, etc.," *New Orleans Medical and Surgical Journal* (new series) 4: 563–601, 1847–1848.

20. L. D. Beauperthuy, "Fiebre Amarilla," *Gaceta Official de Cumana,* vol. 57, May 23, 1854, reprinted in L. D. Beauperthuy, *La Obra,* Caracas: REMAR, 1963, pp. 260–270.

21. A. Agramonte, "The Inside History of a Great Medical Discovery," *Scientific Monthly,* 1: 209–237, 1915, p. 227.

22. At the time, Texas fever, which was also called "Red Water," was destroying enormous numbers of cattle in the United States, chiefly in the warmer seasons. In the same manner that Jenner had listened to the dairy maid who told of the protection afforded by cowpox against smallpox, Smith and Kilborne acted on the suspicions of shrewd cattlemen who believed that cattle ticks spread the disease in some unknown way. Smith and Kilborne took infected cattle from North Carolina to an experimental station in Washington, D.C., and found that of ten uninfected cows placed in the pasture with the infected cattle, eight developed Texas fever and died. When the North Carolina cattle were removed, the pasture remained infective. Then Smith and Kilborne put infected North Carolina cattle with

uninfected cattle in one area and picked the ticks from the North Carolina cattle as soon as they were large enough to be detected. In another area, the ticks were left on the North Carolina cattle; the uninfected cattle in this area became infected and died, while those in the former area remained healthy. Smith and Kilborne established the link; all they failed to discover was the development of the parasite in the tick. (Refs.: C. E. Dolman, "Theobold Smith, 1859–1934," *New York State Journal of Medicine,* 69: 2801–2816, 1969. S. H. Gage, "Theobold Smith; Investigator and Man," *Science,* 84: 117–122, 1936. "Obituary Notice of Deceased Member. Theobold Smith," *Journal of Pathology and Bacteriology,* 40: 621–635, 1935. T. Smith and F. L. Kilborne, "Investigation into the Nature, Causation and Prevention of Texas or Southern Cattle Fever," Washington, D.C.: U.S. Government Printing Office, 1893.)

23. P. Manson, "Further Observations on Filaria Sanguinis Hominis," *Medical Reports,* China Imperial Maritime Customs (special series no. 2) 14: 1–26, 1878. P. H. Manson-Bahr and A. Alcock, *The Life and Work of Sir Patrick Manson,* London: Cassell, 1927.

24. Finlay was born in 1833 in Cuba to a French mother and a Scottish father who practiced medicine and grew coffee in Puerto Principe. After receiving part of his education in France, Finlay earned his M.D. at Jefferson Medical School in Philadelphia and began practicing in Cuba. Finlay was a good physician who came close to finding the solution to yellow fever but who was inhibited by the limitations of not being a trained scientist. For instance, for a time Finlay thought that a common bacterium caused yellow fever. He abandoned the idea after Dr. George M. Sternberg, a trained microbiologist and later the surgeon general of the U.S. Army who created the Yellow Fever Board, refuted it in 1889. (Ref.: C. Finlay, "El Mosquito hipoteticamente considerado como agente de transmisión de la fiebre Amarilla," *Anales de la Real Academía Ciencias Médicas, Fisicas y Naturales de la Habana,* 18: 147–169, 1881–1882, reprinted in *Medical Classics,* 1938, 2: 569–612. C. F. Finlay, *Carlos Finlay and Yellow Fever,* New York: Institute of Tropical Medicine of the University of Havana and Oxford University Press, 1940.)

25. In 1891 Army Surgeon General Sternberg rejected Finlay's experiments and the mosquito theory because he believed that the

insects did not inject anything harmful into humans and that whatever substances the insects ingested in biting humans passed through the anus. (Ref.: G. M. Sternberg, "Dr. Finlay's Mosquito Inoculations," *American Journal of Medical Sciences,* 52: 627–630, 1891.)

26. J. Carroll, "Yellow Fever—A Popular Lecture," *American Medicine,* 9: 907–915, 1905, p. 912. G. Sanarelli, "A Lecture on Yellow Fever with a Description of the Bacillus Icteroides," *British Medical Journal,* 2: 7–11, 1897. G. Sanarelli, "Etiologia e patogenesi della febbre gialla," *Annali d'Igience Sperimentale* (new series) 7: 345–475, 1897. J. Sanarelli, "Le Bacille de la fièvre jaune," *Semaine Médicale,* 17: 253–255, 1897.

27. Surgeon General Sternberg challenged Sanarelli because Sternberg had described an organism he called "bacillus X" that he believed was the same as bacillus icteroides. In his papers, Sternberg hedged about whether the bacterium was the cause of yellow fever, never considering it more than a possible cause. (Ref.: J. Carroll, "Yellow Fever—A Popular Lecture," *American Medicine,* 9: 907–915, 1905, p. 912. W. Reed and J. Carroll, "The Specific Cause of Yellow Fever. A reply to Dr. G. Sanarelli," *Medical News,* 75: 321–329, 1899. G. M. Sternberg, "The Bacillus Icteroides [Sanarelli] and Bacillus X [Sternberg]," *Transactions of the Association of American Physicians,* 13: 61–72, 1898.)

28. Dr. Walter Wyman, who later became surgeon general of the U.S. Public Health Service, reported finding the organism in thirteen of sixteen cases studied. The commission's members were Dr. Eugene Wasdin and Dr. H. D. Geddings. (Ref.: E. Wasdin and H. D. Geddings, "Report of the Commission of Medical Officers, Marine-Hospital Service, Detailed by Authority of the Secretary of the Treasury and the President to Investigate the Cause of Yellow Fever," in *Yellow Fever: Its Nature, Diagnosis, Treatment and Prophylaxis, and Quarantine Regulations Relating Thereto,* Washington, D.C.: U.S. Government Printing Office, 1899, pp. iii–viii.)

29. V. C. Vaughan, "Discussion of G. M. Sternberg, 'The Bacillus Icteroides (Sanarelli) and Bacillus X (Sternberg),'" *Transactions of the Association of American Physicians,* 13: 70–71, 1898.

30. W. Osler, "Discussion of G. M. Sternberg, 'The Bacillus Icteroides (Sanarelli) and Bacillus X (Sternberg),' " *Transactions of the Association of American Physicians,* 13: 71, 1898.

31. George Sternberg, who was born in Otsego County, New York, in 1838, earned his M.D. from the Columbia University College of Physicians and Surgeons and practiced medicine in Elizabeth City, New Jersey, until he joined the army in 1861, during the Civil War. Turning to research in 1875 after a severe attack of yellow fever, Sternberg pioneered in determining the practical value of disinfectants. In 1880 he and Louis Pasteur independently isolated the pneumococcus bacterium, which is one of the many causes of pneumonia. In 1893, when Sternberg was appointed surgeon general, he had authored pioneering textbooks on bacteriology which included photographs taken through microscopes. Sternberg commanded such enormous respect as a bacteriologist that Vaughan, in discussing Sternberg's scientific paper that had criticized Sanarelli, said: "The probabilities are that yellow fever is not due to a bacteria. Of course, we may be mistaken, but I think that if it had been due to such a cause, Sternberg would have discovered the organism." (Refs.: G. M. Sternberg, *Immunity, Protective Inoculations in Infectious Diseases and Serum Therapy,* New York: Wood, 1895. G. M. Sternberg, *A Manual of Bacteriology,* New York: Wood, 1893. G. M. Sternberg, *A Textbook of Bacteriology,* New York: Wood, 1896. M. L. Sternberg, *George Miller Sternberg, A Biography,* Chicago: American Medical Association, 1920. V. C. Vaughan, "Discussion," *Transactions of the Association of American Physicians,* 13: 70–71, 1898.)

32. W. B. Bean, *Walter Reed. A Biography,* Charlottesville, N.C.: University of Virginia Press, 1982. W. B. Bean, "Walter Reed and the Ordeal of Human Experiments," *Bulletin of the History of Medicine,* 51: 75–92, 1977. W. B. Bean, "Walter Reed and Yellow Fever," *Journal of the American Medical Association,* 250: 659–662, 1983. Personal communications with Dr. William B. Bean, 1978, May 15, 1984, and October 1, 1985, and interviews in Farmington, Connecticut, April 27–28, 1984, and Iowa City, Iowa, February 25–28, 1986.

33. Letter from Walter Reed to Emilie B. Lawrence (fiancée), July 18, 1874.

34. William H. Welch, a leading pathologist and bacteriologist, taught three members of Sternberg's Yellow Fever Commission and made suggestions to the team along the way. During his "sabbatical," Reed also gained some experience with malaria. In 1895 Sternberg asked him to study a malaria epidemic in Washington, D.C. Reed concluded that the cause of the epidemic lay not in the drinking water, as most had suspected, but in "the extensive marsh lands lying in and along the Potomac and Anacostia rivers." He had traced it not to mosquitoes but to their habitat. (Ref.: W. Reed, "Malarial Diseases," in *Report of the Surgeon-General of the Army to the Secretary of War for the Fiscal Year Ended June 30, 1896,* Washington, D.C.: U.S. Government Printing Office, 1896, pp. 65–75.)

35. W. Reed, V. Vaughan, and E. O. Shakespeare, *Abstract of Report on the Origin and Spread of Typhoid Fever in U.S. Military Camps During the Spanish War of 1898,* Washington, D.C.: U.S. Government Printing Office, 1900. W. Reed, V. C. Vaughan, and E. O. Shakespeare, "Report on the Origin and Spread of Typhoid Fever in U.S. Military Camps During the Spanish War of 1898," vol. I, Washington, D.C.: U.S. Government Printing Office, 1904.

36. Letter from Dr. James Carroll to Dr. Caroline W. Latimer, March 9, 1905.

37. Letter from Dr. Jesse Lazear to his wife, July 15, 1900.

38. J. A. del Regato, "Jesse William Lazear, '92," *P & S Quarterly,* 16: 10–17, 21, 1971.

39. W. S. Thayer, "Opening of the Surgical Building and New Clinical Amphitheatre of the Johns Hopkins Hospital," *Johns Hopkins Hospital Bulletin,* 15: 379–389, 1904, p. 388.

40. Letters from Dr. Aristides Agramonte to Surgeon General Sternberg, April 18, 1898, and from Sternberg to Agramonte, April 19, 1898.

41. A. Agramonte, "Report of Bacteriological Investigations upon Yellow Fever," *Medical News,* 76: 203–212, 249–256, 1900.

42. J. Carroll, "A Brief Review of the Aetiology of Yellow Fever," *New York Medical Journal and Philadelphia Medical Journal*, 79: 241–245, 307–310, 1904. W. Reed and J. Carroll, "Bacillus Icteroides and Bacillus Cholerae suis. A Preliminary Note," *Medical News*, 74: 513–514, 1899.

43. W. Reed, "The Propagation of Yellow Fever; Observations Based on Recent Researches," *Medical Record*, 60: 201–209, 1901, p. 202.

44. Finlay, in turn, rejected the idea that mosquitoes discharge as excrement in drinking water the mysterious agent that, when swallowed, produced yellow fever. (Ref.: S. Peller, "Walter Reed, C. Finlay, and Their Predecessors Around 1800," *Bulletin of the History of Medicine*, 33: 195–211, 1959, p. 199.)

45. H. R. Carter, "A Note on the Interval Between Infecting and Secondary Cases of Yellow Fever from the Records of Yellow Fever at Orwood and Taylor, Mississippi, in 1898," *New Orleans Medical and Surgical Journal*, 52: 617–636, 1900.

46. A. Agramonte, "The Transmission of Yellow Fever," letter to editor, *Journal of the American Medical Association*, 40: 1660–1661, 1903.

47. Letter from Surgeon General Sternberg to Dr. Aristides Agramonte, May 14, 1900.

48. Agramonte said: "Though born on the island of Cuba, I had practically lived all my life away from a yellow fever zone; it was therefore presumed that I ran no risk in allowing mosquitoes to bite me, as I frequently did, just to feed them blood, whether they had previously sucked from yellow fever cases or not." (Ref.: Agramonte, "Inside History," p. 220.)

49. W. Reed and J. Carroll, "The Etiology of Yellow Fever. A Supplemental Note," *American Medicine*, 3: 301–305, 1902.

50. According to General Albert E. Truby, the commander of the hospital in Cuba, Reed "was apprehensive that the British scientists who had visited him in July and who were probably working along

the same lines, might also get immediate results." (Refs.: H. E. Durham and W. Myers, "Liverpool School of Tropical Medicine: Yellow Fever Expedition. Some Preliminary Notes," *British Medical Journal,* 2: 656–657, 1900. Letter from Dr. Walter Reed to his wife, July 19, 1900. A. E. Truby, *Memoir of Walter Reed. The Yellow Fever Episode,* New York: Hoeber, 1943, p. 127.)

51. Letter from Dr. James Carroll to Surgeon General Robert M. O'Reilly, August 29, 1906.

52. Carroll, "Yellow Fever—A Popular Lecture," p. 912.

53. Military order from Dr. Walter Reed to the Adjutant General, U.S. Army, Sept. 1, 1900. Reed's most recent biographer, William Bean, told me he had not been aware of the date in the order and he did not believe Reed could have traveled without some other order; possibly, he said, the army had lost such a document.

54. Letter from Dr. James Carroll to Dr. William Kelly, June 23, 1906.

55. Agramonte, "Inside History," p. 221.

56. Carroll, "Yellow Fever—A Popular Lecture," pp. 912–913.

57. J. Carroll, letter to the editor, *Journal of the American Medical Association,* June 26, 1903.

58. Agramonte, "Inside History," p. 221.

59. Carroll, "Aetiology of Yellow Fever," p. 245.

60. Agramonte, "Inside History," p. 222.

61. J. Carroll, "The Treatment of Yellow Fever," *Journal of the American Medical Association,* 39: 117–124, 1902.

62. Carroll, "Aetiology of Yellow Fever," p. 245.

63. Agramonte, "Inside History," p. 223.

64. Letter from Dr. Walter Reed to Dr. James Carroll, September 7, 1900.

65. C. W. Latimer, "James Carroll," in H. A. Kelly and W. L. Burrage, *American Medical Biographies,* Baltimore: Norman, Remington, 1920, pp. 201–202.

66. Letter from Dr. James Carroll to his wife, September 28, 1900.

67. Letter from Dr. James Carroll to his wife, September 29, 1900.

68. J. C. Hemmeter, *Master Minds in Medicine,* New York: Medical Life Press, 1927, p. 310.

69. Letter from Dr. James Carroll to Dr. Caroline Latimer, September 26, 1906.

70. Letter from Dr. Jesse Lazear to his wife, September 8, 1900.

71. Telegram from Dr. William Osler to Surgeon General Sternberg, September 26, 1900.

72. Carroll, "Aetiology of Yellow Fever," p. 245.

73. Telegram from Surgeon General Sternberg to Dr. H. M. Hurd, Johns Hopkins Hospital, Baltimore, September 24, 1900. Letter from Dr. Jefferson R. Kean to Mrs. Lazear, September 25, 1900.

74. Letter from Dr. Walter Reed to Dr. Jefferson R. Kean, September 25, 1900.

75. Ibid.

76. Letter from Dr. Walter Reed to Dr. James Carroll, September 24, 1900.

77. Carroll, "Aetiology of Yellow Fever," p. 245.

78. Agramonte, "Inside History," p. 223.

79. A. E. Truby, *Memoir of Walter Reed,* pp. 123–124.

80. Letter from Dr. Leonard Wood to Adjutant General, U.S. Army, November 4, 1900.

81. Memorandum from Dr. Walter Reed, January 11, 1902. Letter from Surgeon General Sternberg to Henry C. Loudenslager, January 21, 1901: "His death is believed to have been due to an experiment which he made upon himself with a view to obtaining positive evidence with reference to the manner in which this fatal infectious disease is communicated to man."

82. P. S. Hench, "Conquerors of Yellow Fever," *Proceedings of the Staff Meetings of the Mayo Clinic,* 16: 790, 1941.

83. Agramonte, "Inside History," p. 223.

84. Carroll's death in 1907 has been attributed to chronic inflammation of the heart resulting from his yellow fever attack. However, according to Osler, Carroll died from a different heart condition, bacterial endocarditis. Whether heart damage from yellow fever contributed to his death can never be fully answered. (Ref.: W. Osler, "Chronic Infective Endocarditis," *Quarterly Journal of Medicine,* 2: 219–230, 1909.)

The yellow fever episode was not Carroll's only self-experiment. In 1904, three years before his death, when he was director of laboratories at the Army Medical School, he experimented on himself to develop a new method of immunization: the oral vaccine. His experimental vaccine was derived from typhoid bacteria isolated from a soldier who had died of the disease in 1898 during the Spanish-American War. (The organism had been kept in continuous culture in the laboratory during the interval.) After the vaccine appeared to work in animals, a call was made for army volunteers to swallow the first doses, and Carroll was among them. Two other physicians—Dr. Harry L. Gilchrist and Dr. Edward B. Vedder—who were involved in the development of the experimental vaccine also swallowed it. But the vaccine trial failed for technical reasons: the cultures were not heated properly, and some typhoid organisms survived. Of twelve men who took the typhoid vaccine and who were not known to have suffered from typhoid fever in the past, seven came down with the infection. They included Gilchrist and Vedder. Carroll, who had had typhoid fever several years earlier, remained well, apparently because of lasting immunity from the previous infection. Although the experiment failed to develop an oral vaccine, it unwittingly succeeded in providing the first experimental proof that typhoid bacteria actually caused typhoid fever. The experiment was also valuable in showing that just a few organisms were needed to start an infection. But scientists and public health officials did not benefit from that knowledge because the army kept the report secret until 1958, by which time other researchers had learned the same information by repeating the experiments on prison volunteers. Army officials also declined to test further oral typhoid vaccines, preferring instead those derived from the one Almroth Wright had made in England in 1896. (See Chapter Five: The Pasteurian Club.) Now an oral typhoid vaccine is marketed in Switzerland. Theoretically, this self-experiment could have caused Carroll's fatal heart condition. (Ref.: W. D. Tigertt, "The Initial Effort to Immunize American Soldier Volunteers with Typhoid Vaccine," *Military Medicine,* 124: 342–349, 1959.)

85. W. Reed et al., "The Etiology of Yellow Fever. A Preliminary Note," *Philadelphia Medical Journal,* 6: 790–796, 1900, p. 796.

86. The *Washington Post,* for example, mocked: "Of all the silly and nonsensical rigamarole about yellow fever that has yet found its way into print—and there has been enough of it to load a fleet—the silliest beyond compare is to be found in the arguments and theories engendered by the mosquito hypothesis." (Ref.: "The Mosquito Hypothesis," *Washington Post,* November 2, 1900.)

87. W. Bean, *Walter Reed,* p. 147.

88. W. Reed, J. Carroll, and A. Agramonte, "The Etiology of Yellow Fever. An Additional Note," *Journal of the American Medical Association,* 36: 431–440, 1901, p. 435.

89. Ibid., p. 438.

90. Letter from Dr. Walter Reed to his wife, December 4, 1900.

91. Durham went on to report on "a fine, small bacillus" that he believed caused yellow fever and made accurate observations on the role of mosquitoes. (Refs.: H. E. Durham, *Report of the Yellow Fever Expedition to Para,* London: Longmans, Green, 1902. H. E. Durham and W. Myers, "Abstract of Interim Report on Yellow Fever by the Yellow Fever Commission of The Liverpool School of Tropical Medicine," *Johns Hopkins Hospital Bulletin,* 12: 48–49, 1901.)

92. Telegram from Dr. Walter Reed to Surgeon General Sternberg, December 15, 1900. Telegram from Sternberg to Reed, December 17, 1900.

93. Loeffler and Frosch, "Berichte der Kommission zur Erforschung der Maul-und Klauenseuche bei dem Institut für Infektionskrankheiten in Berlin," *Zentralblatt für Bakteriologie,* 23: 371–391, 1898, cited by G. K. Strode, *Yellow Fever,* New York: McGraw-Hill, 1951, p. 10. Reed and Carroll, "Etiology of Yellow Fever."

94. G. M. Sternberg, "The Transmission of Yellow Fever by Mosquitoes," *Popular Science Monthly,* 59: 225–241, 1901, p. 229. Letter from Surgeon General Sternberg to Dr. Stanford F. Chaille, February 15, 1898.

95. G. M. Sternberg, "Dr. Finlay's Mosquito Inoculations," *American Journal of Medical Sciences,* 52: 627–630, 1891.

96. Letter from Dr. Walter Reed to Dr. James Carroll, August 23, 1901.

97. J. Guiteras, "Experimental Yellow Fever at the Inoculation Station of the Sanitary Department of Havana with a View to Producing Immunization," *American Medicine,* 2: 809–817, 1901.

98. Letter from Dr. W. C. Gorgas to Dr. H. R. Carter, December 13, 1900.

99. W. C. Gorgas, *Sanitation in Panama,* New York: Appleton, 1915. W. Reed, "Recent Researches Concerning the Etiology, Propagation, and Prevention of Yellow Fever, by the United States Army Commission," *Journal of Hygiene,* 2: 101–119, 1902.

100. W. C. Gorgas, "Sanitation of the Tropics with Special Reference to Malaria and Yellow Fever," *Journal of the American Medical Association,* 52: 1075–1077, 1909.

101. F. L. Soper, "Recent Extension of Knowledge of Yellow Fever," *Quarterly Bulletin of the Health Organization, League of Nations,* 5: 19–59, 1936.

102. A year later, in 1907, the *Journal of the American Medical Association* also promoted Carroll for a Nobel Prize. (Refs.: "Carroll's Promotion and the Nobel Prize," *Journal of the American Medical Association,* 48: 331–332, 1907. "Sanitation in Panama," *British Medical Journal,* 2: 586–587, 1906.)

103. When it was time to test Theiler's yellow fever vaccine, which would be given along with blood serum from a person who had recovered from the disease, Dr. Wray L. Lloyd volunteered to be the first recipient. For this reason blood tests had been started. But then Lloyd developed yellow fever as an occupational hazard of working in the yellow fever laboratory, not from the blood tests. The exposure had occurred days before, and most of his colleagues came down with the viral disease for the same reason. However, "by a queer quirk of fate, he came down with his attack of yellow fever just hours before the intended shot of vaccine," Norton said.

Theiler and others then took the first vaccine, which "was something of a trial to endure" because as much as thirty cubic centimeters of solution was injected beneath the skin of the abdomen. The immune serum was obtained from the worker in the laboratory who had recovered from yellow fever. "Lloyd at one time gave too much and too soon of his blood, for in the middle of a bleeding he collapsed. This is the same man who, interested in a research problem at the University of Western Ontario, had injected himself with a solution of calcium chloride while hooked up to an electrocardiograph machine. He was found by a co-worker in a state of collapse, and only vigorous measures saved his life."

The problem was eased by development of a new yellow fever vaccine. (Refs.: T. W. Norton, *Confidential Monthly Report,* no. 87, The Rockefeller Foundation, October 1, 1946. M. Theiler and H. H. Smith, "The Use of Yellow Fever Virus Modified In Vitro Cultivation for Human Immunization," *Journal of Experimental Medicine,* 65: 787–800, 1937.)

104. P. M. Ashburn, *Why Walter Reed General Hospital Was Named and Located As It Is. An Address to Student Nurses,* unpublished.

105. Bean, "Walter Reed and the Ordeal of Human Experiments," pp. 85–86.

## Chapter Seven: TAMING THE GREATEST KILLERS

1. There is no accurate list of the top ten diseases in the world because the world's network of disease surveillance is based on a crude, voluntary reporting system. Nevertheless, we know that parasitic diseases attack billions of people around the world. An estimated one billion people are afflicted with giant roundworms (ascaris) in the small intestine that in serious cases can obstruct the bowel. When the worms travel through the lungs they can cause fever, coughing, and wheezing. Another billion people have whipworms (trichuris). These infect the large intestine and can cause abdominal pain, bloody stools, diarrhea, and weight loss. Still a third billion have pinworms (enterobius) that can cause severe anal itching and local infections secondary to the scratching. Toxoplasmosis, another parasitic disease which can produce infection of the muscles, lymph system, and eyes, has infected at least 40 percent of the world's population of 4.2 billion people, although it has not made each victim sick. Some of these billions overlap, with one person having more than one kind of parasite, and not all infections are harmful or necessarily fatal. Nevertheless, collectively, the many parasitic diseases are partly responsible for the thirty-year gap—the span of an entire generation—that exists in life expectancy between the developed and the developing worlds.

2. H. H. Scott, *A History of Tropical Medicine,* vol. 1, London: Arnold, 1939, pp. 68–70.

3. J. A. Walsh and K. S. Warren, "Selective Primary Health Care. An Interim Strategy for Disease Control in Developing Countries," *New England Journal of Medicine,* 301: 967–974, 1979.

4. The Maryland malaria vaccine experiments were reported in two research papers, in 1973 and 1975. Clyde self-experimented from the very beginning, although he recorded the fact in only the second paper. "It did not seem necessary at first to mention self-experimentation, because the criticism of using prison volunteers had not yet built up," Clyde said. Interviews with David F. Clyde in New Delhi, India, October 9, 1983, and November 30, 1983. (Refs.: D. F. Clyde et al., "Immunization of Man Against Falciparum and Vivax Malaria by Use of Attenuated Sporozoites," *American Journal of Tropical Medicine and Hygiene,* 24: 397–401, 1975. D. F. Clyde et al., "Immunization of Man Against Sporozoite-Induced Falciparum Malaria," *American Journal of Medical Sciences,* 266: 169–177, 1973.)

5. Mefloquine was then in its experimental stage; it has since proved effective against all types of malaria.

6. "Development of Malaria Vaccines: Memorandum from a USAID/WHO Meeting," *Bulletin of the World Health Organization,* 61: 81–92, 1983.

7. A. Dubini, "Nuovo verme intestinal umano *(Agchylostoma duodenale),* costitutente un sesto genere dei nematoidei proprii dell'uomo," *Annali Universali di Medicina,* 106: 5–13, 1843, translated in B. H. Kean, K. E. Mott, and A. J. Russell, *Tropical Medicine and Parasitology,* Ithaca, N.Y.: Cornell University Press, 1978, Vol. 2, pp. 287–291.

8. Scott, *History of Tropical Medicine,* vol. 2, p. 842.

9. M. C. Hall, "The Use of Carbon Tetrachlorid for the Removal of Hookworms," *Journal of the American Medical Association,* 77: 1641–1643, 1921. M. C. Hall and J. E. Shillinger, "Tetrachlorethylene, New Anthelmintic," *American Journal of Tropical Medicine,* 5: 229–237, 1925.

10. Scott, *History of Tropical Medicine,* Vol. 2, p. 848.

11. A. Looss, "Über das Eindringen der Ankylostomalarven in die menschliche Haut," *Zentralblatt für Bakteriologie und Parisitenkunde,* 29: 733–739, 1901, translated in Kean et al., *Tropical Medicine*

*and Parasitology,* pp. 300–314. A. Looss, "Zur Lebensgeschichte des Ankylostoma duodenale," *Zentralblatt für Bakteriologie,* 24: 441–449, 483–488, 1898.

12. H. A. Bayliss, "Arthur Looss, 1861–1923," *Parasitology,* 16: 335–338, 1924.

13. A. Looss, in Kean et al., *Tropical Medicine and Parasitology,* p. 308.

14. Ibid.

15. Ibid.

16. Ibid., p. 309.

17. Ibid., p. 310.

18. Ibid., p. 309.

19. A. E. Boycott and J. S. Haldane, "An Outbreak of Ankylostomiasis in England. No. II," *Journal of Hygiene,* 4: 73–111, 1904, p. 89. See also A. E. Boycott, "Ankylostomiasis," *Transactions of the Epidemiological Society of London,* 24: 113–142, 1904–1905. A. E. Boycott and J. S. Haldane, "An Outbreak of Ankylostomiasis in England. No. I," *Journal of Hygiene,* 3: 95–136, 1903.

20. A. E. Boycott, "Ankylostoma Infection," *Lancet,* 1: 717–721, 1911. Indisputable evidence that hookworm larvae could enter through the skin had come from an antihookworm campaign in Puerto Rico begun in 1904, after Dr. Bailey K. Ashford discovered that the most prevalent anemia of that island was due to hookworm. (Ref.: B. K. Ashford, "Ankylostomiasis in Puerto Rico," *New York Medical Journal,* 71: 552–556, 1900.)

21. A. Looss, in Kean et al., *Tropical Medicine and Parasitology,* pp. 313–314.

22. Scott, *History of Tropical Medicine,* p. 849.

23. B. E. Washburn, *As I Recall,* New York: The Rockefeller Foundation, 1960, p. vii.

24. In addition to Barlow's scientific publications, I drew from interviews with Dr. Dominic DeGiusti in Detroit, Michigan, April 27, 1980, and with Dr. Horace W. Stunkard, American Museum of Natural History, in New York City, February 10, 1983.

25. C. H. Barlow, "The Life Cycle of the Human Intestinal Fluke *Fasciolopsis buski* (Lankester)," *American Journal of Hygiene,* monograph no. 4, July 1925.

26. C. H. Barlow, "Experimental Ingestion of the Ova of *Fasciolopsis buski;* Also the Ingestion of Adult *Fasciolopsis buski* for the Purpose of Artificial Infestation," *Journal of Parasitology,* 8: 40–44, 1921, pp. 43–44.

27. There was no single specific treatment for flukes at that time, and the several drugs used worked mostly on a hit-or-miss basis.

28. L. S. Iarotski and A. Davis, "The Schistosomiasis Problem in the World: Results of a WHO Questionnaire Survey," *Bulletin of the World Health Organization,* 59: 115–127, 1981.

29. T. Bilharz, "Ein Beitrag zur *Helminthographia humana,*" *Zeitschrift für Wissenschaftliche Zoologie,* 4: 53–76, 1852. T. Bilharz, "Fernere Mittheilungen über *Distomum haematobium,*" *Zeitschrift für Wissenschaftliche Zoologie,* 4: 454–456, 1853.

30. *Schistosoma mansoni* occurs in Arabia, Africa, South America, and the Caribbean; *S. japonicum* in Japan, China, and the Philippines; and *S. haematobium* in Africa and the Middle East.

31. Within two months the female schistosome flukes begin to lay several hundred eggs each day, a process that may go on for much of a victim's life; the flukes usually survive in the body about five to ten years, although the period can be as long as thirty. The eggs, aided by the combined action of enzymes, secretions, and movement of the body's organs, work their way out of the blood vessels and pass into the feces or urine. So many eggs are produced that hundreds,

sometimes millions, remain in the body. It is this fact that causes human disease from an inflammatory reaction that occurs around the eggs and that eventually produces blockage of blood flow to the liver, bladder, lungs, and heart.

As the next step in their life cycle, eggs discharged from the body must reach freshwater, and there they quickly hatch into a form called miracidium. This is the free-swimming larva that must penetrate a specific species of snail in order to complete the life cycle. Miracidium that do not reach such a snail die. Once one miracidium has entered the snail, the young parasite can reproduce asexually into as many as one hundred thousand cercariae, the form that infects humans and other animals. The cercariae are the same size as the miracidium, and the production of overwhelming numbers of cercariae often kills the snail. However, each cercaria that enters a human develops into only one worm, either male or female. When the schistosome parasites mate in the human body, they do not reproduce themselves but produce large numbers of eggs that must leave the body to continue the life cycle.

32. C. H. Barlow, "The Value of Canal Clearance in the Control of Schistosomiasis in Egypt," *American Journal of Hygiene,* 25: 327–348, 1927. J. A. Scott and C. H. Barlow, "Limitations to the Control of Helminth Parasites," *American Journal of Hygiene,* 27: 619–648, 1938.

33. There was one potential risk: the disease might gain a natural foothold in the United States. To Barlow's thinking, ecological factors were extremely important in the transmission of schistosomiasis, and he believed that the answers to questions about the disease were best obtained by studying it in a natural setting, not under the artificial conditions of the laboratory. Further, he wondered whether the inability to infect snails in the laboratory reflected genetic factors of the species selected for study. He knew only one way to find out. (Ref.: C. H. Barlow and H. E. Meleney, "A Voluntary Infection with *Schistosoma haematobium,*" *American Journal of Tropical Medicine,* 29: 79–87, 1949.)

34. Interview with Dr. Dominic DeGiusti in Detroit, Michigan, April 27, 1980. DiGiusti did the parasitology tests in the laboratory on samples taken from Barlow and visited Barlow almost every day

during his stay in the United States. His impression was that Barlow's personality and ethical code would not allow him to give the disease experimentally to anyone else first.

35. Interview with Dr. Julius M. Amberson in Silver Spring, Maryland, February 11, 1983.

36. J. M. Amberson, "Schistosomiasis and Its Control in Egypt," *Naval Medical Bulletin,* 46: 977–1010, 1946.

37. Ibid., p. 993.

38. Ibid.

39. I was unable to locate Barlow's diary through his family or professional colleagues.

40. Amberson, "Schistosomiasis," p. 993.

41. Fouadin was one of two drugs then used to treat this form of schistosomiasis; the other was called tartar emetic. Fouadin was the more convenient, though not necessarily the more effective, choice because its course was shorter and much less toxic than that of tartar emetic. (Ref.: Interview with Dr. Harry Most, New York University, in New York City, February 11, 1983.)

42. L. Greenbaum, "Bilharziasis/Schistosomiasis," *Phoenix,* 1: 1–14, December 1961, p. 10.

43. M. G. Schultz, *The Forgotten Problems of Forgotten People,* Royal Society of Medicine, International Congress and Symposium Series, no. 24, London: Academic, 1980, pp. 57–62.

## Chapter Eight: TOXIC SHOCKS

1. For news accounts of the Japan Air Lines outbreak, see L. K. Altman, "Close Call over Copenhagen—A Near Tragedy Aboard a Jumbo Jet Raises Important Questions About the Rules that Govern the Food Served to Passengers and Crews," *American Medical News,*

April 26, 1976. These articles were based on interviews in Copenhagen with Dr. Poul Effersø, November 26, 1975, Dr. Knud Gaarslev, November 30, 1975, and Dr. Mickey Eisenberg, February and October 1975. L. K. Altman, "Illness on Japanese Jet Is Traced to Alaskan Cook," *New York Times,* February 7, 1975, p. 3. L. K. Altman, "Investigators Link Airline Food Poisoning to Caterer's Meats," *New York Times,* February 5, 1975, p. 2. L. K. Altman, "Some Illness Is Traced to Airline Meals," *New York Times,* November 8, 1975, p. 1.

For the scientific papers about the Japan Air Lines outbreak, see P. Efferson and K. Kjerulf, "Clinical Aspects of Outbreak of Staphylococcal Food Poisoning During Air Travel," *Lancet,* 2: 599–600, 1975. M. S. Eisenberg et al., "Staphylococcal Food Poisoning Aboard a Commercial Aircraft," *Lancet,* 2: 595–599, 1975.

Several other outbreaks of food poisoning have been traced to meals served aboard airplanes. These outbreaks have been due to microorganisms other than staphylococci. In March 1984, for example, salmonellosis caused more than one hundred passengers aboard thirteen British Airways flights to suffer fever, nausea, vomiting, diarrhea, and other intestinal symptoms. The outbreak was caused by a bacterium called *Salmonella enteritidis.* (Refs.: L. K. Altman, "Are Pilots Protected from Contaminated Food?" *New York Times,* March 27, 1984, p. C-2. L. K. Altman, "100 Sickened by Hors d'Oeuvres on 13 Flights," *New York Times,* March 22, 1984, p. A-19.)

2. The word "phage" is shorthand for bacteriophage—any virus that infects bacteria. Since they were discovered in the early 1900s, they have been used to classify staphylococci as well as for genetic studies that established the groundwork for molecular biology.

3. The leading textbook on staphylococci is S. D. Elek, *Staphylococcus Pyogenes,* Edinburgh and London: Livingstone, 1959.

4. The fractured vertebral spine in the remains of a Permian reptile is the oldest known example of osteomyelitis. The spine had been fractured near its base. Because the nature of the fossilization processes usually destroys disease-causing bacteria, the causative organism could not be determined. Some bacteriologists speculate that

it was the staphylococcus. (Ref.: R. L. Moodie, *Paleopathology. An Introduction to the Study of Ancient Evidences of Disease,* Urbana, Ill.: University of Illinois Press, 1923.)

5. A. Ogston, "Report on Micro-Organisms in Surgical Diseases," *British Medical Journal,* March 12, 1881, 1: 369–375.

6. V. C. Vaughan, "Poisonous or 'Sick' Cheese," *Public Health Papers and Reports,* 10: 241–245, 1884.

7. M. A. Barber, "Milk Poisoning Due to a Type of *Staphylococcus albus* Occurring in the Udder of a Healthy Cow," *Philippine Journal of Science,* 9: 515–519, 1914.

8. Barber could not find evidence from blood tests that those who escaped symptoms had developed immunity. Further, he reported that kittens, puppies, and monkeys showed no symptoms after drinking the contaminated milk.

9. G. M. Dack et al., "An Outbreak of Food Poisoning Proved to Be Due to a Yellow Hemolytic Staphylococcus," *Journal of Preventive Medicine,* 4: 167–175, 1930.

10. I did not interview Dack, who died in 1976. The accounts of his experiments were based on his scientific papers, which are summarized and referenced in G. M. Dack, *Food Poisoning,* Chicago: University of Chicago Press, 1949, and an interview with his widow in Elgin, Illinois, November 1, 1976.

11. Microbiologists distinguish between two types of toxins—exotoxins and endotoxins—on the basis of where they are produced in bacteria. Endotoxins are part of the outer membrane of the cell wall of those bacteria that are classified as gram negative on the basis of their reaction to a chemical stain. Though they can cause shock, fever, and other serious problems, they tend to be less toxic than exotoxins, which are not structural components of bacteria but are released by these microorganisms. Some can be fatal in tiny doses. Enterotoxin is the name given to an exotoxin or endotoxin produced in the intestines that affects the walls of the bowel and causes nausea, vomiting, and diarrhea. Staphylococcal enterotoxin is one type that is believed

to be absorbed from the intestines into blood to act elsewhere in the body.

12. F. M. Burnet and C. H. Kellaway, "Recent Work with Special Reference to Interpretation of Bundaberg Fatalities," *Medical Journal of Australia,* 2: 295–301, 1930. "Report of the Royal Commission on the fatalities at Bundaberg," *Medical Journal of Australia,* 2: 2–31, 1928.

13. Interview with Dr. Claude E. Dolman in Vancouver, B.C., 1969 and July 15, 1974. Dolman's key scientific publications are C. E. Dolman, "Bacterial Food Poisoning," *Canadian Journal of Public Health,* 34: 97–111, 205–235, 1943. C. E. Dolman, "Pathogenic and Antigenic Properties of Staphylococcus Toxin," *Canadian Journal of Public Health,* 23: 125–132, 1932. C. E. Dolman, "Staphylococcus Antitoxic Serum in the Treatment of Acute Staphylococcal Infections and Toxemias," *Canadian Medical Association Journal,* 30: 601–610, 1934. C. E. Dolman, "Treatment of Localized Staphylococcic Infections with Staphylococcus Toxoid," *Journal of the American Medical Association,* 100: 1007–1010, 1933. C. E. Dolman, R. J. Wilson, and W. H. Cockcroft, "A New Method of Detecting Staphylococcus Enterotoxin," *Canadian Public Health Journal,* 27: 489–493, 1936.

14. We now know there were two possible reasons they escaped symptoms: First, the toxin may not have been absorbed from the bowel; second, the staphylococcal toxin may have been destroyed by digestive enzymes.

15. Dolman, "Bacterial Food Poisoning," pp. 210–211.

16. C. Garré, "Zur Aetiologie acut eitriger Entzündungen (Osteomyelitis, Furunkel and Panaritium)," *Fortschritte der Medicin,* 3: 165–173, 1885.

17. M. Bockhart, "Über die Ätiologie und Therapie der Impetigo, des Furunkels, und der Sykosis," *Monatshefte für Praktische Dermatologie,* 6: 450–471, 1887.

18. E. Bumm, "Ueber einen abscessbildenden Diplococcus," *Sitzungs-Berichte der Physikalisch-medicinischen Gesellschaft zu Würzburg,* 1885, pp. 1–7.

19. Interviews with Dr. Stephen D. Elek in London, August 13, 1973, and in Lausanne, Switzerland, December 11, 1975, October 23–24, 1978, November 10, 1980, November 3–4, 1981, and November 28, 1983.

For the pertinent scientific papers, see S. D. Elek, "Experimental Staphylococcal Infections in the Skin of Man," *Annals of the New York Academy of Sciences,* 65: 85–89, 1956. S. D. Elek and P. E. Conen, "The Virulence of *Staphylococcus pyogenes* for Man. A Study of the Problems of Wound Infection," *British Journal of Experimental Pathology,* 38: 573–586, 1957.

20. Elek and Conen, "Virulence of *Staphylococcus pyogenes,*" p. 583.

21. At the time doctors knew little about this type of research. In fact, the minimum infecting dose was known only for syphilis, and in that case scientists had been surprised to learn that just fifty of the treponema spirochetes that cause syphilis could produce the venereal infection.

22. Among their volunteers were two medical students. No incision was made, but contaminated stitches were threaded through their skin and the knots tied tightly. A huge, painful abscess developed in each student volunteer; the abscesses disappeared only after antibiotic treatment. In retrospect, Elek and Conen had made a mistake. Normally stitches are made to bring together the lips of torn skin. When infection occurs under such circumstances, pus can drain through the incision. But in this experiment no incision was made, and therefore the pus that formed had no way to escape.

23. Interview with Dr. David E. Rogers in Princeton, New Jersey, March 19, 1984.

24. R. V. McCloskey, "Scarlet Fever and Necrotizing Fasciitis Caused by Coagulase-Positive Hemolytic *Staphylococcus aureus,* Phage Type 85," *Annals of Internal Medicine,* 78: 85–87, 1973. Also, I interviewed Dr. Bruce B. Dan in Atlanta, Georgia, April 19, 1982, and in Bethesda, Maryland, January 5, 1986; Dr. Kathryn N. Shands in Atlanta, April 19 and June 28, 1982; and Dr. Richard V. McCloskey in Philadelphia, February 7, 1983, and in Nutley, New Jersey, June 20–21, 1983.

25. J. Todd et al., "Toxic-Shock Syndrome Associated with Phage-Group-I Staphylococci," *Lancet,* 2: 1116–1119, 1978.

## Chapter Nine:
## FUNGI—INFECTING AND HALLUCINATING

1. *Phytophthora infestans* caused the 1845 potato blight in Ireland that killed five hundred thousand people and led another two million people to emigrate to England, the United States, and elsewhere. (Ref.: H. J. Fuller et al., *The Plant World,* fifth edition, New York: Holt, Rinehart and Winston, 1972.)

2. Dutch elm disease—first recognized as such in 1919—is caused by *Ceratocystis ulmi.* (Ref.: G. A. Strobel and G. N. Lanier, "Dutch Elm Disease," *Scientific American,* August 1981, pp. 56–66.)

3. Other fungal infections such as histoplasmosis, coccidioidomycosis (valley fever) and actinomycosis (lumpy jaw) are potentially fatal because they can invade any organ in the body. These systemic fungal diseases have distinctive geographic patterns. Histoplasmosis is most common in the Mississippi and Ohio river valleys. Coccidioidomycosis occurs throughout the southwestern United States and is most prevalent in the San Joaquin Valley area of southern California.

4. J. E. Edwards, Jr., "Candida Species," in G. L. Mandell, R. G. Douglas, Jr., and J. E. Bennett, *Principles and Practice of Infectious Diseases,* New York: Wiley, 1979, chap. 211.

5. W. Krause, H. Matheis, and K. Wulf, "Experimentelle Fungiamie und Fungiurie durch orale Verabreichung grosser Mengen von *Candida albicans* beim gesunden Menschen (Selbstversuch)," *Arzneimittel-Forschung,* 19: 85–91, 1969. W. Krause, H. Matheis, and K. Wulf, "Fungaemia and Funguria after Oral Administration of *Candida albicans,*" *Lancet,* 1: 598–599, 1969.

6. Interviews with Dr. Wolfgang Krause in Kassel, West Germany, 1973, December 2, 1975, and October 28–29, 1981.

7. G. Volkheimer and F. H. Schulz, "The Phenomenon of Persorption," *Digestion,* 1: 213–218, 1968.

8. Interviews with Dr. Albert Hofmann in Burg-i.-Leimental, Switzerland, September 11, 1978, October 30, 1981, and June 2, 1983. Many years earlier, Hofmann had moved to Burg-i.-Leimental from the home in Basel where he lived when he discovered the effects of LSD-25 and made his famous bicycle trip.

For Hofmann's written accounts, see A. Hofmann, "How LSD Originated," *Journal of Psychedelic Drugs,* 11: 53–60, 1979. A. Hofmann, *LSD—My Problem Child,* New York: McGraw-Hill, 1980. A. Hofmann, "The History of LSD-25 (Lysergic Acid Diethylamide)," *Triangle,* 2: 117–124, 1955. A. Hofmann, "Psychotomimetic Drugs. Chemical and Pharmacological Aspects," *Acta Physiologica et Pharmacologica Neerlandica,* 8: 240–258, 1959.

9. Hofmann, *LSD—My Problem Child,* p. 15.

10. H. C. Wood, Jr., "On the Medical Activity of the Hemp Plant, As Grown in North America," *Transactions of the American Philosophical Society,* 11: 226–231, 1869.

11. S. W. Mitchell, *Injuries of Nerves and Their Consequences.* Philadelphia: Lippincott, 1872, pp. 54–55, 177–178. S. W. Mitchell, "Remarks on the Effect of *Anhelonium lewinii* (The Mescal Button)," *British Medical Journal,* 2: 1625–1629, 1896. A. Waller, "On the Sensory, Motory, and Vaso-Motory Symptoms Resulting from the Refrigeration of the Ulnar Nerve," *Proceedings of the Royal Society of London,* 11: 436–441, 1860–1862.

12. On Good Friday, while alone in a quiet spot in London, Ellis took three mescal buttons and, acting on Mitchell's hint, kept a diary of his kaleidoscopic visions of symmetrical groupings of spiked objects and the play of shadowy colors, particularly the violet halos that played around objects. Ellis, unlike Mitchell, found he could see the visions when lying down in a dark room with open eyes. (Ref.: H. Ellis, " 'Mescal,' A Study of a Divine Plant," *Popular Science Monthly,* 61: 52–71, 1902.)

13. H. Osmond, "Ololiuqui: The Ancient Aztec Narcotic," *Journal of Mental Science,* 101: 526–537, 1955.

14. No other drug has been found to have such a wide range between its active and lethal doses. No human has been known to die from a direct toxic effect of LSD; however, some people have reportedly jumped out of windows or died from similar accidents induced by the mental changes.

## Chapter Ten: LIFETIMES OF SELF-EXPERIMENTING

1. R. W. Clark, *JBS: The Life and Work of J.B.S. Haldane,* New York: Coward-McCann, 1968.

2. Ibid.

3. J. S. Haldane, "On the Air of Buildings and Sewers," *Transactions of the Sanitary Institute of Great Britian,* 9: 395–415, 1888, p. 411. See also: T. Carnelley, J.B.S. Haldane, and A. M. Anderson, "The Carbonic Acid, Organic Matter, and Micro-Organisms in Air, More Especially of Dwellings and Schools," *Philosophical Transactions of the Royal Society of London,* 178: 61–111, 1887. J. S. Haldane, "The Air of Buildings and Sewers," *The Sanitary Record,* October 15, 1887, pp. 152–158.

4. T. Carnelley and J. S. Haldane, "The Air of Sewers," *Proceedings of the Royal Society of London,* 42: 501–522, 1887, p. 508.

5. J.B.S. Haldane, *Keeping Cool,* London: Chatto and Windus, 1940, p. 93.

6. J. Haldane and J. L. Smith, "The Physiological Effects of Air Vitiated by Respiration," *Journal of Pathology and Bacteriology,* 1: 168–186, 1893, p. 186. See also J. Haldane and J. L. Smith, "The Toxic Action of Expired Air," *Journal of Pathology and Bacteriology,* 1: 318–321, 1893.

7. J. S. Haldane, "The New Physiology," *Harvey Society Lectures,* 1916–1917, pp. 21–41. J. S. Haldane, "The Therapeutic Administration

of Oxygen," *British Medical Journal,* 1: 181–183, 1917. J. S. Haldane and J. G. Priestley, "The Regulation of the Lung-Ventilation," *Journal of Physiology,* 32: 225–266, 1905.

8. C. G. Douglas, "John Scott Haldane," *Obituary Notices of the Royal Society of London,* 2: 115–139, no. 5, 1936.

9. J. S. Haldane, "Poisoning by Gas in Sewers," *Lancet,* 1: 220–224, 1896.

10. Ibid., p. 221.

11. "Portrait of J.B.S. Haldane Narrated by Lord Ritchie-Calder," *The Listener, BBC's Weekly Review,* 78: 565–568, 1967, p. 565.

12. J. Haldane, "The Action of Carbonic Oxide on Man," *Journal of Physiology,* 18: 430–462, 1895, p. 435.

13. Ibid., p. 448.

14. J. Haldane, "Notes of an Enquiry into the Nature and Physiological Action of Black-damp, as Met With in Podmore Colliery, Staffordshire, and Lilleshall Colliery, Shropshire," *Proceedings of the Royal Society of London,* 57: 249–257, 1895, pp. 250–251.

15. Ibid., p. 252.

16. Some of the methods are derived from J. Haldane, "Some Improved Methods of Gas Analysis," *Journal of Physiology,* 22: 465–480, 1898, and J. Haldane, "The Mass and Oxygen Capacity of the Blood in Man," *Journal of Physiology,* 25: 331–343, 1900.

17. P. Bert, *La Pression barométrique, recherches de Physiologie Expérimentale,* Paris: Masson, 1878, translated by M. A. Hitchcock and F. A. Hitchcock as *Barometric Pressure, Researches in Experimental Physiology,* Columbus, Ohio: College Book Company, 1943.

18. A. E. Boycott, G. C. Damant, and J. S. Haldane, "The Prevention of Compressed-Air Illness," *Journal of Hygiene,* 8: 342–443, 1908, p. 379.

19. C. Blagden, "Experiments and Observations in a Heated Room," *Philosophical Transactions of the Royal Society of London,* 65: 111–123, 1775. C. Blagden, "Further Experiments and Observations in a Heated Room," *Philosophical Transactions of the Royal Society of London,* 65: 484–494, 1775.

20. J.B.S. Haldane, *Keeping Cool,* p. 73.

21. J. S. Haldane, "The Influence of High Air Temperatures," *Journal of Hygiene,* 5: 494–513, 1905, p. 513.

22. J. S. Haldane, "Acclimatisation to High Altitudes," *Physiological Reviews,* 7: 363–384, 1927.

23. J. S. Milledge, "The Great Oxygen Secretion Controversy," *Lancet,* 2: 1408–1411, 1985. R. Passmore, "Haldane and Barcroft," *Lancet,* 1: 443, 1986.

24. J. S. Haldane, "The Training of the Student of Medicine. An Inquiry Conducted under the Auspices of the Edinburgh Pathological Club. VIII. The Relation of Physiology to Medicine," *Edinburgh Medical Journal,* 20: 255–267, 1918.

25. J.B.S. Haldane, "An Autobiography in Brief," *Perspectives in Biology and Medicine,* 9: 476–481, Summer 1966, p. 476.

26. J.B.S. Haldane, *Keeping Cool,* p. 90.

27. J.B.S. Haldane, *Possible Worlds and Other Papers,* Freeport, N.Y.: Books for Libraries, 1971, pp. 198, 214.

28. Interview with Dr. Martin Case in Ryde, Isle of Wight, England, August 19, 1973.

29. Haldane, *Possible Worlds,* p. 122.

30. Ibid., p. 114.

31. Ibid., p. 84.

32. Ibid., p. 264.

33. Ibid., p. 117.

34. H. W. Davies, J.B.S. Haldane, and E. L. Kennaway, "Experiments on the Regulation of the Blood's Alkalinity. I," *Journal of Physiology,* 54: 32–45, 1920. H. W. Davies, J.B.S. Haldane, and G. L. Peskett, "The Excretion of Chlorides and Bicarbonates by the Human Kidney," *Journal of Physiology,* 56: 269–274, 1922. J.B.S. Haldane, "Experiments on the Regulation of the Blood's Alkalinity. II," *Journal of Physiology,* 55: 265–275, 1921.

35. Haldane, *Possible Worlds,* pp. 118–119.

36. Haldane, *Keeping Cool,* p. 73.

37. W. Alexander et al., "After-Effects of Exposure of Men to Carbon Dioxide," *Lancet,* 2: 419–420, 1939. Haldane, *Keeping Cool,* p. 75.

38. E. M. Case and J.B.S. Haldane, "Human Physiology Under High Pressure," *Journal of Hygiene,* 41: 225–249, 1941, p. 234.

39. J.B.S. Haldane, "Human Life and Death at High Pressure," *Nature,* 148: 458–460, 1941, p. 460.

40. E. M. Case and J.B.S. Haldane, "Tastes of Oxygen and Nitrogen at High Pressures," *Nature,* 148: 84, 1941.

41. Haldane, *Possible Worlds,* pp. 123, 227–228.

42. Interviews with Dr. Robert A. McCance in Cambridge, England, December 22, 1975, February 9, 1977, November 2, 1978, November 26–27, 1980, December 2, 1980, and October 20, 1981. Interviews with Dr. Elsie M. Widdowson in Cambridge, England, February 14, 1977, December 2, 1980, and October 20, 1981. E. M. Widdowson, "Adventures in Nutrition Over Half a Century," *Proceedings of the Nutrition Society,* 39: 293–306, 1980. E. M. Widdowson, "Problems and Pleasures of Human Experiments," *Proceedings of the Nutrition Society,* 17: 15–20, 1958.

43. K. Madders and R. A. McCance, "Effect of Pentose Ingestion on Uric Acid Excretion," *Biochemical Journal,* 23: 1175–1177, 1929. R. A. McCance and K. Madders, "The Comparative Rates of Absorption of Sugars from the Human Intestine," *Biochemical Journal,* 24: 795–804, 1930.

44. R. A. McCance and E. M. Widdowson, "The Chemical Composition of Foods," *Medical Research Council Special Report Series,* no. 235, London, 1940. McCance and Widdowson, *The Composition of Foods,* fourth revised and extended edition of MRC Special Report No. 297, A. A. Paul and D.A.T. Southgate, eds., New York: Elsevier/North Holland, 1978.

45. R. A. McCance, "Effect of Salt Deficiency in Man on Volume of Extracellular Fluids, and on Composition of Sweat, Saliva, Gastric Juice and Cerebrospinal Fluid," *Journal of Physiology,* 92: 208–218, 1938. R. A. McCance, "The Effect of Sudden Severe Anoxemia on the Function of the Human Kidney," *Lancet,* 2: 370–372, 1935. R. A. McCance, "Experimental Sodium Chloride Deficiency in Man," *Proceedings of the Royal Society of London. Series B: Biological Sciences,* 119: 245–268, 1935–1936. R. A. McCance, "Individual Variations in Response to High Temperatures and to Production of Experimental Salt Deficiency," *Lancet,* 2: 190–191, 1938.

46. R. A. McCance and W. F. Young, "Secretion of Urine by Newborn Infants," *Journal of Physiology,* 99: 265–282, 1941. W. F. Young, J. L. Hallum, and R. A. McCance, "Secretion of Urine by Premature Infants," *Archives of the Diseases of Childhood,* 16: 243–252, 1941.

47. The chief risk of polycythemia vera is clots from the excessive number of red blood cells; they can, for example, lead to strokes or gangrene of the legs.

48. R. A. McCance, "Medical Problems in Mineral Metabolism (Goulstonian Lectures)," *Lancet,* 1: 643–650, 704–710, 765–768, 823–830, 1936. R. A. McCance and E. M. Widdowson, "Absorption and Excretion of Iron," *Lancet,* 2: 680–684, 1937. R. A. McCance and E. M. Widdowson, "The Absorption and Excretion of Iron Following Oral and Intravenous Administration," *Journal of Physiology,* 94: 148–154, 1938. R. A. McCance, E. M. Widdowson, and L.R.B. Shackleton, *The*

*Nutritive Value of Fruits, Vegetables and Nuts,* Medical Research Council, Special Report Series no. 213, London: His Majesty's Stationery Office, 1936. E. M. Widdowson and R. A. McCance, "Iron in Human Nutrition," *Journal of Hygiene,* 36: 13–23, 1936.

A brief synopsis of Mrs. Harris's case is reported in E. M. Widdowson, "Adventures in Nutrition," p. 297.

49. R. A. McCance and E. M. Widdowson, "The Fate of Calcium and Magnesium after Intravenous Administration to Normal Persons," *Biochemical Journal,* 33: 523–529, 1939.

50. J.B.S. Haldane, "The Production of Acidosis by Ingestion of Magnesium Chloride and Strontium Chloride," *Biochemical Journal,* 19: 249–250, 1925. J.B.S. Haldane, R. Hill, and J. M. Luck, "Calcium Chloride Acidosis," *Journal of Physiology,* 57: 301–306, 1922–1923.

51. For the eleven days before the planned injections of strontium, the two researchers ate only simple foods such as potatoes so the meals could easily be duplicated later in the experiment. And during the week before the experiment, they collected all their urine and feces for chemical analysis. They wanted to inject forty-seven milligrams of strontium each time, but as a precautionary step they decided to use half that dose. They made up a large solution of strontium and sterilized enough to last through the course of the experiment. When they later increased the dose to the original forty-seven milligrams, they ran out of strontium before the end of the experiment. (Ref.: R. A. McCance and E. M. Widdowson, "The Fate of Strontium after Intravenous Administration to Normal Persons," *Biochemical Journal,* 33: 1822–1825, 1939.)

52. The rationing in the McCance-Widdowson diet was planned to meet much more serious blockade conditions than actually occurred in the United Kingdom in World War II. (Refs.: R. A. McCance and E. M. Widdowson, *An Experimental Study of Rationing,* Medical Research Council, Special Report Series no. 254, London: His Majesty's Stationery Office, 1946. For related experiments, see R. A. McCance, "Bread," *Lancet,* 1: 77–81, 1946. R. A. McCance and E. M. Widdowson, "The Composition and Milling of Wheat," *Proceedings of the Nutrition Society,* 4: 2–6, 1946. R. A. McCance and E. M. Widdowson, "The Digestibility and Absorption of the Calories, Pro-

teins, Purines, Fat and Calcium in Wholemeal Wheaten Bread," *British Journal of Nutrition,* 2: 26–41, 1948. R. A. McCance and E. M. Widdowson, "The Digestibility of English and Canadian Wheats with Special Reference to the Digestibility of Wheat Protein by Man," *Journal of Hygiene,* 45: 59–64, 1947. R. A. McCance and E. M. Widdowson, "Mineral Metabolism of Healthy Adults on White and Brown Bread Dietaries," *Journal of Physiology,* 101: 44–85, 1942.)

Of the four researchers highlighted in this chapter, there is a full-length biography of only one. It is R. W. Clark, *JBS: The Life and Work of J.B.S. Haldane,* New York: Coward-McCann, 1968. In addition: N. W. Pirie, "J.B.S. Haldane," *Biographical Memoirs of the Fellows of the Royal Society of London,* 12: 219–249, 1966. *British Medical Journal,* 1: 617–619, March 21, 1936. The most comprehensive biography of J.B.S.'s father, J. S. Haldane, is C. G. Douglas, "John Scott Haldane. 1860–1936," *Obituary Notices of the Royal Society of London,* 2: 115–139, no. 5, 1936. *Proceedings of the Royal Society of Edinburgh,* 57: 253, 1936–1937.

## Chapter Eleven: DIETARY DEPRIVATIONS

1. J. Goldberger and J. F. Schamberg, "Epidemic of an Urticarioid Dermatitis Due to a Small Mite *(Pediculoides ventricosus)* in the Straw of Mattresses," *Public Health Reports,* 24: 973–975, 1909.

2. Whether pellagra affected the American Indians in the seventeenth century, before the Pilgrims arrived, is a matter of speculation; no evidence supports this thesis, which has been advanced by some writers. (Refs.: D. A. Roe, *A Plague of Corn,* Ithaca, N.Y.: Cornell University Press, 1973, p. 77. Also, C. A. Elvehjem, "Pellagra—A Deficiency Disease," *Proceedings of the American Philosophical Society,* 93: 335–339, 1949. J. P. Gray, "Case of Pellagra of the Insane," *American Journal of Insanity,* 21: 223–227, 1864–1865. This is the unreferenced case cited in E. J. Wood, *A Treatise on Pellagra for the General Practitioner,* New York: Appleton, 1912, p. 29. S. R. Roberts, *Pellagra,* St. Louis: Mosby, 1912, p. 63.)

3. In one case in Mobile, a blood transfusion led to the rapid recovery of a pellagra patient, but the doctor who prescribed it did not appre-

ciate the fact that the blood contained enough nicotinic acid to be curative. (Ref.: H. P. Cole, "Transfusion of Blood in a Case of Pellagra," *Journal of the American Medical Association,* 52: 633–634, 1909. E. L. McCafferty, "Pellagra Among the Colored Insane at the Mount Vernon Hospital," *Gulf States Journal of Medicine and Surgery and Mobile Medical and Surgical Journal,* 14: 228–236, 1909, p. 229.)

4. If the disease was new to American physicians, it was an old problem to doctors in Italy, France, Spain, Germany, and some other countries, where for at least two hundred years endemic pellagra had been linked to maize diets and was known to have a peak incidence in the spring. For many years a leading theory held that pellagra was due to spoiled corn that permitted the growth of an unidentified microorganism that produced an unidentified toxin. (Ref.: Wood, *A Treatise on Pellagra.*)

5. J. F. Siler, P. E. Garrison, and W. J. MacNeal, "Pellagra, a Summary of the First Progress Report of the Thompson-McFadden Pellagra Commission," *Journal of the American Medical Association,* 62: 8–12, 1914, p. 12. J. F. Siler, P. E. Garrison, and W. J. MacNeal, "Further Studies of the Thompson-McFadden Pellagra Commission. A Summary of the Second Progress Report," *Journal of the American Medical Association,* 63: 1090–1093, 1914. J. F. Siler et al., *Third Report of Pellagra Commission of the New York Post-Graduate Medical School and Hospital,* New York, 1917.

6. L. Sambon, "Progress Report on the Investigation of Pellagra," *Journal of Tropical Medicine and Hygiene,* 13: 271–282, 287–300, 305–315, 319–321, 1910.

7. M. Goldberger, "Dr. Joseph Goldberger. His Wife's Recollections," *Journal of the American Dietetic Association,* 32: 724–727, 1956.

8. J. Goldberger, C. H. Waring, and W. F. Tanner, "Pellagra Prevention by Diet Among Institutional Inmates," *Public Health Reports,* 38: 2361–2368, 1923. M. Terris, *Goldberger on Pellagra,* Baton Rouge: Louisiana State University Press, 1964, p. 3. This book is a collection of seventeen of the more significant of Goldberger's fifty-four scientific papers.

9. Some of what Goldberger and his colleagues were about to do repeated self-experiments conducted more than a century earlier, in particular experiments that Michele Francesco Buniva, an Italian researcher, did on himself from 1805 to 1808. Although Goldberger cited Buniva's work in a paper he wrote in 1925, it is not clear, in retrospect, whether he knew about that work before he undertook his own experiments or learned about it later. If he had known from the beginning, the knowledge would have afforded a considerable degree of comfort to an unpalatable series of experiments. Even today, Buniva's work is virtually unknown to nutritional experts. (Ref.: M. F. Buniva, "Memoria sulla pellagra, etc.," *Archivio de l'Accademia de Turin,* vol. 3, 1805–1808, cited in T. Roussel, "Traité de la pellagra et des pseudo-pellagres," Paris: Baillière, 1866, p. 500.)

10. Associated Press, "Wife of Pellagra Conqueror Risked Danger of Disease to Prove Husband's Theory Sound," *New York Times,* May 21, 1929, p. 33.

11. M. Goldberger, "Dr. Joseph Goldberger," p. 726.

12. R. P. Parsons, *Trail to Light. A Biography of Joseph Goldberger,* Indianapolis: Bobbs-Merrill, 1943, p. 312.

13. R. H. Chittenden and F. P. Underhill, "The Production in Dogs of a Pathological Condition which Closely Resembles Human Pellagra," *American Journal of Physiology,* 44: 13–66, 1917.

14. C. A. Elvehjem et al., "The Isolation and Identification of the Anti-Blacktongue Factor," *Journal of Biological Chemistry,* 123: 137–149, 1938. C. A. Elvehjem et al., "Relation of Nicotinic Acid and Nicotinic Acid Amide to Canine Blacktongue," *Journal of the American Chemical Society,* 59: 1767–1768, 1937.

15. M. Goldberger, "Dr. Joseph Goldberger," p. 727.

16. V. P. Sydenstricker, "The History of Pellagra, Its Recognition as a Disorder of Nutrition and Its Conquest," *American Journal of Clinical Nutrition,* 6: 409–414, 1958.

17. N.S.T. Lui and O. A. Roels, "The Vitamins," in R. S. Goodhart and M. E. Shils, *Modern Nutrition in Health and Disease,* Philadelphia:

Lea and Febiger, 1980. V. P. Sydenstricker, "The Impact of Vitamin Research upon Medical Practice," *Proceedings of the Nutrition Society,* 12: 256–269, 1953.

18. R. R. Williams, *Toward the Conquest of Beriberi,* Cambridge, Mass.: Harvard University Press, 1961. A thorough history that contains a bibliography of Eijkman's papers. See also C. Eijkman, "Eine Beri Beri-ähnliche Krankheit der Hühner," *Virchows Archiv für Pathologische Anatomie und Physiologie,* 148: 523–532, 1897. G. Grijns, "Over Polyneuritis Gallinarum," *Geneeskundig Tijdschrift voor Nederlansch-Indië.* 49: 216–231, 1909. G. A. Lindeboom, "Eijkman, C.," in *Dictionary of Scientific Biography,* vol. 4, pp. 310–312.

19. Hopkins discussed the concept of accessory factors, without specifically using the word, in F. G. Hopkins, "The Analyst and the Medical Man," *Analyst,* 31: 385–404, 1906, and then used it in F. G. Hopkins, "Feeding Experiments Illustrating the Importance of Accessory Factors in Normal Dietaries," *Journal of Physiology,* 44: 425–460, 1912.

In terming the missing factors "accessory substances," Hopkins said that "a substance or substances present in normal foodstuffs (e.g. milk) can, when added to the [rat] diet in astonishingly small amount, secure the utilization for growth of the protein and energy contained in such artificial mixtures."

20. C. Funk, "On the Chemical Nature of the Substance which Cures Polyneuritis in Birds Induced by a Diet of Polished Rice," *Journal of Physiology,* 43: 395–400, 1911.

21. Cartier left a vivid account: "Some did lose all their strength, and could not stand on their feet, then did their legs swell, their sinews shrink as black as coal. Others also had all their skins spotted with spots of blood of a purple color: then did it ascend up their ankles, knees, thighs, shoulders, arms, and necks. Their mouths became stinking, their gums so rotten, that all the flesh did fall off, even to the roots of the teeth, which did also almost all fall out." (Ref.: H. P. Biggar, *The Voyages of Jacques Cartier,* Ottawa: F. A. Acland, Publications of the Public Archives of Canada, no. 11, 1924 pp. 204–215.)

22. J. Lind, *A Treatise of the Scurvy,* Edinburgh: Sands, Murray and Cochran, 1753. Lind cited Cartier's experiences. C. P. Stewart and D.

Guthrie, *Lind's Treatise on Scurvy. A Bicentenary Volume Containing a Reprint of the First Edition of "A Treatise of the Scurvy" by James Lind, M.D. with Additional Notes,* Edinburgh: University of Edinburgh Press, 1953, p. 257.

23. Scurvy killed many victims of the 1846 potato famine in Europe (Ref.: E. V. McCollum, "A History of Nutrition," Boston: Houghton Mifflin, 1957, p. 254.) and continued to kill well into the twentieth century. Infant scurvy increased only a few decades ago, when boiled orange juice was fed to children and breast milk substitutes were first used in urban areas of Europe and the United States. (Ref.: H. Chick, "Early Investigations of Scurvy and the Antiscorbutic Vitamin," *Proceedings of the Nutrition Society,* 12: 210–219, 1953.) And in World War I, British troops in the Middle East suffered from scurvy because they were fed preserved, not fresh, lime juice. Sporadic cases occurred elsewhere in Europe when potatoes were unavailable. Even during World War I, patients in a Vienna hospital and residents of a children's home there suffered from scurvy. (Ref.: H. Chick, E. M. Hume, and R. F. Skelton, "The Relative Content of Antiscorbutic Principle in Limes and Lemons," *Lancet,* 2: 735–738, 1918.)

24. Lind, *A Treatise of the Scurvy,* p. 228. Lind's study is cited as the first example of a scientifically controlled clinical experiment. His remedy was based on experiments made at sea on twelve sailors who had developed scurvy. Lind tested various supposed remedies by dividing the twelve sailors into six groups of two each. One group drank a quart of cider each day, another took elixir vitriol three times a day, a third group took two spoonsful of vinegar three times a day, a fourth ate two oranges and one lemon each day, another group had nutmeg three times each day, and the last, two of the sickest sailors, drank seawater. The most sudden and visible improvement occurred in the two who were fed oranges and lemons; one was fit for duty after just six days.

25. In 1795 the Royal Navy began to provide an ounce of lemon juice for each man after his sixth week at sea. Although the dose was less than the amount recommended today, it was effective. (Refs.: F. Bicknell and F. Prescott, *The Vitamins in Medicine,* New York: Grune and Stratton, 1953, p. 390. G. Blane, *Observations on the Diseases Incident to Seamen,* London: J. Murray, 1785. H. Chick,

"Early Investigations of Scurvy and the Antiscorbutic Vitamin," *Proceedings of the Nutrition Society,* 12: 210–219, 1953. A. Newsholme, *Evolution of Preventive Medicine,* Baltimore: Williams and Wilkins, 1927, pp. 191, 196–197.) Later, when the less expensive West Indian limes replaced the expensive Mediterranean lemons, sailors in the British Navy gained the sobriquet "limeys."

26. J. C. Drummond and A. Wilbraham, "William Stark, M.D. An Eighteenth Century Experiment in Nutrition," *Lancet,* 2: 459–462, 1935. W. Stark, *The Works of the Late William Stark, M.D. Consisting of Clinical and Anatomical Observations, with Experiments, Dietetical and Statical,* revised by James Carmichael Smyth, London: J. Johnson, 1788.

27. Stark, *Works,* pp. 89–90.

28. Ibid., p. xi.

29. A. Holst and T. Frölich, "Experimental Studies Relating to Ship Beriberi and Scurvy," *Journal of Hygiene,* 7: 634–671, 1907.

30. C. G. King, "The Discovery and Chemistry of Vitamin C," *Proceedings of the Nutrition Society,* 12: 219–227, 1953, traces the steps in the discovery of vitamin C. Also see J. C. Drummond, "The Nomenclature of the So-Called Accessory Food Factors (Vitamins)," *Biochemical Journal,* 14: 660, 1920. C. G. King and W. A. Waugh, "The Chemical Nature of Vitamin C," *Science* 75: 357, 1932. J. L. Svirbely and A. Szent-Györgyi, "Chemical Nature of Vitamin C," *Biochemical Journal,* 26: 865–870, 1932. J. L. Svirbely and A. Szent-Györgyi, "Hexauronic acid as Antiscorbutic Factor," *Nature,* 129: 576, 690, 1932. A. Szent-Györgi, "Identification of Vitamin C," *Nature,* 131: 225, 1933. A. Szent-György, *On Oxidation, Fermentation, Vitamins, Health and Disease,* Baltimore: Williams and Wilkins, 1939. A. Szent-Györgyi and W. N. Haworth, " 'Hexauronic Acid' (Ascorbic Acid) as the Antiscorbutic Factor," *Nature,* 131: 24, 1933.

31. T. H. Lanman and T. H. Ingalls, "Vitamin C Deficiency and Wound Healing," *Annals of Surgery,* 105: 616–625, 1937. C. C. Lund, "The Effect of Surgical Operations on the Level of Cevitamic Acid

in the Blood Plasma," *New England Journal of Medicine,* 221: 123–127, 1939.

32. Others had tried to find answers to some of these questions through self-experimentation, but none had developed clinical signs of scurvy. In 1935 two Dutch investigators, Marie van Eeekelen and Martin Heinemann, had independently determined their daily vitamin C requirements for periods lasting about one month. Neither developed clinical signs of scurvy or other deficiencies. (Refs.: M. Heinemann, "On the Relation Between Diet and Urinary Output of Thiosulfate and Ascorbic Acid. II. Human Requirements for Vitamin C," *Biochemical Journal,* 30: 2299–2306, 1936. M. van Eckelen, "On the Amount of Ascorbic Acid in Blood and Urine. The Daily Human Requirements for Ascorbic Acid," *Biochemical Journal,* 30: 2291–2298, 1936.)

Then in 1936 another Dutch researcher, H. J. van Wersch, determined his daily requirements of vitamin C over a thirty-one-day period. (Refs.: H. J. van Wersch, "Determination of the Daily Requirements for Ascorbic Acid of Man," *Acta Brevia Neerlandica de Physiologia,* 6: 86–87, 1936. H. J. van Wersch, "Het Verbruik van Vitamine C," *Nederlands Tijdschrift voor Geneeskunde,* 80: 3653–3660, 1936.)

In London in 1937, an investigator lived thirty-seven days on a low-vitamin-C diet to determine the amount of ascorbic acid excreted in the urine. His partner was a volunteer in the preliminary investigations, which were stopped for unspecified "reasons of health." (Ref.: A. E. Kellie and S. S. Zilva, "The Vitamin C Requirements of Man," *Biochemical Journal,* 33: 153–164, 1939.)

33. R. Brandon, *The Spiritualists,* New York: Knopf, 1983, pp. 175–189. W. F. Prince, "A Review of the Margery Case," *American Journal of Psychology,* 37: 431–441, 1926. Thomas R. Tietze, *Margery,* New York: Harper and Row, 1973.

34. Interviews with Dr. John Crandon in Winthrop and Boston, Massachusetts, 1961, May 22, 1972, July 25 and September 4, 1979, and February 1, 1983.

35. Telephone interviews with Mrs. James McGrath and Mrs. Ruth McFadden Miller, who worked in the surgical department at the

Boston City Hospital during Crandon's experiments, September 5, 1979.

36. Dr. David B. Dill was a cofounder in 1926 of the Harvard Fatigue Laboratory at the Harvard Business School. Its chief aim was to measure the physiological effects of everyday life. One goal was to find the toxin that was then believed to cause fatigue. Self-experimentation played a prominent role in these experiments, which, of course, showed there was no such toxin.

37. This episode was omitted from Crandon's scientific articles, and he has always suspected that the medical journal editor removed it because he considered it overly dramatic.

38. J. Lind, *A Treatise of the Scurvy,* Edinburgh: Stewart and Guthrie, 1953, pp. 134–135, 229.

39. C. C. Lund and J. H. Crandon, "Human Experimental Scurvy," *Journal of the American Medical Association,* 116: 663–668, 1941. The other scientific papers are J. H. Crandon and C. C. Lund, "Vitamin C Deficiency in an Otherwise Normal Adult," *New England Journal of Medicine,* 222: 748–752, 1940. J. H. Crandon, C. C. Lund, and D. B. Dill, "Experimental Human Scurvy," *New England Journal of Medicine,* 223: 353–369, 1940.

## Chapter Twelve: THE RED CELL RIDDLE

1. Coombe, a Scots physician, may have been the first to describe pernicious anemia, in 1822. (Ref.: J. S. Coombe, "History of a Case of Anemia," *Transactions of the Medical and Chirurgical Society of Edinburgh,* 1: 194–204, 1824.) Many American doctors call it Addison's pernicious anemia after Dr. Thomas Addison, a physician at Guy's Hospital in London, who described it in 1849 and 1855. (Refs.: T. Addison, "Anaemia—Capsules," *London Medical Gazette,* 43: 517–518, 1849. T. Addison, *On the Constitutional and Local Effects of Disease of the Suprarenal Capsules,* London: Highley, 1855.) In Europe it is often called Biermer's pernicious anemia after Professor Anton Biermer of Zurich, who first called it progressive pernicious (i.e., lethal) anemia. However, it is uncertain whether it was true

pernicious anemia that Biermer described. (Refs.: A. Biermer, "Halt Zunächst einen Vortrag über eine von ihm öfters beobachtete eigenthümliche Form von progressiver pernizioser Anamie," *Correspondenz-Blatt Für Schweiz. Aerzte* 2: 15, 1872, cited in L. Kass, *Pernicious Anemia,* Philadelphia: Saunders, 1976. A. Biermer, *Tageblatt der 42. Versammlung Deutscher Naturforscher und Aertze in Dresden vom 18 bis 24 September 1868.* Dresden: Teubner, 1868, p. 173.)

2. I. Holmgren, "The Nobel Prize for the Year 1934," *Nobel Lectures, Physiology or Medicine, 1922–1941.* New York: Elsevier, 1965, p. 343.

3. Ibid., p. 337.

4. At the turn of the twentieth century, one standard textbook said that "bone marrow has been used with alleged excellent results. Red marrow from the small bones of calves or other young animals should be taken . . ." (Refs.: T. R. Fraser, "Bone Marrow in the Treatment of Pernicious Anemia," *British Medical Journal,* 1: 1172–1174, 1894. H. C. Wood and R. H. Fitz, *The Practice of Medicine,* Philadelphia: Lippincott, 1898, p. 11.)

5. G. H. Whipple, C. W. Hooper, and F. S. Robscheit, "Blood Regeneration Following Simple Anemia," *American Journal of Physiology,* 53: 151–282, 1920.

6. G. R. Minot and W. P. Murphy, "Treatment of Pernicious Anemia by a Special Diet," *Journal of the American Medical Association,* 87: 470–476, 1926.

7. Interviews with Dr. William B. Castle in Boston and New York City, 1961, February 27, 1974, July 17, 1975, and May 17, 1978, and personal communications, April 7, 1969, and March 26, 1984.

Castle's pertinent scientific papers are: L. Berk et al., "Observations on the Etiologic Relationship of Achylia Gastrica to Pernicious Anemia. X. Activity of Vitamin B12 as Food (Extrinsic) Factor," *New England Journal of Medicine,* 239: 911–913, 1948. W. B. Castle, "The Gordon Wilson Lecture. A Century of Curiosity about Pernicious Anemia," *Transactions of the American Clinical and Climatological Association,* 73: 54–80, 1961. W. B. Castle, "Observations on the Etiologic Relationship of Achylia Gastrica to Pernicious Anemia. I. The

Effect of the Administration to Patients with Pernicious Anemia of the Contents of the Normal Human Stomach Recovered after the Ingestion of Beef Muscle," *American Journal of the Medical Sciences,* 178: 748–764, 1929. W. B. Castle, "Treatment of Pernicious Anemia: Historical Aspects," *Clinical Pharmacology and Therapeutics,* 7: 147–161, 1966. W. B. Castle (by invitation) and E. A. Locke, "Observations on the Etiological Relationship of Achylia Gastrica to Pernicious Anemia (Abstract)," *Journal of Clinical Investigation,* 6: 2–3, 1929. W. B. Castle and W. C. Townsend, "Observations on the Etiologic Relationship of Achylia Gastrica to Pernicious Anemia. II. The Effect of the Administration to Patients with Pernicious Anemia of Beef Muscle after Incubation with Normal Human Gastric Juice," *American Journal of the Medical Sciences,* 178: 764–777, 1929. W. B. Castle, W. C. Townsend, and C. W. Heath, "Observations on the Etiologic Relationship of Achylia Gastrica to Pernicious Anemia," *American Journal of the Medical Sciences,* 180: 305–335, 1930. G. R. Minot and W. B. Castle, "The Interpretation of Reticulocyte Reactions. Their Value in Determining the Potency of Therapeutic Materials, Especially in Pernicious Anemia," *Lancet,* 2: 319–330, 1935.

8. E. A. Greenspon, "The Nature of the Antipernicious Anemia Principle in Stomach," *Journal of the American Medical Association,* 106: 266–271, 1936.

9. E. L. Rickes et al., "Crystalline Vitamin B12," *Science,* 107: 396–397, 1948. E. L. Smith and L.F.J. Parker, "Purification of Anti-pernicious Anemia Factor," *Biochemical Journal,* 43: viii–ix, 1948.

10. D. C. Hodgkin et al., "Structure of Vitamin B-12," *Nature,* 178: 64–66, 1956.

11. L. Pauling, "Abnormality of Hemoglobin Molecules in Hereditary Hemolytic Anemias," in *The Harvey Lectures,* New York: Academic, 1955, pp. 216–241. L. Pauling et al., "Sickle-cell Anemia, a Molecular Disease," *Science,* 110: 543–548, 1949. M. B. Strauss, "Of Medicine, Men and Molecules: Wedlock or Divorce?" *Medicine,* 43: 619–624, 1964.

12. Interviews with Dr. Victor D. Herbert in Boston, 1961, and in New York, September, 19, 1979 and July 26, 1976, and personal communi-

cations, March 27, 1969, and February 10, 1984. Herbert's pertinent scientific papers are: V. Herbert, "Experimental Nutritional Folate Deficiency in Man," *Transactions of the Association of American Physicians,* 75: 307–320, 1962. V. Herbert and R. Zalusky, "Interrelations of Vitamin B-12 and Folic Acid Metabolism: Folic Acid Clearance Studies," *Journal of Clinical Investigation,* 41: 1263–1267, 1962. V. Herbert et al., "Minimal Daily Adult Folate Requirement," *Archives of Internal Medicine,* 110: 649–652, 1962.

13. V. Herbert et al., "Value of Fasting Serum 'Folic Acid' Levels," *Federation Proceedings,* 18:246, 1959.

The first descriptions of folic acid deficiency came in the 1930s, and credit is given to Lucy Wills. (Refs.: V. Herbert, in L. Goodman and A. Gilman, "Drugs Effective in Megaloblastic Anemias," *The Pharmacological Basis of Therapeutics,* New York: Macmillan, 1970, chap. 64. L. Wills and H. S. Bilomoria, "Studies in Pernicious Anemia of Pregnancy: Production of Macrocytic Anemia in Monkeys by Deficient Feedings," *Indian Journal of Medical Research,* 20: 391–402, 1932. L. Wills, P. W. Clutterbuck, and P.D.F. Evans, "A New Factor in the Production and Cure of Macrocytic Anemias and Its Relation to Other Hemopoietic Principles Curative in Pernicious Anemia," *Biochemical Journal,* 31:2136–2147, 1937.)

14. Interview with Dr. Louis Sullivan in Atlanta, Georgia, October 8, 1979, and in Davis, California, April 1–2, 1983.

15. Herbert had two daughters and a son who at the time ranged in age from two to seven years. He did not make out a will nor did he change his life insurance policy, because he considered the risk of the experiment negligible. He told his wife about it, but presented it in such a way that he gave her little choice in his decision.

16. Interview with Dr. Ronald Arky, September 4, 1979.

17. Interview with Dr. Lansing C. Hoskins, September 1979.

18. Reflecting on Welch's comments, Herbert said: "It was considered poor form to speak in other than the third person in scientific communications. It would have been considered arrogant to describe one's own research in the first person. I cannot put my finger on just why that was so, but it was. So I spoke in the third person."

19. For this work Herbert received the American Society for Clinical Nutrition's award for outstanding clinical research.

20. The memory of his lawyer mother stimulated Herbert to become a lawyer as well as a physician. He now uses this dual expertise to chair the American Bar Association's committee on life sciences and in legal battles over cases charging nutritional quackery.

In 1977 and 1978 computer surveys of citations of all medical journal articles made by the Institute for Scientific Information showed that Herbert was one of the seventy-seven most frequently cited scientists.

For an overview and a historical perspective of the anemias, see M. M. Wintrobe, *Blood, Pure and Eloquent,* New York: McGraw-Hill, 1980.

## Chapter Thirteen: BLACK AND BLUE AT THE FLICK OF A FEATHER

1. Private hospitals that either have no professional education program or train only a few interns and residents often hire medical students as externs to record medical histories and do routine tests and physical examinations at night. This practice helps the older doctors and gives their younger colleagues clinical experience, as well as a few dollars and possibly room and board.

2. Today, doctors' chief recourse is to treat ITP patients with steroid drugs such as cortisone, which modify the interaction of antibodies and platelets. Steroids, however, only work in some cases. More often, even today, the major therapy is the surgical removal of the spleen, a splenectomy.

3. In the summer of 1972 I talked with Dr. Moore by telephone about scheduling an interview after he returned from vacation. Unfortunately, Moore died from a heart attack during his vacation. He was sixty-three. Moore's chief interest had been in the metabolism of iron, a prime component of red blood cells and often a key factor in anemia. His scientific reputation was based in part on experiments he had done on himself, including the swallowing of radioactive iron to study the way the body uses this element.

4. ITP is sometimes called immune thrombocytopenic purpura. Harrington believes the word "idiopathic" is preferable to "immune" because it more correctly conveys the situation: Doctors do not know what causes it.

5. Nature protects us against bleeding to death from the slightest leakage by forming clots. These clots are formed when huge cells (megakaryocytes) in the bone marrow break up into millions of platelets that travel through the bloodstream to reach an injured blood vessel. There the platelets become sticky to help seal the leak. They release chemicals to promote a chain reaction that, in about a dozen steps taking a few seconds, transforms a gel into a solid clot. It consists of platelets as well as red and white cells, all trapped in a clump. The process is the same whether the blood escapes outside the body or stays within it. If the bleeding is internal, the body, regarding the spilled red cells as debris, immediately takes steps to remove the vital substances. Scavenger cells begin to gobble up the iron in the spilled red cells so the metal can be used in making more such cells. Black and blue marks are a reflection of the blood that pools beneath the skin after tiny blood vessels are torn—before clots stop the bleeding. As the spilled blood is resorbed from beneath the skin, the black and blue marks turn green and then fade to yellow and then tan. After about two weeks the skin resumes its normal hue.

6. Interviews with Dr. William J. Harrington in New York City, April 1, 1974, and in Miami, November 30, 1977, March 28, 1980, September 10–11, 1982, and April 27 and November 5, 1983. Among Harrington's pertinent scientific papers are: W. J. Harrington et al., "Demonstration of a Thrombocytopenic Factor in the Blood of Patients with Thrombocytopenic Purpura," *Journal of Laboratory and Clinical Medicine,* 38: 1–10, 1951. W. J. Harrington et al., "Immunologic Mechanisms in Idiopathic and Neonatal Thrombocytopenic Purpura," *Annals of Internal Medicine,* 38: 433–469, 1953. C. C. Sprague et al., "Platelet Transfusions and the Pathogenesis of Idiopathic Thrombocytopenic Purpura," *Journal of the American Medical Association,* 150: 1193–1198, 1952.

7. Telephone interview with Dr. James W. Hollingsworth from San Diego, California, October 16, 1979.

8. The researchers might have given the woman's blood to a volunteer who was not group O because it is the so-called universal donor. But the circumstance did not arise.

9. Interview with Dr. William C. Moloney in Boston, August 30, 1983.

10. A few years later, Moore repeated the ITP experiment, this time to provide further evidence that it could be induced by quinine. (See Chapter Fourteen: Cancer: Can You Give It to Yourself?)

11. Interview with Dr. Jean Dausset in Paris, November 29, 1983, and personal communications, February 24 and May 16, 1983.

12. A picture of the skin grafts on Dausset's forearms appears in J. Dausset, *Titres et Travaux Scientifiques,* Chatelaudren, 1975, p. 113.

13. In 1920, for example, Dr. Samuel B. Grant and Dr. Alfred Goldman of Washington University Medical School set out to study a syndrome called tetany in which wrists bend and muscles twitch due to an abnormality of calcium or the acid balance of the body. At the time doctors knew that tetany could follow the removal of the parathyroid glands in the neck. But the cause of many other cases of tetany was unknown, and in the course of their own experiments Grant and Goldman found it could result from overbreathing. They used a metronome to help them time their deep breaths at a rate of about fourteen per minute and continued at this rate until symptoms of tetany developed, usually from fifteen to sixty minutes after they began. They realized that tetany could result from overbreathing from their very first experiment. Ten minutes after it began, Grant's fingers began to tingle. Five minutes later, his face felt stiff and he had difficulty in articulating his words. In the second experiment, Goldman's hand went into spasms just after Grant inflated a cuff around Goldman's arm to measure his blood pressure.

In the eighteenth experiment, after overbreathing for about half an hour, Goldman uttered a shrill cry and went into a general convulsion. Every muscle in his body was contracted. He remained rigid for about thirty seconds, and then his limbs, which were stretched out stiff, and his back, which had been arched, began to relax. Goldman suffered no ill effects following the convulsion. The two researchers went on to do a total of twenty-one experiments on themselves. (Ref.:

S. B. Grant and A. Goldman, "A Study of Forced Respiration: Experimental Production of Tetany," *American Journal of Physiology,* 52: 209–232, 1920.)

Chapter Fourteen:
## CANCER: CAN YOU GIVE IT TO YOURSELF?

1. Interviews with Dr. Thomas E. Brittingham III in Fort Worth, Texas, June 11, 1980, November 13, 1982, March 19, 1983, and April 17 and 24, 1983. Among Brittingham's scientific reports are: T. E. Brittingham, "Immunologic Studies on Leukocytes," *Vox Sanguinis,* 2: 242–248, 1957. T. E. Brittingham and H. Chaplin, "The Antigenicity of Normal and Leukemic Human Leukocytes," *Blood,* 17: 139–165, 1961. T. E. Brittingham and H. Chaplin, Jr., "Attempted Passive Transfer of Thrombotic Thrombocytopenic Purpura," *Blood,* 12: 480–482, 1957. T. E. Brittingham and H. Chaplin, "Febrile Transfusion Reactions Caused by Sensitivity to Donor Leukocytes and Platelets," *Journal of the American Medical Association,* 165: 819–825, 1957. T. E. Brittingham and H. Chaplin, "Production of a Human 'Anti-Leukemic Leukocyte' Serum and Its Therapeutic Trial," *Cancer,* 13: 412–418, 1960.

2. This time Moore was testing a theory about the physiological mechanism by which quinine could cause thrombocytopenic purpura (TP). In a two-step experiment, he swallowed a single quinine tablet and then injected into himself a sample of plasma (the liquid portion of blood) from a patient with the disorder. According to Moore's theory, the patient's plasma contained a factor missing from his own blood that was responsible for the bleeding that resulted from the destruction of the platelets.

Moore was correct. Within a few hours of his self-experiment, his platelet count dropped to zero, black and blue marks popped out all over his skin, and his nose bled so severely that doctors had to pack it with Gelfoam. They feared he might develop a stroke from the bleeding, so Moore was taken to Barnes Hospital. He did not, however, cancel Brittingham's interview. (Ref.: R. Steinkamp, C. V. Moore, and W. G. Doubek, "Thrombocytopenic Purpura Caused by Hypersensitivity to Quinine," *Journal of Laboratory and Clinical Medicine,* 45: 18–29, 1955.)

3. J. Dausset, A. Nenna, and H. Brecy, "Leukoagglutinins. V. Leukoagglutinins in Chronic Idiopathic or Symptomatic Pancytopenia and in Paroxysmal Nocturnal Hemoglobinuria," *Blood,* 9: 696–720, 1954.

4. Interviews with Dr. William J. Harrington in Miami, Florida, November 30, 1977, March 28, 1980, September 10–11, 1982, and April 27 and November 5, 1983.

5. K. Gramen, "Accidental Transfusion of Leukemic Blood," *Acta Chirurgica Scandinavica,* 64: 369–373, 1928.

6. Interview with Dr. Seymour Reichlin in Boston, February 1, 1983, and personal communication, October 9, 1984.

7. J. Nooth, *Observations on the Treatment of Scirrhous Tumors of the Breast,* London: J. Johnson, 1806, p. 13.

8. J. L. Alibert, *Déscription des maladies de la peau observées à l'Hôpital St.-Louis,* Paris: Barrois, 1806–1814, p. 118. I could not independently verify this reference, which is cited in W. H. Woglom, *Studies in Cancer and Allied Subjects. The Study of Experimental Cancer. A Review,* New York: Columbia University Press, 1913, p. 43.

9. Senn was particularly concerned about a then-fresh medical journal report by a doctor from the New York State Pathological Laboratory that supported the parasitic origin of cancer; the doctor reported finding varying numbers and forms of parasites in all cancers that he examined. (Ref.: N. Senn, "The Present Status of the Carcinoma Question," *Journal of the American Medical Association,* 37: 804–815, 1901.)

10. T. S. Hauschka, "Immunologic Aspects of Cancer: A Review," *Cancer Research,* 12: 615–633, 1952.

11. G. Domagk, "Die Bedeutung korpereigener Abwehrkräfte für die Ansiedlung von Geschwulstzellen," *Zeitschrift für Krebsforschung* 56: 247–252, 1942. I was unable to determine if Domagk actually produced antibodies in himself, and, if he did, whether he actually used that material to treat another person.

12. C. Forkner, *Leukemia and Allied Disorders,* New York: Macmillan, 1938, p. 28. J. B. Thiersch, "Attempted Transmission of Human Leucemia in Man," *Journal of Laboratory and Clinical Medicine,* 30: 866–874, 1945. J. B. Thiersch, "Attempted Transmission of Acute Leukemia from Man to Man by the Sternal Marrow Route," *Cancer Research,* 6: 695–698, 1946.

13. Interview with Dr. Elmer Brown in St. Louis, July 1, 1983.

14. At the same time that Brittingham was doing the series of ten experiments, he was also conducting a great many other experiments, almost all of them on himself. For example, in an effort to investigate the mechanisms by which drugs could produce aplastic anemia, he swallowed large doses of aminopyrine pills. Aminopyrine is one of the oldest antifever and painkilling drugs, having been synthesized at the end of the nineteenth century. But over-the-counter sales have been prohibited in the United States since 1938, because it is one of the most potent inducers of oft-fatal aplastic anemia. Infections were the major complication that killed patients; if the infection could be treated successfully with antibiotics, the patients usually recovered. For that reason, Brittingham was not concerned about dying from the experiment. "I was just interested in what made low white counts," he said. The drug made Brittingham so nauseated that he could no longer stand it after about two months. He stopped the experiment before he developed aplastic anemia.

In another experiment in 1955, Brittingham received a transfusion from a patient with TTP (thrombotic thrombocytopenic purpura) and did not develop the disease. In this experiment Brittingham did with the white cell what Harrington had done with the platelet. (Ref.: T. E. Brittingham III and H. Chaplin, Jr., "Attempted Passive Transfer of Thrombotic Thrombocytopenic Purpura," *Blood,* 12: 480–482, 1957.)

15. C. C. Sprague et al., "Platelet Transfusions and the Pathogenesis of Idiopathic Thrombocytopenic Purpura," *Journal of the American Medical Association,* 150: 1193–1198, 1952.

16. Interview with Mrs. Thomas E. Brittingham III in Fort Worth, Texas, September 1, 1983.

17. Interview with Dr. Robert M. Heyssel in Baltimore, Maryland, February 1, 1983. Heyssel is now president of the Johns Hopkins Health System in Baltimore.

Heyssel himself would continue the tradition of self-experimentation until about 1960, when his partner developed a serious reaction in a self-experiment done at Vanderbilt Medical School. The two researchers had injected radioactive platelets into themselves in order to confirm their life span. "For whatever reason, his platelets were benign for me but mine were not for him," Heyssel said. Heyssel's partner suffered an anaphylactic reaction, but not as serious as Brittingham's. "That's when I stopped experimenting on myself," Heyssel said. "I used normal volunteers, but not myself."

18. Telephone interview with Dr. Robert T. S. Jim in Honolulu, April 24, 1983.

19. Several years later, however, Brittingham cautioned against inserting needles into the breastbone to do bone marrow tests because too many patients had died from complications when the needle pierced the heart. Instead, he recommended that the needle be put into the hipbone, an anatomically safer area.

20. Brittingham's efforts to determine whether the white cell antibodies, or leukoagglutinins, were beneficial in cancer therapy reflected earlier attempts by others. For example, a pioneering Swedish researcher, Dr. Gustaf Lindstrom, injected leukemia patients with serum from immunized rabbits in 1927. As in Brittingham's experiment, the encouraging results were temporary. (Ref.: G. A. Lindstrom, "An Experimental Study of Myelotoxic Sera. Therapeutic Attempts in Myeloid Leukemia," *Acta Medica Scandinavica. (Supplement)* 22: 1–169, 1927.)

21. In 1958 Dr. Julian Aleksandrowicz, a forty-year-old researcher in Cracow, Poland, performed a similar experiment. He received two transfusions of cancerous cells taken from a patient with chronic lymphocytic leukemia. The injections were given two months apart. Aleksandrowicz did not develop leukemia and was still alive at the age of seventy-five. (Ref.: J. Aleksandrowicz, personal communication, March 16, 1984.)

22. Brittingham did not report this study and many others he did because he disliked writing scientific papers intensely. "You have to work like a dog to put something into decent English, and it takes away valuable time from doing something else or thinking about your work. My mind used to work like a charm when it was free of these unpleasant chores." Brittingham said he found it easier to report his findings at conferences, even though that meant he reached a much smaller audience.

23. D. Tosteson, "Remarks to the Harvard Medical School Class of 1986," June 5, 1986.

24. "The Jewish Chronic Disease Hospital Case," in J. Katz, A. Capron, and E. S. Glass, *Experimentation with Human Beings,* New York: Russell Sage Foundation, 1972, pp. 9–65.

25. Memorial Sloan-Kettering Cancer Center news release, January 23, 1964.

26. E. Langer, "Human Experimentation: Cancer Studies at Sloan-Kettering Stir Public Debate on Medical Ethics," *Science,* 143: 551–553, 1964.

## Chapter Fifteen:
## CHOOSING THE RIGHT ANIMAL

1. The guinea pig seasonal phenomenon has not been verified in experiments conducted in the southern hemisphere, and should be. (Refs.: Interviews with Dr. Lewis Thomas in New York City, 1978. L. Thomas, *The Youngest Science,* New York: Viking, 1983, pp. 182–185.)

2. A. Pope, *An Essay on Man. Epistle II,* M. Mack, ed., New York: Methuen, 1982, originally published in 1733–1734.

3. At Cambridge University, Mines had worked with the drug muscarine, which he had obtained from Sir Henry H. Dale, who in 1936 shared a Nobel Prize for his discoveries of the chemical transmission of nerve impulses. (Refs.: "Death of G. R. Mines," *British Medical Journal,* 1: 142, 1915. "The Late Professor Mines," *Canadian Medical Association Journal,* 4: 1095–1097, 1914. G. R. Mines, "On the Action

of Muscarine on the Electrical Response of the Heart," *Journal of Pharmacology and Experimental Therapeutics,* 5: 425–447, 1913–1914. G. R. Mines and T. G. Brodie, "On Circulating Excitations in Heart Muscles and Their Possible Relation to Tachycardia and Fibrillation," *Transactions of the Royal Society of Canada,* ser 3, sect. 4, 8: 43–52, 1914. "Professor Dies Testing Machine on His Own Heart," *Montreal Star,* November 9, 1914. "Professor G. R. Mines Victim to Science. Met Death on Saturday in Midst of Experiments at McGill. Exact Cause Unknown. Was Alone in Laboratory at Time, and Found Unconscious—Early End to Promising Career," *Montreal Gazette,* November 9, 1914. D. A. Rytand, "The Circus Movement [Entrapped Circuit Wave] Hypothesis and Atrial Flutter," *Annals of Internal Medicine,* 65: 125–159, 1966. A. L. Wit and P. F. Cranefield, "Reentrant Excitation As a Cause of Cardiac Arrythmia," *American Journal of Physiology,* 235: H1–H17, 1978.) In addition, I interviewed Dr. F. C. MacIntosh, a successor to Dr. Mines as chairman of the department of physiology at McGill, on June 14 and 17, 1983; personal communication, June 15, 1983.

4. Professor Alfredo Leonardi of the Mario Negri Pharmacological Institute and members of his staff in Milan told me about Pauletta after they translated interviews with his former colleagues. Antonio Marone was the first coroner in the Cavagna case, and Professor R. Pozzato, then at the University of Milan's Institute for Forensic Medicine, was the pathologist. (Refs.: "Autopsy Protocol No. 39428." Interviews with Professor Alfredo Leonardi in Milan, Italy, January 10–13, 1977, and in New York City, April 16, 1978, and January 19 and 22, 1979, and personal communication, February 16, 1977. Interviews in Milan, Italy, with Dr. Renato Gilioli, January 11, 1977, and Mrs. Paola Cavagna, January 13, 1977.)

5. L. K. Altman, "A Fatally Ill Doctor's Reactions to Dying," *New York Times,* July 22, 1974, p. 1. G. E. Leinbach, "Radiotriolein Revisited: A Study of the 131-I-Triolein Absorption Test Using Radiochemically Pure Triolein in Man," *Journal of Nuclear Medicine,* 13: 252–259, 1972.

6. C. J. Martin and R. Robison, "The Minimum Nitrogen Expenditure of Man and the Biological Value of Various Proteins for Human Nutrition," *Biochemical Journal,* 16: 407–447, 1922, p. 414.

7. J.B.S. Haldane, *Keeping Cool,* London: Chatto and Windus, 1940, p. 87.

8. J. H. Kellgren, "Observations on Referred Pain Arising From Muscle," *Clinical Science,* 3: 175–190, 1938. J. H. Kellgren, "On the Distribution of Pain Arising from Deep Somatic Structures with Charts of Segmental Pain," *Clinical Science,* 4: 35–45, 1939. T. Lewis, "Research in Medicine: Its Position and Its Needs," *British Medical Journal,* 1: 479–483, 1930. T. Lewis, "Suggestions Relating to the Study of Somatic Pain," *British Medical Journal,* 1: 321–325. February 12, 1938. T. Lewis and J. H. Kellgren, "Observations Relating to Referred Pain, Viscero-Motor Reflexes and Other Associated Phenomena," *Clinical Science,* 4: 47–71, 1939. Interviews with Dr. Jonas H. Kellgren in Manchester, England, July 14 and August 16, 1973.

9. J. H. Kellgren, "On the Distribution of Pain," p. 45.

10. P. DeKruif, *Men Against Death,* New York: Harcourt, Brace, 1932, pp. 140–145.

11. J. K. Aikawa, *Rocky Mountain Spotted Fever,* Springfield: Thomas, 1966, pp. 51–55.

Hideyo Noguchi's death from yellow fever in 1928 was officially attributed to an accident. But some have speculated that his death was a suicide in which he deliberately gave himself yellow fever or, perhaps, the result of a self-experiment that went wrong and led to a fatal case of yellow fever. Proponents of the suicide or self-experiment theory do not offer substantiating evidence but cite Noguchi's embarrassment over erroneous claims he made about the cause of yellow fever. In a series of articles from 1919 to 1922, Noguchi reported that a bacterium called *Leptospira icteroides* caused yellow fever, and based on this finding he had prepared and distributed a vaccine and therapy. In 1927, other scientists disproved Noguchi's claims and found that yellow fever was caused by a virus. In 1928, seeking to carry on his research in an area where yellow fever was rife, Noguchi went to Accra, Gold Coast (now Ghana), in West Africa. Six months later, on the eve of his return to New York, Noguchi developed yellow fever. Nine days later he was dead. A week thereafter the director of the research center in Accra, too, was dead of yellow fever. (Refs.: "Dr. Noguchi Is Dead, Martyr of Science," *The*

*New York Times,* May 22, 1928, p. 1. G. Cormer. "W. Hideyo Noguchi," in: *Encyclopedia Americana,* 1975, p. 400. C. E. Dolman. "Hideyo Noguchi," in *Dictionary of Scientific Biography.* Charles Scribner's Sons, Vol. X, pp. 141–45, 1974.)

12. R. A. McCance, "The Practice of Experimental Medicine," *Proceedings of the Royal Society of Medicine,* 44: 189–194, 1951, p. 192.

13. K. Mellanby, *Human Guinea Pigs,* London: Merlin, 1973, p. 151.

14. Dr. Evan O'Neill Kane of Pennsylvania is among the surgeons who have done autosurgery. In 1919 he amputated one of his fingers; it was at a time when amputation was the only way to prevent the spread of infections, and presumably he suffered from a serious one. Kane's second operation on himself was an appendectomy, which he did at age sixty in 1921. He sat propped up by pillows, with a nurse holding his head forward while he was under the effects of local anesthesia. He used mirrors to see the operative area. Two weeks later, he was back in the operating room, doing major surgery on a patient. Then, eleven years later, in 1932, at age seventy, Kane repaired his inguinal hernia under local anesthesia while he was held in a half-sitting position. Witnesses said he laughed and chatted throughout the operation. (Refs.: "Dr. Evan Kane Dies of Pneumonia at 71," *New York Times,* April 2, 1932. "Operates on Himself for the Second Time. Dr. Evan Kane Uses Local Anesthetic—Had Previously Cut Out His Own Appendix," *New York Times,* January 8, 1932. "Pennsylvania Surgeon Operates on Himself, Successfully Removing His Appendix," *New York Times,* February 16, 1921. "Surgeon Who Removed Own Appendix Back at Work 2 Weeks Later," *New York Times,* March 8, 1921.)

15. The heart condition was unrelated to Forssmann's self-experiments.

16. According to the American Medical Association, the number of women doctors in 1985 had risen to a total of 80,725 (14.6 percent) of the total of 552,716 physicians in the United States. In 1957 there were 12,606 women doctors (5.6 percent).

17. O. Metchnikoff, *Life of Elie Metchnikoff,* London: Constable, 1921, p. 104.

18. George Pickering was another of Thomas Lewis' many trainees who became a leader of British medicine. As a young medical investigator working in Lewis' laboratory, Pickering injected a substance into his veins to measure the time it took blood to circulate in his body. At the time doctors were seeking a substance to measure circulation time, and Pickering was testing a natural chemical called histamine. However, each time Pickering did the circulatory test, he got a violent headache. Rather than stop his research project, Pickering went on, because he realized he could turn the unwanted side effect to advantage. He could use histamine as a tool to produce headaches in himself in order to study them. Headaches could not be studied on animals because animals cannot communicate feelings of pain nor point to their source. Each day Pickering injected himself with histamine to produce the headaches. Over the course of a year he tried every combination and permutation he could imagine as a means of understanding, preventing, and stopping those headaches. But for all his pain and efforts, histamine did not help him solve the mystery of one of the most common human disorders. (Ref.: G. W. Pickering, "The Place of Experimental Method in Medicine," *Proceedings of the Royal Society of Medicine,* 42: 229–234, 1949. G. W. Pickering and W. Hess, "Observations on the Mechanism of Headache Produced by Histamine," *Clinical Science,* 1: 77–101, 1939.) Interview with Sir George Pickering, August 29, 1973 and February 1977 in Oxford, England.

19. In 1951 Dr. Louis J. Welt, who became chief physician at the University of North Carolina after teaching at Yale, asked the heads of all departments of medicine in American medical schools for their views on human experimentation as well as the procedures they were adopting on experiments on humans under their jurisdiction. Representatives of sixty-six departments replied—a figure that represented about four-fifths of the medical schools in the country at the time. Only eight of the respondents had set procedures, and only twenty-four favored a committee to review problems in human experimentation and the experiments themselves. The main objections were that procedural documents were viewed as more hindering than helpful and that a committee could not take responsibility,

which must remain in the hands of the medical investigators. Yet, Welt said: "Some recommended the Golden Rule at least as a minimal requirement. They recognize the special interests and motivations of the investigator and hence do not imply that because the investigator is willing to be a subject it is permissible to impose this on others; but, rather, that he has no right to subject others to an experiment in which he himself would not be willing to serve. The ultimate proof of this willingness to serve is, of course, serving." (Ref.: L. J. Welt, "Reflections on the Problems of Human Experimentation," *Connecticut Medicine,* 25: 75–78, 1951.)

20. Directors of hospital clinical research centers where human experiments are done have called for more rigorous training in clinical investigation, whether the research is focused on human studies, laboratory research, or both. (Ref.: B. Sherman and M. Genel, "Human Investigation in the 1980s," *Clinical Research,* 31: 570–571, 1983, p. 571.)

21. E. G. Laforet, "The Fiction of Informed Consent," *Journal of the American Medical Association,* 235: 1579–1584, 1976, p. 1584.

22. Interview with Dr. Rosalyn S. Yalow, October 13, 1977.

23. McCance, "Practice of Experimental Medicine."

24. Treatment of hormonal disorders can be traced to Brown-Séquard's self-experiments with "rejuvenation" injections. In 1888, at age seventy-one, the stocky, gray-haired, bearded Brown-Séquard tried to restore his mental and physical powers by injecting himself with an extract of dog and guinea pig blood, semen, and crushed testicles. Over a period of three weeks he gave himself ten injections. Although he could not determine whether the mixture prepared from a guinea pig was more potent than that prepared from a dog or vice versa, he convinced himself that the injections restored his vigor. "The day after the first subcutaneous injection, and still more after the succeeding ones, a radical change took place in me, and I had ample reason to say and to write that I had regained at least all the strength I possessed a good many years ago. Considerable laboratory work hardly tired me," Brown-Séquard wrote.

It was not a time when researchers did controlled studies in evaluating drugs, and Brown-Séquard was hardly scientific by today's standards in describing the increased powers he believed he gained over his physiological functions. He compared measurements of the jet of urine he produced after meals of similar quantities of food and beverage. There was no specific mention of any change in his sexual powers; that was left to the reader's imagination.

Yet there was an element of objectivity. He tested the strength of his arm muscles with a mechanical device called a dynamometer and compared the results to those he had recorded many years earlier. They "showed a decided gain of strength," he said. The dynamometer was similar to the one Freud had used in 1885 to measure the effects of cocaine on his muscle strength. (See Chapter Three: The Perilous Route to Painless Surgery.)

Brown-Séquard recognized the possibility that he was deceiving himself in interpreting the results afforded by the rejuvenation injections. Of course, his claims were widely disseminated and distorted in press reports, which led to commercial abuse of the extracts before his claims were refuted.

Nevertheless, Brown-Séquard's experiments were of enormous importance to medicine because they stimulated interest in hormonal research, spurring others to search for and to isolate hormones in animals that could be used as replacement therapy in humans with disorders caused by a hormone deficiency. In 1891, two years after Brown-Séquard's rejuvenation experiments, Dr. George R. Murray, an English physician, prepared an extract of sheep thyroid that he injected into a forty-six-year-old woman with severe myxedema, or thyroid insufficiency. Her recovery was dramatic. A year later, thyroid extract was administered in pill form, the first successful replacement therapy for an endocrinological disorder.

When Brown-Séquard died in 1894 at the age of seventy-seven, Louis Pasteur shed tears and the *Lancet,* in addressing Brown-Séquard's rejuvenation experiments, called his teaching and researches "of enormous importance." Today, all doctors learn the Brown-Séquard syndrome in neurology; he discovered that severing half the spinal cord produces a specific set of physiologic changes that correlates with the anatomy of the spinal cord and central nervous system. (Refs.: C. E. Brown-Séquard, *Advice to Students: An Address Delivered at the Opening of the Medical Lectures of Harvard University, November 7, 1886,* Cambridge: Wilson, 1867, pp. 8–9. C. E. Brown-Séquard, "Note on the Effects Produced on Man by Subcutaneous

Injections of a Liquid Obtained from the Testicles of Animals," *Lancet,* 2: 105–107, 1889. "Death of Professor Brown-Séquard," *Lancet,* 1: 906–907, 1894. J.M.D. Olmsted, *Charles-Edouard Brown-Séquard,* Baltimore: Johns Hopkins Press, 1946.)

25. H. G. Wells, *The Salvaging of Civilization: The Probable Future of Mankind,* New York: Macmillan, 1922, p. 42.

# Index

## ABOUT THE AUTHOR

LAWRENCE K. ALTMAN is one of the few medical doctors working as a full-time newspaper reporter. Born in Quincy, Massachusetts, in 1937, Dr. Altman received his A.B. degree, *cum laude*, majoring in government, from Harvard in 1958, and his M.D. from Tufts University School of Medicine in 1962. He has worked for the U.S. Public Health Service's Centers for Disease Control in Atlanta and in West Africa with the World Health Organization, and was a physician at the University of Washington Hospital in Seattle. He joined the science department of the *New York Times* in 1969 and is now senior medical correspondent and "The Doctor's World" columnist. Dr. Altman lives in New York City and serves on the faculty of the New York University Medical School.